Preferential Rules of Origin in the Law of the WTO and PTAS

World Trade Institute Advanced Studies

VOLUME 19

The titles published in this series are listed at *brill.com/wtia*

Preferential Rules of Origin in the Law of the WTO and PTAs

The Challenge of 3D Printing

By

Diana E. Wade

BRILL | NIJHOFF

LEIDEN | BOSTON

Library of Congress Cataloging-in-Publication Data

Names: Wade, Diana E editor
Title: Preferential rules of origin in the law of the WTO and PTAs / edited by Diana E Wade.
Description: Leiden ; Boston, Massachusetts : Brill, 2025. | Series: WTIA, 2405-9331 ; 19 | Includes bibliographical references.
Identifiers: LCCN 2025007223 | ISBN 9789004730588 hardback | ISBN 9789004730595 ebook
Subjects: LCSH: Certificates of origin | Marks of origin–Law and legislation | Industrial property | Three-dimensional printing–Law and legislation | Electronic commerce–Law and legislation | Free trade | Trade regulation | World Trade Organization
Classification: LCC K4640.O74 P74 2025 | DDC 346.04/8–dc23/eng/20250306
LC record available at https://lccn.loc.gov/2025007223

Typeface for the Latin, Greek, and Cyrillic scripts: "Brill". See and download: brill.com/brill-typeface.

ISSN 2405-9331
ISBN 978-90-04-73058-8 (hardback)
ISBN 978-90-04-73059-5 (e-book)
DOI 10.1163/9789004730595

Contents

Preface and Acknowledgements

The origin of this book is the grassy banks of Colico, on the northern shores of Lake Como. In the summer of 2020, during a respite from pandemic restrictions, I took my reading material on the train from Milan to Colico for afternoons in sunshine. I wanted to write about rules of origin, but I was not sure how to approach the topic. As a trademark lawyer, I had asked clients, "Where do your goods come from?" My experience in IP law had also exposed me to innovation in the production of goods. One July afternoon, I happened to read articles on 3D printing and trade, and I came across a few paragraphs on the impact of 3D printing on origin determination. I realized that I wanted to learn more, and so I progressed on the research journey that led to this book.

The shores of Lake Como are invoked in the opening lines of *I promessi sposi* (*The Betrothed*) by Alessandro Manzoni, written in the first half of the 1800s, but set in 1628–1630, a time of geopolitical conflict and plague for northern Italy and Milan. The year 2020 saw Northern Italy at the epicenter of a global pandemic, and also a hub for innovation. Italian engineers, in response to a shortage of valves for breathing apparatus, produced 3D printed replacements. Lake Como was, and still is in some degrees, a location for silk manufacturing and silk product finishing. As will be explained in Chapter 4, at the end of the 20th century, the Lake Como silk industry found itself in a global dispute over whether silk scarves 'originated' in Italy and could bear the label "Made in Italy."

Perhaps it was the fresh air and historic setting of Lake Como that inspired me to write about rules of origin, but the years since 2020 have also demonstrated the significance of origin and innovation on trade and geopolitics. The disruptions to global supply chains led to discussions by governments and industries of "reshoring" or "friend-shoring" and a looking to redesigning manufacturing processes to become less dependent on producers in countries far away. 3D printing falls into this discussion as it offers the possibility to produce a good or part locally. Geopolitical conflicts and wars have raised a heightened sensitivity on where a good originates from, leading to sanctions or boycotts of goods from certain territories. This book focuses on the nexus of advanced manufacturing (or manufacturing with significant digital inputs), rules of origin, trade policy and domestic policy, and the practicalities of identifying origin for internationally trading a good. However, the setting of this book is a world shaped by both great leaps in technology and its promises for development and great challenges to trade, development, and society.

One of the main goals of this book is to take a topic that seems to be a technical and specialized branch of trade law and show that, in fact, rules of origin impact many people and industries and they can be understood, generally. In the writing and publishing of this book, I have had much appreciated help along the way.

First, I wish to thank the Professors and administration at Università commerciale Luigi Bocconi for their support during my dissertation years, including Professors Leonardo Borlini, Georgio Sacerdoti, Paola Mariani, Lillà Montagnani, Eleanor Spaventa, and Laurent Manderieux. Next, I thank Professsors Ilaria Espa, Elisa Baroncini, and Niall Moran for their encouragement of my research and encouraging me to publish it. I also appreciate the comments and insights from moderators and fellow presenters at the PEPA/SIEL 2022 Conference and the SIEL 2023 Conference. I also thank experts on rules of origin that I have spoken with over the years and who have shared their research and perspectives.

I wish to thank the editor of Brill's World Trade Institute Advanced Studies series, the editors at Brill, and the reviewers of my manuscript for this opportunity to publish and share my research.

I take this last paragraph to express my gratitude to friends and family who have listened to me talk about rules of origin and who have followed me on this journey. First, I thank friends old and new: my Barnard College roommates, my PhD cohort, and colleagues and friends in Milan, Treviglio, Gallarate, and Brussels. And most importantly, my largest thanks to my family in Arizona and Texas.

Abbreviations

AB	WTO Appellate Body
AI	Artificial intelligence
AOR	WTO Agreement on Rules of Origin
AfCFTA	African Continental Free Trade Area
AKFTA	ASEAN-Korea Free Trade Area
ASEAN	Association of Southeast Asian Nations
ATIGA	ASEAN Trade in Goods Agreement
CAD	Computer-aided design
CBP	United States Customs & Border Protection
CETA	Comprehensive Economic and Trade Agreement
CIT	Court of International Trade
CPTPP	Comprehensive and Progressive Agreement for Trans-Pacific Partnership
CRO	WTO Committee on Rules of Origin
CTH	Change of Tariff Heading
CVA	Customs Valuation Agreement
DSU	WTO Understanding on Rules and Procedures Governing the Settlement of Disputes
EFTA	European Free Trade Association
EC	European Communities
ECJ	European Court of Justice
EU	European Union
EV	Electronic Vehicle
GAO	Government Accountability Office
GATS	General Agreement on Trade in Services
GATT 1947	General Agreement on Tariffs and Trade
GATT 1994	General Agreement on Tariffs and Trade 1994
GSP	Generalized System of Preferences
GVC	Global value chain
HS	Harmonized Commodity Description and Coding System
HWP	Harmonization Work Programme
ICC	International Chamber of Commerce
IPR	Intellectual property right(s)
IRA	Inflation Reduction Act
ITA	WTO Information Technology Agreement
LDC	Least developed country
LVC	Labor value content
MFN	Most favored nation

MSME	Micro/Small/Medium Enterprise
NAFTA	North American Free Trade Agreement
OECD	Organization for Economic Co-operation and Development
PEM	Pan-Euro Mediterranean Rules of Origin
PTA	Preferential trade agreement
R&D	Research and development
RoO	Rules of origin
RVC	Regional value content
SADC	Southern Africa Development Community
SAFTA	South-Asian Free Trade Area
SBO	Substantive business operations
SCM	WTO Agreement on Subsidies and Countervailing Measures
TCA	Trade And Cooperation Agreement Between The European Union And The European Atomic Energy Community, Of The One Part, And The United Kingdom Of Great Britain And Northern Ireland, Of The Other Part
TFA	WTO Agreement on Trade Facilitation
TPP	Trans-Pacific Partnership Agreement
TRIMS	WTO Agreement on Trade-Related Investment Measures
UAW	Union, United Automobile, Aerospace and Agricultural Implement Workers of America
UK	United Kingdom
UNCTAD	United Nations Conference on Trade and Development
US	United States of America
USITA	US International Trade Administration
USITC	US International Trade Commission
USMCA	Agreement between the United States of America, the United Mexican States, and Canada
USTR	Office of the US Trade Representative
VCLT	Vienna Convention on the Law of Treaties
WCO	World Customs Organization
WTO	World Trade Organization
3D	Three-dimensional

Introduction

The 1980s set the stage for international trade and manufacturing in the first decades of the 21st Century. In 1984, Charles W. Hull filed a US patent for an "Apparatus for production of three-dimensional objects by stereolithography."[1] This patent covers the basic technology of 3D printing, and Hull would found 3D Systems, one of the first companies to commercialize 3D printing machines.[2] In 1986, members of the GATT, the pre-cursor to the World Trade Organization (WTO), met in Punta del Este, Uruguay for talks on a wide range of trade policy issues.[3] Over the next eight years, negotiations among 123 countries led to the formation of the WTO.[4] Across the world, the manufacturing of goods shifted from centralized production to de-centralizing production in diverse facilities – in other words, the rise of global value chains (GVCs).[5] Finally, trade analysts noticed certain activity by national policymakers – extensive use of a legal tool called rules of origin to regulate trade in imported goods.[6] Over 30 years later, the WTO and GVCs have been instrumental to the progress of international trade, and 3D printing offers new potential for manufacturing goods. All three can be linked by rules of origin, and doing so brings to light some important challenges to the legal framework for international trade in this era of digital production and distribution of products.

1 3D Printing and Advanced Manufacturing: Opportunities to Explore Rules of Origin

A webinar held by the Committee on Rules of Origin of the WTO on 21 May 2021 was titled "What drives the utilization of trade

1 US Patent No. 4, 575,330 (Apparatus for Production of Three-Dimensional Objects by Stereolithography), Filed 8 August 1984, issued 11 March 1986. <https://patentimages.storage.googleapis.com/5c/a0/27/e49642dab99cf6/US4575330.pdf> accessed 2 December 2021.

2 Jukka Tuomi, Segei Chekurov and Jouni Partnanen, '3D Printing History, Principles and Technologies,' in Rosa Maria Ballardini, Marcus Norrgård, Jouni Partanen (eds), *3D Printing, Intellectual Property, and Innovation: Insights from Law and Technology* (WoltersKluwer 2017) 2.

3 World Trade Organization (WTO), 'The Uruguay Round' (wto.org) <https://www.wto.org/english/thewto_e/whatis_e/tif_e/fact5_e.htm> accessed 2 December 2021.

4 ibid.

5 Petros C Mavroidis, *The Regulation of International Trade*, vol. 1 (MIT Press 2016) 233.

6 Edwin Vermulst and Paul Waer, 'European Community Rules of Origin as Commercial Policy Instruments?' (1990) 24 J World Trade 55, 55–57.

preferences."[7] The webinar had over 500 registered participants. One of the speakers, Jeremy Harris, remarked that he was pleased "to chat with such a huge group of what some of us refer to as origin geeks. It always felt like a niche topic," but seeing "250 people logged in and paying attention" was "quite gratifying."[8] The number of participants indicates that rules of origin (RoO) is a topic that interests the trade community. For traders and custom officials, these rules are part of the daily practice of shipping goods across borders.

Yet, many legal professionals and researchers may ask themselves: what are rules of origin and what general role do they play in international trade? There are two types of rules: non-preferential rules of origin and preferential rules of origin. Both aim to assign a country or territory (e.g. the EU) to a product, but for different objectives. Non-preferential RoO, applied on a MFN (Most Favored Nation) basis, are used in connection with non-preferential trade policy instruments relating to anti-dumping and countervailing duties, MFN tariffs, and origin markings.[9] Preferential RoO are applied under reciprocal preferential trade agreements (PTAs), such as the USMCA[10] or CETA,[11] or for non-reciprocal preferential treatment under Generalized System of Preference programs (GSPs).[12] For example, under CETA, the preferential rules are used to determine if a good originates in Canada. If so, it is applied a preferential tariff rate when imported into the EU. This book focuses on preferential rules of origin.

If a good does not qualify for a preferential tariff rate, it can still enter the territory of the PTA under the applicable MFN tariff rate.[13] This is the tariff rate that each WTO member lists in their Schedule of Concessions upon accession to the WTO.[14] If bicycles are imported into the EU from Japan or Australia under the EU's MFN tariff rate for bicycles, the same MFN rate must be applied to the Japanese bicycle and to the Australian bicycle. On the other hand, preferential

7 'What Drives the Utilization of Trade Preferences,' conference held 19 May 2021. Videos and presentations available at <https://www.wto.org/english/tratop_e/roi_e/preference_utilization_190521_e.htm> accessed 3 November 2021.

8 Jeremy T Harris, 'Rules of Origin Preference Utilization' (What Drives the Utilization of Trade Preferences, WTO, 19 May 2021) <https://www.wto.org/english/tratop_e/roi_e/s1_harris19may21.pdf> accessed 1 December 2021.

9 Peter Van den Bossche and Werner Zdouc, *The Law and Policy of the World Trade Organization* (Cambridge University Press 2019) 458.

10 Agreement between the United States of America, the United Mexican States, and Canada (USMCA) (entered into force 1 July 2020) ch 4.

11 Comprehensive and Economic Trade Agreement (CETA) (signed 30 October 2016, some provisions entered into force on 21 September 2017).

12 Van den Bossche and Zdouc (n 9) 458.

13 Bernard Hoekman and Stefano Inama, 'Harmonization of Rules of Origin: An Agenda for Plurilateral Cooperation' (2018) 22 East Asian Economic Rev 3, 4–5.

14 Van den Bossche and Zdouc (n 9) 436–437.

tariff rates are specific for each PTA.[15] For example, when importing a Canadian bicycle into the EU, the tariff rate is 0% as established by CETA.[16] If the bicycle originates from Singapore, the rate is 7.00%, as established by the Free Trade Agreement between the EU and the Republic of Singapore.[17]

The Agreement on Rules of Origin (AOR) is one of the legal texts included in the WTO's Multilateral Trade Agreements, and is thus an integral part of the Marrakesh Agreement Establishing the World Trade Organization and is binding on all members of the WTO.[18] Its aim is to harmonize non-preferential RoO which would apply to all uses for non-preferential rules, such as for tariff quotas, anti-dumping duties, or marks of origin for product labels.[19] The Harmonization Work Programme (HWP) was initiated after the entry into force of the WTO Agreement (1 January 1995) and was to be concluded within 3 years.[20] As the HWP's focus turned to designing product specific rules for 5,000 tariff lines, the political interests of Members on suitable origin criteria diverged leading to an impasse in drafting the rules.[21] The Committee on Rules of Origin still continues to meet, though its focus has shifted to non-reciprocal preferential rules of origin for LDCs (Least Developed Countries).[22]

The fate of the HWP does not impact preferential RoO in PTAs nor their application by customs officials as these rules do not come under the HWP mandate.[23] This book will reference non-preferential rules when relevant

15 Andrew T Guzman and Joost HB Pauwelyn, *International Trade Law* (2nd edn, Wolters-Kluwer 2012) 337.

16 Tariff rate found using the European Commission's My Trade Assistant tool, available at: <https://trade.ec.europa.eu/access-to-markets/en/home> accessed 1 December 2021.

17 Tariff rate found using the European Commission's My Trade Assistant tool.

18 The Marrakesh Agreement Establishing the World Trade Organization (15 April 1994) LT/UR/A/2, art II <https://docs.wto.org> accessed 30 October 2021.

19 Van den Bossche and Zdouc (n 9) 458–459.

20 Agreement on Rules of Origin (AOR) (15 April 1994) LT/UR/A-1A/7, art 9:2(a) <https://docts.wto.org> accessed 5 January 2022. A proposal was submitted in 1999 by the Technical Committee on Rules of Origin to the Committee on the Rules of Origin.

21 Stefano Inama, *Rules of Origin in International Trade* (CUP 2009) 47–71; Mavroidis, *The Regulation of International Trade*, vol. 1 (n 5) 225. Mavroidis and Edwin Vermulst note that the Members "managed to find agreement only with respect of 55% of the 2,744 products." Petros C Mavroidis and Edwin Vermulst, 'The Case for Dropping Preferential Rules of Origin' (2018) 52 J World Trade 1, 6 (referring to Committee on Rules of Origin, 'Draft Consolidated Text of Non-Preferential Rules of Origin' (11 February 2010) G/RO/W/111/Rev.5).

22 WTO, "Event marks 25th anniversary of the WTO's Agreement on Rules of Origin' (wto.org 4 March 2020) <https://www.wto.org/english/news_e/news20_e/roi_04mar20_e.htm> accessed 1 December 2021.

23 Peter Van den Bossche, *The Law and Policy of the World Trade Organization: Text, Cases and Materials* (2nd edn, CUP 2008) 437–438; Mavroidis, *The regulation of International Trade*, vol. 1 (n 5) 227.

to the topic under discussion. Regarding preferential RoO, they are brought under the aegis of the WTO through an annex to the Agreement on Rules of Origin, Annex II: The Common Declaration with Regards to Preferential Rules of Origin.

While the study of rules of origin may seem to be reserved for technical specialists, these rules are more than technical elements of international trade. Many actors, including policymakers, lawyers, scholars, businesses, and customs officials, should be involved in the design and implementation of the rules.[24] While knowledge of the Harmonized System Nomenclature for classification of goods and practical experience in customs administration are important for administering rules of origin, Stefano Inama finds that "the time has long gone since the rules were considered as a rather obscure and technical customs issue, with little bearing on trade and economic policy."[25] Another reason for studying preferential RoO is that they can function as a non-tariff barrier to trade due to their complexity while other trade restrictions are dismantled through multilateral or regional efforts to liberalize trade.[26]

Knowledge of how preferential RoO are designed and function will also assist lawyers, policymakers, and scholars in understanding how to regulate and design laws for trade of goods produced within GVCs and with digital technologies. The fragmentation of production processes across the globe has complicated the process of identifying the origin of a good, which in turn can make it more costly for traders to import goods under preferential tariff rates.[27] The expansion of GVCs results not just from trade liberalization, but also from the widespread adaption of information technology.[28] This could bring into question the role of the WTO and a multilateral trade regime in regulating and facilitating trade.[29] Petros C. Mavroidis finds that there is still "a lot that needs to be done for the WTO to keep pace with the current aspirations of the business community in this respect. Importantly, GVCs would greatly benefit from

24 Stefano Inama, *Rules of Origin in International Trade*, 2 ed (CUP 2022) 821; Moshe Hirsch, 'The Politics of Rules of Origin' in Tomer Broude, Marc L. Busch, and Amelia Porges (eds), *The Politics of International Economic Law* (CUP 2011) 328.

25 Inama, *Rules of Origin in International Trade* (2022) (n 24) 821.

26 Olivier Cadot, Celene Carrere, Jaime de Melo, and Bolormaa Tumurchudur, 'Product-Specific Rules of Origin in EU and US Preferential Trade Arrangements: An Assessment' (2006) 5 World Trade Rev 199, 200–201.

27 Paul Brenton, 'Preferential Rules of Origin' in Jean-Pierre Chauffour and Jean-Christophe Maur (eds), *Preferential Trade Agreement Policies for Development: A Handbook* (World Bank 2011) 161.

28 Mavroidis, *The Regulation of International Trade*, vol 1 (n 5) 234.

29 ibid.

more rational, less complicated rules of origin."[30] If this cannot be achieved at a multilateral level, then Mavroidis suggests that "trading nations profiting from their participation in GVCs could find it to their advantage to simplify or rationalize their own national regimes."[31] Lawyers, scholars, and policymakers should study how preferential RoO are designed by national and regional trade administrations and identify where they may be out-of-synch with how goods are made through GVCs.

The preferential RoO chapters of trade agreements are lengthy, at times over 200 pages,[32] but when delving into the details of these chapters, some interesting observations can be made on the use of PTAs to regulate trade. Despite their length, RoO could be categorized as a "shallow" approach to trade law.[33] A shallow integration of goods results from reciprocal exchanges of commitments focused on the reduction of tariffs and discriminatory border measures.[34] "Deep" integration of goods occurs when the focus is turned towards the potential adverse impact of domestic regulation on policy goals.[35] Deep provisions are found in trade agreements in sections linked to labor or environmental standards. Some of the USMCA's preferential rules of origin enter into "deep" territory: traders must demonstrate that the production of a vehicle includes a certain amount of labor paid at a minimum wage rate for the vehicle to obtain USMCA origin.[36] Whether these labor requirements in the rules will result in changes to vehicle production in the USMCA territory will be explored further in this book.

With preferential RoO we also catch a glimpse of united efforts to redesign legal rules. The EU and 22 trading partners in the European and Mediterranean region have agreed to revisions to the Pan-Euro Mediterranean Convention that aim to simplify the product-specific rules as well as the origin certification

---

30 ibid.

31 ibid.

32 USMCA ch 4, the chapter on rules of origin, is 270 pages including annexes. CETA's Protocol on Rules of Origin and Origin Procedures is 206 pages.

33 Joost Pauwelyn, 'Taking the Preferences Out of Preferential Trade Agreements: TTIP as a Provider of Public Goods' reprinted in Joost HB Pauwelyn, Andrew T Guzman, Jennifer A Hillman, *International Trade Law* (3rd edn, WoltersKluwer 2016) 374.

34 Bernard Hoekman and Douglas Nelson, '21st Century Trade Agreements and the Owl of Minerva' (2018), EUI Working Papers, RSCAS 2018/04, 10–11 <https://cadmus.eui.eu/bitstream/handle/1814/50964/RSCAS_2018_04.pdf?sequence=1&isAllowed=y> accessed 23 October 2021.

35 ibid 11.

36 David A Gantz, 'North America's Shifting Supply Chains: The USMCA, COVID-19, and the U.S.-China Trade War' (2020) Rice U. Baker Institute for Public Policy, 16 <https://doi.org/10.25613/0gaq-h036> accessed 8 January 2022.

requirements.[37] Looking at preferential RoO in trade agreements provides an opportunity to study changes in trade law, such as the shift to deeper trade agreements, the practice of trade negotiations, and finally the impact of such agreements on the practice of trade. Such an investigation should consider the growing role of services in the production of tangible goods.

The changes that 3D printing brings to manufacturing may require examining the role of the origin of digital inputs when seeking preferential tariff treatment for goods. How will rules of origin function in identifying the origin of goods made through advanced manufacturing techniques, such as 3D printing, which require minimal human involvement and more digital and automated processing?[38] If the value of a product derives from a digital input, such as a file that instructs a 3D printer, what role should these digital inputs have in determining the origin of a good? These questions provide an opportunity to study where new manufacturing and trade practices start to diverge from existing laws and whether any modifications to such laws are necessary.

Finally, lawyers and legal scholars interested in trade in digital products or trade of goods with significant digital inputs should become familiar with the basic concepts of RoO for services and for goods. Given the WTO moratorium on custom duties on electronic transmissions and provisions in trade agreements prohibiting such duties, tariffs on the transmission of digital files, like the 3D file, are not currently applied.[39] However, as states explore other barriers to trade, for example data localization requirements, understanding where that digital product originated could be useful for scholars and lawyers focusing on the distribution and use of services. This book briefly examines rules of

37 Commission, 'The Pan-Euro-Mediterranean Cumulation and the PEM Convention' (ec.europa.eu) <https://ec.europa.eu/taxation_customs/customs-4/international-affairs/pan-euro-mediterranean-cumulation-and-pem-convention_en> accessed 23 March 2024; Decision No 1/2023 Of The Joint Committee Of The Regional Convention On Pan-Euro-Mediterranean Preferential Rules Of Origin of 7 December 2023 on the amendment of the Regional Convention on pan-Euro-Mediterranean preferential rules of origin. These amendments to the PEM take effect 1 January 2025. All references to the PEM will be to this version.

38 This question is briefly addressed in: National Board of Trade – Sweden, 'Trade Regulation in a 3D Printed World: A Primer' (2016) Kommerskollegium 2016: 1; Ziyang Fan, Jimena Sotelo, and Venkataraman Sundareswaran, '3D Printing: A Guide for Decision-Makers' (January 2020) World Economic Forum – White Paper 13 <http://www3.weforum.org/docs/WEF_Impacts_3D_Printing_on_Trade_Supply_Chains_Toolkit.pdf> accessed 24 October 2021.

39 Rashmi Banga, 'Growing Trade in Electronic Transmissions: Implications for the South' (2019) UNCTAD Research Paper No. 29, 30–31 <https://unctad.org/system/files/official-document/ser-rp-2019d1_en.pdf> accessed 23 October 2021.

origin for services and e-commerce in the context of 3D printing technology and manufacturing.

2 Approach to Exploring Rules of Origin and 3D Printing

Looking at the design of preferential RoO in the context of 3D printing allows us to experiment with modernizing rules in a digital trade environment. Identifying where there is a risk for protectionist intervention, or a risk of generating more confusion for traders, leads us to question how the trade law system should regulate such rules, which are mainly situated in regional and bilateral preferential trade agreements. These considerations also tie into some of the challenges institutions, especially the WTO, face at this moment: what role should multilateralism play in forming a framework for trade and how can organizations modernize along with technological changes to promote trade liberalization and economic development.

The study of rules of origin for 3D printed goods requires assessing two sub-questions. First, what would be the result of applying rules of origin to 3D printed goods? Second, considering this result, how should rules of origin for 3D goods and other advanced manufactured products be designed in trade instruments? Generally, the starting point for determining the origin of a good is to ask: (1) was the good wholly obtained or produced in a given territory?; (2) if not, where did the last substantial transformation to the good take place?

The first step is to identify the points where RoO designed for traditional manufacturing processes is out of synch with additive manufacturing. The second step is to delve into the debate on whether service inputs, such as design and development, should have roles in conferring origin to final goods. This analysis is built from the work of Geraets, Carroll and Willems[40] who have proposed that service inputs be incorporated into the rules of origin analysis, as well as Duy Dinh's examination of the origin of a 3D product within a greater proposal of developments for the rules of origin regime for services.[41]

There are several technical and legal findings. First, it is possible to apply current preferential RoO to 3D printed goods and other advanced manufactured goods. However, there are some potential changes to the origin of the good in comparison to the application of such rules to traditionally manufactured

---

40 Dylan Geraets, Colleen Carroll, and Arnoud R Willems, 'Reconciling Rules of Origin and Global Value Chains: The Case for Reform' (2015) 18 J Intl Economic L 287–305.

41 Duy Dinh, Rules of Origin for Services: From the Early Days of GATS to the Era of Servicification (Edward Elgar 2020).

like goods. Such changes depend on whether 3D printing is deemed sufficient processing in the territory or if the origin conferring value shifts from labor costs to material costs (the printer ink). Secondly, attempting to insert the service input to the origin analysis results in some points of friction due the distinctions between services classifications and goods classifications under WTO instruments and the Harmonized System of Nomenclature. As rules of origin for services in the GATS and in trade instruments designate origin based on the legal seat of the supplier, adjoining the rules for services with rules for goods requires a careful approach legally and technically. Finally, the potential for a service input to confer origin on a good can provide opportunities for policymakers and trade negotiators to strategically design new rules to favor domestic industries or to take advantage of a global production chain to achieve preferential tariff treatment for key goods.

The observations made in applying RoO to advanced manufactured goods set the foundations for the second focus of the book: how could a rules of origin regime that is responsive to changes in technology be developed and supported by international trade organizations and states? The idea of a plurilateral WTO Instrument could be an option, and the scope and limitations of such an Instrument is assessed by comparisons to existing plurilateral agreements. The general finding is that the Instrument would need to cover a narrow range of goods, give parties sovereignty in designing rules, and have some independence from regulations on e-commerce and electronic transmissions.

Next, the book examines how existing resources at trade organizations, such as the WTO and the World Customs Organization, can be applied to assist states in developing a functional rules of origin regime for advanced manufactured goods. The key term that emerges from this review is "collaboration." It will be necessary for organizations, states, traders, and trade and technology experts to work together to devise rules that perform their legal purpose (distinguish goods for preferential treatment), that are not too complex, that minimize negative externalities (such as being too restrictive), and that can be updated as technological methods of production change and the types of goods traded change. Policymakers and lawyers should conduct a comprehensive review of RoO and they should design rules that are predictable and that enhance the legitimacy of the international trade law framework as one that promotes development, innovation, and even-handed trade practices.

The various legal layers (international, regional, national) as well as the various sectors (trade, economics, technology) that RoO can be situated in suggests a multi-disciplinary approach to these rules. WTO case law, national and EU law and legislation, as well as the historical perspective of RoO in the international trade law system will be examined. There has been only one dispute before a WTO panel dealing with the Agreement on Rules of Origin (AOR) – *US-Textiles Rules of Origin* (2003).[42] Authors who have examined preferential RoO for goods in relation to the GATT 1947 and the WTO are Bernard Hoekman, Edmund Vermulst, Petros Mavoridis, Laura Puccio,[43] and Stefano Inama. Duy Dinh, Americo Zampetti and Pierre Suavé,[44] and Richard Baldwin examine rules of origin for services.[45] Some of these authors are economists and all look beyond WTO jurisprudence when examining rules of origin. The economic perspective is briefly examined as it provides data on how traders and customs offices are impacted by rules of origin.

The rise of GVCs and regional and bilateral approaches to regulating trade also requires a comprehensive analysis of international, regional, and political actors in trade relations.[46] While the WTO had an impact on restraining protectionism after the 2008 global financial crisis,[47] the WTO currently finds itself without an Appellate Body due to the expiration of the mandate of the last sitting member on 30 November 2020. This book aims to balance an expectation that the WTO and its Members will continue to work together to improve the international trade system, with a recognition that legal development, at least for RoO, is occurring at the regional and bilateral level.

Rules of origin is a politicized element of trade law: lobbyists for domestic industries and politicians aim to influence the design of the rules in trade agreements, as will be examined in Chapter 3. Various sources – treaties, decisions

---

42 *United States – Rules of Origin for Textiles and Apparel Products* (Panel Report circulated 20 June 2003, adopted 21 July 2003) WT/DS243/R.

43 Laura Puccio, '20 Years After Marrakesh: Reconsidering the Effects of Preferential Rules of Origin and Anti-Circumvention Rules on Trade in Inputs and Global Production Networks' 2014 Eur YB Intl Economic L 173, 173–200.

44 Americo Beviglia Zampetti and Pierre Sauvé, 'Rules of Origin for Services: Economic and Legal Considerations,' in Olivier Cadot, Antoni Estevadeordal, Akiko Suwa-Eisenmann, and Theirry Verdier (eds), *The Origin of Goods: Rules of Origin in Regional Trade Agreements* (OUP 2006) 114–146.

45 Richard Baldwin, '21st Century Regionalism: Filling the Gap between 21st Century Trade and 20th Century Trade Rules' (May 2011) *Policy Insight* (Centre for Economic Policy Research) <https://cepr.org/publications/policy-insight-56-21st-century-regionalism-filling-gap-between-21st-century-trade-and> accessed 9 March 2025.

46 Ernst-Ulrich Petersmann, '20 Years WTO Law and Governance: Some Legal Methodology Problems' (2016) 13 Manchester J Intl Economic L 106, 111.

47 Manfred Elsig, Bernard Hoekman, and Joost Pauwelyn, 'Thinking About the Performance of the World Trade Organization: A Discussion Across Disciplines' in Manfred Elsig, Bernard Hoekman, and Joost Pauwelyn (eds), *Assessing the World Trade Organization: Fit for Purpose?* (CUP 2017) 23.

of customs courts, reports by international organizations, and research on new technologies – are consulted. Stephan Hall calls treaties "the real workhorses of international law because they are used for an array of indispensable tasks ranging from the creation of commercial commitments" to "the regulation of technical matters."[48] The trade instruments examined in this book were selected according to: (1) the geographical scope, (2) the design of the rules, or (3) utilization in demonstrating an element of the rules. The first category includes the PEM and the PEM revisions, the CPTPP, and the USMCA; the second category includes the PEM revisions and the USMCA; and the third category includes ASEAN treaties, the Digital Protocol of the AfCFTA, EU bilateral treaties, and US bilateral treaties.

While a study of RoO requires looking at various legal and non-binding sources, WTO law is still useful for examining related topics. Cases on the use of the Harmonized System Nomenclature (HS) in trade instruments and cases on whether GATT or GATS applies to a measure in a trade instrument are relevant to understanding RoO in relation to GVCs and the servicification of manufacturing. The Trade Facilitation Agreement (TFA), the Information Technology Agreement (ITA), and the 2013 Bali and 2015 Nairobi Ministerial Decisions on Rules of Origin for LDCs will be referred to when proposing suggestions for greater WTO involvement in the design of RoO.

Finally, it is important to examine the activity of the World Customs Organization (WCO). The WCO administers The International Convention on the Harmonized Commodity Description and Coding System (HS Convention) and the International Convention on the Simplification and Harmonization of Customs procedures (Revised Kyoto Convention). As of October 2024, there are 161 contracting parties to the HS Convention, and as of July 2024, 137 to the Revised Kyoto Convention.[49] The WCO also provides dispute settlement mechanisms under the Convention and the HS; in both instances, the parties may agree in advance to make binding the recommendations issued by

---

48 Stephen Hall, 'Researching International Law' in Mike McConville and Wing Hong Cui (eds), *Research Methods for Law* (Edinburgh UP 2007, reprinted 2012) 181–203.

49 World Customs Organization (WCO), 'Position of Contracting Parties to the Harmonized System Convention and Non-Contracting Party Administrations' (wcoomd.org 7 October 2024) <http://www.wcoomd.org/-/media/wco/public/global/pdf/topics/nomenclature/overview/hs-contracting-parties/positions-of-cp/situation_hs.pdf?db=web> accessed 20 October 2024; WCO, 'Conventions: Summary of Positions' (wccomd.org 1 July 2024) <https://www.wcoomd.org/-/media/wco/public/global/pdf/about-us/legal-instruments/conventions-and-agreements/revised-kyoto/sg0230eb.pdf?la=en> accessed 20 October 2024.

the responsible Committees.[50] The 2022 revisions to the HS nomenclature included a new code for additive manufacturing machines.[51]

Additive manufacturing, also referred to as 3D printing, was chosen as the lens through which to examine rules of origin because of the changes it can bring to production and trade in goods. This examination leads to questions on the modernization of trade law, and more specifically, the steps the WTO can take to meet the needs of traders and customs officials as production and trade adapt to changes in technology. Mavroidis argues that:

> [t]he fact that it will be some time before 3D printing can be fully utilized on a wide commercial scale does not mean that similar questions should be like sleeping dogs that can lie a few yards outside the WTO headquarters, and are handled only at the moment when they start to bark. The WTO can become attractive only if it shows the capacity to address similar concerns preemptively, and not only ex post facto (which might be too late).[52]

Through examining changes in manufacturing processes in relation to RoO and the potential impact of such changes on determining origin, this book also looks to how the WTO could intervene in this context and maintain its relevance as a bastion for the regulation of trade and economic development.

3D printing also allows us to consider other elements of trade influenced by the rise of digital technology, such as the regulation of digital transmissions or the hybridization of goods and services. It is debated among analysts at the OECD and UNCTAD about the impact 3D printing will have on international trade, and whether this necessitates imposing custom duties on

---

50 Customs Co-operation Council (WCO), International Convention on the Simplification and Harmonization of Customs Procedures (as amended) (Revised Kyoto Convention) (entered into force 3 February 2006) art 14; WCO, International Convention on the Harmonized Commodity Description and Coding System (HS Convention) (entered into force 1 January 1988), art 10. The legal effect of such recommendations in connection with trade matters within the jurisdiction of the WTO will be discussed in Chapter 1.

51 CECIMO, 'Press Release: CECIMO Appreciates the Approval of a New Product Nomenclature Standard for Additive Manufacturing Machines' (cecimo.eu 25 April 2019) <https://www.cecimo.eu/news/press-release-cecimo-appreciates-the-approval-of-a-new-product-nomenclature-standard-for-additive-manufacturing-machines/> accessed 24 October 2021. Machines for additive manufacturing have HS Code designation 84.85. WCO, 'Chapter 84 - HS Nomenclature 2022 edition' (wccomd.org) <https://www.wcoomd.org/-/media/wco/public/global/pdf/topics/nomenclature/instruments-and-tools/hs-nomenclature-2022/2022/1684_2022e.pdf?la=en> accessed 19 November 2023.

52 Petros C Mavroidis, *The Regulation of International Trade*, vol 3 (MIT Press 2020) 242–243.

the transmissions of digital 3D design files.[53] In general, 3D printing will not entirely substitute traditional, labor-intensive manufacturing, but will compliment such manufacturing through production of specialized parts or customized consumer goods.[54] 3D printing, while expensive, is of interest to the governments and industry of both developed and developing countries.[55] 3D printing has the potential to become a global form of manufacturing and the trade of 3D printed goods could occur under PTAs as well as GSPs (General Systems of Preferences). This global dimension of such trade suggests that legal topics related to services – classification of digital products, a hybridization of the GATT and GATS, and the addition of a Mode 5 for services under GATS – can be examined through 3D printing. However, this book proposes that exploring how rules of origin impact trade of 3D printed goods should not be reliant on an agreement on e-commerce at the WTO or the existence of a Mode 5 for services.

3 Proposals for Rules of Origin in the Era of Advance Manufacturing and Structure of the Book

At the end of the introduction to the webinar on the utilization of tariff preferences, a question was raised on whether there were any plans for the WTO to study reciprocal trade agreements, such as PTAs. The presenter, Darlan F. Martí, responded that there are two limitations to studying PTAs: 1) limited data pool,

53 Rashmi Banga, 'Growing Trade in Electronic Transmissions: Implications for the South' (n 39) ; A Andrenelli and J López González, 'Electronic Transmissions and International Trade - Shedding New Light on the Moratorium Debate' (2019) OECD Trade Policy Paper, No. 233 <http://dx.doi.org/10.1787/57b50a4b-en> accessed 23 October 2021; A Andrenelli and J López González, '3D printing and International Trade: What is the Evidence to Date?' (2021), OECD Trade Policy Paper, No. 256 <https://www.oecd.org/publications/3d-printing-and-international-trade-0de14497-en.htm> accessed 26 November 2021.

54 A Andrenelli and J López González, '3D printing and International Trade: What is the Evidence to Date?' (n 53) 4; Caroline Freund, Alen Mulabdic and Michele Ruta, 'Is 3D Printing a Threat to Global Trade? The Trade Effects You Didn't Hear About,' (2020) World Development Report Policy Research Working Paper, No. 9024, 2–3 <https://openknowledge.worldbank.org/handle/10986/32453> accessed 26 November 2021.

55 See eg, 'GE Nigeria Launches e-learning Portal at Lagos Garage Week 2018' (Africanews.it 7 December 2018), <https://www.africanews.it/english/ge-nigeria-launches-e-learning-portal-at-lagos-garage-week-2018/> accessed 8 March 2025; Ministry of Electronics and Information Technology, 'National Strategy for Additive Manufacturing: Next Generation Digital Manufacturing' (Meity.gov.in 24 February 2022) 1, 3 <https://www.meity.gov.in/writereaddata/files/Additive%20Manufacturing%20Booklet%2014.02.2022.pdf> accessed 23 March 2024 (archived link).

as not all WTO members notify PTA imports to the Secretariat, and 2) efforts to initiate such a study, "rest largely with the WTO Membership and whether or not they believe the assistance of the Secretariat, there too, would be useful" in promoting best practices and conducting research.[56] This points to a greater issue that underlies not just the design of RoO, but the dynamic between state sovereignty and international institutions. For the WTO Secretariat to conduct research on a trade topic, the WTO Members must provide the necessary data and agree to such a study. As Professor Jackson observed, "in order for the world to cope with the challenges of instant communication" and "fast and cheap transportation," the notion of sovereignty must also be updated to something that "can be called 'sovereignty-modern.'"[57] Yet, the world still needs international institutions: "a general perspective suggests that a key lesson of the last one hundred years is that international institutions (including judicial institutions) are critical and are here to stay. They increasingly play a larger role in world and local affairs."[58] How states rely on international organizations to provide legal frameworks for RoO, while acknowledging that rules also fall under the purview of national (or regional) commercial policy, presents an opportunity for trade analysists to examine the tension between sovereignty and international institutions in trade.

This book proposes some recommendations for the design, implementation, and administration of rules of origin at the WTO and at regional and bilateral levels. These suggestions are made in the context of 3D printed goods to demonstrate that as the production and trade of goods changes, so may the design and interpretation of substantive and administrative rules of origin require updating. However, this book does not propose a radical change of the preferential RoO regime, nor does it propose any specific technical recommendations, such as changing one of the formulas used in the *ad valorem* criterion. Yet, the recommendations echo the calls by trade experts for the simplification of the rules. Preferential RoO have a purpose, to distinguish goods that qualify for preferential tariff treatment, but they risk becoming purposeless if they are so complicated that traders forgo preferential tariff treatment, because it is too costly to comply with the rules. Using 3D printed goods as an example, we can

56 Darlan F Martí, 'What Drives the Utilization of Trade Preferences? Lessons from the work of the WTO Committee on Rules of Origin; (What Drives the Utilization of Trade Preferences, WTO, 19 May 2021) <https://www.wto.org/english/tratop_e/roi_e/s1_harris19may21.pdf> accessed 1 December 2021.

57 John H Jackson, 'The Evolution of the World Trading System – The Legal and Institutional Context' in Daniel Bethlehem, Isabelle Van Damme, Donald McRae and Rodney Neufeld (eds), *The Oxford Handbook of International Trade* (OUP 2009) 52–53.

58 ibid 53.

highlight elements in the design of rules in PTAs and trade instruments that could be simplified or where the administration of the rules could be more efficient. Finally, the WTO can have an important role to play in assisting Members in designing and regulating rules of origin. Such activity could result from providing a platform for a plurilateral agreement, or by tapping into characteristics that have been the WTO's cornerstone, such as a provider of technical assistance.

The book is structured as follows:

- Chapter 1 focuses on preferential rules of origin in the context of WTO agreements and jurisprudence. This allows us to see why preferential rules vary considerably in PTAs and why they can perform a discriminatory function. This chapter also introduces the debate as to the legality of preferential rules of origin under WTO law.
- Chapter 2 presents the main criteria for determining the origin of a good: the good was wholly obtained or produced in a territory or it satisfies one (or more) of the three substantial transformation criteria: manufacturing a good results in a change of tariff (line) heading,[59] a completion of a specific manufacturing or operating process, or the meeting of an *ad valorem* percentage requirement. These criteria will be examined in the context of traditional manufacturing techniques. Innovations to the rules found in the revisions to the PEM Rules of Origin and the USMCA will be referenced. Finally, the chapter concludes with an overview of origin certification and procedural requirements for trading under preferential tariff rates.
- Chapter 3 turns towards legal and economic critiques of preferential rules of origin to set the stage for understanding how the design of these rules can be motivated by protectionist trade policies and how the complexity of the rules can discourage traders from seeking trade preferences. With this awareness, the Chapter next questions whether "deeper" provisions, such as on labor or environmental regulations, should be included in rules of origin chapters. The Chapter then initiates an exploration of how the design of rules would be integrated in a framework for trade in a digitally interconnected world. The Chapter concludes with establishing that the 3D file, the digital instructions downloaded into the 3D printer, is a service.
- Chapter 4 mirrors, in part, Chapter 2. The wholly obtained/produced and the three substantial transformation criteria are examined in the context of 3D printed goods. Challenges in applying these criteria to determine the origin of a 3D file are discussed. The Chapter mainly focuses on the *ad valorem*

59 More specifically, the inputs of the good are classified on one tariff line and the final good is classified in a different tariff line.

criterion and signals where the design of rules under this criterion could lead to favoring a domestic industry or impeding third parties from trading with partners of a PTA.
- Chapter 5 links together the topics of each Chapter to provide recommendations for designing rules in the context of 3D printed goods and for making rules generally more functional and trader-friendly elements of trade law. Then, the Chapter explores the possibility of a plurilateral WTO agreement on preferential rules for PTAs while looking at the Bali and Nairobi Ministerial Decisions on Preferential Rules of Origin for LDCs as well as the ITA and the TFA. Next, the Chapter proposes areas where the WTO can utilize its institutional resources and expertise to assist traders with preferential rules when determining the origin of advanced manufactured product. In this way, the WTO could be responsive to the modernization of trade production. Finally, the Chapter presents some recommendations for the design of the rules in PTAs and regional trade instruments.
- The Conclusion provides a summary of the main arguments of this book and proposes some suggestions for the design of rules of origin for advanced manufactured goods.

4 A Quick Note on Terminology

3D File – This book uses the term 3D file rather than CAD file for the file that is downloaded into a printing machine. In designing the file, several steps occur. A 3D model is generated either by scanning an actual object or though designing it using Computer Aided Design (CAD) software. This CAD file is then processed into a STL file, which is a triangulated representation of the design. From this file, the layers for printing the object are calculated.[60]

RoO – This book abbreviates rules of origin as RoO. This applies both to preferential and non-preferential rules. The sources cited may have different versions of abbreviations, such as ROO or ROOs.

Additive Manufacturing and 3D Printing – "Additive Manufacturing" in basic terms is the manufacture of a product by the addition of successive layers of a material. 3D printing is a general term for this type of manufacturing.[61] There are specific methods of 3D printing, which will be examined in Chapter 4.

60 Tuomi, Chekurov and Partnanen (n 2) 5.

61 Andreas Gebhardt, Julia Kessler, and Laura Thurn, *3D Printing: Understanding Additive Manufacturing* (2nd edn, Hanser 2019) 2.

Advanced Manufacturing and Traditional Manufacturing – "Advanced Manufacturing" refers to manufacturing processes that use robotics, 3D printing, and computer modelling as significant elements of the production process.[62] This book uses the term "Traditional Manufacturing" to refer to processes that require a significant human labor component. This could be purely manual manufacturing or the use of machines that require substantial set up, configuration, and operation by human activity.

62 Commission, 'Advanced Manufacturing' (ec.europa.eu) <https://ec.europa.eu/info/research-and-innovation/research-area/industrial-research-and-innovation/key-enabling-technologies/advanced-manufacturing_en> accessed 2 December 2021.

CHAPTER 1

Preferential Rules of Origin in the WTO Legal Framework

This chapter presents preferential RoO in the framework of the WTO and its agreements. Where to situate preferential RoO within the WTO is a question that WTO officials, WTO Members, and trade experts are not quite sure how to answer. Hoekman and Kostecki argue that "the WTO has no rules regarding rules of origin" and Inama finds that the WTO is "conspicuously silent" on the administration of rules of origin.[1] In 2002, the Negotiating Group on Rules of the WTO prepared a "Compendium of Issues Related to Regional Trade Agreements."[2] They found that "No multilaterally agreed guidelines exist, apart from the Common Declaration with Regard to Preferential Rules of Origin annexed to the Agreement, which might be used in dealing with issues raised with respect to RTA rules of origin.[3]" Nearly 30 years after entering into force, the extent that the AOR or the GATT 1994 govern preferential RoO continues to be uncertain.

The first part of the chapter provides a brief overview of the history of RoO as a part of the WTO legal texts. The second part will discuss the debate on the legality of preferential RoO under Article XXIV of the GATT. The third part will introduce the role of the World Customs Organization as administer of the Harmonized System Convention (the HS code), which is used to identify goods in tariff schedules and in preferential RoO in PTAS. The chapter will conclude with a brief discussion on the differences, but also the similarities, between "Local Content Requirements" under the TRIMS and SCM agreements[4] and preferential rules requiring a certain level of local content for a good to qualify for preferential tariff treatment.

---

1 Bernard Hoekman and Michel M Kostecki, *The Political Economy of the World Trading System: The WTO and Beyond* (3rd edn, OUP 2009) 211. Stefano Inama, *Rules of Origin in International Trade* (CUP 2009) 530.

2 Negotiating Group on Rules, 'Compendium Of Issues Related To Regional Trade Agreements, Background Note by the Secretariat, Revision' (1 August 2002) TN/RL/W/8/Rev. 1 <https://docs.wto.org> accessed 5 January 2022.

3 ibid para 40.

4 Agreement on Trade-Related Investment Measures (TRIMS) (15 April 1994) LT/UR/A-1A/13; Agreement on Subsidies and Countervailing Measures (SCM Agreement) (15 April 1994) LT/UR/A-1A/9; both at <http://docsonline.wto.org>.

 | DOI:10.1163/9789004730595_003

1 The Agreement on Rules of Origin: Transitional Provisions for Non-preferential Rules and Guidelines for Preferential Rules

Prior to the WTO, several International Organizations approached, but did not quite embrace, RoO in trade instruments.[5] In the early part of the 20th Century, trade agreements provided for preferential tariff treatment, but did not always rely on rules to determine the origin of goods.[6] The 1923 International Convention relating to the Simplification of Customs Formalities was signed by many of the original GATT members.[7] Article 11 of the Convention endorsed reducing the need for and simplifying the issuance of certificates of origin, while acknowledging that states had the right to verify the origin of imported goods. The GATT 1947, however, did not include RoO. Inama proposes that negotiators focused on establishing the unconditional MFN principle in Article 1 of GATT 1947, and in "a MFN world there is no need to examine the origin of goods," as the same tariff would be applied to identical or like goods irrespective of their origin.[8] A subcommittee of the Preparatory Committee of the United Nations Conference on Trade and Employment, in reference to the article of GATT 1947 on "General Most Favoured Nation Treatment," considered "it to be clear that it is within the province of each importing member to determine, in accordance with the provisions of its law, for the purpose of applying the most-favoured-nation provision whether the goods do in fact originate in a particular country."[9] This emphasis on origin determination as within the "province" of Members is a perception that continues throughout the 21st

5 Stefano Inama, *Rules of Origin in International Trade* (CUP 2022) 2–3.

6 Hironori Asakura, 'The Harmonized System and Rules of Origin' (1993) 27 J World Trade 5, 6.

7 Petros C Mavroidis, *The Regulation of International Trade*, vol. 1 (MIT Press 2016) 216–217; International Convention relating to the Simplification of Customs Formalities (entered into force 27 November 1924) XXX LNTS 775.

8 Inama, *Rules of Origin in International Trade* (2022) (n 5) 3; The General Agreement on Tariffs and Trade (GATT 1947) art I(1): General Most-Favoured-Nation Treatment: "With respect to customs duties and charges of any kind imposed on or in connection with importation or exportation … and with respect to the method of levying such duties and charges, and with respect to all rules and formalities in connection with importation and exportation … any advantage, favour, privilege or immunity granted by any contracting party to any product originating in or destined for any other country shall be accorded immediately and unconditionally to the like product originating in or destined for the territories of all other contracting parties."

9 Preparatory Committee of the United Nations Conference on Trade and Employment, 'Report to Commission A by The Sub-Committee on Articles 14,15,& 24' (15 August 1947) E/PC/T/174, 3–4 <https://docs.wto.org> accessed 5 January 2022; Inama, *Rules of Origin in International Trade* (n 20) 2.

Century and is one of the factors that have complicated reaching a multilateral discipline on RoO.

While GATT 1947 had provisions on regulating the application of marks of origin,[10] these must be distinguished from RoO. Marks of origin are intended to inform consumers of the geographical origin of good as well serve as an identification of origin for customs duties. In order for customs authorities to determine whether the good qualifies for a *preferential tariff rate*, a good must also be accompanied by a certificate of origin demonstrating compliance with the applicable rules of origin of a PTA.[11] Under Article IX, marking requirements may not be discriminatory or unreasonably burdensome which would violate the national treatment provisions of the GATT.[12] In contrast, preferential RoO discriminate by distinguishing goods that qualify for preferential tariff treatment from those that do not qualify, and are thus subject to MFN tariff rates.[13]

There were attempts prior to the formation of the WTO to establish multilateral rules for RoO.[14] In 1953, the GATT Contracting Parties examined a Resolution submitted by the International Chamber of Commerce on a uniform set of rules, but a text on the definition of origin based on this Resolution was not accepted by all the Parties.[15] The 1973 International Convention on the Simplification and Harmonization of Customs Procedures (the Kyoto Convention) provided non-binding guidelines on RoO.[16] However, states and the European Communities (EC) developed and utilized RoO for implementing anti-dumping investigations and measures, textile and apparel quotas, General System of Preferences (GSPs) regimes, and preferential trade agreements.[17]

10 Marks of origin were incorporated by reference into GATT 1994 as Article IX. General Agreement on Tariffs and Trade 1994 (GATT 1994) art 1(a) <https://www.wto.org/english/docs_e/legal_e/06-gatt_e.htm> accessed 8 March 2025.

11 Mavroidis, *Regulation of International Trade,* vol 1 (n 7) 215, 217; M Matsushita, TJ Schoenbaum, PC Mavroidis, M Hahn, *The World Trade Organization: Law, Practice, and Policy* (3rd edn, OUP 2017) 237 (referred to as Matsushita).

12 Matsushita (n 11) 237.

13 Laura Puccio, '20 Years After Marrakesh: Reconsidering the Effects of Preferential Rules of Origin and Anti-Circumvention Rules on Trade in Inputs and Global Production Networks' 2014 Eur YB Intl Economic L 173, 176.

14 Moshe Hirsch, 'Agreement on Rules of Origin' in Rüdiger Wolfrum, Peter-Tobias Stoll and Holger P. Hestermeyer (eds), *WTO – Trade in Goods* (Koninklijke Brill NV 2010) 1103–1104.

15 Asakura (n 6) 6–7.

16 Bernard Hoekman, 'Rules of Origin for Goods and Services: Conceptual Issues and Economic Considerations' (1993) 27 J World Trade 82, 84.

17 WE James, 'Rules of Origin and Rules of Preference and the World Trade Organization: The Challenge to Global Trade Liberalization' in Patrick F J Macrory, Arthur Edmond Appleton and Michael G Plummer (eds) *World Trade Organization: Legal, Economic and Political Analysis* (Springer 2005) 265–266.

By the late 1980s, RoO had become a complex and unwieldly tool which could be utilized for protectionist purposes, and, thus, had an impact on trade covered by the GATT.[18]

1.1 *Non-preferential Rules of Origin in the Agreement on Rules of Origin*

During the Uruguay Round of Negotiations, the participants recognized that some multilateral discipline on RoO was needed.[19] As such, the Agreement on Rules of Origin [AOR] was included with Annex I to the Marrakesh Agreement, which established the Harmonization Work Programme [HWP] for the multilateral harmonization of non-preferential RoO. The three-year limit for the HWP completion passed in 1998. In an article on the 25th Anniversary of the AOR, WTO staff writers note that "[t]he efforts to negotiate global harmonized non-preferential rules of origin … has not delivered final results."[20] The desire of Members to maintain sovereignty in the use of rules of origin as commercial policy instruments is one of the reasons negotiations on harmonization of non-preferential RoO have not progressed towards a conclusion.[21]

Until the HWP is complete, Members are required to administer non-preferential RoO (for anti-dumping duties, safeguard measures, tariff quotas, for example) pursuant to Article 2, "Disciplines during the Transition Period."[22] Under Article 2(c) "Members shall ensure" that "rules of origin shall not themselves create restrictive, distorting, or disruptive effects on international trade."[23] Members shall not use non-preferential RoO to pursue trade objectives directly or indirectly, to impose conditions unrelated to manufacturing

18 Negotiating Group on Non-Tariff Measures, 'Meeting of 30 November 1989' (19 December 1989) MTN.GNG/NG2/14, para 10 <https://docs.wto.org> accessed 26 October 2024; Hirsch, 'Agreement on Rules of Origin' (n 14) 1104.

19 Peter Van den Bossche and Werner Zdouc, *The Law and Policy of the World Trade Organization* (Cambridge University Press 2019) 458; See generally, Negotiating Group on Non-Tariff Measures, 'Points Made in Relation to Rules of Origin: Synopsis by the Secretariat' (13 March 1990) MTN.GNG/NG2/W/54/Rev.1 <https://docs.wto.org> accessed 5 January 2022.

20 The WTO staff writers also mentioned that several speakers suggested that the work done on harmonization of non-preferential RoO was still beneficial for efforts on rule design outside of the WTO and the former chair of the CRO, Stefan Moser, claimed that "many of these rules found their way into free trade agreements." WTO, "Event marks 25th anniversary of the WTO's Agreement on Rules of Origin' (wto.org 4 March 2020) <https://www.wto.org/english/news_e/news20_e/roi_04mar20_e.htm> accessed 1 December 2021.

21 Inama, *Rules of Origin in International Trade* (2009) (n 1) 104–109; James (n 17) 271.

22 Agreement on Rules of Origin (AOR) (15 April 1994) LT/UR/A-1A/7, art 2 <https://docs.wto.org> accessed 5 January 2022; Matsushita (n 11) 238.

23 AOR art 2(c).

or processing, or to discriminate between Members.[24] Further, Members shall ensure that the rules for determining origin under the three criterion (Change of Tariff Heading, *ad valorem* percentage, and manufacturing and processing operations) are clearly defined,[25] administered consistently, uniformly, impartially, and reasonably,[26] and are based on a positive standard.[27]

Article 2 of the AOR was at the center of disputes on changes by the US to its non-preferential rules on non-apparel textile products for administering its textile quota regime pursuant to the WTO's Agreement on Textiles and Clothing.[28] On 22 May 1997, the EU submitted a request for consultations to the DSB arguing that these changes to the rules did not respect Article 2 of the AOR, but both parties reached a mutually agreed solution.[29] On 25 November 1998, the EU submitted a second request for consultations alleging that the US had failed to implement the agreed-upon changes, and on 31 July 2000, the parties again notified the DSB that they had reached a solution on the basis that the US propose to Congress to make agreed-upon changes to the Change of Tariff Heading and processing rules.[30]

In *US-Rules of Origin for Textiles and Apparel Products* (2003), the only decision on the AOR, the Panel established that Members have a wide degree of discretion in designing non-preferential RoO and that restrictive rules can be legitimate measures under the AOR. India argued that the rules were changed by the US to provide greater protection to domestic industries than allowed by a legitimate quota regime.[31] The Panel noted that in this instance the rules were being used to support a "trade policy instrument – quotas – which, by

---

24 ibid art 2(b, d); Hiroshi Imagawa and Edwin Vermulst, 'The Agreement on Rules of Origin', in Patrick FJ Macrory, Arthur Edmond Appleton and Michael G Plummer (eds), *World Trade Organization: Legal, Economic and Political Analysis* (Springer 2005) 612.

25 AOR, art 2(a).

26 ibid art 2(e).

27 ibid art 2(f).

28 Van den Bossche and Zdouc (n 19) 459–460.

29 *United States – Measures Affecting Textiles and Apparel Products*, Request for Consultations by the European Communities (3 June 1997) WT/DS85/1; *United States-Measures Affecting Textiles and Apparel Products*, Notification of Mutually-Agreed Solution (11 February 1998) WT/DS85/9.

30 *United States – Measures Affecting Textiles and Apparel Products (II)*, Request for Consultations by the European Communities (25 November 1998) WT/DS151/1; *United States-Measures Affecting Textiles and Apparel Products (II)*, Notification of Mutually Agreed Solution (31 July 2000) WT/DS151/10; Mavroidis, *The Regulation of International Trade*, vol 1 (n 5) 216.

31 Panel Report, *United States- Rules of Origin for Textiles and Apparel Products* (Panel report circulated 20 June 2003, adopted 21 July 2003) WT/DS243/R para. 6.49.

definition, is trade-restrictive."[32] The Panel confirmed that the provisions regulating non-preferential RoO, Article 2(b)–(d), set out what Members cannot do, and thereby give them the "discretion to decide what, within those bounds, they can do."[33] Thus, Article 2(b)–(d) "does not prevent Members from determining the criteria which confer origin, changing those criteria over time, or applying different criteria to different goods."[34]

However, the Panel clarified that Article 2(b) distinguishes rules of origin from commercial policy instruments. Rules may implement such policy, but they may not be used to pursue trade objectives.[35] Although changes by the US made the rules more restrictive, the Panel found that India did not provide sufficient evidence that the US was using the rules as an additional trade policy instrument or that the restrictive effects of the rules were "not incidental to the pursuit of legitimate objectives."[36]

India also argued that the rules created trade distorting effects in violation of Article 2(c) due to their "sheer complexity," which made it difficult for Indian exporters to engage in trade with the US due to the "complexities" of a commercial production chain between Indian wholesalers and Sri Lanka processers and manufacturers.[37] The US argued that India did not present any evidence that the rules "discouraged exporters from shipping their products to the United States because they simply could not understand them."[38] The Panel responded that "rules of origin are, by their nature, complex."[39] It was unable to accept that the measures had trade disruptive effects, because India did not show that the measures were more complex than necessary or how such complexity disrupted trade, and it did not provide evidence that traders or producers stopped exporting to the US due to such complexity.[40]

This ruling sets out a principle for non-preferential RoO that could potentially influence a ruling on preferential RoO. Rules are complex given differences in types of goods, production processes, costs, and policy objectives, but such complexity does not necessarily mean that the rules create trade distortive effects, even if traders cannot always understand or comply with these

---

32 ibid para 6.8.

33 van den Bossche and Zdouc (n 19) 460. Panel Report, *US-Rules of Origin for Textiles and Apparel Products*, para. 6.23–24.

34 Panel Report, *US-Rules of Origin for Textiles and Apparel Products*, para 6.23.

35 ibid, para. 6.137; Hirsch, 'Agreement on Rules of Origin' (n 14) 1114.

36 *US-Rules of Origin for Textiles and Apparel Products*, para. 6.94–96.

37 *US-Rules of Origin for Textiles and Apparel Products*, para 6.176.

38 ibid, para 6.177.

39 ibid, para 6.179.

40 ibid.

rules. However, a further question is whether it would it be possible to bring a claim before the DSB on preferential RoO.

1.2 *The Common Declaration with Regard to Preferential Rules of Origin*

Provisions on preferential RoO are found in the Common Declaration with Regard to Preferential Rules of Origin, Annex II to the AOR. During the Uruguay Round negotiations, several states including the US and Japan proposed that the AOR should cover preferential RoO, which the EC rejected arguing that preferential rules were based on the relations between the parties of trade arrangements.[41] The Secretariat's Note for a meeting of the Negotiating Group on Non-Tariff Measures references the EC delegation as making the distinction that preferential rules of origin "were only instruments to implement trade policy, rather than elements of trade policy" and "rules applicable to preferential trade could only be examined in the context of bilateral agreements of which they were part, and which were reviewed under Article XXIV of the GATT."[42] Instead, the focus of discussions should be on MFN rules, or non-preferential RoO.[43] This perspective is reflected in the AOR: preferential rules appear as an annex and only as a declaration.

Given the proliferation of regional and bilateral trade agreements since 1995, preferential RoO have multiplied in various formations, without having yet been subject to WTO dispute settlement or multilateral review under Article XXIV or the AOR.[44] As Stefano Inama puts it, the AOR's failure "to regulate preferential rules of origin … leaves an enormous loophole in the multilateral disciplines of rules of origin."[45] While the US proposal in 1989 that preferential RoO should be included within harmonization procedures was not accepted by other Members,[46] there was an understanding among the Members that

41 Hirsch, 'The Politics of Rules of Origin' (n 14) 331–332; Negotiating Group on Non-Tariff Measures, 'Meeting of 30 November 1989' (n 18) para 9; Negotiating Group on Non-Tariff Measures, 'Meeting of 14–15 February 1990' (13 March 1990) MTN.GNG.NG2/16, para 18 <https://docs.wto.org> accessed 6 January 2022.

42 Negotiating Group on Non-Tariff Measures, 'Meeting of 14–15 February 1990' (n 41) para 18. Annex II first appeared a draft of the AOR distributed on 6 June 1991. Negotiating Group on Rule Making and Trade-Related Investment Measures, 'Rules of Origin, Note by the Secretariat' (6 June 1991) MTN.GNG/RM/W/2 <https://docs.wto.org> accessed 6 January 2022.

43 Negotiating Group on Non-Tariff Measures, 'Meeting of 14–15 February 1990' (n 41) para 18.

44 Hirsch, 'The Politics of Rules of Origin' (n 14) 332; Mavroidis, *The Regulation of International Trade*, vol 1 (n 7) 228.

45 Inama, *Rules of Origin in International Trade* (2009) (n 1) 23.

46 Negotiating Group on Non-Tariff Measures, 'Meeting of 30 November 1989' (n 18) para. 9–10.

"some broad and general principles and procedures for the application of rules of origin [should be developed] in order to ensure that they were not abused for protectionist purposes."[47] Thus, the Declaration provides Members some guidelines for preferential RoO.

The first provision of the Declaration recognizes "that some Members apply preferential rules of origin, distinct from non-preferential rules of origin."[48] Preferential RoO are defined as "those laws, regulations and administrative determinations of general application applied by any Member to determine whether goods qualify to the granting of tariff preferences going beyond the application of paragraph 1 of Article I of GATT 1994 [most-favored-nation treatment]."[49] Members must:

> agree to ensure that: when they issue administrative determinations of general application, the requirements to be fulfilled are clearly defined. In particular:
> (i) in cases where the criterion of change of tariff classification is applied, such a preferential rule of origin, and any exceptions to the rule, must clearly specify the subheadings or headings within the tariff nomenclature that are addressed by the rule;
> (ii) in cases where the ad valorem percentage criterion is applied, the method for calculating this percentage shall also be indicated in the preferential rules of origin;
> (iii) in cases where the criterion of manufacturing or processing operation is prescribed, the operation that confers preferential origin shall be precisely specified.[50]

Further, the Declaration requires that "preferential rules of origin are based on a positive standard."[51]

Annex II also encourages transparency and certainty in legal texts and procedures.[52] Article 3(c) requires Members to publish "their laws, regulations, judicial decisions and administrative rulings of general application relating to preferential rules of origin … as if they were subject to, and in accordance

47 ibid para 10.
48 AOR, Annex II, art 1.
49 ibid.
50 ibid Annex II, art 3(a).
51 Negative standards "are permissible as part of a clarification of a positive standard or in individual cases where a positive determination of preferential origin is not necessary." (AOR, Annex II, art 3(b)).
52 Puccio (n 13) 192–193.

with, the provisions of paragraph 1 of Article X of GATT 1994."[53] Under Article X:1, such material must be "published promptly in such a manner as to enable governments and traders to become acquainted with them."[54] In addition, Article X:1 requires publication of agreements affecting international trade policy between governments or governmental agencies and contracting parties. However, the article does not require the publication of confidential information that could impede law enforcement, be contrary to the public interest, or prejudice legitimate commercial interests of public or private enterprises.

Laura Puccio argues that by using the language "as if they were subject to," Article 3(c) of Annex II excludes preferential RoO from the laws, regulations, decisions, and rulings in Article X:1 of GATT 1994, which thus excludes the application of Article X(3)(a) to preferential RoO.[55] Article X: 3(a) requires Members "to administer in a uniform, impartial and reasonable manner all its laws, regulations, decisions and rulings of the kind described in paragraph 1" of Article X.[56] Since the Annex to the AOR references Article X:1 and not Article X:3, a State is not required to keep RoO uniform among different RTAs and FTAs to which it is a party.[57] An examination of several trade instruments reveals that even among those having a common member, such as the ASEAN agreements, there are minor and also significant variations in the design of the RoO.[58]

There are some important distinctions between the disciplines that apply during the transition period for non-preferential RoO under Article 2 of the AOR and the Common Declaration (Annex II) for preferential RoO.[59]

53 Negotiating Group on Rules, 'Compendium Of Issues Related To Regional Trade Agreements, Background Note by the Secretariat, Revision' (n 2) fn 27: "The preamble to the Agreement recognizes that clear and predictable rules of origin and their application facilitates the flow of international trade, and states the desirability that rules of origin themselves do not create unnecessary obstacles to trade. The Common Declaration provides disciplines for preferential rules of origin; in particular, Article 3(c) requires that laws and regulations relating to them be published 'as if they were subject to, and in accordance with, the provisions of Article X of GATT 1994'".

54 GATT 1994, art. X(1).

55 Puccio (n 13) 192.

56 GATT 1994, art X(3)(a). Subparagraph (c) requires the parties to institute or maintain independent tribunals to review administrative rulings.

57 The final subsections of Article 3 and Article 4 of Annex II focus on administrative procedures and notification requirements.

58 *See* Stefano Inama and Edmund W Sim, *Rules of Origin in ASEAN* (CUP 2015).

59 A draft of the Final Act embodying the results of the Uruguay Round of Multilateral Trade Negotiations, circulated 3 December 1990, included a draft of the AOR (but without Annex II as the Members had not yet decided whether preferential RoO should be covered by the Agreement). Footnote 1 of Article 2(d) states: "It is understood that this provision does not apply to rules of origin used for preferential trading arrangements." In that draft,

The obligations against using rules of origin to create restrictive or distortive effects on international trade or the requirements that the rules be applied in a consistent manner established by Article 2 (AOR) do not appear directly or by reference in Annex II.[60] While the Declaration includes provisions similar to Article 2 of the AOR, such as the rules should be clearly defined and based on positive standards, the provisions in the Declaration, Moshe Hirsch asserts, are legally non-binding.[61] Despite this, "it seems that the rules of Annex II exert some pressure upon Members to comply with its standards of conduct" and the legality of rules could be challenged under Article XXIV of GATT.[62] Even if the Declaration is non-binding and does not prohibit rules from having trade distortive effects, the extent to which Members have sovereignty under Annex II to design rules that impact trade is still unknown as no dispute on the substance of the Declaration has come before the DSB.

In *Turkey-Restrictions on Imports of Textile and Clothing Products* (1999), India claimed that the quantitative restrictions imposed by Turkey on imports of textiles and clothing products were inconsistent with the GATT 1994 and the Agreement on Textiles and Clothing.[63] Turkey imposed the restrictions on the basis of harmonizing their import regime with the EC, otherwise the EC would have excluded Turkish products from free trade to prevent trade diversion (i.e., Indian products imported into Turkey and then re-exported to the EC as "Turkish" products).[64] The Appellate Body (AB) found that the measures were inconsistent and proposed that instead of quantitative restrictions, an alternative for meeting the requirements of Article XXIV:8(a) GATT (governing the formation of a customs union) were rules of origin:

> Turkey could adopt rules of origin for textile and clothing products that would allow the European Communities to distinguish between those textile and clothing products originating in Turkey, which would enjoy

---

Article 2(d) is the provision that prohibits the use of non-preferential rules "as instruments to purse trade objectives directly or indirectly." That footnote was absent in the 20 December 1991 draft and is not included in the final text of the AOR.

60 Imagawa and Vermulst (n 24) 612; Moshe Hirsch, 'The Politics of Rules of Origin' in Tomer Broude, Marc L. Busch, and Amelia Porges (eds), *The Politics of International Economic Law* (CUP 2011) 333.

61 Hirsch, 'Agreement on Rules of Origin' (n 60) 1149–1150.

62 ibid 1152.

63 *Turkey-Restrictions on Imports of Textile and Clothing Products* (1999) WT/DS34/14 <https://www.wto.org/english/tratop_e/dispu_e/cases_e/ds34_e.htm> accessed 2 December 2021.

64 Appellate Body Report, *Turkey-Restrictions on Imports of Textile and Clothing Products* (adopted 19 November 1999) WT/DS34/14, para 61.

> free access to the European Communities under the terms of the custom union, and those textile and clothing products originating in third countries, including India. In fact … Turkey and the European Communities themselves appear to have recognized that rules of origin could be applied to deal with any possible trade diversion.[65]

Thus, the AB recognized preferential RoO as means to prevent trade diversion in customs unions, but it did not proceed with interpreting provisions in Annex II of the AOR. The AB does not refer to subparagraph 8(b), governing FTAs. However, the fact that the AB did not examine FTAs in the context of Article XXIV is not unique to disputes that touch upon rules of origin; WTO jurisprudence on FTAs, in comparison to those on antidumping duties or subsidies is sparse.[66] This relative paucity of jurisprudence on the legality of FTAs and also RoO provides the foundation for scholarly debate as to the legality of preferential RoO under Article XXIV.

2 The Legality of Preferential Rules of Origin in Free Trade Agreements

Article XXIV of GATT 1994 regulates PTAs so as to create more trade for all WTO members even though PTAs establish preferences, such as tariff rates that apply only to members of the agreements.[67] In other words, a PTA should not make trade between the third-party countries and PTA countries more difficult.[68] Under Article XXIV: 5(b):

> The duties and *other regulations of commerce* maintained in each of the constituent territories [of a free trade area] and applicable at the formation of such free-trade area or the adoption of such interim agreement … *shall not be higher or more restrictive than the corresponding duties and other regulations of commerce* existing in the same constituent territories

65 ibid para. 62.

66 Manfred Elsig, Bernard Hoekman, and Joost Pauwelyn, 'Thinking About the Performance of the World Trade Organization: A Discussion Across Disciplines' in Manfred Elsig, Bernard Hoekman, and Joost Pauwelyn (eds), *Assessing the World Trade Organization: Fit for Purpose?* (CUP 2017) 32.

67 Peter Van den Bossche and Denise Prévost, *Essentials of WTO Law* (2nd edn, CUP 2021) 139–140.

68 Mavroidis, *The Regulation of International Trade,* vol 1 (n 7) 299.

> prior to the formation of the free-trade area, or interim agreement as the case may be"(my italics).[69]

As Hoekman and Kostecki note, "Article XXIV is entirely silent on rules of origin, which is rather surprising given that they have an important bearing on the effects of a PTA."[70] Preferential rules must be discriminatory to prevent free-riding of the benefits of a PTA. Without such rules, traders could import third-party goods through the cheapest port, entering the PTA territory, and then transport these goods into other locations in the territory.[71]

The question is whether RoO are "a regulation of commerce" that falls under GATT Article XXIV:5. In 2002, the Negotiating Group on Rules in its "Compendium of Issues Related to Regional Trade Agreements" questioned how to define "other regulations of commerce" in Article XXIV:5. The Group noted that "it might have a wider scope for FTAs than for customs unions, especially if, as it has been argued sometimes, FTA rules of origin should be considered as a regulation of commerce in that context."[72] Later in the Compendium, the Group made the following observations in a section called "The qualification of RTA rules of origin as 'other regulations of commerce.'" Under Article XXIV:5:

> distinct interpretations subsist:
> - RTA origin rules constitute an ORC [other regulation of commerce]
> - RTA origin rules do not constitute an ORC, given that by definition they do not affect trade with third parties.
> - A case-by-case examination of the preferential rules of origin in RTAs is needed. That examination would clearly indicate whether these rules had restrictive effects on the trade vis-à-vis third parties.[73]

Further, rules of origin raise questions on "whether it is appropriate to compare the rules of origin of a new RTA with those of an earlier RTA with overlapping membership which it superseded" and "whether diagonal cumulation

69 Under Article XXIV: 8(b), "a free-trade area shall be understood to mean a group of two or more customs territories in which the duties and other restrictive regulations of commerce … are eliminated on substantially all the trade between the constituent territories in products originating in such territories." Similar wording is found in provisions on customs unions – Article XXIV: 5(a) and Article XXIV: 8(a).

70 Hoekman and Kostecki (n 1) 485–486.

71 Puccio (n 13) 176.

72 Negotiating Group on Rules, 'Compendium Of Issues Related To Regional Trade Agreements, Background Note by the Secretariat, Revision' (n 2) para 52.

73 ibid para 78.

schemes contravene WTO rules, as they favour certain third-parties to a particular RTA, while discriminating against the rest."[74] Diagonal cumulation is a core principle of the Pan-Euro Mediterranean Rules of Origin which applies to trade among the EU, EFTA, and countries in the Mediterranean region. This will be examined in the next Chapter.

There is some debate on whether preferential RoO constitute on ORC. In 1993 and 2008, Hoekman questioned whether RoO fall under the term "other regulations of commerce."[75] In 2018, Mavroidis and Vermulst argued that references in Article XXIV GATT (1994) and GSP schemes to "commerce" mean "international commerce" and Article XXIV and the Enabling Clause likely concern "instruments that apply exclusively to imported goods, like custom duties."[76] Rules of origin are "not necessarily" a regulation of international commerce, "since, unlike duties that concern imported goods, rules of origin concern domestic goods as well." Therefore, Article XXIV does not apply to RoO.[77]

Mavroidis and Vermulst find that "the legal basis for enacting preferential rules of origin is shaky" as they are adopted on the basis that, without them, the granting of preferences would be impeded.[78] In a footnote, the authors question why there has been no litigation on preferential RoO and also provide the answer: "for strategic reasons (all WTO members participate in at least one FTA), litigation is not an option" and beneficiaries of GSPs "might legitimately fear total exclusion from preferences in case they complain about the restrictiveness of preferential rules of origin."[79] Elsig, Hoekman, and Pauwelyen note that the absence of disputes under Article XXIV can be explained by "the adage that 'people who live in glass houses shouldn't throw stones.'"[80] In other words, a Member may be unwilling to have its own compliance with Article XXIV questioned by starting a dispute at the WTO claiming violations of the Article by another Member.[81]

Van den Bossche and Puccio assert that a legal basis for preferential RoO can be found in the WTO texts. According to Van den Bossche, Annex II of the

74 ibid. para 79. In paragraph 80, the Group also reported that "[m]ore recently, it has been noted that a harmonization of RTA rules of origin might be desirable in the long run. However, it has been argued that this might not be workable given that those rules derived from production and trade structures in place between the RTAs parties."

75 Hoekman (1993) (n 16) 86 and Hoeckman and Kostecki (n 1) 485.

76 Petros C Mavroidis and Edwin Vermulst, 'The Case for Dropping Preferential Rules of Origin' (2018) 52 J World Trade 1, 11.

77 ibid.

78 ibid 6.

79 ibid 11, fn 16.

80 Elsig, Hoekman, and Pauwelyn (66) 32.

81 ibid.

AOR leads "to the granting of tariff preferences going beyond the application of the MFN treatment obligation."[82] Puccio also finds that in addition to the "tolerance for preferential rules of origin" being established in Annex II, such rules can be legitimated under Article XXIV GATT.[83] However, as under Article XXIV:4 the purpose of a customs union or a free trade area is facilitating trade among the constituents and not raising barriers to trade to third parties, preferential RoO should not impede third parties from trading with the parties of the PTA.[84] Even if an argument can be made that preferential RoO comply with Article XXIV, the possible protectionist impact and trade distorting effect must be taken into consideration.[85] As will be explored further in Chapter 5, this does support some further action from the WTO on preferential RoO.

Finally, Mavroidis finds that Article XX of GATT 1994 should be applicable to rules of origin.[86] Article XX performs a balancing function, allowing Members to deviate from obligations under GATT or GATT 1994 in order to protect societal values and interests.[87] According to Mavriodis, "WTO members are free to decide on origin of goods sold in their market and have to observe an obligation not to discriminate. As a result, we are squarely under the purview of GATT here. Consequently, Article XX of GATT should be applicable."[88] However, Van den Bossche and Prévost note that "Article XX of the GATT 1994 is not available to justify inconsistencies with any other WTO agreement unless it has been expressly or implicitly incorporated."[89] No express reference to Article XX is made in the AOR or Annex II. There have been no disputes brought before the DSB which examine whether Article XX has been implicitly incorporated into the AOR or Annex II.

Although the legal status of preferential RoO under WTO jurisprudence may be in question, states justify the inclusion of such rules in trade agreements, because, as the AB noted in *Turkey-Textiles*, they can prevent trade diversion.[90] The WTO gives Members States discretion in designing preferential RoO, and

---

82 Peter Van den Bossche, *The Law and Policy of the World Trade Organization: Text, Cases and Materials* (2nd edn, CUP 2008) 436.

83 Puccio (n 13) 192–193.

84 ibid 193–194.

85 ibid 175.

86 Mavroidis, *The Regulation of International Trade*, vol 1 (n 7) 477.

87 Van den Bossche and Prévost (n 67) 108.

88 Mavroidis, *The Regulation of International Trade*, vol 1 (n 7) 477.

89 Van den Bossche and Prévost (n 67) 107. In comparison, see Christian Delev, 'Straining the spaghetti bowl: re-evaluating the regulation of preferential rules of origin' (2022) 25 J Intl Economic L 1, 42–43 (finding, however, that XX(d) not likely to justify more restrictive rules in PTAs to prevent trade diversion under a normal trading environment).

90 Puccio (n 13) 174–175; Mavroidis & Vermulst (n 76) 4.

as a result, this has created a wide range of differing preferential rules regimes among FTAs.[91] However, these various preferential RoO do share a common link: the use of the Harmonized Commodity Description and Coding System (HS, HS nomenclature) to identify goods in the lists of product specific rules.

3 The World Customs Organization and the Harmonized System Nomenclature

The WTO is not the only source for international guidelines on rules of origin. Another important name is the World Customs Organization, for two reasons: the Kyoto Convention and the HS Nomenclature. The WTO and the WCO claim distinct jurisdiction on trade matters, but cooperate and assist each other in disputes and with training on trade matters. The Revised Kyoto Convention, administered by the World Customs Organization (WCO), includes guidelines for determining the origin of a good. The 1973 Convention was amended in 1999, and the Revised Convention entered into force 3 February 2006. Promoting trade facilitation independent from, but complementary to the AOR, it aims to limit the use of RoO as trade impediments with guidance on designing the substantial transformation criteria and certification procedures.[92] As of July 2024, the Revised Kyoto Convention has 137 contracting parties.[93]

The 1973 Kyoto Convention provided a standard definition for when a good undergoes an origin conferring "substantial transformation." National or regional courts had determined origin based on two general criteria: the good was wholly obtained in the territory or a transformation to the product occurred in the territory which resulted in a new product.[94] The 1973 Convention defined the "substantial transformation criterion" as the "criterion according to which origin is determined by regarding as the country of origin the country in which the last substantial manufacturing or processing, deemed sufficient to give the commodity its essential character, has been carried out".[95]

91 ibid; Anne van de Heetkamp and Ruud Tusveld, *Origin Management: Rules of Origin in Free Trade Agreements* (Springer 2011) 41.

92 Inama, *Rules of Origin in International Trade* (2022) (n 5) 8–9; Matsushita (n 11) 237–238.

93 WCO, 'WCO, 'Conventions: Summary of Positions' (wccomd.org 1 July 2024) <https://www.wcoomd.org/-/media/wco/public/global/pdf/about-us/legal-instruments/conventions-and-agreements/revised-kyoto/sg0230eb.pdf?la=en> accessed 20 October 2024.

94 Inama, *Rules of Origin in International Trade* (2022) (n 5) 5–6.

95 International Convention on the Simplification and Harmonization of Customs Procedures (Kyoto Convention 1973, signed 18 May 1973, entered into Force 24 September 1974) Annex D.1, Definitions.

The substantial transformation criterion "can be expressed" through a rule requiring a change of tariff heading, a list of manufacturing or processing operations, or an *ad valorem* percentage rule.[96] The 1973 Convention did not select one criterion as a preferred criterion on the basis that differences in manufacturing processes means that one criterion may be better suited for one type of good while a different criterion may be more apt for another type of good, and it gave members flexibility to design rules that combine two criteria.[97]

The 1973 Kyoto Convention did not require Contracting Parties to accept general principles such as MFN, national treatment, and transparency.[98] The 2006 revision, in the Preamble, recognizes that the simplification and harmonization of customs procedures can be accomplished through the modernization of customs procedures to enhance "efficiency and effectiveness" and through "the application of Customs procedures and practices in a predictable, consistent, and transparent manner."[99] While this language has some resemblance to the calls for transparency and predictability in the preamble of the AOR, there is no mention in the annex on rules of origin (Specific Annex K) on not designing rules to create trade distortive effects or not using the rules to pursue trade objectives.[100] While Annex K provides some recommendations on how to design the substantial transformation criteria, there is no requirement that such rules be clearly defined.[101] The convention includes a dispute settlement procedure which encourages the parties to first settle the matter through negotiation. If no settlement is reached, Article 14 states that "Contracting Parties in dispute may agree in advance to accept the recommendations of the Management Committee as binding." A search online and on the WCO's website did not find references to disputes brought under Article 14.

The WCO is also responsible for the development, maintenance, and updating of the Harmonized Commodity Description and Coding System [HS/HS Nomenclature]. The Customs Cooperation Council (CCC) designed a tariff classification system called the Brussels Tariff Nomenclature after World War II.[102] In the 1980s the system was updated and renamed to the HS, and the CCC

96 ibid Annex D.1, Introduction.

97 James (n 17) 269.

98 Edwin Vermulst and Paul Waer, 'European Community Rules of Origin as Commercial Policy Instruments?' (1990) 24 J World Trade 55, 60.

99 Revised Kyoto Convention, preamble.

100 ibid Annex K.

101 ibid.

102 Ian S Forrester and Tashi Kaul, 'Tariff Classification,' in Patrick F J Macrory, Arthur Edmond Appleton and Michael G Plummer (eds), *World Trade Organization: Legal, Economic and Political Analysis* (Springer 2005) 1583.

became the WCO in 1994.[103] The HS was designed for tariffs, trade statistics, data transmission, freight tariffs and transport statistics, and commercial commodity description and coding systems.[104] It is used by governments, international organizations, and the private sector.[105] The HS nomenclature has, in the words of the WTO's website, "become the de facto standard for Members" in their schedule of concessions under Article II of the GATT and is used by almost all members "as a tool to define the products which are covered by certain agreements" even if those Members are not also members of the WCO.[106] The HS is also used in PTAs in at least two places: first, in the schedule of preferential tariffs, which set the tariff rates that differ from the rates in the parties' schedules of concessions at the WTO[107]; secondly, in the product-specific list in the preferential RoO chapter that specify the products that must undergo certain changes within the territory.[108]

While the HS is utilized by WTO Members, the WTO and the WCO have different competencies. The WCO has exclusive competency in the classification of goods in the HS, and the WCO's goal is to make customs administrations more efficient through the use of the HS.[109] Disputes arising from the application of the HS Convention or the classification of a good in the HS should be brought before the WCO's dispute settlement system, even though it can only issue non-binding advisory opinions.[110] While the WTO has competency over trade regulation, panels and the AB at times assess a measure's inconsistency by referring to the HS; for example, when determining whether a measure violates the national treatment principle by treating domestic like products differently from foreign like products.[111] Likeness can be based on how the goods are classified in the HS.[112]

The role of the HS in forming the basis of Members' Schedules of Concessions was examined in *EC-Customs Classification of Frozen Boneless Chicken Cuts* (2005). The AB found that although the HS was not part of the Marrakesh

103 ibid.

104 Asakura (n 6) 8–9.

105 WCO, 'What is the Harmonized System (HS)?' (wcoomd.org) <http://www.wcoomd.org/en/topics/nomenclature/overview/what-is-the-harmonized-system.aspx> accessed 2 December 2021.

106 WTO, 'The WTO and World Customs Organization' (wto.org) <https://www.wto.org/english/thewto_e/coher_e/wto_wco_e.htm> accessed 2 December 2021.

107 Forrester and Kaul (n 102) 1586.

108 ibid.

109 ibid 1584.

110 ibid 1585.

111 ibid 1584–1585.

112 ibid 1588.

Agreement, "there was broad consensus among GATT Contracting Parties to use the Harmonized System as the basis for their WTO schedules … [thus] this consensus constitutes an 'agreement' between WTO Members 'relating to' the *WTO Agreement* that was 'made in connection with the conclusion' of that Agreement, within the meaning of Article 31(2)(a) of the *Vienna Convention*." [italics original][113] Joost Pauwelyn, Andrew Guzman and Jennifer Hillman note the significance of this decision as the HS thus forms part of the relevant context in interpreting the GATT schedule of concessions.[114] While panels and the AB may seek advice from the WCO, Marina Foltea warns this does not suggest "that the WTO dispute settlement organs should, as a matter of law, defer to the WCO interpretations or practice with respect to HS classifications."[115] Yet, she proposed (in 2012) that WCO practice "may be useful in future WTO disputes dealing" with subject matter other than classification disputes, such as "rules of origin."[116] A dispute on RoO could be linked to an interpretation of the HS, because the tariff classification referred to in the change in tariff classification criterion of a PTA is likely the HS given that most members of the WTO are also members of the WCO.

For purposes of RoO analysis, there are some elements of the HS that require familiarity. A country or territory (in the case of the EU) develops a code based on the HS code: the first six digits must be the HS code if the state is a party to the HS convention,[117] and numeric extensions are added by the national or regional customs authorities.[118] The first two digits indicate a Chapter Heading and the subsequent digits indicate subheadings.[119] Generally, the Chapter Heading represents a category of goods, and the subheadings represent degrees of processing of those goods.[120] Additionally, the WTO allows Members

113 Appellate Body Report, *European Communities – Customs Classification Of Frozen Boneless Chicken Cuts* (circulated 12 September 2005, adopted 27 September 2005) WT/DS269/AB/R and WT/DS286/AB/R, para 199.

114 Joost HB Pauwelyn, Andrew T Guzman and Jennifer A Hillman, *International Trade Law* (3rd edn, WoltersKluwer 2016) 184.

115 Marina Foltea, 'The World Customs Organization' in Marina Foltea (ed), *International Organizations in WTO Dispute Settlement* (CUP 2012) 236.

116 ibid 244.

117 Forrester and Kaul (n 102) 1590.

118 Heetkamp & Tusveld (n 91) 7.

119 WCO, 'Frequently Asked Questions' (wcoomd.org 10 June 2020) <http://www.wcoomd.org/en/topics/nomenclature/overview/harmonized_system_faq.aspx> accessed 2 December 2021.

120 Asakura (n 6) 12.

some flexibility in classification of goods within the HS provided that the GATT Articles I:1 (MFN) and II:1 (Schedule of Concessions) are not violated.[121]

While the HS provides a classification system that is accessible to custom officials, traders, and industry analysists,[122] this system poses several challenges in terms of determining the origin of a good. First, it was not designed for origin determination.[123] The progression of subheadings in every Chapter is not consistent in terms of degree of processing, which creates challenges when applying a general change of tariff classification criterion to determine origin.[124] Further, the HS is mainly designed for classifying completed goods, although it does provide some guidance on where to classify unfinished or disassembled goods or goods that are composites of different materials based on their characteristics.[125] The HS is amended every 5 years to keep up to date with technical developments and changes in international trade,[126] but this also means that custom officials and importers must also be aware of these revisions as tariff schedules and product specific rules of origin in trade instruments may not be revised or there may be a delay in revising them.

4 Local Content Requirement – Not to Be Confused with Prohibited Local Content Requirement under the SCM and TRIMS Agreements

Before examining the methods for determining the origin of a traditionally manufactured product, a clarification of the use of the term "Local Content Requirement" is needed. A "Local Content Requirement" can be a provision in a legal text requiring a manufacturer to incorporate a certain level of locally produced inputs into a product to qualify for a benefit such as market access, import licenses, or tax benefits.[127] Local Content Requirements are prohibited

121 Forrester and Kaul (n 102) 1599; Van den Bossche and Zdouc (n 19) 450.

122 Asakura (n 6) 14.

123 ibid 20.

124 ibid 16.

125 Van den Bossche (2008) (n 82) 430; WCO, 'General Rules for the Interpretation of the Harmonized System' (wcoomd.org) <http://www.wcoomd.org/-/media/wco/public/global/pdf/topics/nomenclature/instruments-and-tools/hs-nomenclature-2017/2017/0001_2017e_gir.pdf?la=en> accessed 2 December 2021.

126 Asakura (n 6) 11–12; WCO, 'What is the Harmonized System (HS)?' (n 105). As a result of the HS updates, the Schedule of Concessions and the Information Technology Agreement must be updated so that the codes of the products covered under those instruments correlate to of the amended HS. WTO, 'The WTO and World Customs Organization' (n 106).

127 Holgar P Hestermeyer and Laura Nielsen, 'The Legality of Local Content Measures under WTO Law' (2014) 48 J World Trade 553, 554.

under the TRIMS and SCM Agreements and Article III.4 of the GATT.[128] When reading preferential RoO, for example in the USMCA, one finds the phrase "regional value content" or "local value content," to refer to value produced in the region when manufacturing a good. This value can come from the costs of materials, the labor performed, or the direct overhead costs.[129] Thus a preferential rule can require that a good include a certain amount of inputs produced in the territory to qualify for preferential treatment under the PTA. Is not this a type of Local Content Requirement?

In their article, "The Legality of Local Content Measures under WTO Law," Holgar Hestermeyer and Laura Nielsen "classify local content requirements according to the benefit granted," as they "condition a benefit on the use of local content."[130] However, local content requirements:

> can also be categorized by their method of calculating the domestic content, most commonly by 'value added'. This is normally done referring to the 'rules of origin', which also decide whether a product counts as national for purposes of benefiting from a certain FTA. The construction of these rules can be used and often is used as a policy tool for advancing local industry too.[131]

Although a product specific rule may require a level of local content value, rules of origin are not categorized as prohibited local content requirements. Prohibited local content instruments that lead to obtaining a benefit are licenses, government procurement, financial incentives, such as feed-in tariffs (FIT), financing, and "other financial incentives, including tariffs."[132]

Hestermeyer and Nielsen find that preferential tariff treatment is also used with respect to local content requirements. An example is "Ecuador's imposition of a new tariff on automobile knock-down kits, where a discount of 1% for every 2% of local content is granted."[133] However, they do not connect this example with any reference to RoO. Preferential tariffs in FTAs discriminate against third party imports and this can be achieved through RoO requiring a

---

128 ibid 555; Pierre Sauvé, 'Life beyond local content: exploring alternative measures of industry support in the context of WTO accession' (2016) 1 J Int'l Trade 1, 13.

129 See eg, Agreement between the United States of America, the United Mexican States, and Canada (USMCA) (entered into force 1 July 2020) ch 4, art 4.1 (definition of Total Cost), and art 4.5.

130 Hestermeyer and Nielsen (n 127) 557.

131 ibid.

132 ibid 557–564.

133 ibid 564.

certain level of local content. If traders comply with the rules, they receive a benefit – preferential tariff treatment.

Pierre Sauvé distinguishes RoO as trade policy similar to, but different from, local content requirements. He notes that there has a been a decline in local content requirements since the Uruguay Round due to a state's need to comply with the TRIMS and SCM agreements for accession to the WTO, growing doubts about the efficacy of local content requirements, and the rise of production fragmentation and GVC-driven trade.[134] However, he points out, there has also "been a trend towards using trade policy measures that achieve objectives similar to those of selected performance requirements. These include rules of origin in preferential trade agreements …"[135] Under Article XXIV, Members use PTAs to achieve trade policy aims that enhance the local market, making "extensive use of the rules of origin to increase local value added."[136] As a result of the domestic content requirement, RoO "have similar effects as local content requirements."[137] Sauvé does not delve deeper into the legal implications of why local content requirements are prohibited under the TRIMS and SCM, while rules of origin in PTAs may be permitted, or at least are not contested, even though they can achieve the same aim of requiring producers to use local inputs. What we can take away from these references to RoO in the articles by Hestermeyer and Nielsen and Sauvé is that (1) states use PTAs to achieve trade policy aims, (2) a state may use rules of origins to benefit the local industry, and (3) the use of these rules to achieve such aims is widespread. The work of economists in documenting how RoO lead to protectionists effects in trade will be discussed in Chapter 3.

5 Conclusion

The WTO seems to govern preferential RoO with a light touch. Annex II of the AOR sets guidelines for designing the rules and is silent on preventing preferential RoO in a PTA from having a trade distortive effect. Whether RoO are inconsistent with Article XXIV GATT is open for debate, but what is not debated is that they are widely used by Members of the WTO.

A few notes before looking at the substantial transformation criteria in the next Chapter. Preferential RoO are found in GSPs, and in that context they are

134 Sauvé, 'Life beyond local content' (n 128) 19.
135 ibid.
136 ibid.
137 ibid.

referred to as non-reciprocal preferential RoO, as they are determined only by the preference-giving country. The WTO has shifted its energy away from the HWP for non-preferential rules of origin towards establishing a framework for non-reciprocal preferential RoO. A General Council decision from 2010, "Transparency Mechanism For Preferential Trade Arrangements", requires for PTAs formed under the Enabling Clause, PTAs with LDCs, and any other non-reciprocal preferential treatment, that the notifying member include the "product-specific preferential rules of origin as defined in the PTA" as part of the initial notification of the PTA to the WTO.[138] In 2013, the Bali Ministerial Conference presented multilateral guidelines for rules of origin for LDC non-reciprocal preference schemes to facilitate qualifying for preferences and market access opportunities.[139] In 2015, the Nairobi Ministerial Decision provided further guidelines on rules in non-reciprocal preferential trade arrangements.[140] In this book, non-reciprocal preferential RoO will be referenced when relevant to a certain issue. Chapter 5 includes a more detailed look at the Bali and Nairobi Ministerial Decisions.

The two DSB cases dealing with RoO referenced in this chapter were related to textiles, and although RoO are significant to trade in textiles, this book will not explore textiles in much depth. The rules for textiles in PTAs add an additional level of complexity to the analysis of RoO, and the regulation of trade in textiles underwent significant modifications at the multilateral level before being integrated into the GATT/WTO framework.[141] An examination of RoO in the context of textiles would provide enough material for at least an additional chapter.

In their article on the design of 21st Century trade agreements, Hoekman and Nelson argue that rule-making in the context of shallow trade agreements, those based upon a reciprocal exchange of commitments, are still needed to address the issue of national policies imposing negative international spillovers. This requires "the major trading powers to agree on additional rules of the game for domestic industrial policies that are not captured by existing WTO agreements."[142] They do not refer to rules of origin, but in fact, such rules are

---

138 General Council Decision, 'Transparency Mechanism for Preferential Trade Arrangements' (14 December 2010) WT/L/806, Annex I, para 28(d).

139 WTO, 'Rules of Origin' (wto.org) <https://www.wto.org/english/tratop_e/roi_e/roi_e.htm#documents> accessed 2 December 2021.

140 ibid.

141 Matsushita (n 11) 248–249.

142 Bernard Hoekman and Douglas Nelson, '21st Century Trade Agreements and the Owl of Minerva' (2018), EUI Working Papers, RSCAS 2018/04, 22 <https://cadmus.eui.eu/bitstream/handle/1814/50964/RSCAS_2018_04.pdf?sequence=1&isAllowed=y> accessed 23 October 2021.

motivated by domestic industrial policies that can have negative international spillovers, as will be discussed further in Chapter 3. Before designing new rules of origin for 21st Century trade in products incorporating digital technology, it is necessary to understand what the current rules of the game are. The next chapter will focus on preferential RoO designed to determine the origin of traditionally manufactured goods.

CHAPTER 2

Rules of Origin in the Context of Traditional Manufacturing

The previous Chapter focused on the history of rules of origin in international trade instruments and their position in the multilateral trade law system. However, one finds preferential RoO, and all of their variations, in bilateral and regional trade instruments. In this Chapter, the focus is on the 'nuts-and-bolts' of RoO and the main criteria for determining origin. While the legality of preferential RoO may be questioned, for traders, RoO are not legal theory: non-compliance may result in fines and sanctions. Understanding how these rules function with regards to traditionally manufactured goods will prepare the discussion in Chapter 4 on how 3D printing may disrupt not only the legal purpose of rules of origin but also the administrative processes of determining origin.

The Chapter begins with an introduction to the two main origin criteria: wholly obtained or produced and substantial transformation. Then, the Chapter focuses on the three categories of the substantial transformation criteria: change of tariff heading (CTH), specific manufacturing or operating processes, and *ad valorem* percentage. As Imagawa and Vermulst state, none of these tests are "perfect" and there is no "'one size fits all' rule for the origin determination of thousands of products."[1] The examples in this chapter demonstrate how the rules in PTAs vary from the general guidelines proposed by the Kyoto Convention and Annex II of the AOR. The Chapter will conclude with a brief discussion of the administrative procedures for certifying the origin of a good, the national or regional regulatory offices with judicial and supervisory functions, and the roles of international organizations in origin determination. Examples will mainly come from the Pan-Euro-Mediterranean Cumulation System of Origin Rules (PEM) and the USMCA, but references to the ASEAN Trade in Goods Agreement will be included (ASEAN TIGA).

1 Hiroshi Imagawa and Edwin Vermulst, 'The Agreement on Rules of Origin', in Patrick FJ Macrory, Arthur Edmond Appleton and Michael G Plummer (eds), *World Trade Organization: Legal, Economic and Political Analysis* (Springer 2005) 609.

 | DOI:10.1163/9789004730595_004

The PEM is the basis for the rules of origin of FTAs among the EU, EFTA, and countries in North Africa, the Middle East, the Balkans and Eastern Europe.[2] The Pan-European cumulation system was created in 1997, initially covering the EC, EFTA states, the Central Eastern European Countries, and the Baltic States.[3] In 2005 the "pan-Euro-Mediterranean cumulation system of origin" was established and Turkey and states in the Middle East and North Africa ("The Barcelona Process") were added.[4] The Membership expanded to include states in the Balkans and the Caucasus. The current instrument is the "Regional Convention on the pan-Euro-Mediterranean preferential rules of origin," [the PEM Convention].[5] Comprising 24 contracting parties, it aims to replace 60 bilateral protocols on RoO with a single legal instrument.[6]

The PEM allows for a system of cumulation of certain processing of inputs in Contracting Parties to count for origin qualifying processing.[7] This system of diagonal cumulation will be discussed further in the Chapter. However, traders have found the PEM to be complex due to the product-specific rules and the requirements for certificates of origin.[8] In 2023, the Parties adopted amendments to the PEM Convention aimed at simplifying the determination of origin and demonstration of proof of origin, which came into force on 1 January 2025.[9]

The NAFTA and the USMCA were and are significant in their use of rules of origin to implement trade policy objectives within the North American region. During the NAFTA negotiations, the CTH was not considered adequate for politically and industrially strategic goods, and a regional value content (RVC) requirement was added to the CTH requirements, resulting in restrictive and complex product specific rules for 5,000 products.[10] The NAFTA RoO

2 Commission, 'The Pan-Euro-Mediterranean Cumulation and the PEM Convention' (ec.europa.eu) <https://ec.europa.eu/taxation_customs/customs-4/international-affairs/pan-euro-mediterranean-cumulation-and-pem-convention_en> accessed 23 March 2024.

3 ibid.

4 ibid.

5 ibid; Council Decision of 14 April 2011 on the signing, on behalf of the European Union, of the Regional Convention on pan-Euro-Mediterranean preferential rules of origin (2013) OJ 56 L 54/1.

6 Commission, 'The pan-Euro-Mediterranean cumulation and the PEM Convention' (n 2).

7 ibid.

8 ibid.

9 Decision No 1/2023 Of The Joint Committee Of The Regional Convention On Pan-Euro-Mediterranean Preferential Rules Of Origin of 7 December 2023 (PEM).

10 Stefano Inama, *Rules of Origin in International Trade* (CUP 2009) 278, 287–288; Antoni Estevadeordal and Kati Suominen, 'Rules of Origin in Preferential Trading Arrangements:

subsequently served as the basis for US bilateral agreements, including those in Latin and Central America, Asia and the Pacific.[11] The USMCA amended the NAFTA RoO in some key areas such as cumulation and exporter declarations and added new provisions on sourcing requirements and labor requirements for automobiles.[12] The USMCA represents a regional approach to address 21st Century trade issues, like global value chains and digital technology[13] and also introduces some novel elements to the RoO analysis, especially with regards to automotive parts.[14]

1 The Wholly Obtained or Produced Criterion

Generally, the starting point for determining the origin of a good is to ask: (1) was the good wholly obtained or produced in the territory?; (2) if not, where did the last substantial transformation to the good take place?[15] The first step means determining whether all the inputs of an assembled product have been wholly grown, produced, or manufactured in the territory.[16]

Although each trade agreement includes its version of the wholly produced criterion, the Kyoto Convention is used below as an example. The following products are relevant to 3D printing as they indicate materials that could be used as 'ink':

> Goods produced wholly in a given country shall be taken as originating in that country. The following only shall be taken to be produced wholly in a given country:
> (a) mineral products extracted from its soil, from its territorial waters or from its sea-bed;

Is All Well with the Spaghetti Bowl in the Americas?' (2005) 5 Economia (Spring) 63, 67, 70–71.

11 Estevadeordal and Suominen (n 10) 70.

12 David Gantz, 'The United States-Mexico-Canada Agreement: Tariffs, Customs, and Rules of Origin' (2019) Baker Institute Rep. no. 02.21.19.

13 SDG Knowledge Hub, 'New Trade Agreement between US, Mexico, and Canada Enters into Force,'(sdg.iisd.org 2 July 2020) <https://sdg.iisd.org/news/new-trade-agreement-between-us-mexico-and-canada-enters-into-force/> accessed 2 December 2021.

14 US International Trade Administration (USITA), 'Understanding USMCA' (trade.gov) <https://www.trade.gov/usmca-dayone-0> accessed 2 December 2021.

15 Imagawa and Vermulst (n 1) 604.

16 Anne van de Heetkamp and Ruud Tusveld, *Origin Management: Rules of Origin in Free Trade Agreements* (Springer 2011) 83.

(b) vegetable products harvested or gathered in that country;

…

(f) products obtained by maritime fishing and other products taken from the sea by a vessel of that country;

…

(h) products extracted from marine soil or subsoil outside that country's territorial waters, provided that the country has sole rights to work that soil or subsoil;

(i) scrap and waste from manufacturing and processing operations, and used articles, collected in that country and fit only for the recovery of raw materials;

(j) goods produced in that country solely from the products referred to in paragraphs (a) to (i) above.[17]

A simple example is a wood plate for food produced from timber cut in the forest in the territory, carved in a factory within the same territory and treated with a varnish wholly produced in the same territory. If the wood is sent across the border to be carved, the plate is now part of a global supply chain, albeit a simple one, and the wholly produced criterion cannot be applied. We must look at another criterion to determine origin.

2 The Substantial Transformation Criteria: Change of Tariff Heading, Technical Test, and *Ad Valorem* Percentage

If the product is not wholly obtained or produced in one territory, three rules are applied separately or conjointly to determine the territory in which the substantial transformation occurred. The 1973 Kyoto Convention divided "substantial transformation" into the three criteria: the Change of Tariff Heading, Manufacturing or Processing Operations, and the Ad Valorem Percentage Rule. RoO in PTAs generally follow the parameters of Kyoto Convention, but they are not uniform in the details for the requirements under each of the criteria.

2.1 *Change of Tariff Heading*

Generally, under the CTH criterion, a product undergoes sufficient manufacturing or processing if it falls into a tariff heading different from the heading

17 International Convention on the Simplification and Harmonization of Customs Procedures (as amended) (Revised Kyoto Convention) (entered into force 3 February 2006) Annex K, para 2.

of the materials.[18] PTAs specify which tariff classification system is applied, but most likely it will be the HS as most WTO Members are also contracting parties of the HS Convention.[19] The US and EU use the HS code for the first six numbers and then add unique numbers for heading subdivisions.[20] Referring to the 2022 HS List available at the WCO website, a wood plate falls under Chapter 44: Wood and articles of wood; wood charcoal. The next two digits, the subheading, for a wood plate are 19: tableware and kitchenware, of wood. The last two digits are a further subheading – 90 indicates that the good is made of a wood other than bamboo. Thus, the HS code for a wood plate (not of bamboo) for food is: 4419.90.

It is important to note the distinction between the Chapter and the subheading numbers, because in PTAs the CTH rules specify whether the change must occur at the Chapter level, the subheading level, or even the sub-subheading level. Under the product specific rules for the USMCA (Annex 4-B), for an item falling under 4419 (wooden tableware) to obtain origin there must be "a change to heading 4401 through 4421 from any other heading, including another heading within that group" in the territory. If birch wood [HS 4403.91] is imported into the US from a country other than Mexico or Canada and is carved into a plate [4419.90] in Texas, the plate qualifies as a good originating in the territory, because of the change in subheading (03.91 to 19.90). As another example, take a hamburger bun. The HS code for bread is 1905, and the USMCA product specific rules require a change from any other Chapter. If wheat flour grown and ground in Italy [1001] is imported to the US and is used by an industrial baker in Texas to make the bun [1905], the bun originates in the US, because there has been a change from Chapter 10 to Chapter 19.[21]

18 International Convention on the Simplification and Harmonization of Customs Procedures (Kyoto Convention 1973, signed 18 May 1973, entered into Force 24 September 1974), Annex D.1 (A).

19 Peter Van den Bossche, *The Law and Policy of the World Trade Organization: Text, Cases and Materials* (2nd edn, CUP 2008) 430; WCO, 'What is the Harmonized System (HS)?' (wcoomd.org) <http://www.wcoomd.org/en/topics/nomenclature/overview/what-is-the-harmonized-system.aspx> accessed 2 December 2021.

20 van de Heetkamp and Tusveld (n 16) 7. Eg, on its website for importers and exporters, the DG Trade cautions that "Eight digits is generally considered to be fully qualified for customs purposes ... But the same 8-digit class can represent different products in different countries. For example, 2001.90.30 means 'sweet corn' in the EU-27 classification and 'beans' in the US classification." Commission, 'Access 2Markets: Frequently Asked Questions-What is the Harmonized System' (trade.ec.europa.eu) <https://trade.ec.europa.eu/access-to-markets/en/faqs> accessed 23 March 2024.

21 Agreement between the United States of America, the United Mexican States, and Canada (USMCA) (signed 30 November 2018, entered into force 1 July 2020) ch 4, annex 4-B: Product-Specific Rules of Origin.

While the near universal application of the HS in preferential RoO provides some advantages, the structure of the HS can make it challenging to comply with CTH rules. At first glance, use of the HS nomenclature appears to simplify origin determination; yet, it requires a thorough understanding of the various headings and subheadings for both inputs and finished goods.[22] The HS does not provide explanations for the type or amount of processing of a good or input required to move from one subheading to another, or from one Chapter to another.[23] This lacuna allows traders and policymakers to take advantage of the HS. Producers who do have knowledge of the HS, and who have the flexibility in their manufacturing systems, could establish processing procedures so that the finished product meets a CTH rule.[24] Further, a CTH rule may not necessarily reflect the value created within the territory. For example, assembling goods into a final product may satisfy the CTH rule (the parts are categorized in one HS heading, the final good in another), but the assembly process may be simple and of lower value relative to the materials and other elements of the production process.

Exceptions in a CTH rule occur when the drafters want to limit the geographical scope of the inputs that undergo an origin qualifying transformation in the territory. In essence, as long as the necessary heading change occurs, a good can qualify for origin even if the inputs come from outside of the territory. RoO designers can make CTH rules restrictive by requiring that certain inputs originate in the territory.[25] An example is the product-specific rules for catsup in the NAFTA,[26] which has been transferred to the USMCA. Someone in Texas is preparing a hamburger and spreads catsup on the hamburger bun. For catsup [2103.20] to originate within the USCMA territory, there must be a change from any other chapter, except from subheading 2002.90.[27] Under the HS, "Tomatoes prepared or preserved otherwise than by vinegar and acetic acid" fall under Chapter 20, Subheading 02.[28] Subheading 2002 is divided

22 Imagawa and Vermulst (n 1) 607–608.

23 Petros C Mavroidis, *The Regulation of International Trade*, vol 1 (MIT Press 2016) 222.

24 Hoekman and Michel M Kostecki, *The Political Economy of the World Trading System: The WTO and Beyond* (3rd edn, OUP 2009) 188, 190.

25 Imagawa and Vermulst (n 1) 608.

26 WE James, 'Rules of Origin and Rules of Preference and the World Trade Organization: The Challenge to Global Trade Liberalization' in Patrick F J Macrory, Arthur Edmond Appleton and Michael G Plummer (eds) *World Trade Organization: Legal, Economic and Political Analysis* (Springer 2005) 268.

27 USMCA, ch 4, annex 4-B.

28 WCO, HS Nomenclature 2022 'Chapter 20'(wccomd.org) <http://www.wcoomd.org/-/media/wco/public/global/pdf/topics/nomenclature/instruments-and-tools/hs-nomenclature-2022/2022/0420_2022e.pdf?la=en> accessed 7 January 2022. For the full list of

into two further subheadings: 2002.10: Tomatoes, whole or in pieces; 2002.90: Other. For making catsup, "other" signifies tomato paste. Basically, the tomato paste must originate in the USMCA territory if a catsup is to qualify for preferential treatment under the USCMA. So, if a company in Mexico imports tomato paste from Italy, makes the catsup and then tries to export the catsup to Texas, the catsup will not qualify for preferential tariff treatment.[29] Only catsup made from paste or tomato preparations processed in one of the parties of the USMCA qualifies for preferential tariff treatment.[30]

Product-specific CTH rules can also be coupled with Regional Value Content requirements to make them even more restrictive. This requires that a certain level of value be created within the territory in addition the change of heading. According to Hoekman, all substantial transformation criteria impose value-added constraints which discriminate against low-wage economies.[31] Thus, adding a RVC requirement to a CTH rule narrows the range of processing outside of the territory and increases the amount of processing in the territory.

2.2 *Technical Test or Specific Manufacturing or Processing Operations*

Before discussing the *ad valorem* criterion, a slight detour is necessary to present a second method for determining origin–origin on the basis of specific manufacturing or processing operations performed on the good, also referred to as a "technical test."[32] Under this criterion, a transformation to the materials must occur, but it does not require a change of heading or subheading to occur. While the revised Kyoto Convention no longer includes this method as part of the substantial transformation criteria, states continue to include rules on manufacturing and processing operations.[33]

---

the 2022 HS codes, see WCO, HS Nomenclature 2022 Edition (wccomd.org) <http://www.wcoomd.org/en/topics/nomenclature/instrument-and-tools/hs-nomenclature-2022-edition/hs-nomenclature-2022-edition.aspx> accessed 7 January 2022.

29 Although it may be very tasty, having been made with Italian tomato paste.

30 This catsup exception is also an example of how preferential RoO create trade distortion and protectionism. Laura Puccio' 20 Years After Marrakesh: Reconsidering the Effects of Preferential Rules of Origin and Anti-Circumvention Rules on Trade in Inputs and Global Production Networks' 2014 Eur YB Intl Economic L 173, 177–178; Kala Krishna, 'Understanding Rules of Origin' (February 2005) NBER Working Paper 11150, 8–9.

31 ibid.

32 Imagawa and Vermulst (n 1) 608.

33 Stefano Inama and Pramila Crivelli, 'Convergence on the Calculation Methodology for Drafting Rules of Origin in FTAS Using the Ad Valorem Criterion' (2019) 14 Global Trade & Customs J 146, 147 fn. 2. Duy Dinh, *Rules of Origin for Services: From the Early Days of GATS to the Era of Servicification* (Edward Elgar 2020) 121. For example, the product specific rules for KORUS for products of chemicals lists seven types of processes that confer origin.

A reason for maintaining the "technical test" is that it allows flexibility to address the complexities of producing certain products,[34] for example, the highly specific manufacturing and post-production necessary to create tradeable chemical products.[35] This method may also be useful strategically within the context of assembled goods. When parts for a good are classified under the same heading as the finished good, assembling the parts into that good does not result in a change of heading. Yet a state may want to claim that a substantial transformation has nonetheless occurred; i.e., the act of assembly resulted in a new good having new characteristics, thus the good qualifies for preferential treatment.[36]

The specific manufacturing or processing operations criterion also has some drawbacks. The rules could be devised to exclude certain procedures from conferring origin to protect domestic industries from competition from goods imported under preferential rates.[37] Rules designed for political purposes may not necessarily reflect decision making by producers who locate plants in countries based on economic and management objectives.[38] Focusing on specific manufacturing or operation processes could result in more complex rules as the specific operations would need to be updated as manufacturing operations change with changes in technology.[39] Further, customs officials would need to verify that the production processes performed on inputs in third countries also meet these rules.[40]

2.3 *What Is and What Is Not Sufficient Processing?*

Even if a change of tariff heading or sub-heading occurs when producing the good, there still must be sufficient processing in the territory to confer origin on the good. This will be a key element to explore when considering how 3D printing can shift the origin of a good. Trade instruments do not list every type of processing that confers origin. Instead, many provide examples of operations that do not confer origin. Annex K of the Revised Kyoto Convention

---

United States - Korea Free Trade Agreement (KORUS) (entered into force 12 March 2012) annex 6-A, pt II, s VI.

34 Imagawa and Vermulst (n 1) 608.

35 Customs and Tariff Bureau, 'Outline for Rules of Origin' (July 2017) Japan Ministry of Finance, 3 <https://www.customs.go.jp/roo/english/origin/outline_of_roo.pdf> accessed 2 December 2021.

36 Inama, *Rules of Origin in International Trade* (2009) (n 10) 40–41.

37 James (n 26) 268.

38 ibid 278.

39 Mavroidis, *The Regulation of International Trade*, vol 1 (n 23) 222.

40 Imagawa and Vermulst (n 1) 608.

recommends that operations "which do not contribute or which contribute to only a small extent to the essential characteristics or properties of the goods … should not be regarded as constituting substantial manufacturing or processing."[41] Such operations include

- packing and repacking
- mixing goods of different origin if it does not result in an essentially different product,
- simple assembly operations

Article 6 of the PEM establishes that "the simple assembly of parts of articles to constitute a complete article or disassembly of products into parts" do not confer origin.[42] Other operations that do not confer origin include:

- "simple painting and polishing operations"
- "sharpening, simple grinding or simple cutting"
- affixing or printing labels and "other like distinguishing signs on products or their packaging."[43]

This subsection includes a footnote: "Explanatory notes including a definition of "simple assembly" will be established by the Contracting Parties." Finally, the Japan US Trade Agreement (2019), defines "simple assembly":

- "the fitting together of five or fewer [non-originating] parts … by bolting, gluing, soldering, or sewing or by other means without more than minor processing."[44]

As will be explored in Chapter 4, the definition of terms such as "simple assembly" and "minor processing" could have an impact on determining whether certain steps in the production of 3D printed goods are origin conferring processes.

Traders and customs officials have to decide whether an operation is a minor process which does not result in the good having new characteristics, or an operation that contributes significantly to the essential characteristics or properties of the goods. Further, they will be required to make this determination for each PTA under which preferential treatment is requested. Hoekman in 1993 on RoO wrote that this mélange of rules results partially from the legal texts and partially from the choice of countries in designing different RoO:

---

41 Revised Kyoto Convention, Annex K, art 6.

42 PEM, App. I, art 6(p).

43 PEM App. I, art 6(e),(i),(l).

44 Trade Agreement between the United States of America and Japan (entered into force 1 January 2020), Annex II Tariffs and Tariff-Related Provisions of the US, Product-Specific Rules of Origin, art 19(d).

> Whatever specific test is employed by a country, a general goal is to prevent simple assembly operations and cosmetic processing of a product ... from conferring origin. However, in practice, it is often quite difficult to distinguish in a consistent and neutral manner transformations that are substantial from those which are not.[45]

The rules for determining when a substantial transformation has occurred have multiplied since 1993. This has, Mavoridis writes in 2016, "substantially increased transaction costs for international trade."[46] The next method discussed, the *ad valorem* percentage criterion, is not applied uniformly among PTAs, though there are some shared general principles, which will be discussed in the next section.

2.4 *Ad Valorem Percentage*

This book provides an overview of how the *ad valorem* percentage criterion is utilized by states and will not go into the particulars of how costs are calculated, value quantified, and percentages set. Understanding the basic principles of this criterion, we can understand why the production and trade of parts through the GVCs complicate the determination of the origin of a final product and how RoO can be used as a trade policy instrument that favors a domestic or regional industry.[47] Under the 1973 Kyoto Convention, in determining origin under this criterion, one must consider "the extent of the manufacturing or processing undergone in a country, by reference to the value thereby added to the goods. When this added value equals or exceeds a specified percentage, the goods acquire origin in the country where the manufacturing or processing was carried out." Value generally derives from the cost of labor, manufacturing overhead, and materials – it does not derive from intellectual property rights, investments based on predictions of the good's success in the market, and consumer perceptions on the value of the product.[48]

Trade instruments set out the parameters for determining the *ad valorem* percentage. Generally the value of imported materials (inputs) is the first ascertainable price paid for them within the territory.[49] The instrument will

45 Berard Hoekman, 'Rules of Origin for Goods and Services: Conceptual Issues and Economic Considerations' (1993) 27 J World Trade 82, 85.
46 Mavroidis, *The Regulation of International Trade*, Vol 1 (n 23) 222.
47 James (n 26) 278.
48 Dylan Geraets, Colleen Carroll, and Arnoud R Willems, 'Reconciling Rules of Origin and Global Value Chains: The Case for Reform' (2015) 18 J Intl Economic L 287, 288.
49 Revised Kyoto Convention art 5.

establish whether the value of final goods produced is (1) the ex-works price,[50] the price of the good when it leaves the factory, which does not include costs of transportation, (2) FOB (Free on Board), in which case transportation costs between the factory and port of exportation is included, or (3) CIF, which includes the costs, insurance, and freight up to the port of entry for importation.[51] Sometimes product specific rules allow origin qualification under either criterion, and sometimes both a CTH and an *ad valorem* percentage are needed, making the rules more restrictive.[52] For example, the SAFTA (South-Asian Free Trade Area) regional cumulation provisions require (1) that the transaction value of a good be adjusted to a FOB basis when determining whether the local value threshold was met and (2) the good must undergo a CTH at the four digit level.[53] Thus, it is important for traders to look at the rules for each PTA under which they seek preferential tariff treatment to assess whether a good qualifies for origin.

To calculate the *ad valorem* percentage, the value of originating materials must be distinguished from non-originating materials. Using the hamburger bun example, the flour from Italy is the non-originating material, but the milk from Texas, the butter from California, and the salt from Mexico are originating materials. If the hamburger bun was shipped from the US to Canada, it would qualify for preferential tariff treatment under an *ad valorem* rule if the ingredients from Texas, California, and Mexico, the costs to operate the mixing stands and oven, and the labor of the baker exceed the value of the flour from Italy. The price of materials can be influenced by fluctuations in foreign currency and the cost of labor and manufacturing can be impacted by overhead, the number of different types of goods produced with the materials, units produced, machine hours, and floor space.[54] Further, if materials are dual sourced

---

50 Under PEM, Article 1 (f) the "'ex-works price' means the price paid for the product ex works to the manufacturer in the Contracting Party in whose undertaking the last working or processing is carried out, provided the price includes the value of all the materials used, minus any internal taxes which are, or may be, repaid when the product obtained is exported."

51 van de Heetkamp and Tusveld (n 16) 84–85; ASEAN Trade in Goods Agreement (ATIGA) (entered into force 17 May 2010) art 25(b) (c).

52 Eg, *see* Hasegawa Jitsuya's comparison of product specific rules for machinery in FTA/EPA partners of Japan. Hasegawa Jitsuya, 'Standardization of Complex and Diversified Preferential Rules of Origin' (2021) 55 J World Trade 545, 556–557.

53 South-Asian Free Trade Area (SAFTA) (signed 6 January 2004, entered into force 1 January 2006), Rules of Determination of Origin of Goods, r 9. See also, Ram Singh and Surendar Singh, 'Do Rules of Origin Extend Disproportionate Trade Gains under SAFTA: A Case Study of Bicycle and Textile Industries' (2021) 16 Global Trade & Customs J 59, 63.

54 Inama, *Rules of Origin in International Trade* (2009) (n 10) 296–303; James (n 26) 268.

(identical materials from different origin), the manufacturer must either keep the qualifying material completely separate from non-qualifying material, or mix the material and later calculate what percentage of material in the finished product is qualifying material under the PTA.[55] Focusing on the PEM and the USMCA, the next sections will present a very concise overview of the technical provisions for determining origin.

2.4.1 The PEM

Annex II of the PEM provides a list of product-specific rules based on the HS. PEM contracting parties must use this list in PTAs among other PEM contracting parties. Article 2 in conjunction with Article 4 stipulates that products incorporating non-originating materials shall be considered as PEM originating products if the non-originating materials have undergone sufficient working or processing as set out in the Annex II (PEM) list.[56] Annex II (PEM) also stipulates that for some goods, certain non-originating material may not be used in the manufacture of the product. However, if the total value of the non-originating material which should not be used does not exceed 15%, with some exceptions, of the ex-works price of the product, that non-originating material will not impact the good's ability to qualify for preferential tariff treatment.[57] This is known as the Tolerance Rule.[58] For some items, Annex II (PEM) sets a maximum percentage limit for non-originating materials; once this limit is exceeded, the good or input does not qualify for origin in the contracting party.[59] For many products, Annex II (PEM) includes alternate methods which confer origin on the product. To conclude this brief introduction to the PEM, it should be noted that despite the references to values and percentages, the PEM does not specify how to calculate the total value of the materials or the percentages indicated in Annex II. On the other hand, equations are found in PTAS entered into by the US.

2.4.2 US Trade Agreements

The US has developed two methods to calculate the regional value content (RVC) of a good, also expressed as a percentage, which determines whether the good qualifies for preferential tariff treatment: the "Transaction Value"

55 van de Heetkamp and Tusveld (n 16) 90.

56 PEM, App. I arts 2 and 4.

57 PEM, App. I art 5. The percentages differ for agricultural and textile products.

58 However, the 15% tolerance does not allow traders to exceed a maximum percentage of non-originating materials indicated by the product specific rule. PEM App. I art (5)(2).

59 PEM Annex I, Note 1(a).

method and the "Net Cost" method. The percentage of RVC required under each method varies, and one must look to the product specific lists in a PTA to determine the required percentages. For example, under the USMCA product specific list, Chemical products in Chapter 29 (of the HS) require either 40% RVC under the Transaction Value method or 30% RVC under the Net Cost method; however, for some pharmaceutical products in Chapter 30 the percentages are 60% RVC for the Transaction Value method, and 50% RVC under the Net Cost method.[60] The rules may allow manufacturers or importers to choose either method; however, the Net Cost method can be required for goods such as automotive goods and footwear and inputs for these products.[61] The formulas presented below seem simple; the complexity in determining whether the product meets the RVC threshold derives from calculating the value of the non-originating materials, the value of the originating materials, and excluded costs.[62] The USMCA includes a *de minimis* rule: a good is originating, if the value of all non-originating material that do not undergo a CTH, with certain exceptions, are not more than 10% of the transaction value or the total cost of the good, in addition to any other applicable requirements.[63] If the good is also subject to a RVC requirement, the value of the *de minimis* non-originating material shall be included in the value of all non-originating materials for calculating the RVC.[64]

The formula for the Transaction Value under the USMCA is: RVC = (TV – VNM)/TV x 100. RVC stands for "regional value content", while TV is "transaction value" adjusted to exclude costs incurred in international shipment of the goods, and VNM stands for "value of non-originating material". The instrument specifies that the transaction value is determined according to the WTO's Customs Valuation Agreement (CVA): "the customs value of imported goods shall be the transaction value, that is the price actually paid or payable for the goods when sold for export to the country of importation adjusted in accordance

60 USMCA, Annex 4-B.

61 Inama, *Rules of Origin in International Trade* (2009) (n 10) 288.

62 Jessica Gladstone and Cintia Aquilar Flores, 'Free trade agreements: compliance with rules of origin and utilization of preferential tariffs' (2017) 23 Intl Trade L & Regulation 113, 113–115.

63 USMCA art 4.12(1). The exceptions pertain to the alimentary goods and mineral fuels (see Annex 4-A).

64 ibid art 4.12(2). Other agreements including a *de minimis* rule are: Australia, Chile, Colombia, DR-CAFTA, Panama, Peru, S. Korea and Singapore. Those that do not have a *de minimis* rule are: Israel, Bahrain, Morocco, Jordan. USITA, 'FTA Provisions for *De Minimis* Rule' (trade.gov) <https://www.trade.gov/fta-provisions-de-minimis-rule.> accessed 12 March 2024.

with the provisions of Article 8." There are prohibitions on restrictions on selling the good, on proceeds returning to the seller from subsequent resale of the good, and on the relatedness between the seller and buyer.[65] Under Article 8 of the CVA, the following goods and services "shall be added to the price actually paid or payable for the imported goods," if "supplied directly or indirectly by the buyer free of charge or at reduced cost for use in connection with the production and sale for export of the imported goods":

> materials, components, and parts incorporated in the goods, tools … engineering, development, artwork, design work, plans and sketches, undertaken elsewhere in the country of importation and necessary for the production of the imported goods.[66]

Therefore, the Transaction Value method allows the inclusion of a wide range of costs, including services provided to the manufacturer free of charge by the buyer, when determining whether a good meets the RVC threshold.

RoO under other instruments, such as the ASEAN agreements and the CPTPP, provide formulas under the terms "Build-down" or "Build-up" methods or "direct" and "in-direct" methods.[67] Generally, these formulas take into consideration the value of the originating materials, the non-originating materials, and value adjusted for shipping cost.[68] Those instruments that do not provide a formula, such as CETA and the PEM, still include a reference to the CVA.[69] This reference to the CVA in trade instruments could impact use of the *ad*

65 USMCA, ch 4 art 4.1. Article 8 of the Customs Valuation Agreement requires that the following costs be added to the price actually paid or payable to the imported goods if they are incurred by the buyer but not included in the price actually paid or payable for the goods: commissions and brokerage fees, costs of containers, cost of packing. Agreement On Implementation of Article VII Of The General Agreement On Tariffs And Trade 1994 (Customs Valuation Agreement/CVA) (15 April 1994) LT/UR/A-1A/4.

66 CVA, art 8(b). Also included in the price must be royalties and license fees that the buyer must pay as a condition of sale and "the value of any part of the proceeds of any subsequent resale, disposal or use of the imported goods that accrues directly or indirectly to the seller."

67 Stefano Inama and Edmund W Sim *Rules of Origin in ASEAN* (CUP 2015) 86–92; Comprehensive and Progressive Agreement for Trans-Pacific Partnership (CPTPP), incorporating Trans-Pacific Partnership Agreement (TPP) (signed 8 March 2018) ch 3 art 3.5.

68 van de Heetkamp and Tusveld (n 16) 88–89.

69 For example, under CETA, the value of non-originating materials "is the customs value of the materials as determined under the Customs Valuation Agreement", and the "customs value" is "the value as determined in accordance with the Customs Valuation Agreement." CETA, Protocol on rules of origin and origin procedures, s A.

valorem criterion for 3D printed goods. If the 3D good buyer provides the 3D file to the printer for free, then the value of the design of the file would have to be included in the customs value under the CVA.[70] How to incorporate the value of the 3D file into the origin determination of the 3D printed good will be discussed in Chapter 4.

If an instrument requires use of the Net Cost method, direct labor costs, the costs of materials, and direct overhead costs influence whether the good meets the RVC requirement.[71] The formula in the USMCA is: RVC = (NC − VNM)/NC x 100.[72] RVC is regional value content, NC is net cost of the good, and VNM is value of non-originating material including materials of undetermined origin. The percentage requirement is less under the Transaction Value method, but this does not necessarily mean that the Net Cost method is more favorable for those seeking to meet the RVC threshold.[73] Complications arise in assessing which costs cannot be factored into the Net Cost.[74] For example, the USMCA and CETA provide three options for how to subtract excluded costs to

70 Patricio Díaz Gavier and Julio Gaudalupe Báscones, 'On Article 8.1(b)(iv) of the Customs Valuation Agreement: When is the Value of Certain Services Supplied by the Buyer Relevant for Customs Value (i.e. Engineering, Development, Artwork, Design Work, and Plans and Sketches)?'(2014) 9 Global Trade & Customs J 260, 262. See Case C-509/19, *BMW Bayerische Motorenwerke AG v. Hauptzollamt München* [2020] ECLI:EU:C:2020:694. BMW developed or commissioned the development of software in the EU, which was installed into control units outside of the EU. BMW then imported the control units with the software and released them for free circulation in the EU. When indicating the customs value of the controls, BMW did not account the costs of the development of the software. The German Finance court referred to ECJ the question whether the development costs should be included in the transaction value of the imported product (para 11). The ECJ found that Article 71 (b) of the Customs Code applied to this matter, and thus, "[i]t is therefore irrelevant, for the purposes of determining the customs value of the imported goods, that the product to which the value should be added is an intangible asset, such as software. It follows from the wording of that provision, which expressly refers to 'goods' or 'services', that its scope is not limited to tangible assets" (para 18). Article 71 (1)(b) of the Customs Code mirrors Article 8.1 of the CVA.

71 Vivian C Jones and Liana Wong, 'International Trade: Rules of Origin' (2020) *Congressional Research Service Report*, 3 March 2020, 8 <https://crsreports.congress.gov/product/pdf/RL/RL34524/16> accessed 23 October 2021. Under the USMCA, net costs are "total cost minus sales promotion, marketing and after-sales service costs, royalties, shipping and packing costs, and non-allowable interest costs that are included in the total cost." USMCA art 4.1.

72 USCMA art 4.5.

73 van de Heetkamp and Tusveld (n 16) 89.

74 Inama, *Rules of Origin in International Trade* (2009) (n 10) 291–292; Inama and Sim (n 67) 89.

determine the Net Cost.[75] Under these agreements, only the Net Cost method can be used in connection with automobiles and inputs.[76]

We begin to see why inputs from different countries or regions can complicate the origin determination of the final product. An accounting of originating and non-originating materials in each input must be assessed and factored into the ex-works price if using the PEM or one of the formulas to calculate RVC. If non-originating materials are transformed into an input within the territory, then the trader must determine if this input qualifies for origin status based on whether it met the CTH criterion or if it possesses a certain percent of RVC. This leads to the next significant aspect of RoO: cumulation.

3 Cumulation Provisions: Variations on the *Ad Valorem* Criterion

Cumulation, simply, means the act of accumulating processing of the good or inputs completed in different locations to qualify for a preferential tariff rate in the final import destination.[77] There are three forms: bilateral, diagonal, and full cumulation.[78] An example of bilateral cumulation would be requiring a certain level of sufficient processing within the territory of the FTA, but allowing flexibility in where processing occurs: for example, inputs originating in Party A are sent to Party B; these inputs are sufficiently processed into a final good in Party B and exported back to Party A, qualifying for B origin and preferential tariff treatment. On the other hand, full cumulation allows for the accumulation of any type of processing completed within the territory even if, for example, processing in Party A was not sufficient to confer A origin to the third-party inputs before being imported to Party B to be assembled with other inputs.[79] Then, there is diagonal cumulation, which allows for cumulation of value or processing among countries if they have PTAs with identical rules of origin and cumulation provisions.[80] The PEM is a prime example of

75 USMCA ch 4 art 4.5(8); CETA Protocol on Rules of Origin, s B art 17.

76 USMCA ch 4 art 10(3)(a); CETA Protocol on Rules of Origin, s B art 17 (for purposes of annual quota allocations for vehicles exported from Canada to the EU).

77 Mavroidis, *The Regulation of International Trade*, vol 1 (n 23) 229.

78 ibid.

79 ibid. Commission, 'Common Provisions' [for preferential origin arrangements] (ec.europa.eu) <https://ec.europa.eu/taxation_customs/customs-4/international-affairs/origin-goods/general-aspects-preferential-origin/common-provisions_en> accessed 13 March 2024.

80 Commission, "Common Provisions" (n 79).

diagonal cumulation. Other territories use diagonal cumulation,[81] but as looking at these examples would take us beyond the scope of this book, only the PEM is examined.

3.1 *Cumulation:* PEM

Under the PEM, the origin of a finished product is based on a system of diagonal cumulation relying on a network of PTAs among the Contracting Parties.[82] This concept relies on the absorption, or roll-up principle.[83] Basically, the following PTAs have RoO with identical terms: A–B, B–C, C–D, A–C, and A–D; all are Members of the PEM. In the first country of manufacture (Country A), the non-originating materials acquire origin status through sufficient working or processing. The completed Input-A is imported into Country B. Input-A qualifies as PEM originating material and is incorporated into Input-B, which is imported to Country C, and incorporated into a machine. This machine is then exported to the country of final destination, Country D. The input made from non-originating materials in Country A can be "rolled-up" with the other originating materials and inputs produced in Country B and Country C when determining if the machine qualifies for preferential treatment in Country D.[84]

The PEM revisions allows for full cumulation of most products among all Contracting Parties, with exceptions for textile products.[85] Under Article 7(1), products with originating materials from other Contracting Parties are considered as originating in the exporting Party if more than minor processing is carried out on them,[86] sufficient (i.e. origin conferring) processing is not necessary.[87] If only minor processing is performed, the final good can still obtain

81 Maria Donner Abreu, 'Preferential rules of origin in regional trade agreements' in Rohini Acharya (ed), *Regional Trade Agreements and The Multilateral Trading System* (CUP 2016) 67–71.

82 Commission, 'The pan-Euro-Mediterranean cumulation and the PEM Convention' (n 2).

83 WCO, 'Comparative Study on Preferential Rules of Origin' (wccomd.org 2017) 78. The study includes a graph on the "roll-up" principle <http://www.wcoomd.org/-/media/wco/public/global/pdf/topics/origin/instruments-and-tools/reference-material/170130-b_comparative-study-on-pref_roo_master-file_final-20_06_2017.pdf?db=web> accessed 2 December 2021.

84 van de Heetkamp and Tusveld (n 16) 91.

85 Commission, 'The pan-Euro-Mediterranean cumulation and the PEM Convention' (n 2).

86 Under Article 6 of the PEM (App. I), minor processing includes washing, cleaning, simple painting and polishing, sharpening and simple grinding or cutting, affixing lables or distinquishing signs, and under subsection (p), "simple assembly of parts of articles to constitute a complete article or disassembly of products into parts."

87 This means that the processing on the non-originating material does not need to meet the product specific rule in the Annex II – meeting a certain value added, a CTH, or a manufacture from certain products rule.

origin status of the exporting Party if the value of processing that good there is greater than the material used to make it originating from other Contracting Parties.[88] If no processing or minor processing is done to non-originating material, it retains its non-PEM origin status: i.e, if an input originates from Australia and no processing is done at all to the input in a PEM Party, it cannot be considered part of the materials originating in the PEM Party when exported to another PEM Party.[89]

Drawback provisions must also be considered. A "no-drawback provision" requires that duties are paid on materials imported from third countries at some point during the manufacture of a product, even if the good is reexported from the territory.[90] On the other hand, a drawback provision exempts imported inputs which are further manufactured and reexported from customs duties in the country of manufacture.[91] A partial drawback, i.e., a partial refund on tariff duties, for a limited period is allowed by some agreements, for example with the EU-South Korea FTA[92] The PEM allows drawback for most products, with limitations for textiles and textile products.[93] To sum up, for a product manufactured in the PEM territories, origin depends on the applicable cumulation, processing and drawback rules.[94] As we will see in the next Chapter, cumulation does not necessarily economically benefit traders if they are forced to source costly inputs or materials from within the territory.[95]

Looking at some tariff rates suggests why preferential tariffs are, in theory, more beneficial to a trader. Using the European Commission's My Trade

---

88 PEM App. I, art 7(2).

89 PEM App. I, art 4(1)(2).

90 Commission, 'Common Provisions' [for preferential origin arrangements] (ec.europa.eu) <https://ec.europa.eu/taxation_customs/customs-4/international-affairs/origin-goods/general-aspects-preferential-origin/common-provisions_en> accessed 2 December 2021; van de Heetkamp and Tusveld (n 16) 93.

91 Drawback provisions can lead to tariff circumvention and be an incentive to use third-country materials rather than materials originating under an PTA. Inama, *Rules of Origin in International Trade* (2009)(n 10) 251–252.

92 Free Trade Agreement between the European Union and the Republic of Korea (entered into force 13 December 2015) Rules of Origin, s B, Title IV, art 14.

93 Commission, 'The pan-Euro-Mediterranean cumulation and the PEM Convention' (n 2). PEM App. I, art. 16.

94 PEM is not the only instrument that stipulates these various parameters and Maria Donner Abreu's work on rules of origin provides an extensive survey of trade instruments that include diagonal cumulation, full cumulation, as well as tolerance limits. Donner Abreu (n 81) 62–78.

95 Mavroidis, *The Regulation of International Trade*, vol 1 (n 23) 229.

Assistant calculator,[96] we can compare some of the different preferential rates for importing a passenger motor vehicle into the European Union. The EU Common External Tariff for passenger vehicles (non-electric) under HS 8703.50 is 10%. Under the Economic Partnership Agreement with Japan (2018), to qualify for a 2.5% preferential duty on vehicles, the total value of the non-originating material must not exceed 50% ex-works price or there must be 60% RVC. Using the PEM,[97] for a car imported from Morocco, non-originating materials must not exceed 40% of the ex-works price to qualify for a 0% preferential duty. Finally, under the Viet Nam FTA, the value must not exceed 45% ex-works price of the vehicle for a 3.7% duty.[98]

Despite the complexity preferential RoO appear to create for traders, industries as a whole may be reluctant to forgo them. The Trade and Cooperation Agreement (TCA) allows for full bilateral cumulation. Production on non-originating material, which is then used to complete a good in the UK for re-export to the EU, may be taken into account for determining if the good has UK origin – as long as the production on the non-originating material for the input in the EU is not insufficient production.[99] Had the UK exited the EU without some preferential duty in place, the 10% external tariff rate would have cost the automotive industry billions in pounds.[100] Prior to the conclusion of the TCA, negotiators had reached an impasse on the amount of local material in completed vehicles. The average amount of UK local content in UK automobiles in 2018 was 44%; the EU was requiring 60% to qualify for preferential tariff treatment and had refused third-party cumulation of parts.[101] In the TCA, the rules covering passenger automobiles [87.08-87.11] require a CTH or a "MaxNom

96 Commission, My Trade Assistant Tariff Calculator <https://trade.ec.europa.eu/access-to-markets/en/content> accessed .9 March 2025.

97 Council Decision No 2/2005 Of The EU-Morocco Association Council of 18 November 2005 amending Protocol 4 to the Euro-Mediterranean Agreement, concerning the definition of the concept of 'originating products' and methods of administrative cooperation (21.12.2005) OJ L 336.

98 All results in this paragraph are generated from the My Trade Assistant calculator.

99 Trade And Cooperation Agreement Between The European Union And The European Atomic Energy Community, Of The One Part, And The United Kingdom Of Great Britain And Northern Ireland, Of The Other Part, (TCA) (entered into force 1 January 2021) L 444/14, Article 40.

100 Lisa O'Carroll, 'UK carmakers face higher tariffs as EU rejects component plea' (*The Guardian* 30 Sept. 2020) <https://www.theguardian.com/politics/2020/sep/30/uk-carmakers-face-higher-tariffs-as-eu-rejects-component-plea-brexit> accessed 2 December 2021.

101 ibid.

50% (EXW)",[102] meaning that the maximum value of non-originating materials must not exceed 50% of the ex-works price of the completed good.[103] The maximum amount of non-originating materials for batteries for electric vehicles and for electric vehicles was intended to descend from 70% to 45% and from 60% to 45% on 31 December 2023.[104] However, this deadline was extended to 31 December 2026, as factors ranging from the disruptions to supply chains from the COVID-19 pandemic to competition from subsidized foreign firms slowed down the rate of development of the European and UK electric vehicle industry, and thus the ability for firms in these territories to meet the rules of origin.[105] As will be explored in Chapter 4, the context in which a good is manufactured and the level of innovation in production may not always match the context intended in the rules of origin instrument of a PTA.

3.2 *Cumulation: US Trade Agreements*

There is no unified US approach to cumulation of origin for inputs, but generally there are similarities among groups of US PTAs.[106] In the first group, a good is deemed originating if the good satisfies the applicable requirements for acquiring origin status (such as one of the substantial transformation criteria). These PTA include Australia, Chile, Columbia, DR-CAFTA, Panama, Peru, Singapore, and South Korea.[107] In the second group, a 35% appraisement method is used. The US-Bahrain FTA states that direct costs of processing operations performed in the territory of one or both of the parties and the values of materials produced in one of the territories may be counted without limitation towards satisfying this 35% requirement.[108] This also applies for FTAs with Morocco and Oman.[109] Under the FTAs with Israel and Jordan, there is still a 35% domestic content requirement, but only 15% of that can derive from

102 TCA, Annex 3: Product Specific Rules of Origin.

103 TCA, Annex 2, Note 4(c).

104 TCA, Annex 5: Transitional Product-Specific Rules For Electric Accumulators And Electrified Vehicles.

105 Commission, 'Partnership Council confirms one-off extension of the current rules of origin for electric vehicles and batteries' (ec.europa.eu 21 December 2023) <https://ec.europa.eu/commission/presscorner/detail/en/ip_23_6707> accessed 23 March 2024.

106 USITA, 'FTA Provisions for Accumulation' (trade.gov) <https://www.trade.gov/fta-provisions-accumulation> accessed 2 December 2021.

107 Ibid.

108 United States – Bahrain Free Trade Agreement (signed 14 September 2004, entered into force 11 January 2006) ch 4 art 4.4.

109 USITA, 'FTA Provisions for Accumulation' (n 314).

the value of processing operations or materials produced in the other party.[110] Manufacturers and traders wishing their goods to benefit from preferential tariff treatment must study the applicable PTAs closely to be sure that processing and local material requirements are met.

Under NAFTA, a producer could reduce the value of non-originating material in the product of a good by accumulating any regional value added within the NAFTA territory to the non-originating materials incorporated into the final good.[111] However, the non-originating materials had to undergo a CTH within at least one of the NAFTA countries, all other applicable requirements had to be met, and the RVC calculated using the net cost method.[112] Under the USMCA, a good qualifies for origin if the good is produced in the territory, the good meets the definition of an originating good, and all other applicable requirements are met.[113] The production undertaken on non-originating material in the territory "contributes to the originating status of a good regardless of whether that production was sufficient to confer originating status to the material itself."[114] Thus, even if the processing of non-originating material for an input is not sufficient to confer origin status, the value of that processing can be accumulated with the value of the other processing to complete the final good.

3.2.1 USMCA – Automobiles

The approach to inputs for automobiles has also changed from NAFTA to the USMCA. Under NAFTA, for inputs identified in Annex 403.2, the value of the non-originating materials remains non-originating to the time of calculation

110 Ibid; The Israel Free Trade Agreement further specifies that "[s]uch materials must in fact be products of the importing Party under the country of origin criteria set forth in this Agreement." United States – Israel Free Trade Agreement (signed 22 April 1985, entered into force 1 September 1985) Annex 3 art 5.

111 US Customs and Border Protection (CBP), 'Accumulation' (cbp.gov 28 May 2014) <https://www.cbp.gov/trade/nafta/guide-customs-procedures/other-instances-confer-origin/accumulation> accessed 2 December 2021.

112 North American Free Trade Agreement (NAFTA) (entered into force 1 January 1994) art 402(5)(e) and 404; CBP, 'Accumulation-Factsheet' CBP Publication No. 1141–0620 <https://www.cbp.gov/sites/default/files/assets/documents/2020-Jun/%2316_Accumulation_USMCA%20Informational%20Fact%20Sheet.pdf> accessed 2 December 2021.

113 USMCA ch 4 art 4.11.

114 USMCA ch 4 art 4.11 (3). Article 4.11(2) requires each party to provide that "an originating good or material of one or more of the Parties is considered as originating in the territory of another Party when used as a material in the production of a good in the territory of another Party."

of the RVC of the completed motor vehicle.[115] Under the USMCA, the RVC of each input must be calculated to determine if it is an originating part; further, a passenger vehicle or light truck is originating if certain core parts are originating in the USMCA territory.[116] The RVC of a completed passenger vehicle is 75% using the net cost method.[117] For core parts for passenger vehicles and light trucks that must originate in the USMCA territory, the RVC is 75% (net cost) and 85% (transaction value).[118] Producers of automobiles must verify that processing of non-originating materials in inputs reaches the requisite RVC, otherwise the producers may not be able to satisfy the 60–75% RVC for the entire vehicle. The interpretation of the roll-up of non-originating materials was at the center of a USMCA Panel Dispute. Canada and Mexico argued that if a core part with non-originating materials qualifies for USMCA origin, then 100% of the value of the core part should count to meet the RVC requirement.[119] The US argued that the value of the non-originating materials should be excluded. The Panel ruled in favor of Canada and Mexico in December 2022. There were hopes that the Biden administration would implement the necessary changes to its origin analysis, but as of 2025, industry groups still are unclear of which version of the 'roll-up' principle applies.[120] 3D printing of inputs for automobile parts may have an impact on RVC calculations, as raw materials are not generally sourced in USMCA territory. It will also have an influence in areas in

115 van de Heetman and Tusveld (n 16) 103; Such inputs included components of engines and gear boxes. NAFTA ch 4, Annex 403.2, List of Components and Materials.

116 These parts include the engine, transmission, body and chassis, axles, suspension system, steering system. There is an exception for the battery. USMCA ch 4, app Provisions Related To The Product-Specific Rules Of Origin For Automotive Goods (Appendix), art 3(7), Regional Value Content for Passenger Vehicles, Light Trucks, and Parts Thereof.

117 USMCA ch 4, app Provisions Related To The Product-Specific Rules Of Origin For Automotive Goods, art 3(1)(d).

118 ibid, art 3(2)(d). As under NAFTA, producers of automotive goods can average their costs over a month, quarter, or fiscal year when calculating the RVC of an automotive good or can calculate the average of all vehicles in one of the listed categories produced within a fiscal year. Ibid, art 5.

119 USMCA Panel Report, *United States – Automotive Rules Of Origin* (USA-MEX-CDA-2022-31-01), 14 December 2022, para. 100; Liana Wong and Kyla H Kitamura, 'USMCA: Automotive Rules' (2023) Congressional Research Service Reports, 8 December, 2 <https://crsreports.congress.gov/product/pdf/IF/IF12082> accessed 23 March 2024.

120 Jennifer M. Safavian, 'Comments Concerning the Operation of the United States-Mexico-Canada Agreement With Respect to Trade in Automotive Goods,' Submission to the USTR (17 January 2024) 1 <https://autosdriveamerica.org/wp-content/uploads/2024/02/2024.01.17-Autos-Drive-America-Comments-to-USTR-on-USMCA-ROO-Operation.pdf> accessed 23 March 2024.

which the USMCA has included additional elements to the RoO: the sourcing requirements for steel and aluminum and the labor value content.

3.2.2 Deep Trade Provisions in the USMCA RoO Chapter

The USMCA's RoO is a combination of shallow and deep approaches to trade agreements. The requirements to source steel and aluminum from the Parties were designed to redistribute gains in trade from third-party markets to regional markets (i.e. a shallow approach), and to support the automotive, steel, and aluminum manufacturing sectors in Canada, Mexico, and the US (i.e. a deep approach). A fact sheet of the Office of the US Trade Representative (USTR) titled, "Rebalancing Trade to Support Manufacturing," states in the first paragraph, "The new United States-Mexico-Canada Agreement (USMCA) will create more balanced, reciprocal trade that supports high-paying jobs for Americans and grows the North American economies."[121] One method to rebalance trade is requiring that at least 70% of purchases of steel and aluminum are of originating goods for vehicles to be deemed USMCA originating.[122] Seven years after entry into force of the USMCA, all steel and aluminum must be sourced in the USCMA except for "metallurgical processes involving the refinement of steel additives."[123] In its Fact Sheet the USTR explains that "[t]he United States, Mexico, and Canada have agreed to stronger rules of origin that exceed those of both NAFTA 1.0 and the Trans-Pacific Partnership (TPP), including for autos and automobile parts and other industrial products … The new rules will help ensure that only producers using sufficient and significant North American parts and materials receive preferential tariff benefits."[124]

Another new rule is the labor value content (LVC) rule. For a passenger vehicle to be deemed originating, the producer must demonstrate that 40% percentage of value of the vehicle derives from manufacturing or assembly facilities that pay workers at least $16 per hour.[125] The rules divide this

121 Office of the US Trade Representative (USTR), 'United States – Mexico – Canada Trade Fact Sheet: Rebalancing Trade to Support Manufacturing' (ustr.gov) <https://ustr.gov/trade-agreements/free-trade-agreements/united-states-mexico-canada-agreement/fact-sheets/rebalancing> accessed 13 October 2024.

122 USMCA ch 4, app art 6(1).

123 Ibid, fn 74 to art (6)(1). Additionally, the sourcing requirements do not apply to "raw materials used in the steel manufacturing process, including steel scrap; iron ore; pig iron; reduced, processed, or pelletized iron ore; or raw alloys." If such raw materials are used to produce steel or aluminum based "ink" for printing 3D goods, this exception may be favorable to those ink producers who must source non-USMCA raw materials.

124 USTR, 'United States – Mexico – Canada Trade Fact Sheet' (n 330).

125 USMCA ch 4, app art 7.

percentage into types of labor: a certain number of percentage points must be dedicated to high-wage material and manufacturing expenditure (25 percent), high-wage technology expenditures (no more than 10 percent), and high-wage assembly expenditures (no more than 5 percent).[126] This breakdown into materials, technology, and assembly correlates to the three areas in which 3D printing promises to be disruptive not only in terms of production of goods, but also in origin determination under the substantial transformation criteria. Also interesting from the point of view of 3D printing is that wages for workers involved in R&D and engineering cannot be included in the high-wage material and manufacturing expenditures, but can be included in the technology expenditures.[127] The USTR explains that the high-wage labor requirement will "support better jobs for United States producers and workers by requiring that a significant portion of vehicle content be made with high-wage labor," ensure that such producers and workers "are able to compete on an even playing field," incentivize investment in new vehicles and parts in the US, and encourage more R&D in the region.[128]

Given this attempt to tie trade agreements to domestic policy goals, especially in the context of labor protection,[129] the rules of origin in the USMCA could be seen as a prototype for deep rules of origin. This is an interesting trend from the point of view of the MFN principle with respect to custom duties and provisions in connection with importation and exportation.[130] Any advantage (or disadvantage) must be accorded to all Members unconditionally and the granting of such an advantage cannot discriminate between foreign products based on how the products are made.[131] Regarding the application of the MFN principle in connection with tariffs and labor standards, Hoekman and Kostecki state that "[u]nconditional means 'no strings attached.' For example, a country cannot condition a tariff on exporting countries satisfying a specific

126 Ibid art 7(1).

127 ibid art 7(3) and fn 77.

128 USTR, 'United States – Mexico – Canada Trade Fact Sheet' (n 330).

129 Harlan Grant Cohen, 'What is International Trade Law For?' (2019) 113 The American J Intl L 326, 342.

130 Article I:I GATT 1994 requires that:

> "[w]ith respect to customs duties and charges of any kind imposed on or in connection with importation or exportation ... with respect to all rules and formalities in connection with importation and exportation ... any advantage, favour, privilege or immunity granted by any contracting party to any product originating in or destined for any other country shall be accorded immediately and unconditionally to the like product originating in or destined for the territories of all other contracting parties."

131 Peter Van den Bossche and Denise Prévost, *Essentials of WTO Law* (2nd edn, CUP 2021) 55–57.

labour standard (that is, impose a higher rate on countries that do not satisfy whatever criterion is imposed) even if domestic producers are subject to it."[132] However, this perspective changes "if a country offers *preferential* access … this may be conditioned on satisfaction of certain criteria" (italics original).[133]

Article 2 of Annex II of the AOR defines preferential RoO as "those laws, regulations and administrative determinations of general application applied by any Member to determine whether goods qualify for preferential treatment under contractual or autonomous trade regimes leading to the *granting of tariff preferences going beyond the application of paragraph 1 of Article 1 GATT 1994*" (my italics). While specifying a specific labor standard (16$ minimum wage) or source requirement as a condition for an advantage may not comply with Article I:1 GATT 1994, such conditions could be permitted under Article 2 of Annex II AOR as the tariff treatment sought is preferential treatment and not MFN treatment. Whether the USCMA rules conditioning particular labor use or sources for materials will accomplish the domestic policy goals is yet to be seen, but the rules have raised some debate among industry analysists regarding their efficacy in building a technologically skilled workforce.[134]

Researchers are developing vehicles made of parts of light-weight materials that require minimal assembly.[135] On the one hand, this could mean that the 70% steel or aluminum sourcing requirement is not necessarily an issue for such producers as other metals are also used for ink. On the other hand, this means that such producers devote the majority of expenditures to sourcing metals which can be found only outside the region. As a result, these new types of automobiles may be imported under MFN rates, an occurrence which the Congressional Budget Office predicts will also happen to traditional motor vehicles

132 Hoekman and Kostecki (n 24) 189.

133 ibid.

134 Safavian (n 120) 2; William Alan Reinsch, Jack Caporal, Madeleine Waddoups and Nadir Tekarli, 'The Impact of Rules of Origin on Supply Chains: USMCA's Auto Rules as a Case Study' (April 2019) Center for Strategic and International Studies, 27–28 <https://csis-website-prod.s3.amazonaws.com/s3fs-public/publication/190403_Scholl_RulesofOrigin_WEB_v3.pdf> accessed 24 October 2021; Adam S. Hersh, 'EPI comments to the Office of the United States Trade Representative on the US-Mexico-Canada Agreement with respect to automotive goods' USTR-2023-0013-0011 Comment Submission (Economic Policy Institute 22 January 2024) <https://www.epi.org/publication/us-mexico-canada-agreement/> accessed 23 March 2024.

135 Josh Davis, 'The Strati: a 3D-printed electric car that could be built in 24 hours' *The Guardian* (London, 9 December 2014) <https://www.theguardian.com/technology/2014/dec/09/3d-printed-electric-car> accessed 2 December 2021.

and parts which do not meet the USMCA's stricter RoO requirements.[136] While 3D printing and assembly of 3D printing parts will require a skilled workforce, the value creation may shift from the technician in the factory to the designer sitting at a computer. Further, fewer high-wage workers would be needed to assemble the parts. Thus, 3D printing could throw a wrench in the intention behind the USMCA rules designed to increase manufacturing jobs in the US. Would a 3D printed car meet the requirements under the new rules? Given the special materials used and less labor required, perhaps not.

This example also points to a significant critique of the *ad valorem* criterion: it can discourage efficient manufacturing processes and innovation. Expensive domestic materials and expensive labor-intensive, but not necessarily productive, methods raise the costs expended in the territory in which a good is produced.[137] If it is too costly to purchase domestic materials or use labor-intensive methods, than traders may purchase foreign inputs, use more efficient methods, and trade under the MFN rates. In 1990, Vermulst and Waer noted that the value added test seems to be inconsistent with the evolution of production processes, as "a producer will presumably aim its research and development efforts particularly at finding means of making the technically complex (and therefore initially most expensive) processes more cost-efficient … A test which focuses on value added rather than on the nature of the production process discourages such rationalization techniques."[138] Twenty-six years later, Mavroidis writes that while, "[t]he 'value added' method is clear" it "could act as a disincentive to use the 'cheapest source of supply.'"[139] As 3D printing is seen as a method for more efficiently producing products using less human involvement it provides a testing-ground to examine how the *ad valorem* criterion in existing agreements could constrain traders of 3D goods to choose to trade under MFN rates and how to design *ad valorem* rules to be more responsive to changes in manufacturing.

The previous sections have summarized the RoO framework. Whether a CTH occurred or whether the Net Cost Method for determining RVC must be used are determinations and calculations made across the world daily. Traders must also prove that the good originates from the claimed territory.

136 Congressional Budget Office, *Cost Estimate for H.R. 5430* (December 2019) fn c, <https://www.cbo.gov/system/files/2019-12/hr5430.pdf> accessed 24 October 2021.

137 Imagawa and Vermulst (n 1) 607.

138 Edwin Vermulst and Paul Waer, 'European Community Rules of Origin as Commercial Policy Instruments?' (1990) 24 J World Trade 55, 95.

139 Mavroidis, *The Regulation of International Trade*, vol 1 (n 23) 222.

4 Administration of Rules of Origin: Into the Factory and Customs Offices

The goal of the final pages of this Chapter is to give a glimpse of "rules in origin in practice" and demonstrate why producing 3D printed parts may be appealing to traders. 3D printing promises to reduce the number of parts in automobiles, engines, bicycles, and other goods. Less parts, should, so it seems, result in less work figuring out whether the final good meets the substantial transformation requirements. However, traders would still have to demonstrate proof of origin.

PTAs include administrative procedures for demonstrating that a good originates in the territory. A trader not only has to meet one or more of the substantial transformation criteria, they must also ensure that there is sufficient evidence to support a claim of origin. Additionally, all paperwork must be submitted properly to avoid delays in clearing the goods through customs, being subject to an audit by the customs authorities, or being liable for penalties. This process requires the coordination of manufacturers, suppliers, importers, custom authorities, brokers, lawyers and organizations such as chambers of commerce.[140] While the WTO has a light-touch with regards to a multilateral approach to regulating preferential RoO, there have been some multilateral achievements in facilitating trade since 2009.

The WTO's Trade Facilitation Agreement (TFA), ratified by two-thirds of Members and entered into force in 2017, sets out measures to simplify paperwork, harmonize custom requirements, and reduce the cost of complying with custom procedures.[141] It encourages the creation of a "single-window" for traders to submit documentation for exportation, importation, transit of goods to authorities and to receive responses from such authorities in a timely manner.[142] By October 2024, the implementation rate of the TFA was 79.4%.[143] Reform of customs procedures in trade agreements and the increased participation in international trade by SMEs suggests that the agreement is succeeding in streamlining customs procedures and removing obstacles to participating in

140 van de Heetkemp and Tusveld (n 16) 111–115.

141 WTO, 'Trade facilitation – Cutting red tape at the border' (wto.org) <https://www.wto.org/english/tratop_e/tradfa_e/tradfa_introduction_e.htm> accessed 2 December 2021.

142 Agreement on Trade Facilitation (TFA), WT/L/940 (entered into force 22 February 2017) art 10.4.1 <https://docs.wto.org/> accessed 9 March 2025.

143 WTO, 'Trade Facilitation Database,' (tfadatabase.org 2024) <https://tfadatabase.org/implementation> accessed 20 October 2024.

the global market.[144] Further, under Article 1, Members must promptly publish in a non-discriminatory and easily accessible manner, "laws, regulations, and administrative rules of general application relating to rules of origin."[145]

The Information Technology Agreement (ITA) was signed in 1996 and currently has 84 members who must eventually eliminate import duties on a MFN basis on products such as telecommunications equipment, software, scientific instruments, and computers.[146] In 2015, the list of products was expanded (ITA II) to include new generation technology products such as touch screens and GPS navigation equipment.[147] 54 of 56 participants to the ITA have notified to the WTO the modification of their tariff schedules.[148] The WCO has added a classification code for additive manufacturing machines to the 2022 revisions of the HS.[149] It will be interesting to see if WTO Members amend their tariff schedules to include the new code, and subsequently if the ITA will be amended to include these tariff lines. In a dispute before the US Customs and Border Patrol (CBP), the classification of additive manufacturing machines,

---

144 Nora Neufeld, 'Great Expectations: How the World Trade Organization's Trade Facilitation Agreement Impacts Trade and Trade Cooperation' (2019) 11 Trade, L & Development 11, 29–35.

145 Agreement on Trade Facilitation (TFA), WT/L/940 (entered into force 22 February 2017) art 1.1(e) <http:// docs.wto.org>.

146 WTO, 'Information Technology Agreement – an Explanation' (wto.gov) <https://www.wto.org/english/tratop_e/inftec_e/itaintro_e.htm> accessed 13 October 2024; 'Status of Implementation: Note by Secretariat' (15 March 2024) G/IT/1/Rev.60 <https://docs.wto.org> accessed 20 October 2024.

147 WTO, 'Briefing note: The Expansion of Trade in Information Technology Products (ITA Expansion)' (wto.org 16 December 2015) <https://www.wto.org/english/news_e/news15_e/itabriefingnotes161215_e.pdf> accessed 2 December 2021. In 2024, the delegate from Japan reported to the Committee of Participants on the Expansion of Trade in Information Technology Products that the level of understanding of ICT products, including 3D printers, had deepened in the in the that Asia-Pacific Economic Cooperation region. Committee of Participants on the Expansion of Trade in Information Technology Products, 'Minutes of the Meeting of 11 April 2024' (5 July 2024) G/IT/M/80, para 8.8. <https://docs.wto.org> accessed 20 October 2024.

148 Committee of Participants on the Expansion of Trade in Information Technology Products, 'Status of Implementation: Note by Secretariat' (n 146).

149 Additive manufacturing machines have been given subheadings 8485.10 to 8485.90, WCO, HS Nomenclature 2022 – Chapter 84 (wcoomed.org) <http://www.wcoomd.org/-/media/wco/public/global/pdf/topics/nomenclature/instruments-and-tools/hs-nomenclature-2022/2022/1684_2022e.pdf?la=en> accessed 7 January 2022. See also, WCO, 'The WCO has published the HS 2017/HS 2022 Correlation Tables for the Harmonized System' (wcoomd.org 13 November 2020) <http://www.wcoomd.org/en/media/newsroom/2020/november/the-wco-has-published-the-hs-2017-2022.aspx>. All sources accessed 2 December 2021.

and thus the tariff duty applied to them, was based on the material – plastic or metal – that the machine used for printing.[150]

Traders may consult international organizations other than the WTO for guidance on preferential RoO procedures and trade in goods. The WCO, in addition to the HS and the Kyoto Convention, coordinates with customs authorities in forming regional intelligence liaison offices[151] and programs on addressing and resolving specific issues such as corruption and IPR protection.[152] Finally, the International Certificate of Origin Council of the International Chamber of Commerce (ICC), consisting of officials of national chamber of commerce offices, establishes guidelines for issuing Certificates of Origin by national offices, verifying the authenticity of trade documents, and resolving issues in determining the origin of a product.[153] The ICC prepares positions papers and meets with WTO delegations in Geneva,[154] and has also called for less complex and obscure rules of origin.[155]

Two important documents are a Certificate of Origin and a Bill of Materials. Generally, the exporter provides a Certificate of Origin, issued by the Chamber of Commerce of the exporter's country.[156] For Certificates of Origin for the purpose of PTAs,[157] the ICC requires information on the raw materials, direct labor costs, direct overhead costs, and profit.[158] The ICC must prepare the Certificate

150 CBP Ruling Letter, *The Tariff Classification of a Robo 3D Printer from China* (12 September 2017) NY N289281; CBP Court Decision, *EOS of North America, Inc. v United States* (10 May 2013) Slip Op. 13–59.

151 WCO, 'RILO: A Unique and United Network' (wcomd.org) <http://www.wcoomd.org/-/media/wco/public/global/pdf/topics/enforcement-and-compliance/tools-and-instruments/rilo/rilo-brochure_en.pdf?db=web> accessed 2 December 2021.

152 WCO, 'Activities and Programmes' (wcoomd.org) <http://www.wcoomd.org/en/topics/enforcement-and-compliance/activities-and-programmes.aspx> accessed 2 December 2021.

153 International Chamber of Commerce (ICC), 'Chamber Services: Certificates of Origin' (iccwbo.org) <https://iccwbo.org/world-chambers-federation/chamber-services/certificates-of-origin/> accessed 9 March 2025; van de Heetkemp and Tusveld (n 16) 21.

154 Eg, ICC, 'Builidng Business Engagement ahead of the WTO's 12th Ministerial Conference' (iccwbo.org 24 June 2021) <https://iccwbo.org/media-wall/news-speeches/building-business-engagement-ahead-of-the-wtos-12th-ministerial-conference/> accessed 3 January 2022.

155 ICC, 'Business Recommendations on Rules of Origin in Preferential Trade Agreements' (May 2017) Doc. No. 104–89 <https://iccwbo.org/news-publications/policies-reports/business-recommendations-rules-origin-preferential-trade-agreements/> accessed 9 March 2025.

156 van de Heetkampa and Tusveld (n 16) 114–115.

157 ibid 119–120.

158 ICC, 'Certificates of Origin' (iccwbo.org), <https://iccwbo.org/resources-for-business/certificates-of-origin/> accessed 2 December 2021.

based on the relevant PTA.[159] If a Certificate of Origin from the exporter is not sufficient to demonstrate reasonable care in proving the origin of a good, the importer should also take efforts to obtain documentation of origin on a consistent basis from the suppliers, a process called solicitation,[160] maintain bookkeeping records, and even visit the suppliers' factories.[161] One of the key changes to the procedural rules on origin verification in the PEM revisions and the USMCA are simplifications to the certification process. Finally, the producer seeking preferential treatment for an item made of subcomponents will need to prepare a Bill of Materials (BOM), which contains a list of the subcomponents, their HS codes, value, and country of origin. This BOM will be used to determine whether the product will qualify for preferential treatment, and if made in advance of assembly, can be used to predict whether a good will qualify by comparing the sources of different inputs.[162]

The PTA will determine what documentation is required for proof of origin.[163] Under the USCMA, either the importer or the exporter can submit a certificate of origin. This certificate "need not follow a prescribed format", but does need to contain "minimum data elements" including identification of the certifier, contact information of the exporter (if identity known), producer and importer (all if different from the certifier), description of the good and HS code, the origin criteria under which the good qualifies, and the period of time requested if the certification covers multiple shipments (up to 12 months).[164] The PEM requires (1) importers or exporters to fill out a single origin declaration (called EUR.1) or (2) a declaration of origin on an invoice, delivery note or other commercial document, if the trader is an approved exporter and the total value of the consignment does not exceed 6000 Euros.[165] Documents that can support a declaration of origin include direct evidence of the processes carried out to obtain the goods, documents proving originating status of materials used, and documents proving the working or processing of materials in or outside the relevant Contracting Party.[166]

Traders must also comply with "Direct Transportation" or "Direct Consignment" rules. Under a Direct Transportation rule, it is necessary to ship the good directly from one party to another party to preserve origin status; transit

159 van de Heetkamp & Tusveld (n 16) 119; ICC, 'Certificates of Origin' (n 158).

160 van de Heetkamp & Tusveld (n 16) 129.

161 ibid 185.

162 ibid 160; Mitchell Grant, 'Bill of Materials (BOM)' (*Investopedia* 30 October 2020) <https://www.investopedia.com/terms/b/bill-of-materials.asp> accessed 2 December 2021.

163 van de Heetkamp & Tusveld (n 16) 114.

164 USMCA ch 5 Annex A.

165 PEM App. 1, art 17(1), art. 18(1).

166 PEM App.1, art (31)(3).

through a third-party country could result in the good losing preferential origin status.[167] The PTA will specify what procedures must be followed for a good to retain origin status if shipped through a third-party: for example, evidence showing that the goods remained under supervision of the customs authority, that there was no further processing of the goods, and that they did not enter the market in the country of transit.[168] In the PEM, requirements on shipment are found under Article 14, 'Non-alternation.' Preferential tariff treatment is applied if the goods exported from one Contracting Party into another Contracting Party meet the substantial transformation criteria and "those products are the same as those exported from the exporting Party."[169] Products may be split into different consignments in a third-party, but it is necessary to demonstrate that no alternation to the goods occurred and they remained under customs supervisions.[170] However, in a study by Stefano Inama, Pramila Crivelli and Jonas Kasteng, published in 2021, direct transport rules in preferential trade agreements between the EU and Japan and EU and Switzerland were a factor that led traders to forgo seeking preferential tariff treatment and to trade under MFN rates.[171]

In addition to seeking assistance from international organizations, traders can also look to the rulings of national and regional courts on customs procedures. In the US, decisions regarding international trade and customs duties are made by the Federal Circuit and the Court of International Trade (CIT). The CIT can hear matters related to custom duties throughout the US, decisions by this Court can be appealed to the Federal Circuit, and these decisions can be appealed to the Supreme Court.[172] In Chapter 3, a case before the CIT appealed to the Federal Circuit regarding the 3D files used for printing dental aligners will be discussed. The CIT applies the substantial transformation test developed through case law to determine whether an operation is sufficient to

167 E.g., USMCA ch 4 art 4.18(1).

168 Paul Brenton, 'Preferential Rules of Origin' in Jean-Pierre Chauffour and Jean-Christophe Maur (eds), *Preferential Trade Agreement Policies for Development: A Handbook* (World Bank 2011) 172.

169 PEM, App. 1, art 14(1).

170 ibid art 14(3).

171 Pramila Crivelli, Stefano Inama and Jonas Kasteng, 'Using Utilization Rates to Identify Rules of Origin Reforms: The Case of EU Free Trade Area Agreements' (2021) EUI Working Papers RCS 2021/21 <https://cadmus.eui.eu/handle/1814/70396> accessed 24 October 2021.

172 US Court of International Trade, 'About the Court' (cit.uscourts.gov) <https://www.cit.uscourts.gov/about-court> accessed 2 December 2021.

confer origin to a product.[173] As each matter is fact-intensive, the application of this standard by the court varies for each proceeding.[174]

Nonetheless, these rulings are applied by the US Customs and Border Protection (CBP) to make determinations on whether a product qualifies for preferential treatment under a PTA.[175] When assessing whether an origin qualifying substantial transformation occurred, the CBP "considers the totality of the circumstances and makes such decisions on a case-by-case basis."[176] The primary considerations are "whether such processing renders a product with a new name, character, and use", but also reviewed are "facts on resources expended on product design and development, extent and nature of post-assembly procedures and working skill required during the actual manufacturing process."[177] At times, "the determination will be a mixed question of technology and customs law, mostly the latter."[178] Thus, officials at the CBP take into consideration technology when reviewing whether a good qualifies for preferential treatment, and this will be seen in some of the rulings discussed in the next Chapters.

Under the Customs Modernization Act, the burden is on the importer to provide to the CBP, "with reasonable care," documents sufficient to enable the CBP to "properly assess duties on the merchandise … and determine whether any other applicable requirement of law … is met."[179] In its circular to the trade community, the CBP warns that "[a]n importer of record's failure to exercise reasonable care could delay release of the merchandise and, in some cases, could result in the imposition of penalties or, in certain instances, referral for

173 Monika Brenner, 'Navigating Rules of Origin in the New Trade Environment' Proceeding of the 20th Judicial Conference of US Court of Int'l Trade (cit.uscourts.gov) <https://www.cit.uscourts.gov/sites/cit/files/MBrenner%20CIT%20Nov182019%20.doc.pdf> accessed 2 December 2021; van de Heetkamp and Tusveld (n 16) 151.

174 Jeremy Page, 'Determining Origin in a Predetermined World: The Impact of *Energizer Battery*', Proceeding of the 20th Judicial Conference of US Court of Int'l Trade (cit.uscourts.gov), <https://www.cit.uscourts.gov/sites/cit/files/JPage%20CIT%20Conference%20Article.pdf>; Jason M Kenner, 'A Brief Overview of Several Decisions Discussing Substantial Transformation' Proceeding of the 20th Judicial Conference of US Court of Int'l Trade (cit.uscourts.gov), <https://www.cit.uscourts.gov/sites/cit/files/JKenner%20A%20Brief%20Overview%20of%20Several%20Decisions%20Discussing%20Substantial%20Transformation%20final.pdf> all sources accessed 2 December 2021.

175 Jones and Wong (n 71) 2.

176 CBP, Ruling Letter, *re: U.S. Government Procurement; Country of Origin of Storage Infrastructure Solution Systems; Substantial Transformation* (July 16, 2015) HQ H59758, printed in (5 August 2015) 49 Customs Bulletin & Decisions 54.

177 ibid 54–55.

178 ibid 55.

179 Customs Modernization Act, 19 U.S.C. §1484(a)(1)(B).

criminal enforcement."[180] Personal penalties range from the domestic value of the merchandise in cases of fraud to two times the loss of duties in cases of negligence and to four times the loss in duties for gross negligence.[181] In 2023, a new bill was introduced to the US Senate (Customs Modernization Act 2023) with expansions on the duty to report supply chain information, including for shipments under 800$ (duty-free limit), expansion of liability, and mandatory electronic collection of data prior to entry of the goods in the US.[182] These changes are aimed at the use of complex supply chains and small shipments exemptions to import illicit or counterfeit goods,[183] yet they will likely increase the burden on traders to maintain records on more steps of the production chain and expend more resources in providing data to customs offices.

While the EU is a customs union, the national customs offices implement customs legislation, including the legislation on preferential rules of origin.[184] For example, the Italian national customs office (ADM – L'Agenzia delle accise, dogane e monopoli) administers customs duties as well as issues administrative decisions, such as binding information on origin (BOI, IVO in Italian).[185] Each Member State must also apply penalties for failure to comply with customs legislation, including pecuniary penalties, that are "effective, proportionate and dissuasive."[186] National courts also refer disputes to the European Court

180 CBP, 'What Every Member of the Trade Community Should Know: Reasonable Care' (cbp.gov September 2017) 3 <https://www.cbp.gov/sites/default/files/assets/documents/2018-Mar/icprescare2017revision.pdf> accessed 2 December 2021.

181 Tariff Act of 1930, 19 U.S.C. §1592; CBP, 'What Every Member of the Trade Community Should Know About : Customs Administrative Enforcement Process : Fines, Penalties, Forfeitures and Liquidated Damages' (cbp.gov February 2004) 28 <https://www.cbp.gov/sites/default/files/documents/icp052_3.pdf> accessed 2 December 2021.

182 US Congress, S.3431 – Customs Modernization Act of 2023, introduced 7 December 2023 <https://www.congress.gov/bill/118th-congress/senate-bill/3431/text/is> accessed 23 March 2024.

183 'Cassidy, Whitehouse Introduces Bill To Bring U.S. Customs Laws Into The 21st Century, Stop Illicit Trade' (Cassidy.Senate.Gov 8 December 2023) <https://www.cassidy.senate.gov/newsroom/press-releases/cassidy-whitehouse-introduces-bill-to-bring-u-s-customs-laws-into-the-21st-century-stop-illicit-trade> accessed 23 March 2024.

184 Commission, 'EU Customs strategy' (ec.europa.eu) <https://ec.europa.eu/taxation_customs/customs-4/eu-customs-strategy_en?> accessed 2 December 2021.

185 Agenzia delle accise, dogane e monopoli, 'I.V.O. Binding Information on Origin' (adm.gov.it) <https://www.adm.gov.it/portale/en/-informazioni-vincolanti-in-materia-di-origine> accessed 2 December 2021.

186 Regulation (EC) No 952/2013) of the European Parliament and of the Council of 9 October 2013 laying down the Union Customs Code (recast) (partially entered into force on 1 May 2016) OJ L 269, art 42 (1).

of Justice, and decisions by the Court have led to legislative changes.[187] With the revisions to the Union Customs Code, the EU aims to streamline customs procedures, including a Central Data Hub in which businesses can submit data on supply chains and production processes, engaging online platforms to take accountability on the payment of customs duties and VAT, and enhance cooperation between the national customs offices and their enforcement of regulation impacting importation of goods into the EU.[188]

5 Conclusion

As seen in this Chapter there is much work and not a little risk involved in claiming that a good qualifies for preferential treatment under an PTA. Such activity is made by companies, large and small, worldwide on a daily basis. Preferential RoO aim to ensure that only the chosen goods are granted the reward of preferential treatment. Yet many companies forgo seeking preferential treatment, because of the lack of organizational and financial resources to obtain from suppliers the information required to prove the origin of various inputs and to comply with multiple rules under multiple PTAs.

If 3D printing parts and assembling final goods from those parts may lead to avoiding this paperwork and risk, 3D printing may have its appeal for manufacturers. Instead of importing a part and relying on the supplier to provide verification of its materials, assessing whether there will be enough originating materials, and determining whether the firm has the resources to document all of this – why not simply print the part in the same territory, if not on the same factory floor, as where the final good is assembled? Surely this will save all of those RoO headaches and ensure that the finished product has enough domestic content to qualify for preferential treatment? That is to be explored in Chapter 4. However, before examining how 3D printing could disrupt origin determination under the current rules, the critiques of legal scholars and economists on the disruptive effect of RoO on trade will be discussed in the next Chapter.

187 van de Heetkamp & Tusveld (n 16) 150; Commission, 'Infringements & Case Law" (ec.europea.eu) <https://ec.europa.eu/taxation_customs/infringements_en> accessed 2 December 2021.

188 Commission, 'EU Customs Reform' (ec.europea.eu) <https://taxation-customs.ec.europa.eu/customs-4/eu-customs-reform_en> accessed 23 March 2024.

CHAPTER 3

Exploring Critiques of Preferential Rules of Origin and Positioning Rules in a Framework for Digital Trade

Towards the end of the previous Chapter, the administrative requirements of RoO were introduced, requirements that result in a lot of paperwork. This is the environment that traders operate in. Chapter 3 examines this situation through arguments that RoO do not provide a level playing field for all participants in global trade. The question arises, how to place RoO into a narrative for the international trade law system, i.e., that it provides a legal framework in which all states have an opportunity to develop and prosper through trade.

This Chapter will explore how RoO fit into that framework and how well they would fit into new frameworks being proposed for 21st Century trade. As Hoekman and Nelson propose, 21st Century agreements go beyond reciprocal promises to lower tariffs and other duties towards "creating an institutional environment supportive of global economic activity in a post-industrial world."[1] Harlan Grant Cohen also explores a new framework that is supportive of national political goals such as labor or environmental standards. However, he emphasizes that this system still requires "notions of efficiency, transparency, and even-handedness that undergird and guide trade regulation today" and that can be provided for by the WTO and international agreements.[2] Yet, the studies on RoO referenced in this Chapter suggest that RoO do not instill "efficiency, transparency, and even-handedness" into the trading environment. Finally, if in the data-driven economy there should be no hierarchy of rules, as Shaffer proposes,[3] RoO, which discriminate goods for preferential treatment, do not, as currently written, seem like the best tool for regulating digital trade.

1 Bernard Hoekman and Douglas Nelson,'21st Century Trade Agreements and the Owl of Minerva' (2018), EUI Working Papers, RSCAS 2018/04, 9 <https://cadmus.eui.eu/bitstream/handle/1814/50964/RSCAS_2018_04.pdf?sequence=1&isAllowed=y> accessed 23 October 2021.

2 Harlan Grant Cohen, 'What is International Trade Law For?' (2019) 113 The American J Intl L 326, 339.

3 Gregory Shaffer, 'Trade Law in a Data-Driven Economy: The Need for Modesty and Resilience' (2021) 20 World Trade Rev. 259, 271, 273.

 | DOI:10.1163/9789004730595_005

There is still a possibility that RoO could be a productive and positive legal instrument in a 21st Century trade framework. There will still be a need for rules, because technology could make the trade playing field more uneven. 3D printing, though still an emerging form of manufacturing, shows this. Rashmi Banga, Chief of the Development Research Branch of UNCTAD, raises concerns that 3D printing could undercut much of the benefits arising from tariff preferences in GSPs if digital transmissions are not taxed. A manufacturer from a developed country will be able to take advantage of 3D printing by printing shoes in a 3D printing hub in the territory and thus avoid paying import customs duties.[4] On the other hand, Andrea Andrenelli and Javier López González of the OECD argue that 3D printing manufacturing is still far from replacing traditional manufacturing, and taxing digital transmissions will only raise more barriers to trade.[5] However, neither report approaches the subject of identifying the origin of the digital transmission, which may be relevant if a state is going to tax digital transmissions. On the other hand, the Protocol to the Agreement Establishing the African Continental Free Trade Area (AfCFTA) on Digital Trade proposes identifying the origin of digital transmissions so that there are no custom duties imposed on digital products originating and transmitted electronically from other parties of the Protocol.[6] Thus, rules of origin will be necessary in some capacity in regulating the data-driven economy.

This Chapter is structured along three main parameters: assessing how well preferential RoO fit into the framework of an international trade law system which "increases the size of the pie" for all; exploring whether RoO can or should become "deeper" instruments of trade; and finally, the initial steps into examining how RoO could identify the origin of 3D printed goods, as well as generally situating RoO in the regulation of the data-driven economy.

4 Rashmi Banga, 'Growing Trade in Electronic Transmissions: Implications for the South' (2019) UNCTAD Research Paper No. 29, 30–31 <https://unctad.org/system/files/official-document/ser-rp-2019d1_en.pdf> accessed 23 October 2024.

5 Andrea Andrenelli and Javier López González, 'Electronic Transmissions and International Trade - Shedding New Light on the Moratorium Debate' (2019) OECD Trade Policy Paper, No. 233, 20 <http://dx.doi.org/10.1787/57b50a4b-en> accessed 23 October 2021.

6 African Continental Free Trade Area Secretariat, 'Draft: Protocol to the Agreement Establishing the African Continental Free Trade Area on Digital Trade' (Digital Protocol AfCFTA) (7–10 February 2024) Art. 5 & 6. Available at <https://www.bilaterals.org/IMG/pdf/afcfta_digital_trade_protocol_-_9_february_2024_draft.pdf> accessed 20 October 2024.

1 Rules of Origin: Unpredictable and Not Very Transparent Rules of the Game

If predictability, legitimacy, and efficiency are necessary for an international legal regime for trade, then finding a place for RoO within this framework can be challenging. The AOR recognizes though the third preamble that "clear and predictable rules of origin and their application facilitate the flow of international trade" and desires to ensure that "rules of origin are prepared and applied in an impartial, transparent, predictable, consistent and neutral manner." For various reasons Members have not drafted and implemented consistent preferential RoO. It could be argued that the industrial reality of states and the density of the HS code, for example, does necessitate allocating a certain level of detail and attention to particular products over others.[7] If raising livestock and processing meat is not a key industry for Party A, but Party B may be significantly worse off if third-party shoes are imported into Party A, then it may be reasonable for A and B to develop more detailed RoO for shoes and not include a restrictive rule for meat. In other words, variance among preferential RoO may have some benefits.[8]

Differences in RoOs due to the different industries and level of development of each trading partner (along with any political rationales) nonetheless impact the international trade law system in its goals of promoting liberalization, development, and with more recent agreements, certain environmental standards. According to Moshe Hirsch, different RoO designed to achieve different political goals, "is likely to weaken predictability for producers and traders, destabilize trading relations, and hinder long-term development of international trade."[9] For this reason, reducing the negative externalities of political involvement in the creation and implementation of RoO may help improve international trade. To do this however, it is necessary to understand why RoO are susceptible to political interference.

First, there are some positive aspects about political involvement in RoOs. Regional agreements, such as the PEM, with cumulation provisions can potentially establish some harmony between nations which were once contentious

7 Hasegawa Jitsuya, 'Standardization of Complex and Diversified Preferential Rules of Origin' (2021) 55 J World Trade 545, 560.

8 Hennie Erasmus, Frank Flatters, and Robert Kirk, 'Rules of Origin as Tools of Development? Some Lessons from SADC,' in Olivier Cadot, Antoni Estevadeordal, Akiko Suwa-Eisenmann, and Theirry Verdier (eds), *The Origin of Goods: Rules of Origin in Regional Trade Agreements* (OUP 2006) 288–289.

9 Moshe Hirsch, 'The Politics of Rules of Origin' in Tomer Broude, Marc L Busch, and Amelia Porges (eds), *The Politics of International Economic Law* (CUP 2011) 330.

or even belligerent.[10] RoO can contribute to developing regional value chains through rules requiring a certain amount of local inputs or labor in the region.[11] Finally, cumulation could take the sting out of some of the more restrictive RoO, as according to Hirsch, "establishing a cumulation agreement between several parties provides a significant incentive for producers located in those parties' territories to cooperate and reap the benefits of cumulation in their trade with third parties."[12] A sprinkle of political activity may benefit preferential RoO; however, politicians and industry lobbyists are eager participants in the drafting and implementation of preferential RoO.

One key reason why political attention has turned to restrictive RoO is the gradual reduction of tariff barriers as Member States meet their GATT commitments.[13] As discussed in Chapter 1, local content requirements for obtaining a benefit from a Member State are prohibited under the TRIMS and SCM agreements. States have turned to RoO to bolster the domestic economy by drafting complex rules requiring goods to have a certain percentage of local content, thus imposing a non-tariff barrier to trade.[14] Procedural requirements also can hinder trade. While the TCA preserved the no-duty rate for goods that qualify for origin under the TCA[15], the agreement has a collateral side effect of unleashing paperwork upon traders who must now prove that their products qualify for preferential treatment, and this has impacted small UK firms in trading with the EU.[16] A political decision to preserve a trading relationship by

10 ibid 324.

11 Ram Singh and Surendar Singh, 'Do Rules of Origin Extend Disproportionate Trade Gains under SAFTA: A Case Study of Bicycle and Textile Industries' (2021) 16 Global Trade & Customs J 59, 62.

12 Hirsch, 'The Politics of Rules of Origin' (n 9) 323.

13 ibid 329; Erasmus, Flatters and Kirk (n 8) 289.

14 WE James, 'Rules of Origin and Rules of Preference and the World Trade Organization: The Challenge to Global Trade Liberalization' in Patrick F J Macrory, Arthur Edmond Appleton and Michael G Plummer (eds) *World Trade Organization: Legal, Economic and Political Analysis* (Springer 2005), 275–280; Rhoni Acharya, 'Regional trade agreements: recent developments,' in Rhoni Acharya (ed), *Regional Trade Agreements and the Multilateral Trading System* (CUP 2016) 13.

15 Commission, 'EU-UK: A New Relationship' (www.ec.europa.eu) <https://ec.europa.eu/taxation_customs/united-kingdom_en> accessed 5 January 2022.

16 Paola Mariani and Giorgio Sacerdoti, 'Trade in Goods and Level Playing Field' (2021) Working Paper No. 7/2021, DCU Brexit Institute <https://ssrn.com/abstract=3797021> accessed 23 October 2021. (n 382) 3; Isabelle Ioannides, 'The EU-UK Trade and Cooperation Agreement Two Years On: Unpacking Early Evidence' European Parliamentary Research Service (August 2023), 29–34 <https://www.europarl.europa.eu/RegData/etudes/STUD/2023/747433/EPRS_STU(2023)747433_EN.pdf> accessed 23 March 2024.

keeping tariff rates low may be made hampered by the practicalities of trying to comply with the rules and customs procedures.[17]

Governments understandably want to support and promote the development of an industry and provide jobs for their workforces. Problems arise when RoO are designed to the detriment of third-party importers of final products or intermediate products.[18] As a PTA opens up a domestic market to imports of goods or inputs from the other parties, RoO can be designed to balance such an opening by requiring use of supplies or resources originating from the parties to the agreement.[19] The more restrictive a rule is in requiring local or regional content, the more incentive, so the theory would suggest, a local producer has in using local or regional materials and labor. RoO are drafted to obtain or retain origin for certain goods.[20] These objectives differ according to the different strategic goals of industry supporters and lobbyists.[21] If, for example, painting color designs on tableware is a sensitive industry in Country A, it may want painting to confer origin so as to "obtain" origin of the final product. On the other hand, if stamping of color decals on tableware is a significant industry, Country A may claim that painting is a simple operation which does not confer origin, but draft a rule claiming that stamping confers origin. The section below on the economic critique of RoO presents studies finding that increasing the restrictiveness of the rules does not necessarily result in increasing the use of local or regional material or labor.

The political tinkering with RoO creates information asymmetry between major stakeholders and small businesses and consumers of retail products. The text of the PEM or USMCA is accessible on the internet, so one can, depending on one's access to the internet, find them; understanding them is another matter. Hirsch argues that the language of RoO is a form of veiled protectionism as "their level of complexity often requires special expertise to assess their impact upon a particular sector of the economy. Practically, ROOs and their economic impact are not comprehensible to most citizens, journalists, and policymakers."[22] I.M. Destler provides some insight behind the political drive towards complex rules of origin in the US in the early 1990s. Industries that favored protectionism, such as the automobile and textile industries, "abandoned a strategy of opposition to all new international trade agreements and … looked for

17 Mariani and Sacerdoti (n 16) 3.
18 Hirsch, 'The Politics of Rules of Origin' (n 9) 323.
19 ibid 326–327.
20 Inama, *The Rules of Origin in International Trade* (CUP 2022) 171–172.
21 ibid.
22 Hirsch, 'The Politics of Rules of Origin' (n 9) 328–329.

ways to gain advantage within these agreements."[23] As the 1990s progressed, trade policymakers and drafters sought to carve out benefits for specific industries in RoO and the rules grew more technical to favor those industries that had strong lobbying activities.[24]

Finally, questions on the WTO legality of preferential RoO as Annex II in the AOR could diminish the legitimacy of these rules as legal instruments. Hirsch argues that "the lack of an effective legal regime" makes RoOs more susceptible to being utilized for political aims.[25] Thus, RoO, a widely used means for regulating trade is unpredictable and nontransparent, and unexamined by the DSB. This is problematic, because RoO are trade measures that traders and custom officials deal with on a daily basis.

Rules of origin have been identified as one element tangling up the "spaghetti-bowl" of trade agreements.[26] This is due, as Jagdish Bhagwati argues to the variety of the product specific rules and the political intent to deter competition by raising costs of compliance.[27] Inama and Sim, in their review of the rules of origin in ASEAN agreements, point out that not only are there overlapping rules among the Agreements, a trader importing under an ASEAN agreement can be required to follow two sets of accounting systems for the imported goods: one to determine if the preferential origin status is met, and one to comply with domestic requirements.[28] This additional expenditure can deter traders from seeking preferential tariff treatment if it outweighs the benefit of importing under a preferential tariff rate.

Hasegawa Jitsuya provides another perspective on the high number of preferential RoO in existence. It is necessary to distinguish the diversity of the "content of the rules" from the diversity of "expressing the rules."[29] The "content of the rules", or the "concrete meaning of the rules," focuses on whether a production process confers origin on the good, for example whether plating of steel is sufficient processing.[30] Diversity in content results from the different political and commercial objectives of the parties, and "[w]ithout this

23 IM (Mac) Destler, 'Rules of Origin and U.S. trade policy' in Olivier Cadot, Antoni Estevadeordal, Akiko Suwa-Eisenmann, and Theirry Verdier (eds), *The Origin of Goods: Rules of Origin in Regional Trade Agreements* (OUP 2006) 178.

24 Ibid 178–179.

25 Hirsch, 'The Politics of Rules of Origin' (n 9) 329.

26 James (n 14) 287.

27 Jagdish Bhagwati, *Termites in the Trading System: How Preferential Agreements Undermine Free Trade* (OUP 2008) 68–69.

28 Stefano Inama and Edmund W Sim, *Rules of Origin in ASEAN* (CUP 2015), 87–88.

29 Jitsuya (n 7) 547.

30 ibid 547, fn. 2.

diversity, the conclusion of FTAs/EPAs would not be possible."[31] The complexity of the rules arises from the different ways meeting a certain requirement is expressed in different agreements.[32] For example, a set of PTAS may have a similar approach to whether a good must undergo a CTH and meet a value added percentage. However, as the language, percentages, and formulas differ among agreements, a trader must decipher how to comply with the rules in Agreement A and those in Agreement B, although both confer origin on a good as long as there was a CTH and local value added.[33] While the diversity of the content of the rules results from different policy objectives, Jitsuya proposes that policymakers and trade and customs experts should focus on simplifying and standardizing the expression of the rules so that traders can understand the meaning and purpose of the rule, i.e. what is or is not sufficient processing of a good.[34]

While simplicity and consistency of RoOs is important for SMEs, such elements are important for all firms trading internationally. A study by EY in 2016, based on interviews at multinational corporations, such as General Motors, Nike, Microsoft, and the Walt Disney company, found that 33% of the reported participants managed 10 or more different PTAs and about a third of the participants allocated resources to third parties for assistance in origin analysis and certification.[35] On the other hand, as SMEs are more likely to devote resources on the quality and price of their products rather than customs compliance procedures, high costs of such compliance or the need to use third party advisors may deter them from participating in a particular PTA market.[36] The next two Chapters will explore whether the shift from traditional to advanced manufacturing (including additive manufacturing) presents an opportunity for

31 ibid 560.

32 ibid.

33 ibid 560–563.

34 ibid 563–564.

35 William M Methenitis and Kristine Price Dozier, 'Making sense of a world in motion – a global trade perspective' (2016) EY Global Trade Symposium Report, 10 <http://www.goingglobalskills.com/pdfs/making-sense-of-a-world-in-motion.pdf> accessed 23 October 2021. The EY report of 2018 stressed the need for the harmonization of customs rules to facilitate trade. J Michael Heldebrand, Sharon A Martin, Robert Smith, 'Is trade the disrupter or the disrupted?' (2018) EY Global Trade Symposium Report, 19–23 <https://assets.ey.com/content/dam/ey-sites/ey-com/en_gl/topics/global-trade/global-trade-pdfs/1808-2835224_Global_Trade_Symposium_report_012125-18Gbl.pdf> accessed 23 October 2021.

36 Jessica Gladstone and Cintia Aquilar Flores, 'Free trade agreements: compliance with rules of origin and utilization of preferential tariffs' (2017) 23 Intl Trade L & Regulation 113, 114.

redesigning RoOs that are more aligned with modern trade practices, and also more transparent and supportive of trade by large and small companies. The next part, however, will shift focus to the economic analysis of RoOs as the work in this field provides some important insights on where the trade distorting effects of RoO occur.

2 Economic Perspective: With Preferential Rules of Origin, Some States Have a Bigger Piece of the Pie

Since at least the early 1980s, economists have studied how RoO, in particular preferential RoO, function as a non-tariff barrier to trade. As the years progressed, economists and trade analysts questioned whether RoO achieve their purported goals: preventing trade deflection and increasing manufacturing activity in the parties to a preferential agreement. This section will briefly introduce the work of some economists on RoO.

A study by Estevadeordal, Suominen, and Jeremy Harris of the Inter-American Development Bank examines the restrictiveness and transaction costs of preferential RoO. The "observed" restrictiveness of RoO are the CTH, local value added, cumulation, and de minimis rules in the text.[37] The "effective" or "real" restrictiveness is "the extent that" rules limit:

> both the input and geographical pools, thus increasing the cost of production by requiring firms to use higher-cost regional inputs … As such, it arbitrates the degree to which a producer can globalise production without foregoing the preferential access in an RTA.[38]

This suggests that RoO in PTAs among partners with diverse economies and territories may not be as restrictive (even if complex) because of the large geographic pool for sourcing inputs.[39] PTAs joining a developing country with an advanced economies may be restrictive (though not complex), because the developing country may be constrained to source inputs at a higher cost from the other parties.[40]

37 Antoni Estevadeordal, Jeremy Harris, and Kati Suominen, 'Multilateralising Preferential Rules of Origin around the World' (2009) IDB Working Paper Series, #IDB-WP-137, 30 <https://publications.iadb.org/publications/english/document/Multilateralising-Preferential-Rules-of-Origin-around-the-World.pdf> accessed 23 October 2021.

38 ibid.

39 ibid 31–32.

40 ibid 32.

Conconi, García-Santana, Puccio, and Venturini examine how the restrictiveness of preferential RoO in NAFTA protected NAFTA manufacturers of intermediate inputs.[41] They focused on the production of trousers in Mexico, because Mexico's bargaining power in the NAFTA negotiations was weak and the CTH rule for trousers and the sourcing rules for inputs (cotton yarn, fabrics) were particularly restrictive.[42] Their estimates indicated that the NAFTA RoO significantly decreased the growth rate of imports from third countries relative to NAFTA partners and "in the absence of RoO, Mexican imports of these goods from third countries relative to NAFTA partners would have been 45 percent higher."[43] The authors draw two main conclusions: (1) RoO should be analyzed to understand their implications on GVCs and trade in intermediate inputs within regions; and (2) RoO generate protectionist effects "by substantially increasing the level of protection faced by non-members" and as a result RoO violate GATT Article XXIV.[44]

One indication that preferential RoO are overly restrictive or complex is the underutilization of preferences, by traders in the territory of the RTA. However, quantifying the utilization rate of preferential RoO is not an easy task as data on the use of these rules are not widely available.[45] Studies by Maria Donner Abreu on the utilization of preferences involving the EU, the US, China, Panama, and LAIA (Latin American Integration Association) from 2010–2013 and Inama on GSPs between 1994–2001 both identify the lack of knowledge of a preference scheme or complications in producing the required paperwork as reasons for the underutilization of the rates.[46] Pramila Crivelli, Stefano Inama, and Jonas Kasteng also studied the utilization rates of preferential RoO between 2009 and 2013 for EU Free Trade Area Agreements and the low utilization rates in specific sectors. Reasons for the denial of preferential treatment could be: insufficient documentary evidence on the origin of the good or on compliance with administrative requirements, non-compliance

41 P Conconi and M García-Santana, L Puccio, R Venturini, 'From Final Goods to Inputs: The Protectionist Effect of Rules of Origin' (2018) 108 American Economic Rev 2335, 2338.

42 ibid 2342, 2344.

43 ibid 2362.

44 ibid 2362–2363.

45 Maria Donner Abreu, 'Preferential Rules of Origin in Regional Trade Agreements' in Rohini Acharya (ed), *Regional Trade Agreements and The Multilateral Trading System* (CUP 2016) 79.

46 ibid 80; Stefano Inama, Trade Preferences and the World Trade Organization Negotiations on Market Access: Battling for Compensation of Erosion GSP, ACP, and Other Trade Preferences or Assessing and Improving Their Utilization and Value by Addressing Rules of Origin and Graduation? (2003) 37 J World Trade 959, 970.

with the substantial transformation rules, low preferential margins, and other factors such as duty rebate schemes or drawback provisions.[47]

A study by Ram Singh and Surendar Singh suggests that when trade deflection is profitable, preferential RoO may have a reduced effect in preventing deflection if domestic manufacturing in the preferential territory is inefficient. SAFTA provides cumulation rules for finished bicycles and garments: when importing final goods into India, the regional value added requirement for producers in Bangladesh and Sri Lanka is 20% if the parts originate under SAFTA, or 30% if the parts originate from third parties.[48] Indian bicycle part manufacturers found that a high number of finished bicycles were made in the SAFTA territory from inputs sourced from outside the territory, namely China.[49] As bicycle assembly is a standardized process, firms know which expensive parts need to be sourced locally to meet the regional value added 30% threshold and which inexpensive parts could be sourced from China.[50] Firms in Bangladesh and Sri Lanka also sourced Chinese inputs as India was not a competitive producer of such inputs, in addition to transportation costs, "inadequate economies of scale, trade supply chain and trade infrastructure-related issues."[51] Trade deflection is not only a matter of rerouting parts and reassembling parts to take advantage of preferential rules of origin of PTA, but is also an indicator of the well-being of the PTA's parties' domestic industries.

Preferential RoO also impact intermediate and final goods producers differently. Hoekman in 1993 cautioned policymakers to not overextend the scope of the rules by protecting certain producers of intermediate parts at the expense of final good producers in different areas of the territory.[52] During the 1990s, the drafters of the SADC RoO adopted product specific rules for conferring origin. Hennie Erasmus, Frank Flatters, and Robert Kirk found that these rules were made restrictive partially to protect the South African market from final goods produced in the other PTA territories made from cheap inputs from third

47 Pamela Crivelli, Stefano Inama, and Jonas Kasteng, 'Using Utilization Rates to Identify Rules of Origin Reforms: The Case of EU Free Trade Area Agreements' (2021) EUI Working Papers RCS 2021/21, 3 <https://cadmus.eui.eu/handle/1814/70396> accessed 24 October 2021.

48 Singh and Singh (n 11) 70. The study also looked a similar practice of sourcing Chinese yarn.

49 ibid 63.

50 ibid 66, 70.

51 ibid.

52 Bernard Hoekman, 'Rules of Origin for Goods and Services: Conceptual Issues and Economic Considerations' (1993) 27 J World Trade 82, 91.

parties.[53] The more restrictive CTH rules designed to protect South Africa was likely to be harmful to the development of industries in the other territories as flexibility in sourcing parts from within or without the region was a significant factor that contributed to the growth of these markets.[54] A study in 2024 led by Hoekman on the optimal restrictiveness of RoO found that the AfCFTA was too restrictive in requiring a 40% domestic-value added requirement, as the countries forming part of AfCTFA rely on foreign inputs for production and are varied in their level of domestic industrial development.[55] Instead, the authors propose an optimal level of domestic value added at 26% and varying this percentage based on the degree of development for each country.

This brief introduction to the economics literature on RoO presents some studies that support concerns raised by legal scholars on the trade restrictive effect of RoO. These studies question whether the goal of preventing trade deflection is a sound justification for RoO when they have restrictive side-effects. Yet, in addition to pointing out the flaws in the system, several economists provide potential changes. Their suggestions will be discussed briefly in the next part. A more extensive analysis on revising rules of origin, also taking into consideration the digital trade environment and advanced manufacturing, such as 3D printing, will be discussed in Chapter 5.

3 How Do You Solve a Problem Like Preferential Rules of Origin?

Proposals to correct the inefficiencies of preferential RoO and protectionist tendencies range from getting rid of them altogether to simplifying them. Mavroidis and Vermulst look at some of the authors mentioned above and argue that as non-preferential rules can perform the function of identifying origin of goods for preferential tariff treatment, there is no need for preferential rules.[56] Secondly, preferential rules add to the cost of trade and have not granted advantages to developing countries.[57]

53 Erasmus, Flatters and Kirk (n 8) 280–283.

54 ibid.

55 B Hoekman, C Lippitsch, M Olarreaga, M Sanfilippo, R Ticku, 'Maximising value-added in Africa exports: Understanding the role of Rules of Origin' *IGC Blog* (International Growth Centre 27 August 2024) <https://www.theigc.org/blogs/maximising-value-added-african-exports-understanding-role-rules-origin> Accessed 22 October 2024.

56 Petros C Mavroidis and Edwin Vermulst, 'The Case for Dropping Preferential Rules of Origin' (2018) 52 J World Trade 1, 6–7.

57 ibid 10–11.

Puccio proposed that the restrictiveness of preferential rules should be proportional to the MFN tariff rates. This would help ensure that preferential RoO do not become more trade restrictive than necessary to prevent trade deflection and thus be legal under Article XXIV:5 and Article XXIV:8.[58] Her proposal requires establishing a new single protocol, which would not be a harmonized set of rules. The EU would apply the same rule to all states to which it has an FTA for a particular good that would be proportionate to its MFN applied tariff level.[59] Ideally, the maximum level of restrictiveness for preferential RoO would be decided at the WTO.

A multilateral approach to preferential RoO has been examined by economists. Estevadeordal, Souminen, and Harris are contrary to harmonization of the rules, because it could increase the effective restrictiveness of RoO: if harmonized rules prohibit the use of non-originating materials, this will impact RTAs with small geographic input-sourcing zones disproportionately over those with larger zones.[60] However, a multilateral approach could correct some of the inefficiencies of the RoO found in numerous FTAs. They propose setting a cap on the complexity and restrictiveness of RoO at a multilateral level, such as limiting the range of RoO options (like the calculations for determining value added), to ensure relative similarity among qualifying production methods in sectors across export markets.[61] Another option is for RTAs to "'bind' their rules of origin at existing levels of restrictiveness and then negotiate reductions of these bindings under further negotiations."[62] Olivier Cadot and Jaime de Melo also propose a multilateral approach to bring preferential rules under the aegis of the WTO. However, this requires moving "along three dimensions: harmonization [at the trading bloc level], simplification, and relaxation."[63]

Flexible and relaxed rules are likely to benefit traders in developing countries and SMEs. Erasmus, Flatters and Kirk argue that preferential RoO should be radically reformed by going "back to the basics" so that their only function is to authentic goods so that the rules cannot be used for protectionist uses.[64]

58 Laura Puccio, '20 Years After Marrakesh: Reconsidering the Effects of Preferential Rules of Origin and Anti-Circumvention Rules on Trade in Inputs and Global Production Networks' 2014 Eur YB Intl Economic L 173, 198.

59 ibid 198–199.

60 Estevadeordal, Harris, and Suominen (n 37) 50.

61 ibid. The cap would have to be set relatively high given the variety of methods in existing RTAS.

62 ibid.

63 Olivier Cadot and Jaime de Melo, 'Why OECD Countries Should Reform Rules of Origin' (2008) 23 The World Bank Research Observer 77, 98.

64 Erasmus, Flatters and Kirk (n 8) 292.

In 2014, Dan Ciurnek and Dirk Bienen propose eliminating the costs of complying with preferential RoO for SME by establishing a regime in which there is a presumption of origin for small shipments or shipments worth less than a threshold amount.[65] Small traders could benefit from the rules without being burdened by compliance procedures. Some paperwork would still be required to ensure that this alternative is not used for fraud or circumvention.[66] Yet, by the early 2020's, the proliferation of small parcel shipments into the EU and US, and the concerns over the origin of these goods within such parcels, has led the EU and the US to propose customs reform requiring more documentation for such shipments.

3D printing promises to simplify production of goods and reduce inputs, and thus the need to trace the origin of multiple parts. 3D printing is used for small batch manufacturing. Large companies, which could afford the administrative costs of complying with rules of origin, could take advantage of the small shipment presumption of origin. Or, they could find they have to complete more paperwork given multiple batches of products. Yet, simplifying preferential RoO may not be sufficient, improving the competitiveness of the markets and how goods are produced must still be considered. Revising RoO to prevent protectionist uses requires an examination of how trade is conducted and, possibly, encouraging policymakers to make regulatory reforms in the areas of competition or labor.

4 Should There Be Next-Generation Rules of Origin?

How well do preferential RoO fit into a trade instrument including trade-plus objectives? In his article, "Retooling Trade Agreements for Social Inclusion," Shaffer argues that trade agreements should be assessed, "in terms of their distributional effects and their implications for social inclusion and social stability. Trade offers considerable opportunities that otherwise would not exist, especially for those in countries with small domestic markets that lack capital and require advanced technology."[67] We have seen that RoO can in fact limit

65 Dan Ciuriak and Derk Bienen, 'Overcoming Low Preference Utilization in Preferential Trade Agreements: Presumption of Origin for Small Shipments' (2014) Trade & Development Discussion Paper No. 02/2014, bkp Development Research and Consulting, 19 <https://papers.ssrn.com/sol3/papers.cfm?abstract_id=2460648> accessed 10 March 2025.

66 ibid 21.

67 Gregory Shaffer, 'Retooling Trade Agreements for Social Inclusion' (2019) U Illinois L Rev 1, 7.

global opportunities to small domestic markets and have distributional effects that favor developed countries already playing a role in influencing trade policy. Designing or implementing preferential RoO can also be linked to sensitive social issues.

The origin given to a product may impact a consumer's perception on the quality and essence of the product. The origin of a good can suggest that the good was produced according to certain labor or environmental standards. A change in the country of origin can also impact a consumer's decision to buy a product based on environmental or fair trade concerns.[68] Colombian coffee roasters raised objections during WTO negotiations on the harmonization of non-preferential RoO. They opposed allowing roasting or decaffeinating to be origin conferring processes. This would mean that Colombian coffee beans roasted in the US and EU would be marketed as US and EU products. According to Inama, in the eyes of the Colombian delegation, this "could severely diminish the image value and marketing potential of Colombian coffee as a quality product with a distinct character and taste."[69] Therefore, rules can be designed to protect the reputation of goods that are identified as originating in a certain country or region.

RoO could be linked to issues that are traditionally beyond the WTO's scope. In 2006, Erasmus, Flatters and Kirk raised concerns about using RoO to address labor or environmental issues. While liberalization of trade can impose threats to those areas, "[i]n each case there also exist a wide range of instruments that should be more suitable, more effective and have less costly side effects than Rules of Origin."[70] Over 10 years later, Hoekman and Nelson, Shaffer, and Grant Cohen, who explore how trade law should support and interact with regulations on labor and the environment, have not put forth proposals referencing RoO. According to Grant Cohen, an international law system should grant labor and environmental policymakers more of a role in trade dispute settlement and allow states some flexibility in designing measures based on their level of liberalization.[71] Schaffer addresses the inclusion of labor clauses in trade agreements, and argues that "[t]hey can be used by protectionist interests in advanced industrial economics to block developing country imports, in turn harming workers."[72] He recommends a third-party neutral review to com-

68 Inama, *The Rules of Origin in International Trade* (2022) (n 20) 171.
69 ibid 172.
70 Erasmus, Flatters, and Kirk (n 8) 268.
71 Grant Cohen (n 2) 340–344.
72 Shaffer, 'Retooling Trade Agreements for Social Inclusion' (n 67) 26.

mitments that benefit the domestic labor of the parties.[73] Hoekman and Nelson find that trade agreements should be designed to limit negative spillovers, and international regulatory cooperation should be pursued at the plurilateral level.[74] Whatever the reason for not including RoO, these proposals suggests that it is not necessary to use RoO as means to achieve a regulatory objective.

The USCMA attempts to impose uniformity on wage rates in Canada, US, and Mexico through the Labor Value Content (LVC) provisions in the rules of origin chapter.[75] Aimed primarily to influence Mexican producers to raise wages, the impact has also been felt in the US and in Canada. Since the implementation of the LVC requirement, economists and automotive industry representatives and analysts have noted an increase in the cost of complying with the rules, to the point of questioning whether preferential tariff treatment is worth the time, effort, and money in redesigning manufacturing procedures.[76] A study conducted by the U.S. International Trade Commission (USITC) on the impact of the USMCA's RoO on the automotive industry (published in June 2023) reported that as a result of the LVC rules, there was increased production of vehicles and parts in the US and Canada and a slight increase in employment in the automotive sector, but there were also increased labor costs and increased input costs.[77] The report also notes a sharp rise of imports into the US of parts that did not meet the USMCA requirements and for which duties were paid, a decline of US exports into the USMCA territory (although the US's share of global exports increased), and an increase of exports of light vehicles into the US for which duties were paid. However, the report emphasizes that these minor fluctuations do not truly represent the competitiveness of the US automotive industry, nor should these slight improvements or decreases be necessarily attributed to the USMCA's RoO – since 2020, there was a global pandemic and several shocks to the global supply chain system.[78]

Even accounting for these external factors, there is consensus in the automotive industry that the USMCA's LVC, RVC, and steel and aluminum sourcing

73 ibid.

74 Hoekman and Nelson (n 1) 22–23.

75 David Gantz, 'The United States-Mexico-Canada Agreement: Tariffs, Customs, and Rules of Origin' (2019) Baker Institute Rep. no. 02.21.19, 3–5.

76 Lilian Wong and Kyla H Kitamura (n 327) 1–2.

77 US International Trade Commission (USITC), 'USMCA Automotive Rules of Origin: Economic Impact and Operation', 2023 Report, Pub No 5443, 17 <https://www.usitc.gov/publications/332/pub5443.pdf> accessed 23 March 2024.

78 ibid 77.

requirements are confusing and raise costs, especially for parts suppliers.[79] As part of the USMCA's implementing legislation, the Government Accountability Office (GAO) issued a report on 31 January 2024, on the effectiveness of the Interagency Autos Committee (also established under the USMCA) in coordinating the implementation, enforcement, and verification of the RoO and providing advice on these rules.[80] The GAO also reported that US importers have paid more duties on vehicles and parts since the USMCA entered into force, with most of the imports subject to the 2.5% duty (the MFN rate) coming from Mexico.[81] The GAO found that generally there was coordination among the relevant agencies, as well as the coordination between the CBP and the Department of Labor on the coordination of LVC certification, however there was a need for clear written guidance on the accountability of these agencies in their effectiveness in monitoring the impact of the RoO on automotive trade. The Interagency Autos Committee held a hearing in February 2024, and submissions and statements from economists and industry and union representatives pointed out that the rules have not been successful in preventing the widespread importation of inputs from third parties, particularly, China, and that the USMCA was designed without taking into consideration a shift in consumer preferences and U.S. trade policy towards electric vehicles (EV).[82]

---

79 USTR, 'Report to Congress on The Operation of The United States-Mexico-Canada Agreement with Respect to Trade in Automotive Goods', 1 July 2024, 16 – 17 <https://ustr.gov/sites/default/files/2024%20USMCA%20Autos%20Report%20to%20Congress_0.pdf> accessed 23 October 2024.

80 US Government Accountability Office, 'International Trade: USTR Should Improve Coordination on New Automotive Rules of Origin' Report to Congressional Committees GAO-24-106330 (January 2024) 1 <https://www.gao.gov/assets/d24106330.pdf> accessed 14 October 2024.

81 ibid 5–6.

82 AS Hersh, 'EPI comments to the Office of the United States Trade Representative on the US-Mexico-Canada Agreement with respect to automotive goods' USTR-2023-0013-0011 Comment Submission (Economic Policy Institute 22 January 2024) https://www.epi.org/publication/us-mexico-canada-agreement/ accessed 23 March 2024; Jennifer M. Safavian, 'Comments Concerning the Operation of the United States-Mexico-Canada Agreement With Respect to Trade in Automotive Goods,' Submission to the USTR (17 January 2024) 1 <https://autosdriveamerica.org/wp-content/uploads/2024/02/2024.01.17-Autos-Drive-America-Comments-to-USTR-on-USMCA-ROO-Operation.pdf> accessed 23 March 2024; International Union, United Automobile, Aerospace & Agricultural Implement Workers of America (UAW), 'UAW's Public Comment on Operation of the United States-Mexico-Canada Agreement With Respect To Trade in Automotive Goods' Submission No USTR-2023-0013 (17 January 2024) 4 <https://downloads.regulations.gov/USTR-2023-0013-0013/attachment_1.pdf> accessed 23 March 2024.

Here, we catch a glimmer of how RoO designed on the basis of a particular industrial method, and with particular domestic goals, can quickly become out-of-synch with developments in innovation and international trade if there are no flexibilities included for advancements in manufacturing. While the negotiators and drafters of the USMCA's RoO may not have been able to predict the Inflation Reduction Act (IRA) and the tax credit to purchases of new EV, there was a market for and a growing industry in EV before 2020. The IRA gives up to 7,500$ in tax credit, however, the majority of battery materials and production, in addition to the manufacture of the car, must be sourced from or made in North America. This limits the models of EV that qualify for the credit.[83] There is a loop-hole: EV's that are leased to consumers do not have to meet the strict origin requirements nor be assembled in North America, and studies show a rise in leases in EV since 2023.[84] Automakers are now faced with costs of complying with the USMCA's RoO and the IRA guidelines, in both cases are met with challenges in finding parts and materials that meet the requirements, and in some cases may find a clash. For example, there are no restrictions in the USMCA on sourcing raw materials for batteries from China (though the battery still must meet the 75% LVC rule to qualify for origin); under the IRA, qualifying vehicles cannot contain battery components or raw materials sourced from China.[85] In a letter to Ambassador Tai (the U.S. Trade Representative) on 17 January 2024, the UAW (the union representing automobile workers in the US), pointed out 1) that under the IRA, an automotive manufactured in North America can qualify for the tax credit while not being compliant with the USMCA's RoO, and 2) the lease loop-hole could result in a subsidy for EVs manufactured in Mexico (with foreign materials and inputs) that are not USMCA compliant.[86] US automotive producers proposed to the government reducing LVC and RVC requirements for EV and electric batteries or prolonging the phase-in period for meeting the full RVC requirement, while

83 Elaine Buckberg, 'Clean vehicle tax credit: The new industrial policy and its impact' Stanford Institute for Economic Policy Research (August 2023) 6 <https://siepr.stanford.edu/publications/policy-brief/clean-vehicle-tax-credit-new-industrial-policy-and-its-impact> accessed 14 October 2024.

84 ibid 6–7.

85 William Alan Reinsch, 'Congressional Testimony: USMCA Automotive Rules of Origin: Economic impacts, Competitiveness Effects, and Relevance' Center for Strategic & International Studies (CSIS.org 4 November 2022) <https://www.csis.org/analysis/usmca-automotive-rules-origin-economic-impacts-competitiveness-effects-and-relevance> accessed 23 March 2024.

86 UAW (n 82) 3–4.

some producers suggested more North American components be required for EVs and batteries.[87]

While a pioneer in crafting a deep-RoO regime by adding a trade-plus item, labor, into origin determination, the USMCA's RoO success in achieving a twin goal of boosting domestic manufacturing and increased competitiveness in trade is mixed. The USITC is collecting data and comments for another report, expected to issue in 2025. Stakeholders are invited to submit an extensive questionnaire which inquires on changes to sourcing, including steel and aluminum, changes to assembly, and the impact on new production resulting from the USMCA's RoO.[88] The data by that time may be able to give a better picture of the impact of the rules on trade in automotive goods. It may be that in fact, wages rise, labor conditions improve, and output increases – or producers may decide the efforts in changing their sourcing and production methods is not worth the preferential tariff rate. There may also be a significant technological development that makes it no longer relevant to try to comply with the labor, local content, and sourcing requirements. Whatever the future of the RoO in the USMCA, those policymakers and trade lawyers wishing to merge domestic regulation with trade law may want to think carefully about using RoO to correct any risks to domestic labor or environmental conditions.

As businesses produce and consumers request more "green" and socially conscious goods, should RoO also adapt? On the one hand, identifying the origin of a good may not be enough for socially and environmentally conscious trade. Rules should also verify that products were made with sustainable processes or eco-friendly materials. Perhaps, this means adding a new criterion to the three substantial criteria: sustainable and protects fair labor standards. There are several responses to such a proposal. First, other legal instruments perform such a function such as standards, regulations, and other measures that fall under the administrative umbrellas of environmental, labor, and health ministries. Adding "a socially and ecologically" conscious layer to the RoO determination could be burdensome to traders. Should policymakers draft such rules, they should also consider setting aside resources for technical assistance. One factor to consider is how inclusive the design of such socially and ecologically conscious rules would be. A rather pessimistic view is that

87 USTR, Report to Congress on The Operation of The United States-Mexico-Canada Agreement with Respect to Trade in Automotive Goods' (n 79) 23.

88 USITC, The USMCA Automotive Rules of Origin Motor Vehicle Producer Questionnaire (2024) <https://www.usitc.gov/usmcaautoroo> and <https://www.usitc.gov/research_and_analysis/documents/usmca/usmca_auto_roos_questionnaire.pdf> accessed 10 March 2025.

politicians and industry lobbyists could strategically design rules through non-transparent negotiations that appear to protect environmental or labor standards, but which effectively function to protect certain industries. A more optimistic view is that groups that support conscious trade would collaborate with policymakers and trade officials to develop rules that perform a discriminatory function and are not overly complex.

Perhaps another approach is possible that could keep rules as shallow trade instruments that nonetheless sustain traders wanting to produce and sell goods that are eco-conscious and made with fair labor standards. Technology provides tools for producing more efficiently with less waste and for alleviating humans from certain labor-intensive activity. Access to telecommunication technologies has allowed SMEs to enter the global market. Certainly, technology is not the answer for all trade problems, but it can be utilized to create the type of products that socially conscious consumers are seeking and governments wish to promote. Yet, these green or fair labor products may have difficulty reaching foreign markets due to preferential RoO which were not designed to support trade in such products. This may be unintentional: technology and technical manufacturing processes have developed after the rules were designed. On the other hand, this could be a more systemic issue in designing rules: if they are too specific in how a good qualifies for preferential origin, they can "freeze" the rules of origin analysis to a particular moment in time. A rule requiring a specific CTH or *ad valorem* percentage today may not adequately reflect manufacturing processes a few years later.

Digitalization may be the key for not only innovating and creating greener and safer products, but also for being more competitive in the current trade environment. 3D printing is a technology that could allow firms to produce products with less waste and a skilled workforce, which could lead to better labor standards. However, producers of "socially conscious" 3D printed products will still face the task of assigning origin to the good when seeking preferential tariff treatment. This leads us to the last part of this Chapter: can RoO be applied to digital products, and more generally, what role should RoO play in an international trade law system that regulates digital trade, including trade in 3D digital files?

5 The Role of Rules of Origin in Digital Trade

A data-driven economy requires reconceptualizing the role and design of trade agreements. Schaffer finds that trade agreements "need to be viewed as part of a broader ecology of governance of the new data-driven economy."[89] Further, "there should be *no single system of hierarchical rules* [italics original]. Rather, in a world of radical uncertainty and different preferences ... [a] diversity of regulatory approaches provides greater resilience against the systemic risks posed when single systems fail."[90] Based on these statements, RoO do not seem to be optimal tools for addressing challenges arising from digital trade. RoO are gatekeepers – their primary legal justification is that they discriminate goods qualifying for preferential tariff treatment from those that do not, establishing a form a hierarchy. However, it is not advisable, on the other hand to keep RoO separate from the data-driven economy and this can be demonstrated through 3D printing.

The impact of 3D printing on trade is at the center of a debate on whether custom duties should be applied to electronic transmissions. Rashmi Banga, Chief in the Development Research Branch of UNCTAD, raises concerns that 3D printing for mass producing will negatively impact industrialization in developing countries that do not have the financial or technical resources to establish additive manufacturing at a widespread scale.[91] The growth of electronic transmissions (currently untaxable) supports the growth of 3D printing,[92] and this:

> can also jeopardize two decades of negotiated tariffs on industrial products under the Uruguay Round. 3D printers and electronic transmissions of CAD files can be used to 'print' manufactured products in any country, irrespective of the protection given by the governments to the sectors in the developing countries through their custom duty regime ... If [the] Moratorium on custom duties on ET [electronic transmissions] is made permanent, then in the future the policy space to address the above challenges will be severely limited.[93]

Without applying a tax or tariff regime on electronic transmissions, developing nations will become less competitive than developed nations in international trade and domestic producers will be at a disadvantaged vis-à-vis foreign producers who print in the domestic territory. On the other hand,

89 Shaffer, 'Trade Law in a Data-Driven Economy' (n 3) 271.
90 ibid.
91 Banga (n 4) 30.
92 ibid.
93 ibid 31.

Andrea Andrenelli and Javier López González (authors of the OECD Trade Policy Paper) advocate for keeping the Moratorium permanent as the lack of tariffs reduces barriers to trade and consumers pay less for goods.[94] The authors state that while 3D printing could potentially exacerbate the effects of the Moratorium, the scope of products that can be produced is limited, and 3D printing can actually promote cross-border trade, such as in final products or in inputs.[95]

What these authors do not mention are RoO. If electronic transmissions are taxed, an origin determination could ultimately have an impact on who must pay tariff or taxes on digital transmissions. Banga questions whether trade in digital files should be regulated under GATT or the GATS and whether printing products constitutes cross-border trade.[96] However, the authors of each report did not take the analysis to the next step. If tariffs are to be applied to electronic transmission, will they be applied on the basis of the origin of the 3D file? This would require determining the origin of the file. In the case of the Digital Protocol of the AfCFTA, origin must be determined so that there are no custom duties applied to transmissions of digital products originating in the territory. The preliminary version of the Protocol states that the State Parties "shall adopt an Annex that sets out Rules of Origin for the determination of origin for African-owned enterprises, African digital platforms and African content," while the Annex "shall define the scope of digital products covered by the Protocol taking into account the objective to develop an AfCFTA Digital Market, trade in African products, promotion of African firms and use of African digital platforms."[97] It is here that we see why a discussion of RoO needs to be incorporated into the greater debate of how digital trade should be regulated and under what type of framework WTO members, policymakers, and industries wish to govern the data-driven economy.

The role of RoO in digital trade has started to be questioned. Dylan Geraets, Colleen Carroll and Arnoud R. Willems propose redesigning the rules to incorporate the value of design and R&D into an *ad valorem* criterion for determining the origin of a product.[98] Their article will be examined in more detail in the next Chapter. While the literature on international trade law has started to assess 3D printing's impact on trade, very little work has been done on 3D

94 Andrenelli and López González (n 5) (2019) 6–7.

95 ibid 19–21.

96 Banga (n 4) 30–31.

97 Digital Protocol, AfCFTA art 5.

98 Dylan Geraets, Colleen Carroll, and Arnoud R. Willems, 'Reconciling Rules of Origin and Global Value Chains: The Case for Reform' (2015) 18 J Intl Economic L 287.

printing and rules of origin. *3D Printing: A Guide for Decision Makers,* a study on 3D printing and trade, led by the World Economic Forum, briefly addresses RoO. Two studies were conducted and written by the Swedish National Board of Trade, "Trade Regulation in a 3D Printed World" (2016) and "Rules of Origin for the 21st Century" (2020). In both reports, the Swedish National Board of Trade concludes that while 3D printing challenges traditional methods of producing goods, an entirely new approach to rules of origin is not needed.[99] Duy Dinh has also looked into determining the origin of a 3D product. However, the work of these authors on 3D printing on RoO are several paragraphs to a few pages at most in length. A goal of this book is to expand their initial steps to demonstrate that a more comprehensive review of RoO in the era of digital trade should be considered by policymakers and lawyers and to provide some suggestions on how to design rules that are more predictable and enhance the legitimacy of international trade law to liberalize trade while promoting development.

To start this analysis, it is necessary to understand whether a 3D file is a good or a service, and this implies not only an examination on the classifications of digital products, but also a quick introduction to rules of origin for services. For if the 3D file is a service, we need to understand how to determine the origin of a service. We will start with this investigation and conclude with the analysis on classification.

5.1 *Rules of Origin for Services and Where to Find Them*

Rules for determining the origin of services do exist; you just have to know where to find them. Early in negotiations of the AOR, Members, such as Japan and the EC, pressed to exclude services from the AOR on the basis that rules of origin for services "might be dealt with in another forum."[100] While there is no WTO instrument for rules of origin for services like the AOR, there are several provisions in the GATS that serve an origin identifying function.[101] This section will briefly introduce the rules related to the origin for services, as this

99 Ziyang Fan, Jimena Sotelo, and Venkataramam Sundareswaran (n 38); National Board of Trade, 'Trade Regulation in a 3D Printed World' (n 38) 28; National Board of Trade – Sweden, 'Rules of Origin in the 21st Century' (2020) Kommerskollegium 15 <https://www.kommerskollegium.se/globalassets/publikationer/rapporter/2020/rules-of-origin-in-the-21st-century.pdf> accessed 24 October 2021.

100 Negotiating Group on Non-Tariff Measures, 'Meeting of 14–15 February 1990' (13 March 1990) MTN.GNG.NG2/16 para 17–18 <http://docsonline.wto.org> accessed 26 October 2024.

101 Petros C Mavroidis, *The Regulation of International Trade,* vol 3 (MIT Press 2020) 300.

investigation has been performed by Americo Zampetti and Pierre Suavé,[102] Duy Dinh,[103] and Richard Baldwin.[104]

There are some key differences between rules of origin for goods and for services that must be identified at the outset. How services are provided internationally impacts what type of trade measures can be applied to services. Guzman and Pauwelyn note that "border measures in general, and ad valorem tariffs in particular, are often difficult to apply to trade in services for the simple reason that customs agents in many instances will not be able to observe the service as it 'passes the frontier.'"[105] As the service is provided within borders, any resulting duties from such provision are no longer within the jurisdiction of the customs authorities.[106] Domestic agencies take a more active role in controlling the trade of services by both domestic and foreign service providers through regulations.[107] Even though these measures may be applied behind the frontier, there may still be some preferential treatment available to foreign service suppliers under a PTA. In that case, Zampetti and Sauvé point out that "the need to determine the origin of services and of service providers arises as soon as an international agreement providing for differential treatment between parties and non-parties is entered into."[108]

Zampetti and Sauvé[109], as well as Dinh[110] find that determining the origin of a service under the GATS requires a reading of the definitions found in Article XXVIII with the four modes of supply indicated in Article I:2. The key definitions in Article XXVIII are "service of another Member", "service supplier", and "juridical person of another Member."

102 Americo Beviglia Zampetti and Pierre Sauvé, 'Rules of Origin for Services: Economic and Legal Considerations,' in Olivier Cadot, Antoni Estevadeordal, Akiko Suwa-Eisenmann, and Theirry Verdier (eds), *The Origin of Goods: Rules of Origin in Regional Trade Agreements* (OUP 2006), 114–146.

103 Duy Dinh, *Rules of Origin for Services: From the Early Days of GATS to the Era of Servicification* (Edward Elgar 2020).

104 Richard Baldwin, '21st Century Regionalism: Filling the Gap between 21st Century Trade and 20th Century Trade Rules' (May 2011) Policy Insight (Centre for Economic Policy Research) 3 <https://cepr.org/publications/policy-insight-56-21st-century-regionalism-filling-gap-between-21st-century-trade-and> accessed 9 March 2025.

105 Andrew T Guzman and Joost HB Pauwelyn, *International Trade Law* (2nd edn, Wolters-Kluwer 2012) 594.

106 ibid.

107 ibid 596.

108 Zampetti and Sauvé (n 102) 118.

109 ibid 140–142.

110 Dinh (n 103) 36.

- A "service of another Member" is a service which is supplied "from or in the territory of that other Member" or "in the case of the supply of a service through commercial presence or through the presence of natural persons, by a service supplier of that other Member."[111]
- A "service supplier" is "any person that supplies a service."[112]
- A "person" can be a natural person or a juridical person.
- A "juridical person" is any legal entity validly constituted under the applicable law, and a "juridical person of another Member" is one that is "constituted or otherwise organized under the law of that other Member, and is engaged in substantive business operations in the territory of that Member or any other Member."[113]

How would this translate to 3D printing? The cross-border transmission of the 3D file is a service, supplied by a service supplier, who could be a company or an individual. If the file is sent to a third-party printing facility and printed, that facility is providing a service by means of a commercial presence. Thus, supplying services in the context of 3D printing involves several modes of supply.

Origin is determined by the mode of the service. Mode 1 services are supplied "from the territory of one Member into the territory of any other Member."[114] Mode 2 services are supplied "in the territory of one Member to the service consumer of any other Member."[115] Mode 3 services are supplied "by a service supplier of one Member, through commercial presence in the territory of any other Member."[116] Finally, Mode 4 services are supplied "by a service supplier of one Member, through presence of natural persons of a Member in the territory of any other Member."[117] According to Zampetti and Sauvé, for Mode 1 and 2 services, "the territory from which a service is supplied to the consumer confers origin … even if such a territory is that of the last (and potentially less significant) stage in a multicounty production process or that from which the service is only retailed."[118] For Modes 3 and 4, "the origin of a

111 General Agreement on Trade in Services (GATS)(15 April 1994) LT/UR/A-1B/S/1 art XXVIII f(i)(ii) <http://docsonline.wto.org> accessed 26 October 2024.

112 GATS art XXVIII(g).

113 GATS art XXVIII(l)(m)(i). If the service is supplied through commercial presence, the juridical person must be owned "by persons of a Member if more than 50 per cent of the equity interest in it is beneficially owned by persons of that Member; or it must be controlled "by persons of a Member if such persons have the power to name a majority of its directors or otherwise to legally direct its actions." GATS art XXVIII(m)(ii).

114 GATS art I:2(a).

115 GATS art I:2(b).

116 GATS art I(c).

117 GATS art I:2(d).

118 Zampetti and Sauvé (n 102) 140–141.

service is identical to the nationality of the service supplier that provides that particular service."[119] For a service related to 3D printing, it will be necessary to identify under which Mode the service is being provided in order to identify its origin.

As more trade in services takes place in GVCs, it will be difficult to determine the origin of a service. In his examination of rules of origin for services, Mavroidis proposes that Article XXVIII GATS, by listing the definitions of a natural person of another Member and a juridical person, reproduces "the most frequently encountered bases for attributing origin in the realm of services (namely, nationality and seat of incorporation)."[120] Regarding Zampetti and Sauvé's work on Article XXVIII in the context of the four modes of supply, Mavroidis finds that their "opinion has a lot of merit, even though, precisely because of the emergence of GVCs, defining origin in mode 1 might often prove to be a quixotic test because a service might be sent from country A but might have benefited from inputs in C and D."[121] The next Chapter will examine in more detail how these factors – GVCs and determining the nationality of the service provider – could impact the origin determination of the 3D file as a service input of the 3D printed final product.

Identifying the service supplier is complicated by determining where a corporation or business is incorporated, and where that service originates geographically.[122] An example where uncertainty in defining the service supplier may impact the regulation of trade in services is the application of Article V:6 GATS, which covers economic integration agreements. Subsection 6 provides:

> A service supplier of any other Member that is a juridical person constituted under the laws of a party to an [economic integration] agreement ... shall be entitled to treatment granted under such agreement, provided that it engages in substantive business operations in the territory of the parties to such agreement.[123]

On the one hand, this provision appears to expand the scope of preferential treatment to a service supplier engaging in substantive business operations in the territory, even if owned by a third-party.[124] However, such an effect could

119 ibid 141.
120 Mavroidis, *The Regulation of International Trade*, vol 3 (n 101) 300–301.
121 ibid 301.
122 James (n 14) 287.
123 GATS art V:6.
124 Zampetti and Sauvé (n 102) 142.

be limited or precluded by rules in a PTA restricting preferential treatment to suppliers with headquarters or a more established presence than a subsidiary.

At this point, we begin to find some similarities for rules of origin for services with rules of origin for goods: the restrictiveness of rules of origin for services has an impact on the costs and the efficiency in the trade of services.[125] Policy objectives can include promoting groups of service suppliers, skill development of established suppliers, or attracting foreign direct investment.[126] Liberal rules of origin in a PTA, which still require that foreign companies do not merely establish shell companies, can encourage investment in the territory by third-party providers.[127] Yet, an open services market may lead to disinterest in negotiating preferential treatment for services as well as reduce any bargaining power a PTA member may have with respect to third-parties.[128] Zampetti and Suavé find that proponents "of more restrictive Rules of Origin may be expected to arise in the case of regional agreements that link countries with marked differences in levels of openness towards services trade or foreign direct investment."[129] Limiting the benefits only to service suppliers established in the PTA could have an negative impact on the supply of services if it protects firms from more efficient foreign suppliers, although it may give local firms time to improve the supply of their services.[130] On the other hand, Zampetti and Sauvé argue that more efficient firms can enter the market through acquisition of local firms, and nascent firms, by being protected from foreign competition, have time to improve how they supply services.[131]

The effectiveness of rules on the origin of services in liberalizing or restricting trade is limited by a significant factor: identifying the origin of the service. One major issue is that a digital service, such as a 3D file, can be created in multiple countries before being transmitted to a user of the service. As Members become parties of multiple PTAs with different approaches for identifying service suppliers and liberalization of services, administration of the rules may grow difficult and service suppliers will be faced with costs when determining

125 ibid 123–124.

126 Carsten Fink and Deunden Nikomborirak, 'Rules of origin in services: A case study of five ASEAN countries' in Marion Panizzon, Nicole Pohl, and Pierre Sauvé (eds), *GATS and the Regulation of International Trade in Services* (CUP 2008) 118.

127 Zampetti and Sauvé (n 102) 123–124.

128 ibid 124.

129 ibid 124–125.

130 ibid 125–126.

131 ibid 126.

whether trade in a particular service qualifies for preferential treatment under the agreement.[132]

Richard Baldwin also identifies two other major factors which limit the possibility for writing RoO for deep trade agreements: "the difficulties of determining the nationality of 21st century companies" and "the public-good nature of regulatory reform."[133] Policymakers may design rules centered on the legal nationality of the service provider rather than the economic origin of the service. However, this reduces the discriminatory function of preferential rules of origin, as "they are easy to get around … if [for example] the rule of origin in the Japan- Malaysia EPA provides access only to banks registered in Japan or Malaysia, the rule encompasses all the US and European banks that have affiliates incorporated in Tokyo."[134] According to Baldwin, deep trade agreements do not have the same political objective as rules of origins: "many but not all deeper provisions tend to act as general liberalisations rather than discriminatory liberalisations because it is difficult or impossible to write rules of origin for them that exclude third nations. The deep reasons are the difficulties in establishing the nationality of modern corporations and of services as well as the public-good nature of the many regulatory reforms in deep RTAs."[135] If RoO for services also do not fit well into a framework integrating regulatory objectives, could they at least be incorporated into a framework for the data-driven economy which seeks to balance digital trade liberalization with protecting and promoting development?

This requires a consideration of two debates: should a new mode be created, the Mode 5, and should there be a hybridization of goods and services under a WTO framework. As more and more services become embedded in goods, for example, a smart speaker, Lucian Cernat and Zornitsa Kutlina-Dimitrova[136] propose categorizing these types of services under a "Mode 5" for services. Dinh argues that for goods with Mode 5 service components, the origin determination of the good will require determining the origin of the service embedded within it.[137] As the service input (the 3D file) is a significant part of the additive manufacturing process, a similar need may arise: to identify where a 3D product comes from, the origin of the 3D file must be considered. However, this book proposes that we do not need a Mode 5 for this process.

132 James (n 14) 287.

133 Baldwin (n 104) 15.

134 ibid 16.

135 ibid.

136 Lucian Cernat and Zornitsa Kutlina-Dimitrova, 'Thinking in a Box: A "Mode 5" Approach to Service Trade' (2014) 48 J World Trade 1109.

137 Dinh (n 103) 131.

Next, the debate on the hybridization of a goods-services legal regime focuses on whether the current rules are sufficient to regulate digital trade as the range of digital products varies from electronic transmissions, to products once sold in tangible forms (such as books), to goods-embodying services. The main starting point is the issue of classification: how do we define a digital product, is it a good, service, something in-between? This means exploring how the act of classifying the digital product correlates with the WTO texts and principles developed through WTO jurisprudence.

5.2 *Is a 3D File a Good or a Service?*

Before exploring the classification of digital products further, we should look at the role of classification in international trade law. Nations create a boundary between goods and services based on domestic regulatory objectives. This is a political decision, which differs from state to state. As such, classification at a national level, Smith and Wood argue, "may undermine the legitimacy" of an international lawmaking organization, such as the WTO.[138] At an international level, classifying goods and services is more than just categorizing products, it also is "a matter of maintaining a single policy imperative within the international regulatory framework."[139] Classification thus will likely be a key element of a new framework regulating trade. Under Shaffer's proposal for a data-driven economy,[140] a more flexible approach to goods and service classification would make the international trade law system more resilient to changes. However, this may not assist in making the application of trade laws more predictable to traders. Within the scope of RoO, questions about whether a product is a good or service compounds the complexity of this process and could consequently raise the cost of trade.

The 3D printing industry, still an emerging form of manufacturing, may be impacted by multilateral or plurilateral decisions on how to classify digital products. Several scholars use 3D files as an example of digital trade that does not easily fit within the GATT or GATS silos. R.S. Neeraj, Joshua P. Meltzer, and Schaffer refer to 3D printing in articles focusing on barriers to the transmission of data flow and regulating cross border transmissions. Meltzer[141] and

138 F Smith and L Woods, 'A Distinction without a Difference: Exploring the Boundary between Goods and Services in the World Trade Organization and the European Union' (2005) 12 Columbia J Eur L 1, 5.

139 ibid.

140 Shaffer, 'Trade Law in a Data-Driven Economy' (n 3) 271.

141 Joshua P Meltzer, "Governing Digital Trade," (2019) 18 World Trade Rev (2Supp) s35.

Schaffer[142] refer to 3D printing in one sentence, while Neeraj[143] devotes two paragraphs to 3D printing. Sauvé[144] and Peng each refer to 3D printing in one sentence in their articles on whether there should be a hybridization of GATT and GATS for digital trade.[145] While barriers to transmission of data, regulating digital trade, and the goods/services dichotomy are relevant to the regulation of the international transmission of 3D files, these articles do not address identifying the origin of the 3D printed good and the role of the 3D file as an input in the production process of the good. Classification would be the start of the process of identifying the origin of a digital transmission,[146] such as a 3D file.

5.2.1 Transmission of 3D Files and E-Commerce

The first step is to determine whether a 3D file electronically transmitted across a border is a product of e-commerce. The definition of e-commerce varies based on political or regulatory purposes, in particular for controlling the cross-border flow of data.[147] The WTO E-Commerce Work Programme attempted to distinguish when a transaction falls under the GATS or GATTS, but eventually defined "electronic commerce" as "the production, distribution, marketing, sale or delivery of goods or services, by electronic means"[148] to avoid the goods-services dichotomy.[149] Another linguistic twist is that e-commerce is often referred to as "digital trade" in trade instruments.

While e-commerce may invoke the retail behemoths like Amazon and Alibaba, digital trade suggests a broader category of products accessible through digital technology or incorporating digital technology.[150]

– For example, Recital 8 of the EU E-Commerce directive, states "The objective of this Directive is to create a legal framework to ensure the free movement

142 Shaffer, 'Trade Law in a Data-Driven Economy' (n 3) 263.

143 RS Neeraj, 'Trade Rules for the Digital Economy: Charting New Waters at the WTO' (2018) 18 World Trade Rev (2Supp) s126.

144 Pierre Suavé, 'To Fuse, Not to Fuse, or Simply Confuse? Assessing the Case for Normative Convergence Between Goods and Services Trade Law' (2019) 22 J Intl Economic L 356.

145 Shin-yi Peng, 'A New Trade Regime for the Servitization of Manufacturing: Rethinking the Goods-Services Dichotomy' (2020) 54 J World Trade 718, 704.

146 Farrokh Farrokhina and Cameron Richards, 'E-Commerce Products Under the World Trade Organization Agreements: Goods, Services, Both or Neither?' (2016) 50 J World Trade 793, 800–801.

147 See eg, Susan Ariel Aaronson and Patrick Leblond, 'Another Digital Divide: The Rise of Data Realms and its Implications for the WTO' (2018) 21 J Intl Economic L 245.

148 WTO, 'Electronic Commerce' (wto.org) <https://www.wto.org/english/thewto_e/minist_e/mc11_e/briefing_notes_e/bfecom_e.htm> accessed 24 October 2021.

149 Peng (n 145)718.

150 Neeraj (n 143) s123.

of information society services between Member States …"[151] While, under Recital 18, "information society services" in addition to the selling of goods online, "also include services consisting of the transmission of information via a communication network."[152]

- CETA states "electronic commerce means commerce conducted through telecommunications, alone or in conjunction with other information and communication technologies."[153]
- The TCA has no definitions for "e-Commerce" or "digital trade," but states that the objective of the Digital Trade Title is to "facilitate digital trade, to address unjustified barriers to trade enabled by electronic means and to ensure an open, secure and trustworthy online environment for businesses and consumers".[154] However, it does state that "Electronic transmissions shall be considered as the supply of a service within the meaning of Title II [Services and investment]."[155]

For the electronic transmission of a 3D file to fall under the category of e-commerce in EU legal instruments, it is likely necessary to classify it as a service.

The US Department of Trade considers digital trade to be a "broad concept, capturing not just the sale of consumer products on the Internet and the supply of online services, but also data flows that enable *global value chains*, services that enable *smart manufacturing*, and myriad other platforms and applications"[my italics].[156] Chapter 19 of the USMCA defines a "digital product" as "a computer program, text, video, image, sound recording, or other product that is digitally encoded, produced for commercial sale or distribution, and

151 Council Directive 2000/31/EC of 8 June 2000 on certain legal aspects of information society services, in particular electronic commerce, in the Internal Market (Directive on electronic commerce) [2000] OJ L178/1.

152 ibid.

153 Comprehensive and Economic Trade Agreement (CETA) (signed 30 October 2016, some provisions entered into force on 21 September 2017) ch 16 art 16. 1.

154 Trade And Cooperation Agreement Between The European Union And The European Atomic Energy Community, Of The One Part, And The United Kingdom Of Great Britain And Northern Ireland, Of The Other Part, (TCA) (signed 30 December 2020, entered into force 1 January 2021) L 444/14, Heading I, Title III ch 1 art 196.

155 ibid art. 203(1) A "'service' means any service in any sector except services supplied in the exercise of governmental authority." (Heading I, Title II, art 124 (o). Further, the TCA prohibits imposing custom duties on electronic transmissions (Heading 1, Title III, ch 3 art 203(2)).

156 USTR, 'Key Barriers to Digital Trade' (USTR.gov 31 March 2017) <https://ustr.gov/about-us/policy-offices/press-office/fact-sheets/2017/march/key-barriers-digital-trade> accessed 24 October 2021.

that can be transmitted electronically."[157] In a footnote, the Agreement clarifies that "[t]his definition should not be understood to reflect a Party's view that digital products are a good or are a service."[158] Peng argues that with this footnote, "difficulties related to differences in treatment between goods and services are managed in the context" of the Digital Trade Chapter, and that "[s]uch an approach, to a large extent, relieves pressure from the debates about the classification issues in the digital age."[159] Under the USMCA's Digital Trade Chapter, a 3D file would at least be a digital product, but whether it is a good or service would have to be determined under a different chapter or instrument.

5.2.2 Classification of Goods and Services – Is a New Hybrid Category Necessary?

Until some hybridized regime for digital products is established, it will be necessary to find a way to categorize 3D files under the GATT or GATS to proceed with the origin analysis of 3D printed products. Using the work of Smith and Woods on defining goods and services allows us to identify some challenges in determining whether 3D files should be classified as goods or services for purposes of origin determination. Their approach is based on Article 31(a) of the VCLT, which instructs that the terms of a treaty shall be interpreted "in good faith in accordance with the ordinary meaning to be given to the terms of the treaty in their context and in the light of its object and purpose."[160] The Appellate Body has found the DSU to allow application of the Vienna Convention to interpret WTO rules.[161]

In reviewing the Oxford English Dictionary definitions for the ordinary meaning of goods and services, Woods and Smith identify two adjectives that indicate that a product is a good, "tangibility" and "tradability."[162] A product must have material form, i.e. tangibility, and there must also be a transfer of physical ownership of the product, i.e. tradability.[163] However in the context

157 Agreement between the United States of America, the United Mexican States, and Canada (USMCA) (signed 30 November 2018, entered into force 1 July 2020) ch 19, art 19.1. The definition of "digital product" does not include "digitized representation of financial instruments, including money."

158 USMCA, ch 19, art 19.1, fn 1.

159 Peng (n 145) 716–717.

160 Smith and Woods (n 138) 40; Vienna Convention on the Law of Treaties (VCLT) (entered into force 27 January 1980) 1155 UNTS 331, art 31(1).

161 Smith and Woods (n 138) 40; Understanding on Rules and Procedures Governing the Settlement of Disputes (DSU) (15 April 1994) LT/UR/A-2/DS/U/1 art 3(2) <http://docsonline.wto.org> accessed 7 January 2022.

162 Smith and Woods (n 138) 41.

163 ibid 44.

of trade, different interpretations (based on different political motivations) on which aspect of the good is the tangible element can lead to conflicting classification systems.[164] As classification is a matter of national policy, it is necessary for the WTO to formulate a "coherent policy on classification based on objective criteria which reflects the goals of the organization itself" if such international classification is to replace one founded on national policy objectives.[165] Relying on "tangibility" and "tradability" as the key determining factors for classification raises some complications when looking at products with significant service inputs, like 3D printed goods.

The WTO's DSB has also addressed, though not in the context of RoO, whether a "good" must be a tradeable item. Under Article 1.1(a)(1)(iii) of the SCM Agreement, a subsidy shall be deemed to exist if, "there is a financial contribution by a government or any public body within the territory of a Member ... i.e. where: a government provides goods or services other than general infrastructure, or purchases goods."[166] The Panel found in *US-Softwood Lumber (III)* that while "goods" in Article 1.1(a)(1)(iii) "includes tradeable products, there is no reason to limit its meaning to only such products," and when goods are provided by the government, nothing in the provision suggests that "the goods in question need to be tradeable products with a potential or actual tariff line."[167] The Appellate Body (AB) found in *US-Softwood Lumber IV*, that when interpreting the English word "goods," the dictionary meaning of "tangible and moveable property" was a starting point of the interpretation, but when looking at the ordinary meaning of the words "biens" and "bienes", the concept of goods includes immoveable property, and thus "goods" should be interpreted broadly to mean tangible property and possessions.[168] The AB then found that Article 1.1(a)(1)(iii) "does not preclude that there may be 'goods' in the sense of Article 1.1(a)(1)(iii) that are not actually 'imported' or traded."[169] However, the AB made it clear that "'[g]oods in Article 1.1(a)(1)(iii) of the SCM Agreement and 'products' in Article II of the GATT 1994 are different words that need not

164 ibid.

165 ibid 49.

166 Agreement on Subsidies and Countervailing Measures (SCM Agreement) (15 April 1994) LT/UR/A-1A/9, art 1.1(a)(1)(iii).

167 Report of the Panel, *United States – Preliminary Determinations with Respect to Certain Softwood Lumber from Canada (US-Softwood Lumber (III))* (27 September 2002) WT/DS236/R, paras 7.23, 7.27–28.

168 Report of the Appellate Body, *United States – Final Countervailing Duty Determination with Respect to Certain Softwood Lumber from Canada (US-Softwood Lumber IV)* (19 January 2004) AB-2003-6, WT/DS257/AB/R, paras 58–59.

169 ibid para 62.

necessarily bear the same meanings in the different contexts in which they are used," and thus it was not necessary for "goods" under the SCM Agreement to be tradeable and capable of having a tariff classification.[170] As the design and administration of preferential RoO are intrinsically linked to tariff lines, it may be challenging to argue that the non-necessity of tradability under the SCM agreement could be extended to RoO provisions that apply to goods.

It could also be argued that for hybrid-products, there must be some element which is tangible and tradable for it to be considered a good. However, in *Canada-Renewable Energy*, the AB found that the language of "purchases goods" in Article 1.1(a)(1)(iii), also encompasses the purchase of electricity.[171] Electricity does have a HS classification, and, while R.S. Neeraj does not reference the finding in *Canada-Renewable Energy*, he argues that the "flow of data constitutes a good."[172]As electricity, "essentially the flow of electrons" falls under HS 2716.00, and "for the purpose of WTO law, electricity comes under the purview of GATT," there is "no reason to treat the flow of data any differently from that of the flow of electricity for the purposes of classification under international trade law."[173] As the next Chapter will suggest, there are some complications when applying the CTH criterion. It could be questioned if a change from the Heading for electricity to the Heading for a finished bicycle frame by downloading a file into an 3D printing machine is the type of transformation the drafters of RoO rules had in mind when designing the product-specific rules. Farrokhina and Richards, in their review of discussions at the WTO by Members on the good-services dichotomy, note that some Members argue that GATT could be applied to digital products as there is no language specifying that GATT applies to tangible goods, while other Members argue that there are no tariff lines for digital products and thus it is impossible to apply GATT.[174]

James Munro points out that while there is no specified tangibility requirement, a key limitation for applying GATT to digital products is that ownership of many digital products are not transferred to the consumer upon purchase.[175]

170 Ibid para 63–61.

171 Reports of the Appellate Body, *Canada-Certain Measures Affecting The Renewable Energy Generation Sector & Canada – Measures Relating to the Feed-In Tariff Program* (*Canada-Renewable Energy*) (6 May 2013) 3AB-2013-1, WT/DS412/AB/R; WT/DS426/AB/R paras 5.127–128.

172 Neeraj (n 143) s128.

173 ibid.

174 Farrokhina and Richards (n 146) 801–802.

175 James Munro, 'Pushing the Boundaries of "Products" and "Goods" under GATT 1994: An Analysis of the Coverage of New and Unorthodox Articles of Commerce' (2013) 47 J World Trade 1323, 1347–1349.

When a consumer purchases a license to use software or a movie file, they do not possess the right to resell or transfer that file to another party. Munro's analysis of the words "good" and "products" in GATT suggests that these terms apply to products whose ownership is assigned rather than licensed upon a commercial transaction, and thus GATT applies to goods whose property rights are transferred upon transfer of the good.[176] This distinction would be relevant when a company designs 3D files and licenses them to a manufacturer across a border, who is either part of the vertical supply chain or independent from the company creating the file. There has been no change in ownership of the 3D file, thus, GATT measures do not apply. Who would own the 3D printed good, the company that licensed the 3D file or the manufacturer which printed it, is an interesting legal question for further research.

5.2.3 Classifying the 3D File

While we can debate whether a 3D printed good deriving from a 3D file is an example of the hybridization of goods-services, this book takes the position that 3D files are services on the basis of their intangibility. In a US Federal Circuit Court case, *ClearCorrect Operating v. International Trade Commission,* a dental aligner company, ClearCorrect, sought an injunction on the transmission of files (data) from outside the US on the basis that aligners printed in the US from such files would infringe ClearCorrect's patent rights. The legal question was whether the International Trade Commission (ITC), a federal and quasi-judicial agency that analyzes trade issues, had jurisdiction to issue the injunction in this instance and whether the Customs and Border Protection (CBP) can regulate the transmission of data. The Court ruled that while the CBP can regulate, the ITC has jurisdiction over articles of commerce, and "articles" means "material things," and "electronic transmissions" are not "material things."[177] Neeraj finds that the "implications of this ruling are hard to miss: there is a growing incidence of servicification of manufactured products and in the future it will be difficult to reason against this blurring of boundaries between goods and services."[178] In the future, blurring of boundaries may occur. However, until such a time, the *ClearCorrect* decision, while having no legal impact on WTO law, nonetheless coincides with the WTO's jurisprudence in considering goods under GATT to be material items.

176 ibid.

177 *ClearCorrect Operating v. International Trade Commission*, 810 F. 3d 1283, Court of Appeals, Federal Circuit 2015; Matthew Rimmer, 'ClearCorrect: Intellectual Property, 3D Printing, and the Future of Trade' (2019) 23 Gonzaga J Intl L 55, 66–68; Neeraj (n 143) s126.

178 Neeraj (n 143) s126.

The AB has identified intangibility as an element of a service. In *US-Measures Affecting Trade in Large Civil Aircraft*, also a dispute under the SCM Agreement, the AB found that "it may be difficult to separate goods from services, for instance, where services are an input or processing step in the production of goods."[179] However, the AB did attempt to distinguish goods from services, by stating that "'Goods' are tangible items. They are often contrasted against 'services', which are intangible ... As opposed to goods, typical features of services include their immaterial, invisible, intangible, and non-storable, and transitory nature."[180] Whether a particular measure at issue could fall under both GATT 1994 and GATS, the AB specified in *EC-Bananas* that such measures include those "that involve a service relating to particular good or a service supplied in conjunction with a particular good," but "whether a certain measure affecting the supply of a service related to a particular good is scrutinized under the GATT 1994 or the GATS, or both, is a matter that can only be determined on a case-by-case basis."[181]

This is not quite the same issue with RoO, as we are not determining whether GATS or GATT apply to RoO in an FTA. Preferential rules applied to goods will be assessed under the AOR Agreement, Annex II. However, we do need to understand whether a digital file is a service to apply GATS provisions on origin to 3D files. As 3D files are intangible and immaterial when transmitted electronically, they could be considered services. On the other hand, they are not transitory in nature, as they can be stored and used multiple times; however, I still find the 3D file to be a service.

If we consider 3D files to be services, the next step is to determine whether GATS applies to digital services. Ines Willemyns argues that GATS "remains the relevant framework for digital services," although none of the legal provisions "expressly regulate digital services."[182] GATS is technologically neutral and general provisions (such as determining the origin of a service) which are not dependent on the specific commitments undertaken by Members, could

179 Appellate Body Report, *United States – Measures Affecting Trade in Large Civil Aircraft (Second Complaint)*, WT/DS353/AB/R (12 March 2012, adopted 23 March 2012) para 619 fn 1295.

180 ibid.

181 Appellate Body Report, *European Communities - Regime for the Importation, Sale and Distribution of Bananas* (9 September 1997, adopted 25 September 1997) WT/DS27/AB/R, para 221.

182 Ines Willemyns, 'GATS Classification of Digital Services – *Does "The Cloud" Have a Silver Lining?*' (2019) 53 J World Trade 59, 72–73.

apply to digitally enabled or digitally transmitted services.[183] She concludes that "truly new services are rare, if they exist at all. Most digital services are services that have existed for many years, but can now be supplied in a different way, through the internet, boiling down to the transmission and processing of data."[184] When considered in this light, the 3D file is a digital version of a very old service – the design of a blueprint to construct an object or a structure. The creation and transmission of a 3D file for the purposes of constructing a tangible item could be classified generally as a service under the GATS and thus the origin provisions of GATS discussed above could apply to 3D files.

Sam Fleuter has looked into the categorization of 3D files under GATT or GATS, concluding that 3D files should be treated as services under GATS. The goal of his article, "The Role of Digital Products under the WTO: A New Framework for GATT and GATS Classification," is not only to decide whether a 3D file is a good or service, but "to use WTO treatment of additive manufacturing as a bellwether for the legal treatment of other new technologies as they arise."[185] The aim of this book on RoO for advanced manufacturing is similar in that by examining how changes in technological production impact origin determination, we can start to design rules that are more responsive to the trade environment. Fleuter examines whether a 3D file is a good or service by referring to the four-part test in *EC-Abestos* for determining if two products are alike for purposes of tariff or tax treatment.[186] While we could treat the 3D file as the same as the finished product, this would only work for highly customized and unique goods, like dental aligners. In this instance, applying a tariff on the 3D file would be the same as applying a tariff on the imported aligner.[187]

For products other than unique products like dental aligners, subjecting the 3D file to a tariff or tax, but not applying any duties to goods printed from that file in the territory does not result in like treatment with traditionally manufactured goods under the GATT.[188] The importer of the file only has to pay one

---

183 ibid 63. Willemyns does not discuss rules of origin in her article.

184 ibid 79–80.

185 S Fleuter, 'The Role of Digital Products under the WTO: A New Framework for GATT and GATS Classification' (2016) 17 Chicago J Intl L 153, 161.

186 ibid 166–167. The factors for determining likeness under GATT art III:4 are: the physical properties of the products, the end uses of the products in the market, the consumer's tastes and habits concerning the products, and tariff classification, Appellate Body Report, *European Communities – Measures Affecting Asbestos and Asbestos-Containing Products* (12 March 2001, adopted 5 April 2001) WT/DS135/AB/R paras 142–146.

187 Fleuter (n 185) 167–168.

188 ibid.

duty when importing the file, but can print 100 widgets in the territory without having to pay any duties on those widgets. The importer of 100 traditionally manufactured like-widgets must pay duties for 100 widgets. Whether 3D printed products can be deemed like to traditionally manufactured products is a complex question given the physical and chemical differences between the materials used in traditionally manufacturing and the materials used in 3D printing.[189] However, before beginning a GATT Article I or III analysis of 3D printed products and traditionally manufactured products, it is first still necessary to identify the origin of the 3D printed product.

Fleuter next compares the 3D file to blueprints. A printed blueprint is a set of instructions.[190] Likewise, a designer using CAD software programs can render a design of a good which then is converted into a file that provides instructions for the production of that good.[191] However, Fleuter notes that with a blueprint, a service must be rendered in order for the good to materialize from those instructions.[192] Files for 3D printing can be downloaded into the printing machine and the machine manufactures the good, thus there is an importation of services without much domestic job creation (although there is some set up and post-production processing).[193] We can conclude that while blueprints and 3D files are similar, they are not perfect substitutes when comparing the treatment of 3D printed goods to traditionally manufactured goods under WTO law.

The act of designing as a type of service is regulated under GATS. The Agreement defines services as including "any service in any sector except services supplied in the exercise of governmental authority."[194] The WTO has categorized the act of designing architectural and engineering blueprints as a service.[195] The Swedish National Board of Trade stated in its report on 3D printing that "3DP can involve a number of different services activities, including (a) designing and engineering computer-aided design (CAD) files …" and "[t]hese activities are regulated under the General Agreement on Trade in Services

189 National Board of Trade – Sweden, 'Trade Regulation in a 3D Printed World: A Primer' (2016) Kommerskollegium 2016: 1, 28–29.

190 Fleuter (n 185) 168.

191 ibid.

192 ibid.

193 ibid.

194 GATS art I:3(b).

195 WTO, 'Architectural and Engineering Services' (wto.org) <https://www.wto.org/english/tratop_e/serv_e/architecture_e/architecture_e.htm> accessed 24 October 2021.

(GATS)."[196] In his book on Rules of Origin for services, Dinh identifies the designer of a CAD file as a service provider.[197]

In light of the arguments above and the creation and use of 3D files, the design of the 3D file is a service, and it is a service input in the production of a 3D printed good. We are stepping away from the exercise of deciding if the 3D file is a good or service or understanding whether measures impacting trade in 3D files are consistent under GATT or GATS. As Neeraj and Fleuter alluded to, the value of a 3D file comes from the design of the file, and these aspects, the design process and its value, will be key elements for a rules of origin analysis.

6 Conclusion

This chapter has both looked to the present and to the future of preferential RoO. It is challenging to place these rules within an international trade law framework that seeks to utilize transparency, predictability, and evenhandedness in regulating trade. Rather, studies by economists have demonstrated that traders are potentially deterred from trading in foreign markets because of the complexity of the rules. However, the fact remains that preferential RoO are included in PTAs and they continue to be used by states as legal tools. The question then becomes: what do we do with preferential RoO? One approach is to find ways to make major adjustments to the technical and procedural elements of the rules. This will be discussed in Chapter 5. Another suggestion could be to make the rules "deeper" by also requiring that certain environmental or labor standards are met in the production of goods to qualify for a preferential tariff rate. This, however, raises some challenges at legal and practical levels and may not help in the simplification of the rules. Further this approach is at risk of being subverted by political and industrial groups using such socially conscious initiatives to maintain protection of domestic industries. Technological innovation, such as 3D printing, has allowed manufacturing to be more geographically diverse, efficient, and socially conscious. This book proposes that some of the challenges, concerns, and hopes for preferential RoO can be addressed by examining the rules in the context of technology and manufacturing.

A RoO system that supports digitalized manufacturing could allow RoO to find a place within an international trade law framework aimed at liberalizing

196 National Board of Trade, 'Trade Regulation in a 3D Printed World' (n 38) 24.

197 Dinh (n 103) 20.

trade and promoting development. The first step of this analysis was looking at RoO for services in general. The next step was to determine if a 3D file could be a service. The final step was to place this digital service as a service falling under the GATS rules of origin.

It may be possible to design RoO so that they can provide a predictable trading environment and support digital trade. However, first it is necessary to understand where the current rules are 'out-of-sync" for products whose value is created in the design stage. Understanding these points of friction can give us some ideas on how to modify the rules. Now, we are ready to delve deeper into additive manufacturing and examine how it will complicate the origin determination process.

CHAPTER 4

Preferential Rules of Origin in the Context of 3D Printing

This chapter will apply existing RoO regimes for goods and services to 3D printed products. Undergoing this process identifies issues in origin determination that may arise with regards to 3D printed products and other goods produced with manufacturing processes that have a significant digital technological component. This approach also provides an opportunity to think about some underlying issues on the interpretation and application of RoO for both goods and services. First, it brings into question the perspective that a good's value lies in the manufacturing stage or in the raw materials used to make the good. Is it time for scholars, trade specialists, and customs offices to take into more consideration the value of research, design, and innovation when determining the origin of a good? Yet, this leads the analysis away from tangible material and physical labor to the intangible – ideas, creativity, data files – and into the realm of services. While the GATS provides a framework for determining the origin of services, the provision of services complicates the analysis when an accumulation of activity from multiple territories and multiple producers.

By determining the origin of the tangible 3D printed product, we can achieve several analytical steps. First, we can identify the points where a RoO determination for goods based on traditional manufacturing processes is out of synch with additive manufacturing. Second, we can delve into the debate on whether service inputs, such as design and development, should have individual roles in conferring origin to final goods. For this chapter, the service input is the digital file which is downloaded into the printing machine and which provides the instructions to the machine to manufacture the good.

Determining the origin of a service input for a 3DP good leads to an uneasy alliance between RoO for goods and RoO for services. Trade experts and economists emphasize the rise of the importance of "servicification" of manufacturing and the increasing role of services as key inputs in GVCs as part of the fourth industrial revolution.[1] If we start to consider a service input like a digital

1 Shin-yi Peng, 'A New Trade Regime for the Servitization of Manufacturing: Rethinking the Goods-Services Dichotomy' (2020) 54 J World Trade 718, 699–726; Duy Dinh, *Rules of Origin for Services: From the Early Days of GATS to the Era of Servicification* (Edward Elgar 2020) 5–6,

 | DOI:10.1163/9789004730595_006

file as the crucial input of a tangible product, this may require linking the origin determination of a good to the origin determination of a service. If the file is the input with the highest economic value,[2] and we continue to use economic value as a basis for origin determination, it could be argued that the origin of the final good is dependent on the origin of the service.

The analysis in this Chapter proceeds on a few assumptions. First, that there are no tariffs or taxes on digital transmissions. Second, there are no restrictions to the transmission of digital files between states. While both issues are in fact more rich in debate, discussing these issues in depth would lead us away from the main argument of this Chapter. The Chapter begins with an analysis of origin determination of a 3D printed good with the Wholly Produced Criterion. Next the chapter examines origin determination under the substantial transformation criteria. First, the change of tariff heading (CTH) criterion is looked at and issues of whether printing is a form of simple processing and simple assembly will be discussed. Next, the Chapter presents whether a digital file can undergo a substantial transformation under the CTH. Finding it challenging to combine the CTH for goods with an origin determination for services, the Chapter will proceed to examine how the origin of the service could be factored into the *ad valorem* approach. While this approach could provide a means for factoring the service input into the origin determination, several key issues remain including how to value the 3D file and how to identify the source of the file.

1 The Likelihood that a 3D Printed Product Can Be Wholly Produced in a PTA Territory

RoO for goods are generally divided into two main categories: origin is determined based on whether the good is (i) wholly produced or obtained in the territory or (ii) whether the good has undergone a substantial transformation in the territory. As a first step, we need to consider if origin can be conferred on a 3D printed product on the basis of being wholly obtained in the territory.

66–67; Patrick Low, "The Role of Services in Global Value Chains," in Deborah K Elms and Patrick Low (eds), *Global Value Chains in a Changing World* (WTO Publications 2013) 61–81.

2 Lucas S Osborn, *3D Printing and Intellectual Property* (CUP 2019) 17; Ana Nordberg and Jens Schovsbo, "EU Design Law and 3D Printing: Finding the Right Balance in a New E-Ecosystem' in Rosa Maria Ballardini, Marcus Norrgård, Jouni Partanen (eds), *3D Printing, Intellectual Property and Innovation: Insights from Law and Technology* (WoltersKluwer 2017) 281; Andreas Gebhardt, Julia Kessler and Laura Thurn, *3D Printing: Understanding Additive Manufacturing* (2nd edn, Hanser 2019), 71–72.

Under the PEM and USCMA, a good is wholly obtained if it is produced exclusively from products specified in the rules. These products include minerals, plant matter, animal products, fish or shellfish, and scrap material.[3] If all the raw materials of the ink are sourced in the territory and the good is printed in the territory, then it seems possible that the 3D printed good is wholly produced in the territory. However, this means that a predominate factor in determining origin is the source of the materials.

Biological material such as plant matter used for steaks[4] and plastic or metal derivatives used for inputs for automobiles, airplanes, and other machinery call into question whether a 3D printed good can be wholly obtained in a territory. A "traditional" steak is wholly obtained in Switzerland if the cow is born, raised, and butchered in Switzerland. A 3D printed steak is made from an ink consisting of pea and rice proteins and seaweed.[5] A company in Switzerland wanting to print steaks will have to source seaweed that is farm-grown in Switzerland or import the seaweed, which may grow along the shores of a country outside of the EFTA territory. Another criterion must be used to determine the origin of 3D printed steaks in Switzerland. Most 3D printers for products for industrial purposes use ink which are proprietary composites of resins,[6] nylon powders (including glass, carbon or aluminum),[7] plastic filaments,[8] and metal powders or wires.[9] Further, the 3D printing machine vendors design the machines to use specific composites and require that the ink be sourced from the same vendor or from a certified provider.[10] Thus, the territory of the maker

3 Decision No 1/2023 Of The Joint Committee Of The Regional Convention On Pan-Euro-Mediterranean Preferential Rules Of Origin of 7 December 2023 (PEM) App I art 3; Agreement between the United States of America, the United Mexican States, and Canada (USMCA) (signed 30 November 2018, entered into force 1 July 2020) art 4.3.

4 Gareth Rubin, 'How do you like your beef ... old-style cow or 3D-printed?' *The Guardian* (10 November 2019) <https://www.theguardian.com/technology/2019/nov/10/3d-printed-meat-european-restaurant-menus-environment> accessed 24 October 2021.

5 Agnieszka de Sousa, 'A Realistic Steak is Fake Meat's Holy Grail' (*Bloomberg Business* 22 November 2019) <https://www.bloomberg.com/news/articles/2019-11-22/fake-meat-companies-are-racing-to-3d-print-steaks> accessed 24 October 2021.

6 Jukka Tuomi, Segei Chekurov and Jouni Partnanen, '3D Printing History, Principles and Technologies,' in Rosa Maria Ballardini, Marcus Norrgård, Jouni Partanen (eds), *3D Printing, Intellectual Property, and Innovation: Insights from Law and Technology* (Wolters-Kluwer 2017) 8.

7 ibid 11.

8 ibid 21.

9 ibid 25.

10 Iñigo Flores Ituarte, Siavash H Khajavi and Mika Salmi, 'Current and Future Business Models for 3D Printing Applications,' in Rosa Maria Ballardini, Marcus Norrgård, Jouni

of the ink must also be taken into consideration along with the territory of all the raw materials used to create that ink.

As the ink for a 3D printed product is a mixture of various materials sourced from various territories, the use of 3D printing may result in the divergence of two policy goals: increasing manufacturing jobs and increasing exports qualifying for preferential treatment. Although US and EU policymakers promote the adoption of 3D printing as a means to reshore manufacturing jobs,[11] a good produced with 3D printing machines may not qualify as having EU or US origin. The political goal of manufacturing goods on the "home" territory may be achieved, but the additional goal of increasing the production of "national" or "regional" products would not be achieved when looking at the RoO. For example, two major suppliers of ink for 3D printing solutions, Solvay and Sandvik, are multi-national organizations with manufacturing facilities worldwide.[12] Even if Solvay Italia supplies the polymer filaments to a factory outside of Milan to print gears for automobiles, all of the chemicals used to create the ink filaments may not have been produced in Italy or within the EU.[13] A criterion

---

Partanen (eds), *3D Printing, Intellectual Property, and Innovation: Insights from Law and Technology* (WoltersKluwer 2017) 47–48; Gebhardt, Kessler, and Thurn (n 2) 72.

11 Opinion of the European Economic and Social Committee, 'Living tomorrow. 3D printing – a tool to empower the European economy' (own-initiative opinion) (2015/C 332/05) C 332/36, 8 October 2015; N Deliyanakis, M Lindberg, E Mascalchi et al. 'Trends in advanced manufacturing R&I – Advanced manufacturing projects and what they tell us about the future of the manufacturing industry' Pub. Office of the EU (2023) <https://data.europa.eu/doi/10.2777/209329> accessed 23 March 2024; E Calza, J Soguero Escuer, J Fabiani, G de Prato, Advanced Manufacturing Study. Preliminary findings on EU's Advanced Manufacturing industry in the global landscape, Pub. Office of the EU (2024) 9–10 <https://publications.jrc.ec.europa.eu/repository/handle/JRC137761> accessed 25 October 2024; The White House, 'President Obama Launches Advanced Manufacturing Partnership' (Obama White House 4 June 2011) <https://obamawhitehouse.archives.gov/the-press-office/2011/06/24/president-obama-launches-advanced-manufacturing-partnership> accessed 24 October 2021; 'America Makes' (Americamakes.us) <https://www.americamakes.us/about/> accessed 24 October 2021; The White House, 'Fact Sheet: President Biden Announces New Actions to Strengthen America's Supply Chains, Lower Costs for Families, and Secure Key Sectors' (Biden White House 27 November 2023) <https://bidenwhitehouse.archives.gov/briefing-room/statements-releases/2023/11/27/fact-sheet-president-biden-announces-new-actions-to-strengthen-americas-supply-chains-lower-costs-for-families-and-secure-key-sectors/> accessed 10 March 2025.

12 'About Solvay' (solvay.com) <https://www.solvay.com/en/our-company> accessed 24 October 2021; 'About Us' (home.sandvik) <https://www.home.sandvik/en/about-us/> accessed 24 October 2021.

13 'Solvay in Italia' (solvay.it) <https://www.solvay.it/it/solvay-in/index.html> accessed 24 October 2021; 'Additive Manufacturing Solutions' (solvay.com) <https://www.solvay.com/en/chemical-categories/specialty-polymers/additive-manufacturing> accessed

other than the wholly produced criterion is required for the printed gear to have EU origin under the PEM.

Finally, we must think about the role of the 3D file as an origin conferring service. We could say that the 3D printed product consists of two inputs – the intangible 3D file and the tangible ink. If the 3D file is designed in France and downloaded in the factory in Milan and printed with 100% Italian ink, the product will still qualify as a product originating in the PEM territory. However, if the 3D file is designed in and transmitted from Japan to the printer in Milan, the product is no longer wholly produced in the EU and does not qualify for PEM origin under the wholly produced criterion.

The international journeys of digital files for the printing of dental aligners and hearing aids provides a glimpse into how the adoption of additive manufacturing by other industries could result in goods that do not meet the wholly produced criterion if the 3D file is an origin conferring input of the product. The dental aligner[14] and hearing aid industries[15] were early adopters of additive manufacturing at a widespread scale. Align Technology, based in the United States, has been producing dental aligners since at least 1998 and has been manufacturing its clear aligners in Mexico since 2000.[16] Dentists and orthodontists around the world scan patients' mouths and send the digital files to be modelled at Align Technology facilities in Costa Rica.[17] The completed digital models are then sent to Mexico for printing and distribution. Similarly, in the hearing aid industry, Sonova has been using 3D printing to mass produce

24 October 2021; The USITA reports that the additive manufacturing market in Italy is estimated to be $600 million – $1 billion and is used in the automotive, aerospace, biomedical and fashion and design industries. USITA, 'Italy – Country Commercial Guide: Advanced Manufacturing' (trade.gov 23 January 2024) <https://www.trade.gov/country-commercial-guides/italy-advanced-manufacturing> accessed 24 March 2024.

14 Structo, 'Part 1: The Birth of Clear Aligners' (*Structo3D* 18 July 2017) <https://www.structo3d.com/blogs/blog/part-1-the-birth-of-clear-aligners> accessed 24 October 2021; Align Technology, 'Align Technology Announces Plans to Assume Operations From Its Manufacturing Services Provider,' (Align Technology Investor Release 22 December 2008) <http://investor.aligntech.com/static-files/de067378-b820-409a-ba5a-fa79087f2fb6> accessed 24 October 2021.

15 Ana Lucia Abeliansky, Immaculada Martínez-Zarsoso and Klaus Prettner, '3D Printing, International Trade, and FDI' (2020) 85 *Economic Modelling* 298, 301; "3D Printing Technology for Improved Hearing," (Sonova.com 2020) <https://www.sonova.com/en/story/innovation/3d-printing-technology-improved-hearing> accessed 24 October 2021.

16 Align Technology Investor Release (2008) (n 14).

17 Align Technology, 'Align Technology Expands Operations in Costa Rica with New Facilities to Support Continued Long-Term Growth,' (Align Technology Investor Release 25 July 2018) <http://investor.aligntech.com/news-releases/news-release-details/align-technology-expands-operations-costa-rica-new-facilities> accessed 24 October 2021.

custom-made hearing aids since 2001.[18] Practitioners scan silicone impressions of the ear canal and further processing is done digitally.[19] Once the hearing aid shell is complete, Sonova reports that "the file with the three-dimensional structure is stored in a central database and transmitted to the 3D printers at the production site,"[20] which are located in Latin America, North America, Asia, and Oceania.[21] These examples demonstrate that business leaders using 3D printing to transform an industry may not choose to concentrate all stages of production in one territory or re-shore production,[22] but instead, break up the production process in various territories.

Factoring the 3D file as a service input into origin determination makes it challenging to meet the wholly produced criterion. However, even with traditional manufacturing, the wholly produced criterion is not frequently applied to products that consist of several parts. Instead, the change of tariff classification criterion or the value-added criterion are usually used.

2 From Ink to Printed Product: A Change of Tariff Heading, but Is It Sufficient Processing to Qualify for Origin?

At first glance, the CTH seems like a suitable method for determining the origin of a 3D printed good. The purpose behind the CTH is to ensure that a certain amount of processing of the good occurs in the territory of the PTA.[23] Putting polymer filaments produced in Country Y into a 3D printing machine in Country X, hitting the "print" button, and hours later finding a gear for an automobile in the bed of the printer seems like there has been sufficient processing in Country X. The polymer filament would be classified in HS Chapter 39 and the finished gear or piston for a motor vehicle in Chapter 87.[24] Lucas S. Osborn in his book on 3D printing and intellectual property law refers to a 3D printing

18 Sonova, '3D Printing Technology for Improved Hearing' (n 15).

19 ibid.

20 ibid.

21 Abeliansky, Martínez-Zarsoso and Prettner (n 15) 301.

22 Ziyang Fan, Jimena Sotelo, and Venkataraman Sundareswaran, '3D Printing: A Guide for Decision-Makers' (January 2020) World Economic Forum – White Paper, 13 <http://www3.weforum.org/docs/WEF_Impacts_3D_Printing_on_Trade_Supply_Chains_Toolkit.pdf> accessed 24 October 2021.

23 Anne van de Heetkamp and Rudd Tusveld, *Origin Management: Rules of Origin in Free Trade Agreements* (Springer 2011) 83.

24 WCO, 'HS Nomenclature 2022 Edition' (wccomd.org) <http://www.wcoomd.org/en/topics/nomenclature/instrument-and-tools/hs-nomenclature-2022-edition/hs-nomenclature-2022-edition.aspx> accessed 7 January 2022.

method called Stereolithography (SLA), which "uses ultraviolet light to cure (harden) successive layers of a liquid photopolymer."[25] He states that "[w]atching this process can be somewhat surreal because the part slowly arises from a vat of liquid goo."[26] Indeed, that seems like a perfect example of a substantial transformation.

Yet, a few analysts examining RoO in the context of 3D printing differ in their assessments of whether the CTH is suitable for determining the origin of 3D printed products. With regards to the CTH, the Swedish National Board of Trade wrote in one of its reports on 3D printing that applying the CTH criterion may be more viable than the *ad valorem* criterion, because substantial transformation occurring as a "CTC [change in tariff heading] would be fulfilled when the 'ink' (classified in one specific HS-code) is printed into a product (classified in a different HS-code from the 'ink')."[27] On the other hand, the study conducted by Ziyang Fan, Jimena Soleto, and Venkataraman Sundareswaran calls into question the use of the CTH as it may be difficult to determine whether the last substantial transformation takes place "at the design stage or at the time of printing."[28] The authors then argue that with 3D printing, the CTH would not function as a discriminatory method for determining origin as almost any 3D printed good must undergo a change from the Heading for the ink to the Heading of the printed good.[29]

If the CTH criterion loses its discriminatory function, transshipment from third-party territories into the territory of one of FTA parties could arise. For example, Countries X and Y have an FTA with a tariff rate for automobile gears at 5%. Country Z is a third party. Producer Y in Country Y wants gears produced by Company Z. However, Producer Y must pay a 10% tariff when importing gears from Country Z. To circumvent the 10% tariff, Company Z designs Z-3DGear in Country Z, and prints Z-3DGear in Country X, at a printing lab. As Z-3DGear is printed in Country X, under the CTH, Z-3DGEAR now originates in Country X and can be imported into Country Y under the 5% preferential rate.[30] On the other hand, a gear traditionally manufactured in Country Z is

25 Osborn (n 2) 34.

26 ibid.

27 National Board of Trade – Sweden, 'Trade Regulation in a 3D Printed World: A Primer' (2016) Kommerskollegium 2016: 1, 27–28.

28 Fan, Sotelo and Sundareswaran (n 22) 14.

29 ibid.

30 If the Customs and Border Protection determines that printing was just for purpose of circumventing, the good becomes non qualifying for origin under USMCA. "Non-Qualifying Operations: Each Party shall provide that a good shall not be considered to be an originating good merely by reason of ... a production or pricing practice in respect of which it

still subject to the 10% tariff. If printing Z-3DGear in Country X and shipping it to Country Y is cheaper than paying the 10% tariff, Company Z has an incentive to stop producing its gears in Country Z, print the gears in Country X, and ship to Country Y; thus, also competing with traditional gear manufacturers in Country X for business in Country Y.

Questioning whether the last substantial transformation takes place at the time of printing leads to the greater question of what type of processing is printing in the context of RoO. Preferential RoO require a certain level of processing of the good to occur in the territory. For example, in PEM, the word "sufficient" is used: products produced with non-originating materials qualify for origin status if the non-originating materials have "undergone sufficient working or processing in that Contracting Party."[31] The emphasis is on sufficient – it is not any processing whatsoever. The level of processing required may be specified in the annexes of the RoO chapter or the chapter may also specify what does not constitute sufficient processing. It is not simply a question of whether there was a transformation and where it last occurred. A further analysis is needed of whether printing a part or the assembly of printed parts meets the minimum requirements of processing under the PTA. Putting plastic filaments in a 3D printing machine and printing a gear likely results in a change of tariff heading. However, is this sufficient processing in the territory to confer origin on the gear?

2.1 *Is Printing and Post-Processing Sufficient Processing?*

Simple processing and simple assembly are those, in the words of the Kyoto Agreement, "which do not contribute or which contribute to only a small extent to the essential characteristics or properties of the goods."[32] Under the PEM, operations which do not confer origin are: simple painting, polishing, "washing, cleaning; removal of dust, oxide, oil, paint or other coverings."[33] Therefore, we need to consider to what extent the act of printing contributes towards the essential characteristic or properties of the printed good. Tuomi, Chekurov and Partnanen report that products printed through the Stereolithography process must be "submerged in a chemical bath to remove excess

may be demonstrated, on the basis of a preponderance of evidence, that the object was to circumvent this Chapter." USMCA art 4.19.

31 PEM App I art (2)(b).

32 International Convention on the Simplification and Harmonization of Customs Procedures (as amended) (Revised Kyoto Convention) (entered into force 3 February 2006), Specific Annex K ch 1(6).

33 PEM App I art (6).

resin and then placed in an ultraviolet oven to cure it further."[34] Metal parts made through the binder jetting process are printed from a mixture of plastic and metal powders, and then "sintered to remove the plastic" to leave "an empty metal matrix" which is "subsequently infiltrated with bronze or similar metal."[35]

Another type of extrusion technology used for industrial printers, fused layer modeling (FDM), builds parts (for eyeglass frames, for example) by feeding plastic cords through a nozzle, the plastic melts, and a second nozzle extrudes support material in a different type of plastic; this process is repeated and each layer fuses to the other by means of the heat of the previous layer.[36] In post-processing the supports can be removed manually or with a bath, and as Gebhardt, Kessler, and Thurn note, the polishing of the part "requires manual working skills and needs time, and results in high surface quality and surprisingly good results."[37]

All of these processes listed above in making a 3D printed product are washing, cleaning, and removing of coverings. However, in order for these processes to confer origin on the good under the PEM they must be sufficient processing, in other words, they must be more than simple polishing, painting, or washing. Could such post-processing be sufficient processing?

Under the ASEAN-Korea FTA, the post-processing for the Stereolithography and binder jetting methods could possibly be considered a processing that confers origin status. Under Rule 8, "Non-Qualifying Operations," a good does not obtain origin status in the territory of the Parties if:

> the following operations are undertaken exclusively by itself or in combination in the territory of that Party ... Simple[4] washing, cleaning, removal of dust, oxide, oil, paint or other coverings.[38]

Footnote 4 clarifies that:

> "simple" generally describes an activity which does not need special skills, machines, apparatus or equipment especially produced or installed for carrying out the activity.[39]

34 Tuomi, Chekurov and Partnanen (n 6) 7; See also Gebhardt, Kessler, and Thurn (n 2) 50.

35 Tuomi, Chekurov and Partnanen (n 6) 15.

36 Gebhardt, Kessler, and Thurn (n 2) 50–51.

37 ibid 52.

38 ASEAN-Korea Free Trade Area (AKFTA)(entered into force June 2007) Annex 3 (Rules of Origin) r 8.

39 AKFTA Annex 3 r 8 fn 4; van de Heetkamp & Tusveld (n 23) 95.

In the case of Stereolithography post-processing, a proprietary post-processing kit may be included with the purchase of the printer or can be sold separately by the printer manufacturer.[40] A case could be argued that the post-processing of 3D printed parts made through the Stereolitography or binder jetting methods are not simple operations and could contribute towards the essential characteristics of the final good.

On the other hand, the material extrusion method, which extrudes melted material from a single nozzle, is one of the most commonly used methods for 3D desktop printers or low-cost 3D printing.[41] The post-processing entails submerging "the part in an ultrasonic bath to remove the water-soluble support material."[42] Ultrasonic baths are widely available and are used to clean various items such as laboratory equipment and sunglasses.[43] Post-processing of a printed good made under this method would likely be considered insufficient processing.

In sum, the post-processing of 3D printed goods may or may not be "sufficient" processing. This presents the possibility that the current rules regarding sufficient and insufficient processing will have to be interpreted with some understanding of how the post-processing of 3D printed goods differs from post-processing in traditional manufacturing operations. However, a more complicated issues lies with the "printing" part of the additive manufacturing process. How much processing occurs when one instructs the machine to print with a click of the mouse?

Referring to the US – Japan Agreement, the act of printing by itself may not qualify as origin conferring processing. The Agreement defines "simple assembly" as:

> the fitting together of five or fewer parts all of which are non-originating (excluding fasteners such as screws, bolts, etc.) by bolting, gluing, soldering, or sewing or by other means without more than minor processing.[44]

3D printing machines are complex technological instruments which require specialized equipment and laser optics to melt the "ink" and print the good.[45]

40 FormLabs, 'Post-elaborazione' (formlabs.com) <https://formlabs.com/it/negozio/post-processing/> accessed 24 October 2021.

41 Tuomi, Chekurov and Partnanen (n 6) 21.

42 ibid 22.

43 'Results for 'Ultrasonic Bath' (amazon.com) <https://www.amazon.com/Ultrasonic-Bath/s?k=Ultrasonic+Bath> accessed 24 October 2021.

44 US-Japan Trade Agreement, Annex II Tariffs and Tariff-Related Provisions of the US, Product-Specific Rules of Origin art 19 (d).

45 Tuomi, Chekurov and Partnanen (n 6) 3–4.

However, the factor under examination in RoO is not the complexity of the machine. If one categorizes 3D printing as a form of "bolting, gluing, soldering" or "fitting" together by means of melting and layering liquid substance over a period of time, then, at least under the U.S.–Japan Agreement, it could be argued that 3D printing is a form of minor processing.

3D printing can be a form of producing requiring special skill and or a hobby requiring a desktop printer. For example, Iñigo Flores Ituarte, Siavash H. Khajavi and Mika Salmi in their chapter for the book, *3D Printing, Intellectual Property and Innovation: Insights from Law and Technology*, write that 3D printing requires a "high level of competence and knowledge to be able to utilize the technology as well as its related digital systems."[46] Yet in the same paragraph, they also state that "[s]tartup companies are also teaching children to 3D model with their hands, reducing the learning curve on technical drawing and 3D modelling" and present a picture of five-year old child sitting before a laptop computer and a desktop 3D printing machine.[47] With regards to the printing of prosthetics, Osborn in his book on 3D printing and intellectual property law, states:

> The accessibility of the technology to relatively unskilled workers has given rise to a worldwide, open source network of people who seek to provide 3D printed prosthetics to everyone in need, regardless of income. The technology is accessible enough that teenagers are using it to make prosthetics for others.[48]

However, he also states that "3D printing is not currently easy for nonexperts" though tools are widely available."[49] The above quotes demonstrate that it is not easy to state whether the printing part is sufficient to confer origin, nor is it entirely clear how much skilled technical work is required to process a 3D printed good.

Companies have set up 3D printing services like a copier service. A customer sends the company the 3D file with specifics on how many goods to print and where to send the goods, and the company prints and ships the goods.[50] This type of print-on-demand business model calls into question how much

---

46 Flores Ituarte, Khajavi and Salmi (n 10) 41.

47 ibid 41–42.

48 Osborn (n 2) 16.

49 ibid 25.

50 3D printing orders can be sent to UPS stores in the US. Mohammad E Arbabian and Michael R Wagner, 'The Impact of 3D Printing on Manufacturer-Retailer Supply Chains,' (2020) 285 Eur J Operational Research 538, 539; Osborn (n 2) 24; Flores Ituarte, Khajavi and Salmi (n 10) 52–55.

origin-conferring processing is actually done to these products. Gebhardt, Kessler, and Thurn note that although intensive training is needed for operating industrial printers, "[m]anual handling has to be eliminated or at least reduced to a minimum … The operation is free of human interaction. Parallel operation of multiple machines operated by one operator is possible."[51] Thus, printing implies a lot of processing by machines, but not by humans. If printing is sufficient processing, the origin of a product could be determined simply by where a print-shop is located, and thus producers would need to be attentive as to the locations where they sub-contract printing operations.

Further, is the level of processing performed by engineers at Boeing when printing components for a spacecraft any greater than the level of processing performed by a college student printing dental aligners with a university printer?[52] What type of evidence would be required to demonstrate to customs officials that sufficient processing occurred? These are administrative questions that may need to be asked when seeking origin certificates for 3D printed goods. To conclude this analysis on assembly, we must consider two further elements of 3D printing: (1) it can reduce or eliminate the need for "tooling" and thus reduce or eliminate a step in the production process; and (2) 3D printing reduces the number of parts to be assembled to form the final good.

The use of digital technology and CAD files in manufacturing predates the invention of 3D printing. CNC (Computer Numerical Control) manufacturing is a form of subtractive manufacturing. It is less adaptable than 3D printing in manufacturing complex parts in certain materials such as plastics, and it is more labor intensive.[53] CNC technology dates back to at least the 1940s and was in widespread use by the 1980s,[54] when the first patents for 3D printing technology were filed.[55] A CNC machine consists of multiple tools and a computer. A CAD file is downloaded and programs the automation of the tools to

51 Gebhardt, Kessler, and Thurn (n 2) 28–29.

52 Osborn (n 2) 25; Hope King, 'College student 3D prints his own braces' (CNN.com 16 March 2016) <https://money.cnn.com/2016/03/16/technology/homemade-invisalign/> accessed 24 October 2021; Richard Aston, '3D Printing Done Right' (*Innovation Q*) <https://www.boeing.com/features/innovation-quarterly/nov2017/feature-thought-leadership-3d-printing.page> accessed 24 October 2021.

53 Alkaios Bournias Varotsis, '3D printing vs. CNC machining' (3D Hubs), <https://www.3dhubs.com/knowledge-base/3d-printing-vs-cnc-machining/> accessed 24 October 2021.

54 Goli Mohammadi, 'The History of CNC Machining, Part 1 & 2' (Bantam Tools) <https://medium.com/cnc-life/history-of-cnc-machining-part-1-2a4b290d994d> <https://medium.com/cnc-life/history-of-cnc-machining-part-2-the-evolution-from-nc-to-cnc-4b9fe1653536> both accessed 24 October 2021.

55 Tuomi, Chekurov and Partnanen (n 6) 2.

remove material and to shape the good.[56] While both CNC and 3D printing machines rely on digital files to operate, there are some differences between the two types of manufacturing that can impact the decision to use one method or the other. 3D printing is preferable if a low volume order or a single item is needed, and in this situation it is faster and relatively cheaper than CNC.[57] On the other hand, for mass orders for products that are not intricate or geometrically complex, CNC manufacturing can achieve economies of scale and be more cost efficient.[58]

The differences between CNC manufacturing and 3D printing also relate to the extent of processing performed under each method. CNC manufacturing requires humans to set up the machine and the tools in the machine; it is this set-up calibration which incurs the most cost of production.[59] The operator must affix the materials directly in the machine's components and attach tooling such as drills.[60] This manual set-up makes CNC manufacturing labor intensive, while the 3D printing process reduces the need for such labor expenditure.[61]

The question of how much human intervention is needed to print goods leads back to the legal issue of what level of processing occurs during 3D printing. It is questionable whether printing in-and-of-itself qualifies as "sufficient" processing under the PEM. Compared to CNC machines consisting of bits, drills, mills, and other components that must be calibrated by humans, relying on the 3D printer's software to calibrate the machine and clicking print with a mouse to initiate printing seems like minor processing.[62] On the other hand, 3D printing may not be categorized as "simple" processing under agreements such as the ASEAN-Korea FTA, which qualifies "simple" processing as not requiring special skills or machines. Operating industrial and complex 3D printers does require training. According to Bournias Vartosis, post-processing "is the most labor-intensive aspect of the 3D printing manufacturing workflow."[63] However, some determination on whether post-processing done to 3D

56 'Understanding CNC Machining' (Thomas Publishing Company) <https://www.thomasnet.com/articles/custom-manufacturing-fabricating/understanding-cnc-machining/> accessed 24 October 2021.

57 Bournias Varotsis (n 53); Gebhardt, Kessler, and Thurn (n 2) 142.

58 Flores Ituarte, Khajavi and Salmi (n 10) 36; Gebhardt, Kessler, and Thurn (n 2) 138–139, 143.

59 Flores Ituarte, Khajavi and Salmi (n 10) 36.

60 'Understanding CNC Machining' (n 56).

61 Bournias Varotsis (n 53).

62 Gebhardt, Kessler, and Thurn (n 10) 72–74.

63 Bournias Varotsis (n 53).

printed goods is "sufficient" processing or is another form of simple washing, painting, or baking would still be necessary.

One non-preferential RoO dispute is an example of how rules on processing may disrupt expected or desired origin determinations. The requests for consultations to the DSB referenced in Chapter 1, *US-Measures Affecting Textiles and Apparel Products*, originate in part from changes to US rules requiring more processing steps to be completed on silk products in Europe if the silk did not originate in the country in which the processing was performed.[64] This rule impacted the Italian silk apparel industry, such as scarves and ties, as under the rules, a scarf could no longer bear the label "Made in Italy," but "Made in China." If the silk was sourced from China, a finished product had to bear the label "Designed in Italy" or "Crafted in Italy".[65] Under the new rules there was not sufficient processing performed in Italy on the raw material (silk) such that the final product underwent a sufficient transformation to qualify for Italian origin.

The Italian perspective was that the sewing and processing to the silk done in the Italian factories and artisanal boutiques were in fact skilled processing and being unable to use the label "Made in Italy" would impair trade with the US.[66] In its Request for Consultations, the EC argued that the additional processing requirements did not respect Article 2 of the AOR which prohibits use of rules of origin as instruments to pursue trade objectives directly or indirectly or to create restrictions or disruptions on international trade. As a result of the rules, EC producers were losing access to the US market because the silk goods no longer were identified as originating in Europe.[67] The US agreed to exempt silk scarves and silk finished products from the changes to the rules of origin:

64 *US – Measures Affecting Textiles and Apparel Products*, Request for Consultations by the EC; *US- Measures Affecting Textiles and Apparel Products*, Notification of Mutually-Agreed Solution; *US – Measures Affecting Textiles and Apparel Products* (*II*), Request for Consultations by the EC; *United States- Measures Affecting Textiles and Apparel Products* (*II*), Notification of Mutually Agreed Solution (31 July 2000) WT/DS151/10.

65 Committee on Ways and Means – US House of Representatives, 'Overview and Compilation of U.S. Trade Statues' (2003 edn, US Government Printing Office June 2003), 75–76.

66 John Tagliabue, 'Italian Silk Industry Upset by a New U.S. Trade Law' *New York Times* (New York, 10 April 1997) Section D p 4 <https://www.nytimes.com/1997/04/10/business/italian-silk-industry-upset-by-a-new-us-trade-law.html> accessed 6 January 2022.

67 *US – Measures Affecting Textiles and Apparel Products,* Request for Consultations by the EC, 1–2; *US – Measures Affecting Textiles and Apparel Products* (*II*), Request for Consultations by the EC, 1–2.

products did not have to be labeled as "Made in China", but could qualify for EC origin if two or more specified processes occurred to the silk fabric in the EU.[68]

While this dispute regards non-preferential RoO, it does demonstrate how the recategorization of sufficient processing can disrupt the intended origin of a product, and how this could disrupt trade of a product if such intended origin is a marketable aspect of the product. We can then think about this issue in the context of 3D printing. An FTA between A and B requires two steps of sufficient processing in the territory for origin qualification. However, some producers, wishing to innovate or be more efficient, print the product using materials from territory C. If one of these processing steps in A (printing) is considered simple processing by territory A, the good does not qualify for origin, and instead is given C origin based on the origin of the ink. For the producers, they may have an unpleasant surprise, like the scarf producers in Italy, of finding out that their goods no longer originate in territory A, and this could impede their ability to trade their products in territory B. At this point it is apparent that trying to apply a small portion of the language in RoO to determine the origin of a 3D printed good leads to a legal riddle whose key perhaps lies in defining the terms "sufficient", "minor," and "simple" in connection with a specific technology.

2.2 *3D Printing: Fewer Parts to Assemble, but Is Assembly Simple?*

Another challenging legal puzzle that 3D printing brings in terms of the CTH criterion is the promise to reduce the number of components of a finished good.[69] For example, GE Aviation reduced the number of parts in a turbopop engine from 855 (sourced from different contractors) to twelve (printed by one manufacturer).[70] A prototype for a printable electric car, Strati, reduced the number of parts from 25,000 to forty-nine.[71] Further, objects that have ball bearings or multiple rotating gears can be printed in one printing session

---

68 *US- Measures Affecting Textiles and Apparel Products (II)*, Notification of Mutually Agreed Solution, 2–3; Committee on Ways and Means 'Overview and Compilation of U.S. Trade Statues' (n 808) 75–76.

69 Kati Suominen, *Revolutionizing World Trade: How Disruptive Technologies Open Opportunities for All* (Stanford UP 2019) 21.

70 'Additive Manufacturing: Aviation and Aerospace Industry' (*GE Additive*) <https://www.ge.com/additive/additive-manufacturing/industries/aviation-aerospace> accessed 24 October 2021 (archived link).

71 Josh Davis, 'The Strati: a 3D-printed electric car that could be built in 24 hours' *The Guardian* (London, 9 December 2014) <https://www.theguardian.com/technology/2014/dec/09/3d-printed-electric-car> accessed 2 December 2021.

(single-pass print jobs).[72] Osborn states that these types of "print jobs eliminate the need to assemble parts, saving time and obviating the need for assembly expertise."[73]

If we eliminate expertise in assembly, then the assembly of a good constituted from 3D printed parts could be a form of simple assembly. For example, under the ASEAN-Korean FTA, simple assembly is: "an activity which does not need special skills, machines, apparatus or equipment especially produced or installed for carrying out the activity."[74] Further, if the number of parts are reduced to five or less (such as for a bicycle frame),[75] and the ink is non-originating material, then assembly of the good would also be categorized as simple assembly under the US-Japan Agreement, which defines "simple assembly" as:

> the fitting together of *five or fewer parts* [my emphasis] all of which are non-originating (excluding fasteners such as screws, bolts, etc.) by bolting, gluing, soldering, or sewing or by other means without more than minor processing.[76]

Therefore, goods which may have qualified for origin under the CTH criterion under traditional manufacturing methods through the assembly of multiple parts (i.e. sufficient processing), may no longer qualify for origin under that criterion when made by additive manufacturing: printing significantly reduces the number of parts necessary for a good and may reduce or eliminate any special skill to assemble those parts.

These last paragraphs have led us into linguistic, technical, and legal knots regarding the application of the CTH criterion to determine the origin of a 3D printed good. At first glance, it appears an adept method: material categorized in one heading is transformed into a printed good categorized in another heading. However, this could mean that nearly all 3D printed goods would be able to gain origin status with this method.[77] The CTH criterion meets its legal function under a preferential RoO regime when it discriminates between

72 Osborn (n 2) 10.

73 ibid.

74 AKFTA, Annex 3 (Rules of Origin) fn 4; van de Heetkamp and Tusveld (n 23) 95.

75 Aysha M., 'The Top Bicycles Made with 3D Printing Technologies,' (*3D Natives* 30 September 2023) <https://www.3dnatives.com/en/ranking-3d-printed-bikes-220920204/#!> accessed 10 March 2025.

76 US-Japan Trade Agreement, Annex II Tariffs and Tariff-Related Provisions of the US, Product-Specific Rules of Origin art 19 (d).

77 Fan, Sotelo and Sundareswaran (n 22) 14.

qualifying and non-qualifying goods. Rules limiting simple assembly or processing operations from conferring origin aim to ensure that the CTH criterion maintains its discriminatory function by requiring a certain level of processing to occur in the territory.[78] It is necessary to identify in the production of 3D goods what steps are "sufficient processing" to continue to apply the CTH criterion as a method for determining origin. Finally, the promises of 3D printing to reduce the number of components of a final good from hundreds to under a dozen and to eliminate assembly expertise could relegate the assembly of 3D printed goods into the category of "simple assembly." To continue to use the CTH criterion and preserve its discriminatory function, it will be necessary to qualify the assembly of fewer parts as assembly still requiring a high level of processing.

2.3 *Application of the Technical Test and Preliminary Conclusions*

At this point, we should look at the "working process" or "technical test" criterion mentioned briefly in Chapter 2. The same concerns arise: in order for a technical working process to confer origin, it must be more than simple processing and assembly. If 3D printing is simple processing, it would not pass the technical test/working process criterion. Rules based on one type of processing that does not require the same technological system as 3D printing may not be applicable to determining the origin of the 3D printed goods. Thus, 3D printing also complicates the use of the "working process or operations" criterion to determine the origin of 3D printed goods.

We can derive the following possible choices regarding the use of the CTH or "working process or operations" criteria to determining the origin of 3D printed goods.

1. Apply CTH rules based only on heading or subheading changes: the "ink" is in one heading, the "good" in another, a substantial transformation has occurred. However, this means that nearly all printed goods undergo a substantial transformation, and thus the method is not very discriminatory.
2. Categorize 3D printing as a form of simple assembly: By removing or significantly removing human time, labor, and processing required to manufacture a good, 3D printing is a form of simple assembly. Even though a change of heading has occurred, there has not been sufficient processing of the good to undergo a substantial transformation in the territory to qualify for preferential origin status.

78 Bernard Hoekman, 'Rules of Origin for Goods and Services: Conceptual Issues and Economic Considerations' (1993) 27 J World Trade 82, 85.

3. Attempt to qualify what is "simple" and "not simple" in 3D printing: This requires different sets of legal and technical definitions of "simple" for traditional manufacturing methods and additive manufacturing methods. Further, it requires differentiating "simple" based on various 3D printing methods and post-production processing.

Manufacturers who adopt additive manufacturing could try to influence what level of processing confers origin through lobbying.[79] Inama's concerns regarding traditional manufacturing are also applicable to additive manufacturing: "countries may be interested in 'obtaining' origin even if the amount of working and processing is minimal," and conversely, "a country may have an interest in 'retaining' origin even if the exported product is processed in a third country before being sold to consumers."[80] A country, for political or strategic reasons, could claim that printing and post-processing confer origin, and thus retain origin even when the parts are sent to another country for assembly; or a country could claim that printing and post-processing are not sufficient processing, and obtain origin when the parts are sent to the country for assembly. If 3D printing becomes a widespread manufacturing process, it may simplify manufacturing, but it may not simplify origin determination.

We can begin to examine the role of the 3D file in determining the origin of a 3D printed good. If the 3D file is the input with the most value, how will that change the origin analysis of the final good in relation to the tangible inputs. If, as Dinh proposes, smart manufacturing requires acknowledging the role of service inputs, and thus the origin of those inputs, how does one proceed with the origin analysis for the final product? To begin this analysis, a question that must be addressed is whether it is possible to apply the "substantial transformation" criteria to a 3D file.

3 Determining the Origin of a 3D Printed Good under CTH with Service and Tangible Inputs

As a preliminary step, it is necessary to recall some fundamental distinctions between RoO for services and RoO for goods. An important difference is that under the GATS framework the origin of a service is determined by the legal nationality of the service supplier, while under the RoO regime for goods, the

79 Stefano Inama, *Rules of Origin in International Trade* (CUP 2022) 171.

80 ibid.

location where the most economic value was created is a key determinant of origin.[81] There is disagreement on whether it is possible to apply the "substantial transformation" criteria to services. Dinh proposes that as more and more products become hybrids of goods and services, the "common characteristics between goods and services may permit an importation of RoO for goods into the field of services trade to facilitate a 'product-based' approach."[82] However, this may mean reconsidering the meaning of the word "transformation" in the context of RoO. Hoekman concludes that the substantial transformation test and change in tariff heading criteria are "not workable in the services context."[83] Presuming that a service does not exist before it is sold, "most trade in services will be 'substantial transformations' of whatever inputs are used."[84] Likewise, the insufficient information regarding the production of services and their non-storability also makes it difficult to assess whether and when any change occurred.[85] Zampetti and Sauvé, in 2006, also asserted that the substantial transformation test and the change of tariff heading criteria cannot function for services.[86]

Dinh's response is that these scholars incorrectly identify the CTH criterion as distinct from substantial transformation rather than considering the CTH as a subset of the substantial transformation criteria.[87] "Substantial transformation" in the context of RoO for goods means that the changes occurring to the materials and inputs create a sufficient level of economic value in the territory. If one considers the activity of the creation of the service from the perspective of generating economic value, it is not impossible to apply a form of the substantial transformation test to services: the origin of the service is where the last significant economic activity occurred.[88] We can identify through an origin analysis of a 3D printed good whether it is feasible to apply a criterion similar to the CTH to a service input.

81 Dinh (1) 98–99.

82 ibid 145.

83 Hoekman, 'Rules of Origin for Goods and Services' (n 78) 89.

84 ibid.

85 ibid.

86 Americo Beviglia Zampetti and Pierre Sauvé, 'Rules of Origin for Services: Economic and Legal Considerations,' in Olivier Cadot, Antoni Estevadeordal, Akiko Suwa-Eisenmann, and Theirry Verdier (eds), *The Origin of Goods: Rules of Origin in Regional Trade Agreements* (OUP 2006) 119; Dinh (n 1) 146.

87 Dinh (n 1) 147.

88 ibid 149.

3.1 *Differences between Classification of Services under* GATS *and Classification of Goods under the* HS

Although the service classification system under GATS serves a classification function like the HS Nomenclature, it is not interchangeable in its framework and purpose. Under the GATS, each Member's Schedule of Commitments and the Sectorial Classification List are based on the Central Product Classification system overseen by the United Nations Statistical Commission.[89] In a Member's schedule, the services are categorized under 12 broad categories of sectors and then under subcategories; however, a service may not be categorized in more than one sector or subsector.[90] "Horizontal" commitments on limitations or undertakings apply to all of the sectors listed in the schedule.[91] The Member also indicates any limitations on market access or national treatment of a particular service sector based on the mode of supply of the service ("Vertical" commitments).[92] Such commitments are the results of negotiations among Members to reduce or eliminate barriers to market access.[93] However, many Members maintain significant limitations to market access in service sectors.[94] Service sectors that are not listed in a Member's schedule are not liberalized and are not subject to the specific commitments listed in the schedule.[95] Further, Members can indicate which sectors are subject to MFN exemptions.[96] Finally, a Member may modify a commitment after 3 years of its entry into force, provided that the Member enters into negotiations on compensatory adjustments with any Members whose benefits are being modified.[97]

On the other hand, the classification of goods serves distinct purposes both at the level of the WTO and at the level of a Member's custom office. Similar to

89 WTO, 'Guide to reading the GATS schedules of specific commitments and the list of article II (MFN) exemptions' (wto.org)<https://www.wto.org/english/tratop_e/serv_e/guide1_e.htm> accessed 24 October 24 The Sectorial Classification List and the 1993 Guidelines are "supplementary means of interpretation" under VCLT art 32(a) (Vienna Convention on the Law of Treaties (VCLT) (entered into force 27 January 1980) 1155 UNTS 331).

90 M Matsushita, TJ Schoenbaum, PC Mavroidis, M Hahn, *The World Trade Organization: Law, Practice, and Policy* (3rd edn, OUP 2017)(referred to as Matsushita) 560–561.

91 WTO, 'Guide to reading the GATS schedule of specific commitments' (n 89).

92 ibid.

93 Peter Van den Bossche and Werner Zdouc, *The Law and Policy of the World Trade Organization: Text, Cases and Materials* (4th edn, CUP 2019) 521–523.

94 Dinh (n 1) 21.

95 Matsushita (n 90) 586; Ines Willemyns, 'GATS Classification of Digital Services – Does "The Cloud" Have a Silver Lining?' (2019) 53 J World Trade 59, 64.

96 WTO, "Guide to reading the GATS schedule of specific commitments" (n 89).

97 General Agreement on Trade in Services (GATS)(15 April 1994) LT/UR/A-1B/S/1, art XXI.

the GATS, under the GATT, tariff levels are determined through negotiations, whether through a multilateral round of negotiations under the principle of reciprocity or through specific undertakings such as the Information Technology Agreement (ITA).[98] The Schedule of Concessions that each WTO Member enters into upon accession to the WTO is based on the HS.[99] This schedule identifies the bound tariff rate that each Member agrees to uphold: the Member will not raise tariffs above this rate.[100] The Member may choose to lower this MFN tariff rate; however, states may be cautious not to lower the rate to the level of any preferential tariffs in a PTA, as this would diminish the margin of preferences granted to PTA partners.[101] Some members have indicated bound tariffs for nearly all heading lines at low rates, while developing countries tend to bind tariffs for fewer heading lines and with higher rates.[102] If a good does not appear in the Schedule of Concessions, the Member is still required to comply with the GATT national treatment and MFN obligations with respect to trade of that good. A Member can modify or withdraw a concession through negotiations with other Members, but under certain conditions and restrictions.[103] A Member's Schedule of Concessions is changed frequently: 1) whenever a new Member accedes to the WTO, 2) whenever the HS code is updated, and 3) after sectorial negotiations, such as those for the ITA.[104]

While the HS nomenclature and the UN nomenclature provide systems for classifying goods and services (respectively), new digital products require traders, trade lawyers, and trade policymakers to determine what classification system to use, which is an act of interpretation.[105] Smith and Woods argue (in the general context of WTO law), that the decision of which classification methodology to use impacts which WTO law applies, but the HS and the UN classification systems do not necessarily consider WTO goals of trade liberalization."[106] The issue of sovereignty also arises when Members decide which products to

98 van den Bossche and Zdouc (n 93) 424–436.

99 'World Tariff Profiles 2023' (WTO, ITC & UNCTAD 2023) 2. <https://www.wto.org/english/res_e/publications_e/world_tariff_profiles23_e.htm> accessed 10 March 2025.

100 WTO, 'What is a WTO Schedule' (*Goods Schedules e-Library*) <https://goods-schedules.wto.org/what-is-a-wto-schedule> accessed 24 October 2021.

101 Matsushita (n 90) 510.

102 'World Tariff Profiles 2023' (n 99) 2.

103 van den Bossche and Zdouc (n 93) 447–450.

104 WTO, 'Schedules of Concessions,' (WTO.org) <https://www.wto.org/english/tratop_e/schedules_e/goods_schedules_e.htm> accessed 24 October 2021.

105 F Smith and L Woods 'A Distinction without a Difference: Exploring the Boundary between Goods and Services in the World Trade Organization and the European Union' (2005) 12 Columbia J Eur L 1, 18.

106 ibid 19.

include in GATT and GATS schedules and a Member may choose to classify a product which could be a good or service under one of the methodologies on the basis of a domestic political consideration.[107]

The AB has determined that a boundary exists between GATT and GATS measures, but it has not established definitive rules on how to draw the boundary line. The decision is made on a case-by-case basis and the Member must explain and provide evidence supporting that the measure affects trade in goods or in services.[108] If no dispute is raised, then the classification decision of the Members or international organizations is not in question.[109] However, taking away the classification decision from a Member during a dispute, Smith and Woods argue, "in circumstances where it does not wish to make a commitment in a specific service sector undermines its sovereignty over decisions it had not ceded to the WTO."[110]

The points raised by Woods and Smith resonate with the points raised in Chapter 1 regarding Annex II of AOR on preferential RoO. The HS nomenclature is nearly always the nomenclature used in product specific rules; thus, preferential RoO are linked to a system that is independent of the WTO. The AOR, by only providing guidelines for preferential RoO, allows Members sovereignty in designing them. Deciding whether a product is a good and is subject to a preferential tariff is an act of classification, an act over which Members retain a significant degree of sovereignty. Thus, by relying on the HS Nomenclature, which is removed from the WTO, preferential RoOs become even more removed from the scope of the WTO. As the next Chapter will show, trying to bring RoOs within the multilateral system and designing RoOs that apply to both goods and services will entail a reexamination of the tenacity of Members' sovereignty on RoO.

Ines Willemyns identifies three elements in connection with GATS classification[111] which highlight the distinction between services classification and goods classification under the HS system. First, "GATS classification is based upon the outputs provided by service suppliers. Footnote 9 to the GATS excludes input services from the market access obligation in Article XVI GATS."[112] Rules of origin using the CTH based on the HS look at the inputs involved in the

107 ibid.

108 Matsushita (n 90) 559–60, 566, referencing, Appellate Body Report, *European Communities - Regime for the Importation, Sale and Distribution of Bananas* (9 September 1997, adopted 25 September 1997) WT/DS27/AB/R, para 221.

109 Smith and Woods (n 105) 22.

110 ibid.

111 Willemyns (n 95) 68.

112 ibid.

production of the good: has an input undergone enough processing in the territory to result in a product categorized in a different heading or subheading.[113]

Secondly, according to Willemyns, with its decision in *China-Audiovisuals*, "the Appellate Body opened the door to an evolutionary interpretation of Members' commitments."[114] The AB in *China-Audiovisuals* found that China's GATS Schedule included sound recording services distributed over the internet, although at the time the Schedule was concluded, the term "distribution" was intended to mean distribution through tangible items such as CDs.[115] According to the AB, the terms in the GATS schedule were "sufficiently generic" and what they could be applied to "may change over time."[116] Limiting their meaning to the time when the Schedule was adopted would mean that "very similar or identically worded commitments" in the Schedules of different Members "could be given different meanings" depending on the date of adoption or the date of a Member's ascension to the treaty.[117] This would "undermine the predictability, security, and clarity of the GATS."[118] Pauwelyn, Guzman, and Hillman note that the AB was able to reach this decision because it based "its textual and contextual interpretation of the words in [the phrase 'sound recording distribution services'], rather than with reference to broader criteria of 'services' and 'goods.'"[119] Willemyns acknowledges the scholarly debate as to whether *China-Audiovisuals* allows for covering new services in existing commitments and whether digital services are in fact a new breed of service or "merely the 'digitised' versions of already existing services."[120]

On the other hand, there is no similar evolutionary interpretation of the HS code. The HS code is updated every five years by WCO, which takes into consideration requests from the private sector to incorporate new products into the code.[121] For example, as there was no HS code for additive manufacturing machines, CECIMO, an industry group, coordinated with the European

113 Dinh (n 1) 118.

114 Willemyns (n 95) 68–69.

115 Appellate Body Report, *China – Measures Affecting Trading Rights and Distribution Services for Certain Publications and Audiovisual Entertainment Products* (21 December 2009) WT/DS363/AB/R paras 338–372, 386–397.

116 ibid para 396.

117 ibid para 397.

118 ibid.

119 Joost HB Pauwelyn, Andrew T Guzman, Jennifer A Hillman *International Trade Law* (3rd edn, WoltersKluwer 2016) 694.

120 Willemyns (n 95) 69.

121 WCO, 'Amending the HS' (wcoomd.org) <http://www.wcoomd.org/en/topics/nomenclature/activities-and-programmes/amending_hs.aspx> accessed 24 October 2021.

Commission in proposing to WCO a new code for these machines; WCO accepted the proposal and a code was included in the 2022 revisions.[122] This updating of the HS nomenclature also helps to avoid WTO members from taking reclassification initiatives independently that may violate GATT Articles II:3 and II:5, which prohibits reclassification that impairs the value of any of the concessions in the Schedule of Commitments.[123] For example, by reclassifying goods, Members could place like goods in different headings; thus, previously "like" products could be given discriminatory treatment without violating GATT Article I on the basis that they are no longer under the same HS heading.[124] If no new HS is created for a new product, Members could strategically classify the product with existing products based on certain characteristics and this could result in impeding market access to certain Members or nullifying a trade concession.[125]

Third, Willemyns proposes that an "integrated approach" in classifying services within the GATS should be applied rather than "distinguishing the production of the service from its distribution" as "the GATS defines the supply of a service as including its production, distribution, marketing, sale, and delivery of a service."[126] Under the application of the HS for custom duties and in tariff schedules, how a finished good is imported or exported or how an input is distributed to a manufacturer has no influence on determining what heading or sub-heading the good or input falls under.[127]

There are some fundamental differences between the approach to classifying services using the GATS framework. The approach to classifying goods under the HS complicates incorporating the origin of a service input into the origin analysis for a 3D printed good under the CTH criterion. As the first step in determining the origin of the 3D file is determining what type of service it is, some classification system for services is required. However, the GATS classification system and the HS do not have the same objectives in identifying a product and where it is should be categorized within the system. While the

122 CECIMO, 'Press Release: CECIMO Appreciates the Approval of a New Product Nomenclature Standard for Additive Manufacturing Machines' (cecimo.eu 25 April 2019) <https://www.cecimo.eu/news/press-release-cecimo-appreciates-the-approval-of-a-new-product-nomenclature-standard-for-additive-manufacturing-machines/> accessed 24 October 2021. CECIMO is the European Association of the Machine Tool Industries and related Manufacturing Technologies.

123 Matsushita (n 90) 230.

124 ibid.

125 ibid.

126 Willemyns (n 95) 69.

127 Van de Heetkamp and Tusveld (n 23) 7.

GATS classification system can be used to classify a service input, when combined with an origin analysis of the tangible inputs under the HS nomenclature, a truly hybrid origin analysis results, a legal Minotaur with the head of GATS and the body of the HS.

3.2 *Do 3D Files Undergo Substantial Processing or a Substantial Transformation?*

Rather than progressing down that legal puzzle, let us look at some other aspects that demonstrate why it will be difficult to apply the CTH criterion to determine the origin of 3D printed good when considering the 3D file as a manufacturing input. First, we must assume (1) the creation of a 3D file is a type of service covered by GATS and (2) we have been able to determine the origin of this service. The next step is to consider whether processing that occurs to the file is like the processing of a good that triggers a change of tariff heading or sub-heading under the product-specific rules of a PTA.

First, the 3D file for a 3D printed good is something intangible that nonetheless is preserved as a file. The service is not transitory, but persists as a file that is transmitted and then downloaded into the 3D printing machine. Is the step of going from the 3D file creation to the downloading of the file into the machine a substantial transformation? This is where the concept of processing plays a role.

It could be arguable that the creation of the 3D file is like a harvesting a raw coffee bean that has potential to be transformed into a roasted coffee bean. It is not universally accepted that roasting coffee confers origin on the coffee bean based on where such roasting takes place. However, at least in the US[128] such processing is sufficient to confer origin. Thus, it could be argued that a 3D file is similar to a coffee bean: the file that has the potential to be a 3D good (i.e., raw bean) transforms into the realization of a 3D good (roasted bean) by means of printing (roasting). A trader who obtains a file from another country could still claim that sufficient processing of the 3D file occurred by the act of printing the good. Beyond requiring international lawmakers, custom officials, and traders to compare digital code transmissions to roasting of coffee, this examples also shows how trying to integrate a service input into the CTH or operating process would complicate origin determination.

Another way to think about this issue is: when going from a digital blueprint to printed parts is there a CTH capable of being a substantial transformation under the CTH criteria? This would require treating data as a form of electricity

128 CBP, *Notice of Issuance of Final Determination Concerning Roasted Coffee* (21 November 2017) 82 Federal Register 55387, 55387-55388.

(as Neeraj proposes)[129] and thus classifying the 3D file under the HS code for electricity. Downloading the file, which instructs the machine to operate, and later obtaining a printed part seems like a transformation. However, let us think about this transformation from the perspective of a printed blueprint. Under the HS, hand drawn originals or photocopies of "plans for drawings for architectural, engineering, industrial, commercial, topographical or similar purposes", fall under heading 4906. "Other printed matter," which could potentially include paper copies of blueprints created with a CAD program, fall under 4911. We have a blueprint for a gear for a vehicle. Under PEM sufficient processing occurs for when there is "Manufacture from materials of any heading, except that of the product."[130] Would the act of looking at the CAD printout and comprehending how to manually calibrate a machine to pour metal to form a gear constitute a CTH? This would suggest that human thought is sufficient processing; a type of processing that the HS is not designed to capture. There is no tariff line (yet) for human or AI thought processing. Thus, it is questionable whether downloading a digital blueprint into a machine which, using computer reasoning, imparts instructions to print a good is substantial transformation under the CTH criterion.[131] Further, under the PEM, energy, fuel and other goods [such as electricity] "which do not enter, and which are not intended to enter, into the final composition of the product" are not taken into account in the origin analysis of the good.[132]

At this point, we have entered a legal and linguistic labyrinth and the best way to exit is to direct our focus on whether a service input can be factored into an *ad valorem* origin analysis. First, we will examine the practice of determining the value of a good considering only the tangible inputs in the context of the printing and processing process. Next, we will consider factoring in the value of the design of the 3D file in the origin determination. However, this will require understanding how much value a 3D file has. Then, we can then try to integrate it into the origin determination for a 3D printed good. This will lead us to a concluding question: even if it is possible to add the value of a service

129 RS Neeraj in 'Trade Rules for the Digital Economy: Charting New Waters at the WTO' (2018) 18 World Trade Rev (2Supp) s126s, 128.

130 PEM Annex II, Product Specific Rule, 8708.

131 Neeraj (n 129) 128, proposes that as "electricity, which is essentially the flow of electrons, falls under the Harmonized System of Tariff Nomenclature (HS 2716.00) and, for the purpose of WTO law, electricity comes under the purview of GATT" there is "no reason to treat the flow of data differently from that of the flow of electricity for the purposes of classification under international trade law."

132 PEM App 1, art 11. Other RoO instruments also indicate such "neutral elements."

input to the value of the inputs traditionally used to determine origin, is that a practice that creates a more or less predictable trading environment?

4 *Ad Valorem* Criterion: Which Input Has the Most Value and Where Is It Created?

As discussed in Chapter 2, the *ad valorem* approach is used to determine whether a good meets the regional value content requirement (RVC) or the value added (VA) threshold indicated in a PTA. An RVC or an VA threshold percentage is sometimes included as an additional requirement to a CTH for a particular good. In determining this percentage, the value of the raw materials will likely always be included.[133] This requires distinguishing the value of the non-originating materials from the value of domestic or regional materials.[134] However, a PTA will not always specify how to determine the value of a particular material. The PEM,[135] USMCA, and CETA for example indicate that the "value of the materials" is the "customs value" as determined under the Customs Valuation Agreement (CVA).[136] As the Agreement distinguishes materials from "engineering, development, artwork, design work, plans and sketches", this likely excludes factoring in the value of a CAD file into the total value of materials.

The ex-works price or transaction value (if using the CVA as a basis for determining the overall value of the product) requires the importer to identify the price paid or payable to the producer.[137] This price incorporates fixed costs, such as the rent or mortgage for the factory, insurance, maintenance, interest paid for capital goods used in production of the good, direct overhead costs, and rental costs or operation costs required to use a machine or a space in a factory for production of the good.[138] The price payable can also incorporate the costs of research and design expenditures, such as salaries or wages, related to the product if including such costs is part of the ordinary course

133 van de Heetkamp and Tuveld (n 23) 84.

134 ibid 87–88.

135 PEM app I, title I, art 1 (definitions).

136 Agreement On Implementation Of Article VII Of The General Agreement On Tariffs And Trade 1994 (Customs Valuation Agreement) (CVA) (15 April 1994) LT/UR/A-1A/4, art 8(1)(b).

137 PEM app I, title I art 1 (definitions).

138 Van de Heetkamp and Tuveld (n 21) 85–87; Will Kenton, 'Direct Costs' (*Investopedia* 27 June 2020) <https://www.investopedia.com/terms/d/directcost.asp> accessed 24 October 2021.

of trade.[139] Thus, it may be possible to include costs related to the design of 3D file, such as the wages of the designers, in this category. If an instrument requires the net cost method, sales promotion, marketing, and after sales services are not included in the calculation.[140] For the purposes of comparing the origin of a 3D printed good with that of traditionally manufactured good using an *ad valorem* criterion, we will look at this from a high level and not delve into the weeds of cumulation.

4.1 *Value of Traditional Manufacturing Inputs: Materials, Labor, and Direct Overhead*

The following inputs are significant for the *ad valorem* criterion: the raw material that is processed (value of materials), human labor that produces the good (direct labor), and the costs to operate the factory in which the good is produced (direct overhead).[141] Looking at these three inputs suggests that when the *ad valorem* criterion is applied to a 3D printed good, the origin may differ from when the criterion is applied to a similar good produced though traditional manufacturing.

4.1.1 Value of Materials and Ink

Let us start with the value of materials. Much of the raw material, "ink", for 3D printed goods are proprietary mixes of plastics or metals. The value of any non-originating material is the customs value, i.e., the price payable or paid for the goods when sold or imported.[142] To determine the value of "ink" for purposes of tariff treatment, the producer must assess the value of any non-originating materials, the value of any originating materials, manufacturing costs, and any

139 van de Heetkamp and Tuveld (n 23) 86; Ian Forrester and Omar E Odarda, 'The Agreement on Customs Valuation' in Patrick F J Macrory, Arthur Edmond Appleton and Michael G Plummer (eds), *World Trade Organization: Legal, Economic and Political Analysis* (Springer 2005) 538, 549.

140 The USMCA requires the Net Cost method to determine the RVC for motor vehicles. When determining the annual quota of exports of motor vehicles from Canada to the EU, sufficient production on the non-originating materials must be determined. This is satisfied when "production in which the value of all non-originating materials used does not exceed: (a) 70 per cent of the transaction value or ex-works price of the product; or (b) 80 per cent of the net cost of the product. CETA requires the Net Cost method to determine the quota allocation." Comprehensive and Economic Trade Agreement (CETA) (signed 30 October 2016, some provisions entered into force on 21 September 2017), Protocol on Rules of Origin and Origin Procedure, Table D. 1.

141 *See* eg, USMCA art 4.5, and definition for "total cost."

142 *See* eg, CETA, Protocol on Rules of Origin and Origin Procedure, s A, "value of non-originating material".

transportation costs. Plastic resins and mixes of metal for professional use are costly to produce as (1) the materials are rare or (2) created by specific providers for use with locked-in machines.[143] Thus, the ink will likely be a significant input of the total value of the 3D printed good.[144]

A key factor is the where the material is sourced. In a report produced for the EU Commission's Executive Agency for SMEs, the researchers identified that aluminum, titanium, and magnesium were critical material for ink.[145] While the EU is a producer of aluminum, there is no significant production of magnesium or titanium in the EU.[146] Russia, China, Japan, and Kazakhstan are producers of titanium[147] and Russia, China, Kazakhstan, the US, Brazil, Israel, and Turkey are producers of magnesium.[148] As the EU Commission promotes 3D printing to reshore manufacturing, let us consider what impact the sources of these metals may have on an origin determination of a product printed in the EU. With respect to titanium, these source countries are not members of the PEM. Even if the metal powder is produced in the EU, if the value of the raw metal exceeds any value incurred processing the metal, then the metal-powder is a costly non-originating material. If there are no original

143 3D Learning Hub, 'How Much Does 3D Printing Cost' (Sculpteo 2024) <https://www.sculpteo.com/en/3d-learning-hub/basics-of-3d-printing/how-much-to-3d-print/> accessed 25 March 2024; Flores Ituarte, Khajavi and Salmi (n 601) 48; The European Economic and Social Committee was critical of the lock-in distribution method for ink-printers, as it requires the use of expensive raw materials, limits supply, and decreases incentives for businesses to develop new materials. Eur Economic & Social Committee, Opinion of the European Economic and Social Committee, 'Living tomorrow. 3D printing (n 11) para. 3.2.3.

144 National Board of Trade, 'Trade Regulation in a 3D Printed World' (n 27) 27.

145 Duchêne V and others, *Identifying Current and Future Application Areas, Existing Industrial Value Chains and Missing Competences in the EU, in the Area of Additive Manufacturing (3D printing)* Final Report for the Commission Executive Agency for Small & Medium-Sized Enterprises (Publications Office Eur Union 2016) 21 <https://data.europa.eu/doi/10.2826/72202> accessed 8 January 2022.

146 ibid. A report for the Executive Agency for SME of the Commission notes, "The strengths of Europe in metal 3D printing are therefore dependent on materials that are sourced outside of Europe." There is a potential for Europe to produce recycled aluminum metal for 3D printing. D Kretz and E Van de Velde, *Advanced Technologies for Industry - Product Watch: 3D Printing of Hybrid Components*, Report for the Commission Executive Agency for Small & Medium-sized Enterprises (Publications Office Eur Union 2021) 20, <https://data.europa.eu/doi/10.2826/581451> accessed 8 May 2022.

147 Ike Brannon, 'Titanium Production's Perilous U.S. Future' (*Forbes* 29 April 2019) <https://www.forbes.com/sites/ikebrannon/2019/04/29/titanium-productions-perilous-u-s-future/?sh=652a00776a72> accessed 24 October 2021.

148 International Magnesium Association, 'About Magnesium' (intlmag.org) <https://www.intlmag.org/page/basics_about_mg_ima> accessed 8 January 2022.

materials incorporated into the powder, then all of the ink, and thus, all of the value of the material, is non-originating value. On the other hand, if the metal powder incorporates magnesium to a significant extent sourced from Israel and Turkey, the powder may qualify as originating material in a PEM Contracting Party. Identifying the geographical source of the material and its value may become further complex if firms, such as Ford and Nissan have begun to do, re-use spent 3D powder for printing parts to make 3D printing a more sustainable form of manufacturing.[149]

This example demonstrates two outcomes for determining the origin of a 3D printed product: 1) under bilateral agreements between parties that are not providers of raw materials, there is a likelihood that ink may be a non-originating material with a high value; or 2) under regional trade agreements, there is a greater possibility that the powder or a resin mix can qualify as originating material, provided that one of the countries are a main source for the ingredients of the powder or mix. If the geographic pool established by the PTA includes several countries, this increases the likelihood that one of the metals will be local material, and a trader seeking to import 3D printed goods to other PTA states may not find any increased restrictiveness of the rules. On the other hand, under a small geographic pool, a trader may find that they have to source the materials from third parties, reducing the percentage of local content incorporated into the 3D printed good. Even if the trader can meet a Labor Value Content rule, the rules may still be more effectively restrictive for 3D printing, because 3D printing also reduces the amount of local labor required to produce the good.

4.1.2 Labor Value – How Much Human Labor Does It Take to Produce a 3D Good?

3D printing analysts portend the reduction of labor in the production stage, processing stage, and assembly stage. While training the workforce to operate 3D printers and post-processing equipment will take time, funding, and effort,[150] once such training is complete, the time and effort to produce a 3D good is expected to be less than the labor required to produce traditionally manufactured goods.[151] This returns to the question of whether there is

149 David Greenfield, 'Ford and Nissan Use HP 3D Printing to Address Production Sustainability,' (May 2021) Automotion World 20–22 <https://www.automationworld.com/factory/3d-printing-additive-manufacturing/article/21366376/ford-and-nissan-use-hp-3d-printing-to-address-production-sustainability> accessed 10 March 2025.

150 Osborn (n 2) 25; Eur Economic & Social Committee, 'Living Tomorrow. 3D printing' (n 11) para 3.4.

151 Flores Ituarte, Khajavi and Salmi (n 10) 36–37, 57; Abeliansky, Martínez-Zarsoso and Prettner (n 15) 289.

sufficient processing during the printing and post-processing process so as to be a "substantial transformation" and confer origin on the printed good. Further, RoO may eventually need to take into account how much artificial intelligence (AI) contributes to the value creation of the 3D printed product. As Grant Cohen reports, "automation may be a bigger structural threat to labor than trade" and AI will require states to redefine how they provide for the welfare of workers.[152] This impact on labor could arise in the context of additive manufacturing.

While the EU and the US see 3D printing as a means to increase manufacturing jobs, 3D printer manufacturers and users, however, look towards AI to reduce the human labor component of the processing and post-processing procedures in 3D printing.[153] As Flores Ituarte, Khajavi, and Salmi write "[m]ore and more of these kinds of solutions will open up new markets for 3D printing in high scale manufacturing."[154] Thus, as the extent of human labor in processing diminishes, the role the value of labor plays in determining origin also diminishes. The simplification of production, processing, and assembly praised by industrialists and analysts in the context of 3D printing has a different outlook from the perspective of RoO within the context of deeper trade instruments that incorporate provisions meant to protect labor. A low level of human labor in 3D printing is an example of how developments in technology can increase efficiency in manufacturing. Traders and producers may choose such efficiency over meeting preferential tariff rate requirements and trade under the MFN rates, or choose to focus on foreign markets that do not have RoO with labor provisions.

4.1.3 Direct Overhead Costs and New Business Models for 3D Printing

Finally, 3D printing may generate less direct overhead costs than traditional manufacturing. One of the main limitations for a widespread adoption of 3D printing is the cost of the machines and the limited range of suppliers, although prices are gradually decreasing and more vendors are entering the market.[155] 3D printing promises to reduce the unit cost of producing a good because less waste is produced and it is easier to customize or modify the production of

152 Harlan Grant Cohen, 'What is International Trade Law For?' (2019) 113 The American J Intl L 326, 342.

153 Flores Ituarte, Khajavi and Salmi (n 10) 59; Adam Zewe, 'AI-driven tool makes it easy to personalize 3D-printable models' (MIT News 15 September 2023) <https://news.mit.edu/2023/ai-driven-tool-personalize-3d-printable-models-0915> accessed 23 March 2024.

154 Flores Ituarte, Khajavi and Salmi (n 10) 59.

155 ibid 49; Abeliansky, Martínez-Zarsoso and Prettner (n 15) 289.

the good than in traditional manufacturing.[156] Further, the current practice in the 3D printing industry of Fab Labs or using third-party providers to print the good rather than purchasing a machine also has an impact on reducing the direct overhead of producing the 3D printed good. A manufacturer may assign the task of printing to a retailer in order to produce the goods closer to the local market and save on transportation costs.[157] A manufacturer may also seek out a third-party company that rents the excess capacity of its machines to be closer to a geographical market or to avoid purchasing machines or rental space for housing such machines.[158] This suggests two things: 1) direct overhead costs may be less than traditional manufacturing direct overhead costs, if using a printing method that is more efficient; and 2) the geographical location of where a good is printed may be a strategic firm decision based on how close the printing venue is to the market the manufacturer wishes to reach. This last point may not have an impact on the firm if the good is sold in the local market of the printer. However, if the firm wishes to export that good to a foreign market, such strategic decisions may have an impact on whether the good qualifies for preferential tariff treatment when the value of direct overhead is compared to the value of other inputs.

In conclusion, as 3D printing promises to reduce labor and direct overhead costs to operate machinery, but as the costs of ink will likely continue to be high given the complexity of the materials, the value of materials could be more influential in determining where the value of the good is created. Reshoring of manufacturing by 3D printing without adopting or increasing the domestic or regional production of ink, may result in the production of printed goods in the territory that have an origin based on the origin of the ink. If the ink's origin is a territory not part of the PTA that the manufacturer wishes to take advantage of, then the manufacturer will be required to pay MFN tariffs or the tariff rate under a PTA with the territory where the ink originates. If the 3D file and research and engineering conducted for developing the 3D printed product are included as part of the price payable under direct costs, this may result in origin being designated on the basis of where such costs occurred.

Yet, the greatest value creation in a 3D printed good may not lie in the printing process, but in the 3D file. If true, this requires us to take two steps before incorporating the value of the file into the *ad valorem* analysis for determining the origin of the good: 1) assign some sort of quantifiable value to the file, and

156 Flores Ituarte, Khajavi and Salmi (n 10) 36–37, 58; Abeliansky, Martínez-Zarsoso and Prettner (n 15) 289.

157 Arbabian and Wagner (n 50) 539.

158 Flores Ituarte, Khajavi and Salmi (n 10) 58.

2) identify the origin of that file. While the trade law literature is mostly silent on determining the monetary value of the file, the intellectual property law field provides some starting points for understanding why the 3D file may be the most valuable input in 3D printing.

4.2 *Value of the 3D File*

An IP right is an intangible asset that can be assigned a monetary value. IP rights include copyright, patents, trademarks, designs, and trade secrets. While scholarship in this field is still exploring what type of IP right a 3D file is,[159] there are some general aspects about IP rights as an asset that could allow us to think of the 3D file as an asset with a potential monetary value. According to the World Intellectual Property Office (WIPO), "The value of an IP asset essentially comes from the right the owner of that asset has to exclude competitors from using it. For an IP asset to have a quantifiable value it should: generate a measurable amount of economic benefits to its owner/user; and enhance the value of other assets with which it is associated."[160] Such value "can be derived through: direct exploitation of the IP by integrating it within the product; sale or licensing of the IP to a third party; and other means, such as raising barriers to entry or reducing the threat of substitutes."[161] The value can be calculated by estimating the economic income the IP right is expected to generate, the price paid to transfer ownership of a similar IP right, or the cost of a similar or identical IP asset.[162]

It is important to note that this valuation is not intended to quantify how much economic value is generated in the creation of the IP right; we are not calculating the cost of labor, materials, and direct overhead that went into drawing the figure, or designing the software, or inventing the patentable subject matter. Further, the particular design technology determines how much human effort goes into the creation of the file. Designing a 3D file using software programs such as CAD is relatively less labor intensive than using a 3D

159 ibid 16–18; Mikko Antikainen and Daniël Jongsma, 'The Art of CAD: Copyrightability of Digital Design Files' in Rosa Maria Ballardini, Marcus Norrgård, Jouni Partanen (eds), *3D Printing, Intellectual Property and Innovation: Insights from Law and Technology* (WoltersKluwer 2017) 257–274; Nordberg and Schovsbo (n 2) 275–302.

160 World Intellectual Property Office, 'Valuing Intellectual Property Assets' (WIPO.int), <https://www.wipo.int/en/web/business/ip-valuation#:~:text=The%20value%20of%20an%20IP,with%20which%20it%20is%20associated> accessed 10 March 2025.

161 ibid.

162 ibid; D Sharma and A Kumar, 'Methods for Intellectual Property Valuation' in Irene Calboli and Maria Lillà Montagnani ed., *Handbook on Intellectual Property Research* (OUP 2021) 599–602.

scanner to create a 3D file of an existing object.[163] In their article on the impact of 3D printing on EU design law, Ana Nordberg and Jens Schovsbo state that "Creating a CAD file can be as easy as taking a picture and using an app on a mobile phone.[164]" However, the user must still clean up the file or fill in missing information, which requires skill and effort.[165] Thus, IP valuation is not a perfect paragon to the type of value quantified in RVC or Value Added Thresholds for goods.

Yet, we need to understand in what way the file is a valuable asset. If a highly-paid GE engineer designs a file for printing the part of an engine of a plane, one could claim that the value of the file is equivalent to how much the engineer was paid. On the other hand, a designer at an SME who is paid a fraction of a GE engineer's wages, designs a 3D file for a particular innovative product. Is this file worth less because the designer is paid less? What if this innovative product becomes a highly sought after product, one that people will be willing to pay above market rate for?

IP valuation allows us to understand that the value of an intangible asset resides in its ability to generate income by the utilization of that asset. A 3D file's worth can be derived by integrating it within the production chain of a product, by selling or licensing the file to a third party who then downloads the file and prints the good, or by reducing competition (for example, the file for a lightweight bicycle made of printed parts that has a particular innovative function that makes these bicycles impossible to reproduce without the file). Osborn states that once 3D printing becomes widespread, "digital objects will have almost as much value as tangible objects, and in some ways will embody more value" as multiple copies of the tangible object can be printed from the file.[166] It is not exactly clear if this is the type of value trade analysts are thinking of when making references to the value of a 3D file.[167] Yet, the value of a 3D file can be associated with how much potential income it can generate by being the set of instructions used to print multiple goods or to customize a certain good for multiple consumers.[168] A business, as a part of its overall risk management and planning strategy, may perform an IP valuation analysis for its IPR portfolio,[169] which could include the IPRs associated with the 3D file

163 Antikainen and Jognsma (n 159) 260–261.
164 Nordberg and Schovsbo (n 2) 298.
165 Antikainen and Jognsma (n 159) 261; Osborn (n 3) 37.
166 Osborn (n 3) 17.
167 Neeraj (n 129) s126.
168 Norberg and Schovsbo (n 2) 281.
169 Jennifer McCollough, 'The Basics in Valuation of Intellectual Property Assets' Federal Lawyer 64 (August 2017) 7–10.

design. Thus, the owner of the 3D file input may already have such information available to use for a RoO analysis.

In the traditional manufacturing sector, IPR owners generally grant an exclusive or other type of license with limitations to manufacturers not only to keep a close watch over who is using the IPR, but also to protect against product liability claims that could arise from use of the product incorporating the IP. This is especially relevant for trademarks, which represent a certain level of standard of quality,[170] and designs which provide the patterns for the products.[171] Thus for IP right owners who have worked with traditional manufacturers in industries such as the automotive, aerospace, and medical products industries, these IPR owners may continue to closely control which additive manufacturers use 3D files to print products with trademarks by granting licenses which indemnify or limit liability for defective products.[172] In this scenario, it would be relatively imaginable, given a close relationship between the IPR owner and the manufacturer, to determine the economic value of the 3D file because the IPR owner could receive accounting reports from the manufacturers. If it is possible to identify the origin of the 3D file, then by using the economic value identified for the 3D file using IP valuation processes, it may be possible to designate the 3D file as a distinct origin conferring input which contributes value to the finished product under an *ad valorem* formula.

Yet, 3D files are not considered by all industry participants to be an asset that must be exclusive to one owner, and this could impact a 3D file's value. Although the income-method looks to the future, the process itself requires calculations and formulas to arrive at the net present value of the asset.[173] This relies on obtaining the necessary information about the asset, projected cash flow, and the rate of discounting.[174] In sectors focused on products for

---

170 Conrad Weinmann, 'Trademark Licensors and Product Liability Claims - A European Perspective' (2005) The Trademark Reporter 1394.

171 For a design to be granted intellectual property protection, it must be ornamental and not necessary for the product to function. However, this ornamental part may be designed to contribute to the overall safety and functioning of the product. William A. Dreier, "A Question of Liability: Who's to Blame When Products Developed by Licensees Cause Unforeseen … ?", reprinted from (2000) New Jersey LJ April 3 <https://norrismclaughlin.com/articles/category/a-question-of-liability-whos-to-blame-when-products-developed-by-licensees-cause-unforeseen> accessed 25 October 2021.

172 Valentina Nieß and Susanne Wende, 'Intellectual Property and Product Liability Challenges in Three-Dimensional Printing' (2017) 6 IEEE Consumer Electronics Magazine October 128, 128–129.

173 Sharma and Kumar (n 162) 601–602.

174 ibid 606.

individual consumers, the 3D printing industry is one of knowledge-sharing and file-sharing.[175] Platforms such as Thingiverse provide downloadable 3D files that can be modified, reshared with platform users, and then printed by various users.[176] Individuals wishing to customize a certain product can modify the file or go to a 3D printing shop, select materials or provide their own materials, and print the good.[177] Embracing the sharing-culture will require a reassessment of determining the economic value of the 3D file. If multiple, potentially unknown persons will be printing an unknown quantity of goods, with or without modifications, even if a license is required to download the file, the IPR owner would have to keep track of all of the licensees and then follow up with them to find out how many goods were printed and what was ultimately done with the goods. If this process is complicated and time-consuming, and if the number of licensees and printed goods is a constantly changing quantity, it may be challenging to determine the economic value of the 3D file. Given this uncertainty in the economic value of the 3D file and the number of 3D printed goods, Jimena Sotelo and Venkataraman Sundareswaran of the World Economic Forum, propose applying a VAT or sales tax to 3DP files rather a tariff of customs duty on the cross-border transmission of the 3D file.[178]

The challenges discussed in the paragraph above suggest that determining the economic value of the 3D file input is complex. Yet, it is a necessary step. Next, an origin must be assigned to the service input, and this means deciding whether to continue using the GATS framework under Mode 1 or Mode 3. This means identifying who is the provider of the service and pinpointing a specific geographical location from which that service was provided.

---

175 Nordberg and Schovsbo (n 2) 300–301.

176 Flores Ituarte, Khajavi and Salmi (n 10) 43.

177 ibid 53. Due to malleability of 3D files, IP legal practitioners advise IPR owners to develop IP enforcement strategies that take advantage of these aspects of additive manufacturing, not only to protect IP rights, but also to protect public safety. Elizabeth Ferrill and E Robert Yoches, 'IP Law and 3D Printing: Designers Can Work Around Lack of Cover,' (*Wired*) <https://www.wired.com/insights/2013/09/ip-law-and-3d-printing-designers-can-work-around-lack-of-cover/> accessed 25 October 2021 (archived link); Justin E Pierce, 'IP Strategies for the Rise of 3D Printing' (Venable LLP 14 April 2015) <https://www.venable.com/insights/publications/2015/04/ip-strategies-for-the-rise-of-3d-printing> accessed 25 October 2021.

178 Jimena Sotelo and Venkataraman Sundareswaran, 'Would a Digital Border Tax Slow Down Adoption of 3D printing?' (*World Economic Forum* 08 January 2020) <https://www.weforum.org/agenda/2020/01/would-a-digital-border-tax-slow-down-adoption-of-3d-printing/> accessed 25 October 2021.

4.3 *Hybridization of RoO: In Search of the Origin of the Service Input*

GATS RoO were designed primarily to address discrete services which are supplied by one provider based in one country to one customer as a final end product.[179] GATS V:6, in referring to FTAs liberalizing trade in services, specifies that such agreements apply to service suppliers that engage in substantive business operations (SBO) in the territory of the parties.[180] As Pierre Latrille's survey on PTAs reveals, the majority use the GATS terminology in connection with provisions related to the RoOs for services.[181] This may mean that the provisions on determining origin in existing PTAs is not in-synch with the creation and trade of services in the digital trading environment. Just as GVCs and the fragmentation of the processing of goods complicate origin determination of goods, GVCs for services also complicate the origin determination for services under the GATS framework.[182]

Dinh questions whether the GATS-based model of origin based on the territory of the legal supplier is still relevant in the era of hybrid products and GVCs for services inputs.[183] If value is created at multiple points during the creation of a digital product, such as a 3D file, assigning origin to the legal supplier may not adequately identify where the greatest economic value of the service is created.[184] Instead of attaching the GATS RoO supplier-approach to the RoO for goods, he calls for designing an integrated RoO regime over the long term and improving the current RoO for GATS in the short term by clarifying GATS definitions such as service supplier and ownership, as well as ensuring the compliance of PTAs with GATS requirements.[185] Even if some all-in-one goods-services RoO is a long-term goal, it is necessary to start considering the implications of including the value of service inputs into the origin determination of a good and whether some action should be taken in the near future with regards to redesigning RoO.

First, we start with the assumption that the 3D file is the most significant input in terms of value of a 3D file good and this value can be quantified. There is some possibility that the value of the 3D printed could be incorporated into an *ad valorem* analysis as part of the direct overhead costs or other costs. The

179 Dinh (n 1) 107–111; Zampetti and Sauvé (n 86) 143.

180 GATS art V(6).

181 Pierre Latrille, 'Services Rules in Regional Trade Agreements: How Diverse or Creative are They Compared to the Multilateral Rules?' in Rhoni Acharya (ed), *Regional Trade Agreements and the Multilateral Trading System* (CUP 2016) 446.

182 Zampetti and Sauvé (n 86) 143.

183 Dinh (n 1) 108–111.

184 ibid 149.

185 ibid 158–161.

ASEAN TIGA RoO state that the costs of research, development, design, and engineering can be incorporated into the direct overhead cost when calculating whether the good meets the 40% RVC under the direct method.[186] Therefore, under such a RoO regime, the value of the research, development, and design of the 3D file could be included in determining whether the 3D printed good meets a certain level of RVC. However, it must be noted that not all ASEAN TIGA-based FTAs clearly state what constitutes direct overhead costs.[187]

In their article, "Reconciling Rules of Origin and Global Value Chains: The Case for Reform," Geraets, Carroll, and Willems argue that RoO for goods should be redesigned to incorporate the value of services in determining origin as service inputs contribute significantly more value to the final product. They use the Apple iPhone 4 as an example, citing studies by Kraemer, Linden, and Dedrick which calculated that the manufacturing of the phone in China adds only 1.8% to the final value of the phone, and most of the value resides in designing the software and user interface of the phone.[188] Geraets, Carroll, and Willems argue that design, R&D, marketing, and transport should be considered value-adding steps in the production process (instead of including costs of such services in the direct overhead costs), as the "value added at these steps

186 ASEAN Trade in Goods Agreement (ATIGA) (signed 26 February 2009, entered into force 17 May 2010) ch 3 arts 29(1) and arts 29 (2)(d); Dinh (n 1) 132–133.

187 Stefano Inama and Edmund W Sim, *Rules of Origin in ASEAN* (CUP 2015) 87–89; The ASEAN-Australia-New Zealand Free Trade Agreement (entered into force January 2010) ch 3, art 5, states that "overhead costs" can be included in the direct formula, but simply defines overhead cost as the "total overhead expense" (art 5 (c)); The ASEAN-India Free Trade Agreement (entered into force 1 January 2010) (Annex 2 r 4) states that direct overhead costs can be included in the direct method, but does not define direct overhead costs; the AKFTA (Annex 3 r 4) allows using the direct overhead costs in the build-up method, but likewise does not define direct overhead costs; and the Regional Comprehensive Economic Partnership (signed 15 November 2020)(ch 3 art 3.5) also allows for a Direct/Build Up formula including direct overhead costs, but defines direct overhead cost as "the total overhead expense."

188 Dylan Geraets, Colleen Carroll, and Arnoud R Willems, 'Reconciling Rules of Origin and Global Value Chains: The Case for Reform' (2015) 18 J Intl Economic L 287, 295; J Dedrick, K L Kraemer and G Linden, 'Who Profits from Innovation in Global Value Chains?: A Study of the iPod and Notebook PCs,(2010) 19 Industrial & Corporate Change 81. A study by Gary Gereffi and Joonkoo Lee found that for the iPhone 4, which had a final factory price of $194.04, in terms of value added, $80.05 was created in South Korea, which supplied the display panels and memory chips, and only $6.54 of value came from assembly in China. Thus, in terms of the iPhone 4, the largest portion of the US trade deficit "incurred not with China, but via indirect exports from Korea and other high-value component suppliers." Gary Gereffi and Joonkoo Lee, 'Why the World Suddenly Cares about Global Supply Chains,' (2012) 48 J Supply Chain Management 24, 27.

generally exceeds the value of the production or assembly activities."[189] A new approach to RoO is needed "in which the value added during these stages of the production process is taken into account in the origin determination."[190] They propose adding language in PTAs such as a good is originating where "more than 50% of the final value of the good, as determined by the customs value, has been added in the territory of one of the parties, taking into account the following stages of the production process: research and development, artwork, design, intellectual property, manufacturing, marketing ..."[191] If the design, development, and IP rights in the 3D file are more significant than any value created by the production and post-processing and the "ink," then, such language would allow for the value of the 3D file to play a key role in determining the origin of the 3D printed good.

Dinh and Geraets, Carroll, and Willems acknowledge that choosing origin based on economic value creation of the service input could result in a change in the origin of the final product. Dinh explores how applying the "substantial transformation" test could also change the origin of a service. If a subsidiary or branch in Country A is more active than the parent company headquartered in County B in creating and providing a service, then Country A is the origin as a substantial transformation of the service occurred in Country A.[192] Geraets, Carroll, and Willems use the example of a Nike T-shirt.[193] Under a RoO, the T-shirt originates in Bangladesh. However, if design and marketing are taken into account, then the T-shirt would originate in the US and custom duties would be determined on the basis that the T-shirt is a US T-shirt despite being manufactured in Bangladesh.[194]

As identifying the origin of a service based on where economic value is created can be complicated, it may be more feasible to use the current GATS framework of assigning origin to the territory where the supplier is legally based. A RoO system based on the legal origin of the service supplier may be more appealing from a political perspective: if the current RoO system for goods skews unduly towards the location of manufacturing, adding the service input valuation could skew the value in favor of the service suppliers, who choose to be legally located in a different territory for strategic and fiscal

189 Geraets, Carroll, and Willems (n 188) 299–300.

190 ibid.

191 ibid 301. The authors acknowledge that this would mean interpreting the CVA to provide for services in the determination of customs value.

192 Dinh (n 1) 154–155.

193 Geraets, Carroll, and Willems (n 188) 302.

194 ibid.

reasons.[195] Further, as Hoekman and Nelson point out, when constructing "a global production structure, an essential part of such a strategy is to apply proprietary technology (product, process and managerial) to a corporate strategy involving a complex mix of exporting, direct investment and arm's length contracting … as part of the overall production process."[196] The focus is on an environment in which services and intermediate inputs "can be exchanged efficiently and securely."[197] While firms "still have an interest in traditional trade policy disciplines," they are more interested in a trade environment "with good protection of property rights, reliable communication, and consistent, market-conforming regulatory environments."[198]

Identifying the origin based on where the most economic value of the 3D file is created may be further complicated by whether the file is licensed to an outside firm or distributed to subsidiaries. Final goods can be printed close to the customer or to a small regional market. 3D printing, if adopted on a widespread basis would, on the one hand, create multiple "value shops" such as consultancy, engineering, and R&D services in addition the physical structure in which the good is printed.[199] Taking an economic value approach, the value that confers origin would be created in one of those "shops." Yet, firms may prefer that the origin be based on the geographical territory in which the supplier has its legal seat.

A US Customs ruling on the origin of dental aligners provides an example of how origin can be a strategic firm decision. Align (the owners of the Invisalign brand and technology) is headquartered in the United States.[200] Scans of a patient's teeth created by a dentist or orthodontist in the US are sent to Pakistan and transformed into a series of digital models as required for the

195 R Soprano, 'Brexit and the EU-UK Free Trade Agreement: Dos and Don'ts When Drafting Rules of Origin' (2019) 18 J Intl Trade L & Policy 96, 103.

196 Bernard Hoekman and Douglas Nelson, '21st Century Trade Agreements and the Owl of Minerva' (2018), EUI Working Papers, RSCAS 2018/04, 5 <https://cadmus.eui.eu/bitstream/handle/1814/50964/RSCAS_2018_04.pdf?sequence=1&isAllowed=y> accessed 23 October 2021.

197 ibid.

198 ibid.

199 Sébastien Miroudot and Charles Cadestin, 'Services in Global Value Chains: From Inputs to Value-Creating Activities' (2017) OECD Trade Policy Papers No. 197, 28,<https://www.oecd-ilibrary.org/trade/services-in-global-value-chains_465f0d8b-en> accessed 25 October 2021. The authors take the notion of "value shop" from the work of C Stabell and Ø Fjeldstad 'Configuring Value for Competitive Advantage: On Chains, Shops, and Networks' (1998) 19 Strategic Management J 413.

200 CBP, Ruling Letter, *Re: Country of Origin Marking of Orthodontic 'Aligners'* (1 March 2001) HQ 562012, MAR-05 RR:CR:SM 562012 BLS.

treatment of the patient. Files of the digital models are then sent to Mexico where they are printed into the plastic models. Align requested a ruling letter from the Commercial Rulings division of the CBP which could be submitted with the printed plastic models upon importation into the US. Align asked that the CBP determine that the plastic models originated in Mexico (under the NAFTA RoO) so that upon importation into the US the models were subject to certain preferential NAFTA marking requirements. The National Commodity Import Specialist found that the applicable CTH occurred when the plastic sheets (non-originating to Mexico) were printed into the models of the teeth, and so the models originated in Mexico. Thus, the NAFTA marking requirements could be applied to the models upon importation into the US.[201]

This example demonstrates that firms may not always be interested in having a product's origin be based on where the most work to the 3D file is done. We could imagine a RoO system which factors in the value of service inputs into an *ad valorem* criteria. Align may not report Pakistan as the location where most of the value is created, even though most of the work on the 3D files is done there. Instead, Align may argue that most of the R&D, engineering, marketing, and innovation is done in the US. Thus, the finished product, the printed models, originate in the US, although the models are designed in Pakistan and printed in Mexico.

This reasoning could be applied to other industries using 3D printing (hearing aids, parts for planes, vehicles and bicycles, consumer goods) and suggests that origin could be strategically concentrated in certain countries. Geraets, Carroll, and Willems suggest that if R&D and other services are factored into RoO, "it is likely that more products would be found to originate in one of the developed economies (EU, USA, Japan)."[202] This would impact revenue from customs duties as a developed country would have to forgo duties when importing products (since they actually originate in the country), though reduced prices could stimulate consumer demand.[203] The impact this type of RoO regime would have on development goals of the WTO and national political objectives will be discussed in the next Chapter. Shifting the origin conferring value from traditional manufacturing inputs to service inputs could result in shifting the origin of a good to territories that have significant and strong service sectors, especially in the field of R&D and digital design.

It would be necessary to examine the corporate structure of firms providing 3D design services. Firms providing digital products internationally establish

201 ibid.

202 Geraets, Carroll, and Willems (n 188) 301–302.

203 ibid.

legal seats or head operating offices in territories to benefit from favorable tax or legal environments.[204] Companies which may have manufacturing establishments in certain countries may choose to select the headquarter territory as the country of origin if able to factor in the value of service inputs. As Miroudot and Cadestin report in their study on services in GVCs, "[h]eadquarter economies, for example, have a higher share of employment in headquarter services that are in-house by definition" such as Luxembourg, Switzerland, Germany, and the Netherlands rather than, for example, the Czech Republic, Slovak Republic, Hungary, or Turkey.[205] The authors find that in terms of value created by labor costs, "jobs associated to service support functions are generally more high-skill and account for a larger share of the labour compensation. The fact that companies spend more on such jobs is an indication of the productivity and additional income they expect out of the servicification."[206] Services outsourced, also have a value to the firm.[207] On the one hand, a company developing a 3D file, which outsources the final design of the file to another company in another country, may wish to "retain" origin of the file by claiming that the outsourced design work does not add a sufficient level of value to the file. On the other hand, if the company wants the 3D file to originate in the country in which the outsourcing design occurs, it could claim that significant value was created in the outsourced country, and thus "obtain" origin for that file in that country. As further modification or downloading of the 3D file into printers may implicate use of IP licenses, firms may also need to conciliate the origin of the file with the territory in which it prefers to be taxed on revenues deriving from IP rights and assets connected to 3D files.[208]

The RoO regime with services input could impact whether 3D printed goods would qualify for EU origin if the 3D file design is the most valuable input.

---

204 Petros C Mavroidis, 'And You Put the Load Right on Me: Digital Taxes, Tax Discrimination, and Trade in Services' (2020) 12 Trade, L & Development 75, 78–79.

205 Miroudot and Cadestin (n 199) 19; See also Catherine Barnard with Jukka Snell, 'Free Movement of Legal Persons and the Provision of Services,' in Catharine Barnard and Steve Peers (eds), *European Union Law* (3rd edn, OUP 2020) 438.

206 Miroudot and Cadestin (n 199) 19.

207 ibid. The countries included: Austria, Belgium, Brazil, Bulgaria, Canada, Czech Republic, Denmark, Estonia, Finland, France, Germany, Greece, Hungary, India, Ireland, Italy, Korea, Latvia, Lithuania, Luxembourg, Mexico, Netherlands, Poland, Romania, Slovak Republic, Slovenia, Spain, United Kingdom, United States.

208 For example, Google transferred its intellectual property holdings from Ireland to the US after closing its "double Irish" tax loophole subsequent to changes in the US tax law implemented by the Trump Administration. Richard Waters, 'Google to end use of 'double Irish' as tax loophole set to close' *Financial Times* (London, 1 January 2020) <https://www.ft.com/content/991f11ae-2c51-11ea-bc77-65e4aa615551> accessed 25 October 2021.

The EU has expressed concern that it did not have a significant level of 3D file design capability and that innovative firms were being acquired by non-EU companies.[209] One out of three advanced manufacturing companies in the EU is owned by US firms.[210] If the value of the 3D file is created outside of the EU by another firm or a subsidiary, then even if printed in the EU, the product would not qualify as an EU originating product. On the other hand, 34% of foreign-owned firms are ultimately owned by EU firms.[211] If other types of services are factored into the value creation, then a company which has its legal seat in Ireland or Luxembourg could argue that due to corporate structure, the location of certain personnel, or communication patterns, the majority of the value is created in the legal headquarters in Ireland or Luxembourg.[212] This would be a strategic use of the SBOs language under the GATS RoO framework. For example, a company in the EU wants to ship printed goods to Canada. It could argue that even though design work on a file is done in Pakistan, the SBOs of the supplier are in Ireland, and therefore benefit under CETA preferential rates when importing to Canada (provided it can demonstrate that it has an effective and continuous link with Ireland).[213]

209 Eur Economic & Social Committee, 'Living Tomorrow. 3D printing' (n 11) para 3.2.6; Kretz and Van de Velde (n 146) 21.

210 Calza et. al. (n 11) 22.

211 ibid.

212 Council Directive 2000/31/EC of 8 June 2000 (Directive on Electronic Commerce) Recital 19: "The place at which a service provider is established should be determined in conformity with the case-law of the Court of Justice according to which the concept of establishment involves the actual pursuit of an economic activity through a fixed establishment for an indefinite period; this requirement is also fulfilled where a company is constituted for a given period; the place of establishment of a company providing services via an Internet website is not the place at which the technology supporting its website is located or the place at which its website is accessible but the place where it pursues its economic activity; in cases where a provider has several places of establishment it is important to determine from which place of establishment the service concerned is provided; in cases where it is difficult to determine from which of several places of establishment a given service is provided, this is the place where the provider has the centre of his activities relating to this particular service."

213 Answer given by Ms. Malmström on behalf of the European Commission (14 November 2018) E-004978/2018 <https://www.europarl.europa.eu/doceo/document/E-8-2018-004978-ASW_EN.html> accessed 25 October 2021 "The term 'substantive business operations' is a well-known concept used in Articles V(6) and XXVIII(m) of the World Trade Organisation (WTO) General Agreement on Trade in Services … The Commission considers, as is also stated in the context of the Commission Declaration on the meaning of the term 'substantial business activities' in Article 8.1 of the Comprehensive Economic Trade Agreement (CETA), that a corporation established in the territory of our trading partner could benefit from the agreement only where it can establish that it has substantive

Further, under the E-commerce Directive, the establishment of a service provider "involves the actual pursuit of an economic activity through a fixed establishment for an indefinite period."[214] A company could argue that a designer in a third-party country to the PEM is only temporarily hired to design or work on a file; the "actual pursuit of economic activity" is conducted in a headquarters or other fixed office with SBO within the PEM territory, and thus, the value of the file could be cumulated with any value created by other inputs created in other PEM Contracting Parties. As a result, not only will importers and custom officials need to verify the source of the "ink" and quantify the labor hours and direct overhead expenditures for printing the good, they will need to provide evidence that the value generated by the service inputs does in fact originate in Ireland.

Firms operating in the EU market would have to consider whether they are providing a service covered by the E-Commerce Directive and the Services Directive,[215] whether they are providing services regulated by another EU or national instrument, or whether, due to printing activity, they are in fact goods producers. *Asociación Profesional Élite Taxi v. Uber Systems Spain SL*, an ECJ decision, suggests that lawmakers and courts examine whether a service provider is providing just an information service.[216] The Spanish taxi association argued that Uber's activity in Spain could be classified as unfair practices under its competition laws, which require licenses and authorizations to commercially transport passengers.[217] The Court was asked to determine if the application service (the app, the digital service) provided by Uber is in fact a service in the field of transport, which is out of the scope of the Services Directive.[218] This would then bring the service under Article 58, paragraph 1 of the TFEU,[219] allowing Spanish courts to decide if Uber should be subject to the

business activities in the foreign territory having an effective and continuous link with the trading partners' economy, in the sense of establishment as applied under the EU Treaty."

214 Directive on Electronic Commerce, Recital 19.

215 Directive 2006/123/EC of the European Parliament and the Council of 12 December 2006 on services in the internal market (Services Directive) [2006] OJ L376/36. Firms providing platforms for electronic transmission of the 3D file will have obligations under the Digital Services Act (2022) and the Digital Markets Act (2022).

216 Case C-434/15, *Asociación Profesional Élite Taxi v. Uber Systems Spain SL* [2017] ECLI:EU:C:2017:364.

217 ibid para 14–15.

218 ibid para 42.

219 Consolidated versions of the Treaty on European Union and the Treaty on the Functioning of the European Union (TFEU) [2012] OJ C 326, 1, art 58(1).

same regulations as taxi operators.[220] The Court found that without the Uber app, drivers would not be led to provide transport services and the passengers would not use such services.[221] Additionally, Uber exercises control over the conditions of the drivers and the fares. As a result, the digital service (the app) formed an integral part of an overall service, transport, and could not be classified as an information society service.[222] Consequently, the digital service (the app) is excluded from the scope of the Services Directive and the Directive on Electronic Commerce and could be subject to national regulations.[223]

While 3D printing files are not transport services, they can be used to produce medical products.[224] Healthcare services are also excluded from the Services Directive.[225] Application of the Directive on Electronic Commerce must not be prejudicial to the level of protection for public health at the Union and national level, and Members States may take measures to derogate from Article 3(2) for the protection of public health.[226] A 3D file design company that connects hospitals or medical services providers with 3D manufacturers or transmits files to 3D printers in the medical facility, could potentially be seen as providing a medical service, and thus, the 3D file could be subject to Union and national regulations on health. If the 3D file producer exercises control over how the product is printed, how many copies are printed, training of the printer operator, and use of the products, it could possibly be argued that the 3D file producer is also the producer of the printed medical equipment and thus subject to additional regulations.

Firms may be hesitant to single out the 3D file as an independent origin conferring input. Declaring the 3D file as an input on a customs form may lead into an investigation on whether they are providing services that are subject to additional regulations. In this case, such firms may want to bundle up the costs of service designs in the direct manufacturing costs of printing the good. On the other hand, national and EU regulators may want to keep an eye on 3D file providers and monitor whether they are just providing an information service or whether the creation and transmission of a 3D file is part of the provision of another type of service or a product that requires a certain level of safety controls.

---

220 *Asociación Profesional Élite Taxi v Uber*, paras 44, 47.

221 ibid para 39.

222 ibid para 40.

223 ibid para 50.

224 Duchêne, et. al. (n 145) 52–54, 61–64.

225 Services Directive, preamble 22.

226 Directive on Electronic Commerce, preamble 11, art 1(3), art 3(2), art 3(4). Art 3(2) prohibits Member States from restricting "the freedom to provide information society services from another Member State."

The Directive on Electronic Commerce and Services Directive apply to services provided by service providers established in the EU.[227] 3D file producers (service providers) established outside the EU would not be eligible for the protections offered under these directives. This would be an incentive for 3D file producers to argue that the 3D file design and transmission services are provided by firm established in the EU. One industry where this type of strategic value placement could be applied is the automotive industry, which already has an intricate relationship with RoO. Companies like BMW are using 3D printing technology and machines to print spare and replacement parts closer to a particular market.[228] For example, we can imagine that Mercedes-Benz has a 3D printing facility in Germany to print replacement parts for older models. Under traditional RoO, the value of the ink for those parts may be more significant than the labor or overhead costs expended to print those parts. Thus, if the ink is non-originating material, it is likely that the part would not qualify for EU origin.

If Mercedes-Benz begins to produce an innovative electric car for the mass market which has a reduced number of parts, and most of those parts are printed parts, then the fact that the non-originating ink has significant value could impact the origin of the car under an *ad valorem* criterion (recall that simple assembly does not create origin conferring value). Mercedes-Benz would want to incorporate the value of any R&D and 3D file design into the RoO analysis if the majority of the value created by these services occurs within the EU. Then, Mercedes-Benz could select a particular legal office or headquarters to justify that the value of the 3D files is created in the EU. Another industry which could also strategically locate value creation for 3D files, and thus the 3D printed goods, is the aerospace industry as companies such as GE and NASA are using 3D printing technology to print parts for engines.

5 Conclusion

This chapter started with applying the wholly produced criterion and the three substantial transformation criteria to determine the origin of a 3D printed good. When these criteria are applied without any modifications to a 3D

227 Electronic Commerce Directive, art 3(1), Services Directive, preamble 16.

228 Vincent Bonneau and others, 'The disruptive nature of 3D printing' (2017) Digital Transformation Monitor <https://ati.ec.europa.eu/sites/default/files/2020-07/The%20disruptive%20nature%20of%203D%20printing%20%20%28v1%29.pdf> accessed 25 October 2021 (archived link).

printed good, one finds that the CTH criterion may no longer have a discriminatory function as all 3D printed goods undergo a change of heading when they go from ink to printed item. Using the *ad valorem* method, the value created from the production of a 3D printed good appears to be weighted in the raw materials, rather than in the printing, post-processing, and assembly. This could potentially offset the political goals behind including labor value content requirements in RoO, such as those in the USMCA, which aim to increase the value of labor in goods production.

Is it necessary to design a new RoO framework in which the origin of the 3D file is incorporated into the analysis of the 3D printed good? This chapter presented the legal and technical challenges to such an approach. The GATS framework is not commensurate with the RoO framework developed in the AOR, the Kyoto Convention, and numerous PTAs for several reasons. The GATS classification system has a different intention and purpose from the HS nomenclature which forms the basis of product specific lists in PTAs. The AB has allowed for an evolutionary interpretation of services classification, while the HS is designed to discourage such an interpretation of classifying goods. Further, GATS provisions for Mode 1 services (which would apply to cross-border transmissions of 3D files) locate origin within the territory of the service supplier, which is not always where the most economic value of the service is created. Whereas, under the RoO framework for goods, the geographical location where the most economic value is created is the origin of the good.

Adding an origin determination for services to the origin determination of a 3D printed good may be an uneasy alliance. In terms of creating a more predictable and transparent trading system, this hybrid may not assist in reducing the paperwork and resource expenditure for firms seeking preferential tariff treatment. There could be opportunities for large firms or Member states to lobby for "retaining" or "obtaining" origin of the 3D file based on where the firms have substantial business operations.

However, we should continue to explore whether there can be some redesign of RoO. As the last pages of this Chapter demonstrated, under traditional manufacturing methods a good originates in Bangladesh, but under a RoO system that incorporates 3D file design, the good originates in the US. Rules that shift origin could impact suppliers, producers, and customers who were relying on origin to be Bangladesh. As the global 3D printing market size is valued over 20 billion USD,[229] perhaps we should consider the concerns of Rashmi Banga

229 Fortune Business Insights, '3D Printing Market Size, Share, & Industry Analysis' (Fortunebusinessinsights.com March 2024) <https://www.fortunebusinessinsights.com/industry-reports/3d-printing-market-101902> accessed 23 March 2024.

of UNCTAD about the impact of 3D printing on the industries of countries that do not have advanced technological infrastructure and training programs.[230] Shaffer also warns that while the free flow of data (like a 3D file) can enhance efficiency and welfare gains, it can also "exacerbate inequality in ways that can threaten social stability and international cooperation."[231] While labor and social concerns should be addressed at the national level, trade agreements "must accommodate (and not foreclose) mechanisms that enable states to address labor and other social concerns."[232] This Chapter has demonstrated that when RoO are applied to determine the origin of data flows, there may be unexpected results to the origin of the final good, which may impact social or labor objectives. If a trader in Bangladesh now finds that he or she has a factory full of US goods, they might not be able to take advantage of a non-reciprocal preferential tariff rate under a GSP as the goods do not "originate" in Bangladesh. This would then offset the intended goal of the non-reciprocal preferential tariffs, which is to foster development.

Finally, a RoO regime which incorporates high value service inputs will add more paperwork to customs procedures as traders will also have to prove the origin of the service. There could be benefits to including the input in the origin analysis to trade, development, innovation, and the growth of a digitally skilled workforce. These benefits should not be forgone because no one can understand how to seek preferential tariff treatment or which tariff applies to the final good. The next chapter will explore whether it is possible to design RoO for 3D printed goods and other goods with a significant service input that are not unwieldy and that allow states to achieve some policy goals without the rules themselves creating unnecessary obstacles to trade.

---

230 Rashmi Banga, 'Growing Trade in Electronic Transmissions: Implications for the South' (2019) UNCTAD Research Paper No. 29, 30–31 <https://unctad.org/system/files/official-document/ser-rp-2019d1_en.pdf> accessed 23 October 2021.

231 Gregory Shaffer, 'Trade Law in a Data-Driven Economy: The Need for Modesty and Resilience' (2021) 20 World Trade Rev. 259, 279.

232 ibid 280.

CHAPTER 5

Preferential Rules of Origin for Advanced Manufactured Products

An Opportunity to Modernize Perspectives on Preferential Rules of Origin

Preferential rules of origin are a technical element of trade law, but they serve an important role in the practice of trade. Addressing preferential RoO in the context of advanced manufacturing allows an understanding of where the rules are wobbly in their functionality. For example, the emphasis in the *ad valorem* criterion on labor and manufacturing overhead may mean an under-reporting of value creation in the design and engineering stages of production, and thus origin is assigned to the territory in which most of the value is not created. The use of the CTH criterion raises questions on what HS code a printed product or input falls into and whether a CTH is a sufficient transformation to confer origin. Additionally, the changes to manufacturing and to GVCs that 3D printing and advanced manufacturing can bring also provides an opportunity to consider the simplification of cumulation rules and direct transport rules.

Considering rules of origin in the context of 3D printing allows an examination of arguments on linking goods and services origin determinations and to identify some possible issue points. Emphasis is given to the value of the 3D file and the creation of digital design file by some of the scholars referenced earlier. However, questions remain as to the implications, both at the level of international trade law and at the level of customs administration. This chapter suggests that linking rules of origin to service origin determinations and e-commerce regulation may not be an easy fit. Identifying the areas of friction presents an opportunity to consider the merits of a hybridized goods-services regime and the role of preferential RoO in the digital trade environment.

Exploring how protectionist, or just inefficient, application of current rules to 3D products and how the design of new rules could reproduce some of the unsavory elements of preferential RoO presents the opportunity to consider whether it is time for plurilateral oversight of such rules. In fact, Mavroidis argues that while 3D printing is still a growing form of manufacturing, the WTO should explore how to determine the origin of 3D printed products:

> The fact that it will be some time before 3D printing can be fully utilized on a wide commercial scale does not mean that similar questions should be like sleeping dogs that can lie a few yards outside the WTO

 | DOI:10.1163/9789004730595_007

> headquarters, and are handled only at the moment when they start to bark. The WTO can become attractive only if it shows the capacity to address similar concerns preemptively, and not only ex post facto (which might be too late).[1]

This chapter explores whether it is possible to craft a WTO instrument on preferential RoO for advanced manufactured products (RoO Instrument) by looking at the development of the Information Technology Agreement (ITA) and the Trade Facilitation Agreement (TFA), both plurilateral agreements. Additionally, an examination of the Nairobi Ministerial Decision on preferential Roo for LDCs provides an opportunity to see how Members may respond to another RoO Instrument.

The success of any RoO Instrument would require the willingness of Members to concede some sovereignty on designing rules. Guidance at an international level would allow parties of PTAs to design rules that perform a discriminatory function, but are not overly restrictive. This means that both the WTO and its members should consider modernizing the perspective that preferential RoO lie beyond the aegis of the WTO. As Professor Jackson commented:

> In the context of international law, based heavily on nation-state sovereignty and supremacy ideas, governments and societies consenting to become members of such institutions must do so with the realization that the institutional structures will not be frozen in time, and that such consent will inevitably bring surprises.[2]

Technological means to produce goods are not frozen in time; they change and the practice of trade thus adapts. As such, if institutional organizations remain frozen in regulating trade based on one type of manufacturing due to reluctance or resistance from Members to modernize, the value and the benefits that the organization can bring to trade may become overshadowed by perceptions that the organization is "outdated." The possibility that the WTO can change its approach to RoO should not be a surprise to its Members as the need to find solutions to the design and implementation of preferential RoO is shared by Members. This means, however, that the WTO and Members

1 Petros C Mavroidis, *The Regulation of International Trade, vol 3* (*MIT Press 2020*) 242–243.

2 Prof. Jonathan H Jackson Jackson, 'The Evolution of the World Trading System – The Legal and Institutional Context' in Daniel Bethlehem, Isabelle Van Damme, Donald McRae and Rodney Neufeld, *The Oxford Handbook of International Trade* (OUP 2009) 31.

should also re-examine what it means to have sovereignty over preferential RoO design in a technologically advanced, highly connected digitalized trading environment.

This Chapter ties together the various discussions on rules of origin presented throughout this book. The questions on the legality of the rules under the WTO agreements presented in Chapter 1 are reexamined. Modest recommendations based on the technical aspects of the rules discussed in Chapter 2 are proposed. Further suggestions on how to make the rules more efficient and user-friendly are proposed based on the work of the economists presented in Chapter 3. A deeper examination of how to link rules of origin for goods to rules for services and e-commerce regulation is discussed based on the exploration of origin determination for 3D printed products in Chapter 4.

The Chapter returns in Part 1 to the arguments on the economic costs of preferential RoO, and then presents a summary of the trade policy concerns and the need to simplify rules both substantively and procedurally. Part 2 explores how to design rules that include the origin of 3D file input or a different type of digital file input without reliance on a hybridization of the goods-services regime. Part 3 examines how RoO for 3D printed goods could be connected to, but not dependent on, a WTO agreement on e-commerce regulation. Part 4 presents a proposal for a WTO Instrument on RoO for Advanced Manufactured goods. Part 5 examines how the WTO Secretariat and the Committee on the Rules of Origin can tap into the resources of the organization to provide assistance to the trade community in designing and complying with RoO for advanced manufactured products. As RoO are mainly found in PTAs, Part 6 provides some recommendations for making the rules beneficial tools for traders and reducing overly discriminatory elements for trade in advanced manufactured goods and for trade in general. Part 7 offers some conclusions on the Chapter.

1 Rules of Origin for 3D Printed Goods and Other Advanced Manufactured Goods: Economic and Trade Policy Concerns

Exploring how to design RoO for 3D printed goods is an opportunity to reexamine issues that beset preferential RoO in RTAs generally. This Part will briefly summarize the arguments raised by the legal and economic analysts regarding preferential RoO for traditional manufactured products and then demonstrate where these concerns are linked to goods produced with advanced manufacturing methods, such as 3D printing.

Fissures within the preferential RoO system result from the lack of transparency in drafting and implementation of the rules. While some political tinkering may be inevitable in the design of trade laws, there is a high level of lobbying and involvement of politicians in the design of these rules. In exchange for agreeing to open domestic markets to foreign products and inputs, industry groups and politicians seek to benefit by the design of rules that will protect or bolster domestic markets despite foreign goods entering the market under a preferential tariff rate. This is achieved through rules that are obtuse, not generally made known to the public for comment and criticism, and for which, Hirsch argues, there is no accountability mechanism.[3] Using the RoO chapter in trade agreements to obtain political domestic objectives may not necessarily benefit the domestic industry. The comments issued by the American automotive industry show that rules designed to favor traditional manufacturing, such as *ad valorem* percentage rules or regional value content rules, may clash with the use of new technologies to reduce labor costs and to make and source parts where it is most efficient.

The complex design of the rules is a source of economic inefficiency. In addition to untangling the "spaghetti bowl" of RTAs, traders and customs officials must decipher the formulas, exceptions, sub-exceptions, and product-specific instructions in RoO chapters. MSMEs (micro, small, and medium enterprises) in both developed and developing countries may not have the legal or financial resources to obtain assistance on determining whether a good made of multiple parts qualifies for preferential treatment under a RTA. As a result, some traders forgo seeking the preferential tariff rate and instead trade under the MFN rates. Further, the rules can be designed to favor certain industries or practices while not promoting practices that are efficient like sourcing inputs from outside the territory (e.g. SADC and AfCFTA)[4] or attempting to regain losses from inefficient manufacturing by means of restrictive rules (e.g. SAFTA).[5]

3 Moshe Hirsch, 'The Politics of Rules of Origin' in Tomer Broude, Marc L Busch, and Amelia Porges (eds), *The Politics of International Economic Law* (CUP 2011) 328.

4 Hennie Erasmus, Frank Flatters, and Robert Kirk, 'Rules of Origin as tools of development? Some lessons from SADC,' in Olivier Cadot, Antoni Estevadeordal, Akiko Suwa-Eisenmann, and Theirry Verdier (eds), *The Origin of Goods: Rules of Origin in Regional Trade Agreements* (OUP 2006) 280–282; Stefano Inama, *Rules of Origin in International Trade* (CUP 2022) 824; Bernard Hoekman, Christian Lippitsch, Marcelo Olarreaga, Marco Sanfilippo, Rohit Ticku, 'Maximising value-added in Africa exports: Understanding the role of Rules of Origin' *IGC Blog* (International Growth Centre 27 August 2024) <https://www.theigc.org/blogs/maximising-value-added-african-exports-understanding-role-rules-origin> Accessed 22 October 2024.

5 Ram Singh and Surendar Singh, 'Do Rules of Origin Extend Disproportionate Trade Gains under SAFTA: A Case Study of Bicycle and Textile Industries' (2021) 16 Global Trade & Customs J 59, 69–71.

The adoption of additive manufacturing in developing or emerging countries indicates that developing rules of origin for 3D products to bolster domestic advanced manufacturing is not just of interest to governments in Europe and North America.[6] GE has set up advanced manufacturing hubs and training programs in Nigeria,[7] and the Ministry of Electronics and Information Technology in India produced a paper proposing that additive manufacturing "could revolutionize India's manufacturing and industrial production landscape," "augment India's efforts to position itself as the Manufacturing Hub of the world," as well as increase the goods "Made in India."[8] India has argued against a permanent moratorium on duties on electronic transmissions on the basis that it needs to support its developing digital manufacturing and trade sectors by limiting the entry of digital products from third countries.[9]

The hearing aid and dental aligner industries have demonstrated that 3D manufacturers print and ship 3D printed goods all over the world,[10] and it is possible that other industries will import and export 3D printed goods. A 3D printing industry may hire lobbyists to influence politicians to design rules to support their domestic market position. Suppose a Moroccan manufacturer prints and assembles components of a dashboard and a company in Germany wishes to import the semi-completed vehicles for final assembly

6 Richard A D'Aveni, 'How 3-D Printing Can Jumpstart Developing Economies' (*Forbes* 19 March 2019) <https://www.forbes.com/sites/richarddaveni/2019/03/19/how-3d-printing-can-jumpstart-developing-economies/?sh=12bcfedd4400> accessed 2 November 2021; https://www.usaid.gov/sites/default/files/2022-12/3D_Printing_Primer.pdf.

7 'GE Nigeria Launches e-learning Portal at Lagos Garage Week 2018' (Africanews.it 7 Decem-ber 2018), <https://www.africanews.it/english/ge-nigeria-launches-e-learning-portal-at-lagos-garage-week-2018/> accessed 8 March 2025.

8 Ministry of Electronics and Information Technology, 'National Strategy for Additive Manufacturing: Next Generation Digital Manufacturing' (Meity.gov.in 24 February 2022) 1,3 <https://www.meity.gov.in/writereaddata/files/Additive%20Manufacturing%20Booklet%2014.02.2022.pdf> accessed 23 March 2024 (archived link).

9 Communication from India and South Africa (10 March 2020) WTO Work Programme on Electronic Commerce <https://docs.wto.org> accessed 29 October 2021. At the WTO'S 2024 Ministerial Conference, India did agree to a continuation of the Work Programme on E-Commerce and the continued Moratorium on customs duties on electronic transmissions. Ministerial Decision, 'Work Programme On Electronic Commerce' (2 March 2024) WT/MIN(24)/38, WT/L/1193 <https://docs.wto.org> accessed 23 March 2024.

10 Caroline Freund, Alen Mulabdic and Michele Ruta, 'Is 3D Printing a Threat to Global Trade? The Trade Effects You Didn't Hear About,' (2020) World Development Report Policy Research Working Paper, No. 9024, 2–3 <https://openknowledge.worldbank.org/handle/10986/32453> accessed 26 November 2021; Ziyang Fan, Jimena Sotelo and Venkatarman Sundareswaran '3D Printing: A Guide for Decision-Makers' (January 2020) World Economic Forum – White Paper, 13 <http://www3.weforum.org/docs/WEF_Impacts_3D_Printing_on_Trade_Supply_Chains_Toolkit.pdf> accessed 24 October 2021.

taking advantage of the PEM diagonal cumulation possibilities between Morocco and the EU.[11] Under the PEM product specific rules for accessories for automobiles, the value of the non-originating material for a dashboard must not exceed 50% of ex-works price of the product.[12] If the value of the non-originating material in the ink used to print the dashboard is worth more than 50% of the total value (including labor value and overhead value), then the dashboard does not qualify as originating under the PEM. At this point, policymakers in Germany, wanting to bolster domestic final assembly automotive plants, may encourage customs officials in Morocco and Germany to interpret "assembly" to ensure that printing a product is not "simple assembly" which confers no or minimal value, but is sufficient processing that produces value that exceeds the value of any non-originating material in the ink.

To expand this example on a broader level, the possibility for 3D printing to shift the origin of a good also presents an opportunity for lawmakers and politicians to design rules that favor or protect a domestic industry, and to do so with closed-door negotiations and technically complex formulas, calculations, and provisions – the same problems that underlie the current RoO regime for traditional manufacturing. Therefore, the design of rules for 3D printed products, or the redesign of existing rules to encompass advanced manufacturing techniques more generally, should, ideally, be conducted with transparency and with some restraints on use of these rules for protectionist purposes.

Next, the resources saved in printing a good should not be expended in trying to determine whether the good qualifies for preferential treatment. Designing rules, both substantive and procedural, for advanced manufactured products could be an opportunity for simplifying preferential RoO. There should be a careful balance. As Inama states, rules that are ambiguous leave "too much space to interpretation and little guidance" to the customs officials and private industry actors that must implement the rules.[13] On the other hand, overcrowding the RoO chapter with definitions, product-specific lists,

11 For a list of countries to which diagonal cumulation applies, see Commission, 'Notice concerning the application of the Regional Convention on pan-Euro-Mediterranean preferential rules of origin or the protocols on rules of origin providing for diagonal cumulation between Contracting Parties to this Convention," (30 March 2020) OJ 2020/C 322/03, tables 1,2, and 3.

12 Decision No 1/2023 of The Joint Committee of The Regional Convention on Pan-Euro-Mediterranean Preferential Rules Of Origin of 7 December 2023 on the amendment of the Regional Convention on pan-Euro-Mediterranean preferential rules of origin (PEM), Annex II, Product Specific Rules, HS code 8708.

13 Inama, *Rules of Origin in International Trade* (CUP 2009) 459–60.

Annexes, and formulas is also dissatisfactory, because it creates confusion on interpreting the various textual elements in relation to each other.[14]

Economists propose that newly designed rules should be more receptive to the level of economic development and geographical size of the territories covered by trade instruments. The dental aligner industry has demonstrated that the design work and printing of aligners occur in Pakistan, Costa Rica, and Mexico. It is possible that entrepreneurs or government funded manufacturing facilities in developing countries could turn their attention to printing and exporting goods. Designing procedural rules for 3D printed goods having flexibility based on the size and economic status of the producer could be taken into consideration. While a system exempting producers from LDCs with proving origin for small shipments or paying duties may allow such producers to devote resources to adopting advanced manufacturing, the customs modernization legislation proposed in the EU and the US is aimed against the use of small shipments to evade customs duties, anti-dumping duties, and other restrictions. Therefore, the US and the EU may want to consider setting aside resources to 1) identify those LDCs that do not pose a high risk of being a conduit for transshipment or a source of large amounts of small packages, and who can thus be exempt from a tariff or VAT for small shipments, or 2) provide training so that these LDCs can provide the requested data and verifications without having to divert resources from the development of manufacturing industries.

Preferential RoO should be examined with more attention because the facility for these rules to become tools of domestic interests ties into the greater discussion of the purpose of the international trade law system as providing a framework for liberalization of trade.[15] Advanced manufacturing techniques such as 3D printing can expand the participation of developing countries and MSMEs in international trade. However, such potential may be limited if some of the unsavory elements of preferential RoO persist, because the rules are unchanged or protectionist measures are integrated into the design of any new rules. New types of inputs, new final goods, and new methods for producing products present an opportunity for examining how preferential RoO function as legal instruments and whether changes should be made so that utilization rates increase. An investigation into advanced manufacturing also requires considering the role of the 3D file in both the creation of the final good and its contribution to the overall value of the final good. Even if it is

---

14 ibid 468.

15 Gregory Shaffer, 'Retooling Trade Agreements for Social Inclusion' (2019) U Illinois L Rev 1, 339.

possible to include the 3D file as an independent origin conferring input in the origin determination analysis, scholars and policymakers should carefully consider how to design such rules, and whether such rules should be linked to e-commerce provisions in WTO instruments and PTAs.

2 Modernizing Preferential RoO: Linking Origin Determination of the 3D File to the Origin of the 3D Printed Good

Identifying and incorporating the origin of the digital file into the origin analysis of the 3D printed good requires looking at the approaches to RoO in the GATS, Annex II of the AOR, and in PTAs and finding points where these instruments can interconnect. This part revisits these approaches, but also focuses on some of the technical implications of a combined RoO regime, and finally links the principle objective of preferential RoO, their discriminatory function, with the principle of sovereignty in the era of the international trade of advanced manufactured goods.

2.1 *Technical Considerations for RoO for Advanced Manufactured Products*

A printed bicycle frame is assembled into a bicycle that is powered by pedaling, but which also includes a smart speaker. The customs official looking at the HS, the preferential RoO, and the Tariff Schedule, would wonder what is this product, a bicycle or a smart-speaker?[16] How do customs official assess whether the 3D file for the bicycle or the R&D for the smart-speaker qualifies as origin conferring value? Should customs officials interpret instruments like the HS and RTAs for technologically advanced products which do not easily fit into preexisting product lines or wait until the HS and RoO are updated.

The greater issue for combining the origin of services and goods inputs is the risk of augmenting the complexity of the rules. As the number of goods having a significant service input in terms of the overall value of the good increases, the case grows, some trade analysts argue, for including the origin of

16 The HS code for a non-stationary, non-motorized bike is 8712 and a motorized bike is 8711. A CBP ruling in 2019 classified the Sony Smart Wireless Speaker with Built-in Voice Assistant as HS 8518.22: heading 8518"Microphones and stands therefor; loudspeakers, whether or not mounted in their enclosures … audio-frequency electric amplifiers; electric sound amplifier sets; parts thereof" and subheading.22 "Multiple loudspeakers, mounted in the same enclosure." CBP, Ruling Letter '*The Tariff Classification of a Smart Speaker from China*' (16 October 2019) N306364.

the file into the origin analysis of the tangible good.[17] Yet, how would customs offices interpret such rules? RoO drafters should work with politicians, industry representatives, and customs representatives to understand the role of the 3D file in 3D printing and how to determine its origin using the substantial transformation criteria.

Next, we explore whether it is necessary to include the origin of the 3D file as a potentially origin conferring input of the 3D printed product. This also means understanding how much value is created in the 3D file and comparing it to the other components for which value can be given: materials, labor, and direct overhead. The GATS rules of origin regime is based on the legal origin of the service provider.[18] However, the location of the legal seat of the company could have been chosen for taxation and corporate strategic reasons. For example, GE is incorporated in New York State.[19] If GE establishes a branch to print goods in Nairobi, several questions arise: (1) do the goods originate in Kenya based on value created in printing and post-processing? (2) if the file was designed in Nairobi, is Kenya the country of origin, or is the US, given that it is GE's legal seat? and (3) would GE prefer that the goods come from Kenya in order to benefit from a GSP or a RTA to which the US is not a party, but Kenya is a party?

Given these factors, the design of rules incorporating the digital file as an input could become industrial and political strategic tools. To minimize the potentially trade distortive impact of incorporating the service input into the origin analysis some limitations on the application of rules to promote domestic industries or some exceptions for small traders may need to be inserted into the rules. For example, rules that in effect favor countries of 3D file design may mean that traders in countries that print and post-process goods may find it more challenging to trade under the preferential rate of the RTA. This may have been an intended political choice by one of the parties or an unintended consequence. To minimize negative effects, the rules could provide for options, such as under the *ad valorem* method: the origin is 1) where the input is created with the highest value relative to the other inputs (favoring parties with a stronger 3D file design industry), or 2) where the cumulation of the value

17 Duy Dinh, *Rules of Origin for Services: From the Early Days of GATS to the Era of Servicification* (Edward Elgar 2020) 134–135; Dylan Geraets, Colleen Carroll, and Arnoud R Willems, 'Reconciling Rules of Origin and Global Value Chains: The Case for Reform' (2015) 18 J Intl Economic L 287, 300–302.

18 Dinh (n 17) 111–112.

19 'Certificate of Incorporation' (GE.com 2019) fn 1, <https://www.ge.com/sites/default/files/GE_Certificate_of_Incorporation_Effective_December_9_2019.pdf> accessed 3 November 2021.

of the materials, processing, and direct costs in a territory is higher than the 3D file (favoring parties with a stronger manufacturing industry). Alternative methods for qualifying for origin in RoO have already been established (as seen in PEM and USMCA) for traditional manufacturing methods and could be applied to rules for advanced manufactured products.

Likewise for GSPs, flexible provisions could achieve two objectives: the country can still trade under the preferential rate and improve its manufacturing industry by adopting technologically advanced methods of production. If a country wants to adopt 3D printing, but does not yet have the capability to design 3D files within the country, it may import files designed by third parties, which may have high economic value. To prevent the high-value third party file input from disqualifying the finished good from the preferential rate under the GSP, the preference-granting country could design rules that allow the preference-receiving country to assign more value to the 3D manufacturing process. On the other hand, designing rules that include the 3D file as an input, but in effect favor traditional manufacturing methods, may negatively impact developing countries or emerging countries that are focusing on improving their digital design industries. Efforts at increasing local services production should focus on the quality and cost of such services to the businesses exporting printed goods. As a study led by Hoekman shows, in Uganda, services input intensity does not positively moderate "the relationship between participation in international trade and firm productivity. Rather, [they] find some evidence that a higher share of total expenditures on services inputs attenuates the positive relationship between trade status and productivity."[20] This may result from the majority of service inputs being of domestic origin, which may not be "up to the standard to be internationally competitive." It is not simply enough to encourage developing countries to increase service inputs in their manufacturing processes, but training, know-how, and resources are necessary to bring the level of these inputs to those produced in digitally advanced economies.

We can identify the following initial conclusions. First, it is recommendable not to design multilateral harmonized rules of origin for products with digital service inputs. The rate of technical skill acquirement in 3D designing and printing is uneven in developed and developed countries and within industries.[21] Critical to the design of rules is the transparency and balance

20 B Hoekman, M Sanflilippo, F Santi, R Ticku, 'Trade, productivity, and services input intensity' *Rev of World Econ* (30 July 2024) 12 <https://link.springer.com/article/10.1007/s10290-024-00548-2> accessed 25 October 2024.

21 Mohammad E Arbabian and Michael R Wagner 'The impact of 3D Printing on Manufacturer-Retailer Supply Chains,' (2020) 285 Eur J Operational Research 538, 538–539; Freund, Mulabdic, and Ruta (n 10) 3.

of the negotiation process: developed economies like the US and the EU are increasingly becoming global service providers while also investing political and financial resources in supporting domestic manufacturing. Heavyweight industries like the automotive and the aerospace industries, as well as HP for consumer and medical products,[22] are adopting 3D printing. This means that industries and politicians in countries like Japan, which have a strong exports in automotives,[23] but are building the 3D printing industry through collaborations with non-Japanese firms,[24] may push for rules that confer origin on parts printed in Japan to allow it to maintain its position in terms of global trade of vehicles. Lobbying and political pressure could induce negotiators to favor rules that strategically confer origin on certain products from certain countries, but are trade distortive due to the high costs of compliance or simply being out-of-synch with how goods are produced and traded by MSMEs. The need to reduce this potential risk provides support for a plurilateral instrument negotiated under the aegis of the WTO, however, not as a harmonized set of rules.

2.2 *Determining the Value of 3D File*

We must consider the legal implications given that RoO for services are regulated by the GATS. As Dinh has argued, a RoO regime for services based on the economic origin of the service input may allow for an integrated goods-services origin determination as origin determination for goods is determined by where the most economic value is created.[25] However, services are created through global value chains. An economic approach for determining the origin of a service would require identifying the value for each input in that chain and may prove an additional burden on trade.[26] It may be challenging to trace drafts of 3D files transmitted among office branches or among contractors in different countries and also identity the value at each stage. Policymakers

22 '3D Printers – From Adoption to Scale: A complete 3D Printing Journey' (hp.com 2025) <https://www.hp.com/us-en/printers/3d-printers.html> accessed 11 March 2025.

23 'Japanese Foreign Trade in Figures' (santadartrade.com July 2021), <https://santandertrade.com/en/portal/analyse-markets/japan/foreign-trade-in-figures?url_de_la_page=%2Fen%2Fportal%2Fanalyse-markets%2Fjapan%2Fforeign-trade-in-figures&&actualiser_id_banque=oui&id_banque=0&memoriser_choix=memoriser> accessed 3 November 2021.

24 USITA, 'Japan Additive Manufacturing and 3D Printing' (trade.gov 15 June 2020) <https://www.trade.gov/market-intelligence/japan-additive-manufacturing-and-3d-printing> accessed 3 November; Davide Sher, 'Japanese additive manufacturing is rising' (*3D Printing Media Network* 7 December 2020) <https://www.3dprintingmedia.network/japanese-additive-manufacturing-is-rising/> accessed 3 November 2021.

25 Dinh (n 17) 133–134, 140–142.

26 ibid 140.

would need to consider whether and how to cumulate value created in different countries. The rules would have to include procedures for obtaining a certificate of origin of the service and custom offices. Would such evidence be the same required for goods: invoices, purchase orders, or affidavits listing the contributions of each designer? Further, some 3D files are created as part of the opensource/sharing economy and made available for little or no cost. A free digital file does not necessarily reflect the economic value of time spent designing it, so how does one assign this file a value when it is an input in determining origin of the final good? Tracing the economic origin of an intangible item transmitted across the globe in addition to the economic origin of the tangible inputs of a good could bring the rules further away from scholarly and policy goals of simplifying the rules to encourage trade under preferential rates.

A GATS regime of rules of origin based on the legal origin of the service provider seems simpler, but, some complications do arise. First, firms may have strategic reasons for being legally based in one country and outsourcing design work to branches or contractors in a different country. Further, with the rise of remote working, designers can make 3D files and transfer them through remote servers to other designers or offices across the world. Claiming that a file originated from the legal seat of a company does not entirely acknowledge the global aspect of production of the file. A benefit of basing origin on legal status is that there are domestic and regional regulations and cases on business establishment and substantive business operations that can be consulted if a question arises as to which entity is the producer of the file and where this entity is located.[27]

Next, the GATS Schedules of Commitments and the GATT Schedules of Concessions were designed with different objectives on preventing trade distortion and encouraging trade liberalization. A possible clash could arise: using the HS code one determines that the 3D printed good is eligible for a very low preferential tariff rate. However, consulting the GATS schedule of Commitments, first identifying the category the 3D file falls under, and then, the level of liberalization for that particular service, one may determine that the same country has not liberalized its design services to the same extent that it has liberalized trade in the type of good that is 3D printed. Thus, if the 3D file is the input with the most significant value of the final product, policymakers and customs administrations may determine that the 3D printed good should

27 Mavroidis, *The Regulation of International Trade*, vol 3 (n 1) 301; Catherine Barnard with Jukka Snell, 'Free Movement of Legal Persons and the Provision of Services,' in Catharine Barnard and Steve Peers (eds), *European Union Law* (3rd edn OUP 2020) 471, 475–477.

not be granted the preferential tariff rate, because allowing such 3D products under the lower rate would expose the design service industry to competition and allow for a higher level of liberalization in design services than intended in the GATS schedule.

Focusing more on the technical aspects of the rules, how would a rule incorporate the value of file design into the value-added formulas? Definitions for the terms in the value-added formula, such as what costs can be included or excluded in the assessment, are set out in RoO chapters. Costs related to design services can be included in the category of direct cost[28] and the ASEAN TIGA specifically references "research, development, design, and engineering" as part of direct costs.[29] RoO for goods produce a certain level of uncertainty, but it is an uncertainty that the trade community has come to expect and has developed means for addressing through customs administrations, private enterprises that assist traders with paperwork, and organizations like the ICC. Additionally, there are customs rulings and trade court decisions that traders and officials can consult.

Adding the valuation of design work as an originating input into the origin assessment will require practitioners, customs officials, and trade assistance industries to adapt. This could be beneficial in the long run, but inject a further element of uncertainty into the system in the short term. From the point of view of the trader and the customs officials, there is potentially additional legal risk. EU and US customs administrations require traders to be responsible for the accuracy of the documents they submit; good faith reliance on the statements of subcontractors and third-party suppliers is not sufficient to avoid penalties if customs officials determine that there was false information in the supporting documents and statements. The trader will have to verify the chain of the design creation in addition to verifying the source of the materials and the labor performed.

This value of 3D file could be subjective. A handcrafted necklace made with raw materials by a micro-enterprise in a developing country takes time to create as the materials must be processed and the beading is intricate. This necklace would have a relatively high labor value. It would also perhaps have a "deeper" value as it is an example of a MSME participating in international trade while

28 Edwin A Vermulst, 'Rules of Origin as Commercial Policy Instruments – Revisited' (1992) 26 J World Trade 61, 66; Anne Van de Heetkamp and Rudd Tusveld, *Origin Management: Rules of Origin in Free Trade Agreements* (Springer 2011), 86; Agreement between New Zealand and Singapore on a Closer Economic Partnership (CEP agreement 2000) (signed 14 November 2000, entered into force 1 January 2001) Annex I, s 2, art 6.

29 ASEAN Trade in Goods Agreement (ATIGA) (signed 26 February 2009, entered into force 17 May 2010), ch 3 art 29 (2)(d).

preserving traditional, culturally significant manufacturing methods. Thus, its "worth" in a deep trade perspective could be high, even though the materials are not expensive. Now, this micro-enterprise has designed a 3D file for parts of the necklace, prints the parts using plastic resins, and assembles those parts with hand-made parts from traditional materials. She can make and sell more necklaces; it would seem that this micro-enterprise is better off. The likelihood that the trader could export the necklaces under preferential rules that do not include a service input may be reduced. Assembling fewer pieces of the necklace could be classified as "simple assembly." The costs of labor have been reduced relative to the costs of the plastic materials, which do not originate in the territory.

If the rules allow for the value of the service input to be considered for origin determination, the micro-enterprise must prove that when the value of the 3D file is added to the value of labor and any originating materials, then most of value creation occurred in the territory. If she has just started 3D design, she may have expended hours creating the design which would have taken a trained designer an hour to create. Is the design of the micro-enterprise more valuable because it took more time to design? Or, is it less valuable given that a skilled designer would be able to produce a similar design in less time? In that situation, should we assign more value to the 3D design because the trader is a start-up who has adopted additive manufacturing technology? By allowing the trader to trade under the preferential rate, we can encourage her to remain in trade and to continue to promote her cultural heritage While such a subjective assessment may satisfy the deeper provisions of a trade agreement, how would customs offices, which rely on documents supported by accounting principles, audits, and valuation formulas, assess the "deeper" value created by making the necklace with 3D printed parts.

This part took proposals to include the value of the service input in origin determination of the final good a few steps further into both the technical and policy implications of designing preferential RoO that incorporate services inputs. From the "shallow" perspective, complications arise when designing the rules to include the service inputs: the GATS Schedules of Commitments and GATT Schedules of Concessions, the AOR Annex II, and the GATS provisions relating to origin of a service were not negotiated for a hybrid system. A mixed rules of origin regime may require a new round of reciprocal exchanges of benefits. This is not impossible: where there is a political will, there is a way. If the industry grows significantly, industry lobbyists, customs officials, and customs organizations may begin to pressure policymakers and lawmakers to design such rules. The aim of the proceeding paragraphs was to highlight where some of the issues that underly RoO for traditional manufacturing (protectionism, lack of transparency, complexity) could arise in the context for rules for advanced manufacturing techniques. These paragraphs also linked such a proposal to the greater discussion in trade law on the inclusion of deeper provisions in trade agreements.

New rules could be designed in a shallow manner, based on reciprocal exchanges and technical expertise, but they may not correlate with some other objectives in a PTA such as promoting new technological means of production, labor safety, or environmental sustainability. RoO chapters are not necessarily the place to insert a deep agenda. However, if policymakers, lawmakers, governments, lobbyists, and industry actors are going to expend efforts into designing a new rules regime, it is an opportunity to design rules that are more receptive to a modernizing trade law framework. One of the elements of this modern framework, e-commerce regulation, does have a connection to rules of origin. However, rules of origin for products with digital inputs should not be dependent on the WTO e-commerce negotiations, as there is no consensus among Members on the regulation of electronic transmissions now and unlikely in the near future.

3 RoO: Connected to, but Not Dependent on, E-Commerce Regulation

The WTO's moratorium on custom duties for electronic transmissions has persisted since 1998, and digital commerce chapters in FTAs and agreements dedicated to digital commerce include provisions on withholding custom duties on electronic transmissions.[30] A study for UNCTAD reports that several developing countries, such as Cambodia, Rwanda, Uganda, and Togo, could be potential adopters of advanced manufacturing and criticize the Joint Statement Initiative (JSI) on E-Commerce, of which 91 WTO Members participate, for not giving enough focus on to how to design rules beneficial for countries

30 Eg, Agreement between the United States of America, the United Mexican States, and Canada (USMCA) (signed 30 November 2018, entered into force 1 July 2020) ch 19 art 19.3(1); Comprehensive and Progressive Agreement for Trans-Pacific Partnership (CPTPP), incorporating Trans-Pacific Partnership Agreement (TPP) (signed 8 March 2018), ch 14 art 14.3; Trade And Cooperation Agreement Between The European Union And The European Atomic Energy Community, Of The One Part, And The United Kingdom Of Great Britain And Northern Ireland, Of The Other Part, (TCA) (signed 30 December 2020, entered into force 1 January 2021) L 444/14, Heading I, Title III, ch 3 art 203(2); Mark Wu, 'Digital Trade-Related Provisions in Regional Trade Agreements: Existing Models and Lessons for the Multilateral Trade System' (2017) RTA Exchange (ICTSD and IDB), 11–13.

that have yet to develop e-commerce and additive manufacturing markets.[31] These countries argue that a permanent moratorium distorts trade by allowing foreign digital goods to enter the markets duty-free, thus depriving these countries of revenue and stunting the growth of local entrepreneurs and MSMEs.[32] In 2018 Indonesia established a new tariff line for digital goods, but with a 0% rate. The Tariff line is 99.01 – Software and other digital goods transmitted electronically, and includes subheading 9901.90.00 – Other software and digital goods.[33] At the WTO Ministerial Conference in 2017, Indonesia submitted a statement arguing that the extension of the moratorium should only apply to "the electronic transmissions and not to products or contents which are submitted electronically."[34] India and South Africa, referencing this statement, submitted a statement to the WTO arguing not only should digital content be excluded from the moratorium, but also cautioned against extending the moratorium to cover services.[35] For "[i]f services are also included, such an interpretation would mean that WTO Members are agreeing to a completely duty-free trading environment, in other words, a fully liberalised digital economy."[36] In such a scenario, tariff revenues could not be collected on the transmission of 3D files. The Protocol to the AfCFTA on Digital Trade establishes that there shall be no custom duties to digital products that originate in the territory (though internal taxes and fees may be applied).[37] The RCEP, however,

31 Pamela Coke Hamilton and Shamika N Sirmimanne (supervisors), 'What is at Stake for Developing Countries in Trade Negotiations on e-Commerce?: The Case of the Joint Statement Initiative' (2021) UNCTAD: Division on Intl Trade & Commodities & Division on Technology & Logistics, 35 <https://unctad.org/system/files/official-document/ditctncd2020d5_en.pdf> accessed on 29 October 2021. As of 2024, there are only 8 African Members that are part of the JSI, and India is not included in the 16 Asian countries.

32 ibid 9–11, 33–34. See also, Susan Ariel Aaronson and Thomas Struett, 'Data is Divisive: A History of Public Communications on E-commerce, 1998–2020' (2020) CIGI Papers No. 247, 17, 19–20, <https://www.jstor.org/stable/resrep27511> accessed 3 November 2021.

33 Ministry of Finance Regulation No. 17/PMK.010/2018 on the Second Amendment of Regulation No. 6/PMK.010/2017 on Stipulation of Goods Classification System and Import Duty on Imported Goods ("Regulation 17"). 'Indonesia Tax Information' (Deloitte 30 April 2018) 4 <https://www2.deloitte.com/content/dam/Deloitte/id/Documents/tax/id-tax-info-apr2018.pdf> accessed 29 October 2021.

34 'Statement by Indonesia: Facilitator's Consultation on Electronic Commerce, MC11 declaration, and other relevant plenary sessions', delivered on 13 December (20 December 2017) WT/MIN(17)/68 <https://docs.wto.org/> accessed 29 October 2021.

35 Communication from India and South Africa (10 March 2020) WTO: Work Programme on Electronic Commerce <https://docs.wto.org/> accessed 29 October 2021.

36 ibid para 5.1.

37 African Continental Free Trade Area Secretariat, 'Draft: Protocol to the Agreement Establishing the African Continental Free Trade Area on Digital Trade' (7–10 February 2024),

provides for the possibility of adjusting the "current practice of not imposing custom duties on electronic transmissions" between the Parties subject to the outcome on WTO Ministerial Decisions on customs duties, thus leaving a door open for the potential to impose custom duties.[38]

Among territories with a developed e-commerce market, such as China, the EU, and US, opinions on regulating data transmission and storage differ.[39] The use of such measures would impact the transmission of a 3D file, and could ultimately influence a company to design and transmit files in certain countries. Eighty of the Members of the JSI have agreed to a stabilized text of the agreement covering unsolicited commercial messages, electronic signatures and authentication, e-contracts, open government data, consumer protection, and flexibilities for LDCs and developing countries.[40] The text establishes that "[n]o Party shall impose customs duties on electronic transmissions between a person of one Party and a person of another Party"; however, "[t]aking into account the evolving nature of electronic commerce and digital technology," the Parties shall after 5 years, and periodically thereafter, assess the impact of this provision and whether any amendments are appropriate.[41] A decision on lifting the moratorium on duties on electronic transmissions at a multilateral level has been deferred until the 2026 Ministerial Conference.[42]

At this point, we can consider the relation of RoO to provisions regulating e-commerce in trade agreements. Should rules on determining the origin of an electronic transmission be included in chapters or sections dedicated to e-commerce? There is some argument in favor of this: rules on identifying the origin of data may assist lawmakers, policymakers and dispute settlement bodies in understanding whether one a party allegedly violates one of the provisions in the e-commerce chapter. However, adding such rules to an

art 6. Available at <https://www.bilaterals.org/IMG/pdf/afcfta_digital_trade_protocol_-_9_february_2024_draft.pdf> accessed 20 October 2024.

38 Regional Comprehensive Economic Partnership (RCEP) (signed 15 November 2020), art 12(11).

39 Aaronson and Struett (n 32) 16–17; Susan Ariel Aaronson and Patrick Leblond, 'Another Digital Divide: The Rise of Data Realms and its Implications for the WTO' (2018) 21 J Intl Economic L 245, 245–272.

40 Joint Statement Initiative On Electronic Commerce, 'Communication' (26 July 2024) INF/ECOM/87 <https://docs.wto.org> accessed 25 October 2024. The Members that did not agree to the stabilized text are Brazil; Colombia; El Salvador; Guatemala; Indonesia; Paraguay; the Separate Customs Territory of Taiwan, Penghu, Kinmen and Matsu; Türkiye; and the United States.

41 ibid. para 11.3 and 11.5.

42 Ministerial Decision, 'Work Programme On Electronic Commerce' (2 March 2024) WT/MIN(24)/38, WT/L/1193 <https://docs.wto.org> accessed 23 March 2024.

e-commerce chapter risks bogging down the e-commerce chapters with rules not related to the free flow of data and protecting access to digital markets.

Even if there is no multilateral resolution on customs duties for electronic transmissions, the prohibitions against duties in recent agreements brings into question whether determining the origin of a design file may lead to imposing a duty where none was intended. For example, the origin of a 3D printed good is determined using an *ad valorem* formula that includes the value of the 3D file. While being designed, the file is transmitted to several parties of the PTA and is finally transmitted to the Party where the file is downloaded into the printer. After assessing the value of the printing, post-processing, and direct costs, it is determined that the element with the most value is the 3D file, and the origin of the good is the origin of the 3D file. The tariff rate for the finished 3D printed good is now based on the country of origin of the 3D file. In the PTA, the e-commerce chapter requires no duties on electronic transmissions. Yet, a duty would be effectively placed on an electronic transmission, because the origin of the good, and thus the tariff duty rate, is based on the 3D file which must be electronically transmitted (if not sent in the mail on a thumb-drive).

Analysts and policymakers should also consider how to design such rules in terms of cumulation of value. A PTA exists for Country A, Country B, and Country C. There are no custom duties on electronic transmissions, but a 5% preferential rate on bicycle parts is imposed. The rule is an *ad valorem* rule in which origin is determined by where the most value was created. Country A produces a 3D file of a bicycle frame and sends it to Country B for printing and processing; no tariff is assessed on the file. The frame is imported into Country C. The customs office in Country C must then decide how to assess tariff duties:

1. Does Country C allow the bicycle frame to enter duty free because the highest value element is a digital file, which is electronically transmitted, and thus, should not be subject to custom duties;
2. Or is the value of the digital file cumulated with the other value created in processing the bicycle frame in Country B and thus, a 5% tariff is applied on a finished product originating in Country B;
3. Or is origin assigned to Country A, as that is where the most value was created, even though there are no customs duties on the electronic transmission of the 3D file, a duty is still applied to the tangible product produced from the file, the 5% rate between Country A and Country C?

If the last two scenarios occur, this may give an incentive for producers in Country C to seek domestic 3D file designers and printers, diverting trade in 3D files away from Country A and Country B. Further, if Country A sends files to Country B for printing of bicycle frames, then the 0% duty on electronic transmissions may benefit traders in Country A and producers in Country B who have adopted advanced manufacturing, but may disadvantage producers who still use traditional manufacturing techniques when trading with C. There is a new source of domestic competition for traditionally manufactured parts (although this may be considered as a positive push to innovate and adopt new technologies).

This example points to two significant issues with including the 3D file in the origin analysis, the first that it will require synthesizing two different frameworks for trade: a lighter-touch approach to e-commerce with a very heavy-handed approach to rules of origin. For example, the digital trade chapter in the USMCA is 10 pages long with one annex of one page,[43] the Rules of Origin chapter is 14 pages, however the annexes on exceptions, the product specific rules, an appendix on product specific rules for automotive goods, and tables of automotive parts total to 256 additional pages.[44]

Secondly, as Shaffer states, a new digital trade agreement should accommodate "regulatory flexibility" as well as "the interface and interoperability of different regulatory systems that reflect varying national practices and preferences."[45] At the level of EU PTAs, Jan A. Micallef finds that while the parties proclaim interest in regulating the transmission of data, they are cautious in establishing obligations in provisions on e-commerce, and instead rely on review clauses, freedom to adopt and maintain safeguards, and general agreements to cooperate on data regulation.[46] In contrast, preferential RoO are intricate so that non-originating goods are not granted preferential rates. Rules of Origin in PTAs are negotiated as reciprocal (in theory) arrangements. This exchange is based on the condition that each party can withdraw a commitment if the other party does not adhere to its reciprocal commitment.[47]

There is a risk that a including the 3D file in the origin analysis will lead traders to circumvent rules that were negotiated for specific strategic purposes. Country A, which has a strong domestic bicycle parts industry, may agree to

43 USMCA ch 19.

44 USMCA ch 14. This ratio is also reflected in CETA. The chapter on electronic commerce has 2 pages, the Protocol on Rules of Origin and Origin Procedures, 206 pages. CETA ch 16 (Electronic Commerce) and Protocol on Rules of Origin & Origin Procedure.

45 Gregory Shaffer, 'Trade Law in a Data-Driven Economy: The Need for Modesty and Resilience' (2021) 20 World Trade Rev. 259, 273.

46 Jan A Micallef, 'Digital Trade in EU FTAs: Are EU FTAs Allowing Cross Border Digital Trade to Reach Its Full Potential?' (2019) 53 J World Trade 855, 867–869; See also Wu (n 30) 7–9.

47 Bernard Hoekman and Douglas Nelson, '21st Century Trade Agreements and the Owl of Minerva' (2018), EUI Working Papers, RSCAS 2018/04, 12 <https://cadmus.eui.eu/bitstream/handle/1814/50964/RSCAS_2018_04.pdf?sequence=1&isAllowed=y> accessed 23 October 2021.

lower its tariff rate for bicycle parts to 5% in exchange for Country B, which has a strong kitchen appliances industry, lowering its tariff rate for dishwashers. Both countries agree to 0% duties on electronic transmissions. The MFN rate for bicycle frames is 15%. Country A produces a 3D file, sends the file to Country C, and there are no duties on electronic transmissions. Country C is not part of the PTA with Country A and Country B. The trader in Country C exports the printed bicycle frames to Country B, claiming on the certificate of origin that the frames originate from Country A, because the highest value created was in Country A (on the basis of 3D file), and thus a 5% tariff should be applied, instead of the 15% MFN rate. Country C is able to take advantage of the Country A-B FTA without having to liberalize its domestic dishwasher or bicycle industries to the same extent of Country A or Country B.

When examining the implications of including the digital file in the origin analysis, policymakers, lawyers, and lobbyists should consider the relation of the RoO chapter to provisions banning custom duties on electronic transmissions or negotiated tariff rates for certain key products. Basing the origin of a finished good on the origin of a 3D file could impinge upon the rate of liberalization negotiators are willing to agree to. If the product originates on the basis of the 3D file, and a 0% rate is applied, this may satisfy policymakers who want few restrictions on e-commerce trade, however it may dissatisfy negotiators focusing on industries that are cautious about liberalizing trade in finished products. On the other hand, determining that the final good originates in a territory because the 3D file originates there and then assigning the tariff rate of the finished good can apply a duty on the basis of an electronic transmission. This suggests that policymakers that want the design file to be part of the origin analysis of an advanced manufactured good should communicate with those drafting e-commerce chapters as there could be conflicting provisions within the same agreement on applying preferential tariff rates to goods whose origin is based on the digital file and applying no tariffs on electronic transmissions.

We also need to consider designing procedural rules. Analysts propose that e-commerce is one area where domestic regulatory bodies should be allowed to participate in the international trade law system given their effectiveness in addressing market failures and the impact of standards and procedures on voters (and thus, traders).[48] Preferential RoO, on the other hand, establish a procedural foundation for customs officials to process vast quantities of goods daily.

48 ibid 10, 14.

RoO chapters include rules on verification of origin, tracing requirements and forms that must be filled out. Ideally, this new drafting activity would not add complex procedures. Local customs offices will need to be trained in assessing the origin of the electronic transmission. While traders may seek guidance directly from the trade offices or their representatives in the commercial service, international organizations like WCO and ICC have roles in the daily practice of clearing goods through customs. Such organizations would likewise be involved in interpreting RoO of a digital service and providing guidance. Finally, the private market of companies offering trade assistance would be tasked with understanding where and how such rules fit into the RoO system established by prior RTAs and instruments and how to clear 3D printed products through customs offices.

These are issues that are not raised in e-commerce chapters, because the purpose of those chapters is to regulate the flow and trade of data. However, expanding RoO to include the digital file as an origin conferring input brings trade of such files into the ambit of procedural and administrative aspects of origin determination. It is quite possible that someone may request the electronic transmission of a 3D file from a foreign designer and then never print anything. In that case, it could be argued that the trade is a solely regulated by e-commerce measures. However, when a 3D file is designed for the purpose of being printed, such as a part for a GE appliance or Mercedes-Benz vehicle, and this part is then exported, it may become necessary to distinguish the regulation of the trade of the 3D file under the e-commerce provisions from the application of the rules in the RoO chapter to the same 3D file, if the digital file also has the potential to have an origin conferring function.

This section has assessed where rules of origin for a 3D file would intersect with a WTO instrument on e-commerce and data, as well as with provisions in e-commerce chapters in trade agreements. It is likely that a 3D file transmitted by means of digital technology is an article of e-commerce and will be subject to regulations in e-commerce chapters or stand-alone digital trade agreements. If rules of origin for digital services like 3D files are included within existing RoO chapters in RTAs or plurilateral instruments, or added as annexes, there should be some sensitivity to provisions on e-commerce so that complying with or enforcing the provisions of one chapter does not lead to a conflict with the objectives and rights established in the other chapter.

Part III took the proposal that goods should be granted origin based on where they are designed several steps closer towards exploring how such a RoO regime would fit within the WTO framework, PTAs, and the practice of customs administration. The next part explores how and to what capacity the

WTO could be involved in negotiating an Instrument on RoO for goods with digital file inputs and assisting Members and traders in understanding RoO.

4 A Proposal for a WTO Instrument on Preferential RoO for Advanced Manufactured Goods

Designing rules of origin for goods with service inputs like 3D printed goods presents an opportunity for reconsidering the role of the WTO in providing a legal framework for preferential RoO. As the stalled negotiations on the HWP for non-preferential rules of origin suggest, Members may be reluctant to cede sovereignty in a politically sensitive area of trade policy in exchange for a multilateral regulation of preferential RoO, even if such an approach may ultimately make the system more evenhanded and less susceptible to influence by domestic protectionary interests. A WTO instrument on preferential RoO nonetheless is still worth considering, especially as the changes advanced manufacturing can bring to goods production can lead to changes in conducting and regulating trade: reshoring, a shift from labor-intensive to automotive production, a shift from natural to synthetic materials for production, as well as reliance on certain mineral and metals for inputs such as the ink in 3D printing.

4.1 *Initial Considerations*

As an initial step into this discussion, let us review some proposals by legal scholars and economists in situating preferential rules of origin within the WTO, an exercise that seems as if one is trying to fit a square peg into a round hole. The title of the article by Mavroidis and Vermulst, "The Case for Dropping Preferential Rules of Origin," neatly presents their perspective. They argue that as the MFN rules of origin "can serve as the vehicle to ascertain origin of goods, and based on this decision, to grant preferential treatment to goods originating in beneficiary countries,"[49] preferential rules, "are not functionally necessary."[50] The authors suggest that MFN rules would perform this task, "especially so if the HWP, which aims at simplifying the existing rules, were to eventually succeed."[51] With regards to harmonization, Hoekman and Kostecki propose that it would help prevent the use of rules as a non-tariff barrier and suggest

49 Petros C. Mavroidis and Edwin Vermulst,'The Case for Dropping Preferential Rules of Origin' (2018) 52 J World Trade 1, 1.

50 ibid 10.

51 ibid 6.

that Members use the non-preferential rules under the Kyoto Protocol instead of the preferential rules found in PTAs.[52]

The removal of preferential RoO would perhaps reduce the number of rules traders must interact with, yet there is still the question of how under MFN rules the origin of a 3D printed good would be determined. Lawmakers and policymakers would be confronted with the task of determining whether and to what extent a digital file service input should be incorporated into the origin analysis of the tangible good. It will still be necessary to consider whether there should be a revision of the three substantial transformation criteria.

While harmonization may reduce the costs of complying with RoO under multiple PTAs, it may not necessarily reduce the administrative cost of complying with a particular PTA for a MSME.[53] Simplification of the certification process has started to appear in some RoO instruments. The revisions of the PEM include one certification process instead of the EUR.1 and EUR.MED certificates.[54] The USMCA now allows importers to complete the certificate of origin, allowing them to control and verify the information on the certificate.[55] The importer can also forgo the certificate and submit a "minimum set of data elements."[56] The EU has an electronic self-certification system, called the REX system (Registered Exporter system).[57]

While some trade and economic scholars encourage simplification of rules of origin, they do not advocate for harmonization due to the different levels of development and different trade practices of WTO Members. Erasmus, Flatters, and Kirk, argue that the focus should be on a "radical reform of Rules-of-Origin regimes, and not on harmonization."[58] Instead, we should "consider the effects

52 Bernard Hoekman and Michel M Kostecki, *The Political Economy of the World Trading System: The WTO and Beyond* (3rd edn, OUP 2009), 487–488.

53 Dan Ciuriak and Derk Bienen, 'Overcoming Low Preference Utilization in Preferential Trade Agreements: Presumption of Origin for Small Shipments' (2014) Trade & Development Discussion Paper No. 02/2014, bkp Development Research and Consulting, 17–18 <https://papers.ssrn.com/sol3/papers.cfm?abstract_id=2460648> accessed 10 March 2025.

54 Commission, 'Guidance: Transitional PEM Rules of Origin' (v1.1–27 August 2024) Brussels, 27 August 2024, TAXUD/A6/AM/MO, 20–22.

55 David Gantz, 'The United States-Mexico-Canada Agreement: Tariffs, Customs, and Rules of Origin' (2019) Baker Institute Rep. no. 02.21.19, 6; USMCA ch 5 art 5.2.1; USITA, 'Understanding USMCA' (trade.gov) <https://www.trade.gov/usmca-dayone-0> accessed 2 December 2021.

56 USMCA ch 5 art 5.2.3; USITA, 'Understanding USMCA' (n 55).

57 Commission, 'REX-Registered Exporter system' (ec.europa.eu) <https://ec.europa.eu/taxation_customs/online-services/online-services-and-databases-customs/rex-registered-exporter-system_en> accessed 3 November 2021.

58 Erasmus, Flatters and Kirk (n 4) 292.

of alternative Rules of Origin in light of their only necessary function and to discard their use for protection and other distorting and counterproductive uses."[59] Estevadeordal, Harris, and Suominen point out that full harmonization is likely to meet resistance as states may not be willing to adopt rules based on those of other states.[60] However, these authors still proposed (in 2009) that multilateral disciplines on preferential RoO within the WTO that aim to reduce complexity and restrictiveness of these rules may be beneficial for the trading system.[61] Since that time there have been developments in plurilateral agreements to regulate trade.

4.1.1 WTO as a Forum for Negotiations on a RoO Instrument

Before examining how a plurilateral agreement could encompass preferential RoO for 3D printed goods or advanced manufactured goods, it is necessary to briefly acknowledge the shift from negotiating multilateral agreements towards plurilateral agreements. The stagnation of the Doha Round and the expansion of the WTO Membership has led to questioning as to the Members' ability to negotiate and conclude multilateral agreements in the near future.[62] The proliferation of PTAs is both seen as a reaction to the difficulties in negotiating multilateral agreements as well as an interest in developing deeper trade agreements.[63] On the other hand, the successful completion of the plurilateral agreements, the Information Technology Agreement and the Trade Facilitation Agreement, indicates that there was, and perhaps continues to exist, an interest in negotiating trade instruments within the WTO framework. The 2015 Nairobi Decision on Preferential Rules of Origin for LDCs suggests a possibility of addressing the regulation of preferential RoO within the WTO. However, the ITA, the TFA, and the Nairobi Decision also regulate trade within a narrow range of tariff lines, procedural issues, or countries. The reasons why these plurilateral agreements and the Nairobi Decision were successful will be discussed below and will be examined in the context of developing a WTO instrument on Preferential RoO.

A WTO Instrument on Preferential RoO could require Members to minimize negative externalities that can arise with preferential RoO. Hoekman and

---

59 ibid.

60 ibid.

61 ibid.

62 Bernard Hoekman, 'Urgent and Important: Improving WTO Performance by Revisiting Working Practices' (2019) 53 J World Trade 373, 374.

63 ibid; C Boonekamp, "Regional Trade Agreements and the WTO," in Carlos A Primo Braga and Bernard Hoekman (eds), *The Future of the Global Trade Order* (2nd edn, Eur U Institute 2017), 211.

Mavoridis argue that the modernization of the WTO as an organization that supports "plurilateral domain-specific cooperation" requires it to "bolster its capacity to be a forum for constructive policy dialogue based on analysis of the negative policy spillovers created by domestic policies."[64] Preferential RoO can cause negative spillovers by raising the costs to trade under preferential rates and diverting trade from third parties. There is reason for the Secretariat to invest resources in studying preferential RoO. Primo Braga and Hoekman propose that for channeling "more of the energy that currently is invested in PTAs towards rule-making under the WTO umbrella," a necessary condition is "more collective learning about the experiences of PTAs in dealing with" policy areas that cause negative externalities.[65] There is a large body of PTAs with preferential RoO that the Secretariat can consult, analyze and build recommendations upon.

The WTO provides a forum for reciprocal negotiations, although some scholars caution that the notion of reciprocity is more nuanced. A new agreement may better reflect the outcome of a strategic negotiation of an agreement that is acceptable, but not optimal, for all rather than a common understanding on the trade issue that initiated discussions.[66] While Members may have a baseline objective to make preferential RoO less susceptible to domestic protectionist pressures and negative spillovers, given the politically sensitive nature of some industries, like textiles and automotives, there may be some concessions that could make the preferential RoO Instrument not very stringent in requiring Members to limit the restrictiveness of the rules.

Nonetheless, reciprocal exchanges on preferential RoO for advanced manufactured products centered on tariff reductions may improve the chance that a concluded agreement relatively balances the benefits for all parties. Once "deeper" issues enter the discussions, such as labor wage rates or environmental regulations for ink or energy consumption, Members, with more resources, could use their economic and geopolitical weight to turn the negotiations in their favor. L. Alan Winters points out that negotiating tariffs is more straightforward than negotiating regulations as "tariffs may be tweaked to reach acceptable agreements" and are "owned" by trade ministries simplifying the

---

64 Bernard Hoekman and Petros C Mavroidis, 'WTO Reform: Back to the Past to Build for the Future' (2021) 12 Global Policy (Sup. 3) 5, 6.

65 Carlos A Primo Braga and Bernard Hoekman, 'The Future of the Global Trade Order' in Carlos A Primo Braga and Bernard Hoekman (eds), *The Future of the Global Trade Order* (2nd edn, Eur U Institute 2017) 23.

66 Joseph Michael Finger, 'The GATT/WTO System and National Trade Policies: Which Comes First?' in Manfred Elsig, Bernard Hoekman, and Joost Pauwelyn (eds), *Assessing the World Trade Organization: Fit for Purpose?* (CUP 2017) 418.

bureaucratic process whereas regulatory issues are "owned" by other ministries and "often have a rather all-or-nothing character."[67] As a result, regulatory issues give "a strong first mover advantage to a bloc that can arrive at the global negotiating table with a ready-made proposal."[68] If Members keep a preferential RoO Instrument as a "shallow" agreement, there is a possibility that reciprocity could lead to a mutually beneficial (or at least somewhat beneficial) result given the tradition of such negotiations within trade ministries. On the other hand, should these rules include "deeper" provisions (which may be beneficial – rules on environmental standards for ink to reduce pollution could produce positive externalities), trade ministers and the WTO would need to be careful that the inclusion of regulatory issues does not transform the negotiations into an "either/or" condition from one or a few of the parties. The success of the ITA and the FTA derives partially from the ability of the negotiators to side-step contentious political issues due to the limited scope of the products or practices covered by the agreements.

4.1.2 First Plurilateral Success Story: Information Technology Agreement

Key factors for the success of the ITA and the ITA expansion were the focus on tariffs, the relatively narrow range of goods covered, the support of the IT industry, and a general interest to arrive at an agreement. First, the ITA is a Critical Mass Agreement (CMA), meaning that its disciplines apply only to the Members who are signatories to the agreement, but its benefits apply to all Members.[69] The ITA resulted from negotiations to gradually eliminate tariffs on information-technology products.[70] The 14 parties accounted for 80% of world trade in IT products[71] and as Members joined, the ITA's coverage expanded to 97% of world trade in such products.[72] This high level of coverage reduces the risk of free riding by the non-signatories.[73] For the expansion negotiations, the

67 L Alan Winters, 'The WTO and RTAs: Is It All Over for Multilateralism?' in Manfred Elsig, Bernard Hoekman, and Joost Pauwelyn (eds), *Assessing the World Trade Organization: Fit for Purpose?* (CUP 2017) 359–360.

68 ibid 360.

69 Gary Winslett, 'Critical mass agreements: the proven template for trade liberalization in the WTO' (2018) 17 World Trade Rev 405, 418.

70 Ministerial Declaration on Trade in Information Technology Products (Singapore, 13 December 1996) WT/MIN(96)/16, p 1 <http://docs.wto.org> accessed 30 October 2021.

71 ibid. The parties included the EC, at that time 15 states, and other states or customs unions in the process of acceding to the WTO in the Singapore Ministerial Conference in 1996.

72 Ministerial Declaration on the Expansion of Trade in Information Technology Products (ITA Expansion) (Nairobi, 16 December 2015) WT/MIN(15)/25.

73 Rudolf Adlung and Hamid Mamdouh, 'Plurilateral Trade Agreements: An Escape Route for the WTO?' (2018) 52 J World Trade 85, 88.

Members agreed only to include IT products and refrained from requesting concessions on unrelated products as a condition for accepting the inclusion of another Member's IT product in the list.[74] However, informal deals between China, the US, and EU regarding contested IT products took place before the ITA expansion could be concluded.[75] Additional important factors were that the IT industry was in favor of the expansion, other domestic industries did not become involved or express interest in the discussions, and non-tariff domestic regulations were kept out of the negotiations.[76] Finally, the ITA focuses on tariff reduction, a benefit that is relatively easy to convey to voters: lower or no tariffs means less expensive IT products.[77] The ITA's success derives from: a general interest in reducing tariffs on a limited number of goods, general interest in reaching an agreement and streamlining the negotiation process, industry support, and a benefit that can be easily explained to voters.

4.1.3 Second Plurilateral Success Story: Trade Facilitation Agreement

A key factor in the TFA's success are the flexibilities it offers to developing countries in implementing commitments. Like the ITA, its origin is found in the Singapore ministerial conference.[78] There was also an understanding among Members for the need for a multilateral agreement on trade facilitation.[79] Developing countries initially expressed reluctance in negotiating from concern of being legally responsible for modernization of customs procedures for which they did not have technical or financial resources.[80] However, not only did developing countries agree to become parties if given flexibilities in implementing commitments, other Members supported including special and differential treatment provisions in order to conclude the agreement.[81] With regards to enforcement, the TFA includes an expert advisory group which assists Members in understanding their obligations under the agreement and in resolving implementation problems before recourse to the DSU.[82] The TFA's

74 Winslett (n 69) 418. Adlung and Mamdouh report that during the negotiations for the original ITA, there may have been some concessions by the US to the EU with regards to liberalizing its liquour imports (n 73) 96, fn 33.

75 Winslett (n 69) 419.

76 ibid 419, 422.

77 ibid 420.

78 Ministerial Declaration on Trade in Information Technology Products (Singapore) (n 70).

79 Alex Ansong, 'Single Undertaking, Different Speeds: Pliable Models for Decision-making in the WTO' (2018) 21 J Intl Economic L 395, 409.

80 ibid 409–410.

81 Ibid.

82 TFA art. 18; Bernard Hoekman and Charles Sabel, 'Plurilateral Cooperation as an Alternative to Trade Agreements: Innovating One Domain at a Time' (2021) 12 Global Policy (Sup. 3) 49, 57.

success derives from an understanding of the need for an agreement on trade facilitation and a general willingness to consider the concerns of developing members. Considering the ITA and TFA as examples of successful plurilateral negotiations, would it be possible to conclude a plurilateral agreement for preferential RoO for 3D printed goods and goods with a significant digital service input under the WTO?

4.1.4 Potential Plurilateral Success Story: Rules of Origin?

Looking at developments in the design of preferential RoOs in PTAs as well as the interest of WTO members in CMAs, Hoekman and Inama argue that a plurilateral agreement on RoO is feasible, albeit for non-preferential rules of origin. The complex design of rules, the variations by Members of the rules, and the reduction of efficiency resulting from different rules for different products amounts to a non-tariff barrier to trade.[83] Simplification and convergence of the non-preferential rules would reduce the cost to trade.[84] The authors focus on a plurilateral WTO instrument for non-preferential rules, because arguably preferential rules "fall out of the ambit" of the WTO.[85] However, they examine what they call the "convergence" of preferential RoO resulting from Southern Hemisphere and Asian Members modelling RoO on PEM or NAFTA in PTAs.[86]

Hoekman and Inama propose that WTO Members consider a CMA for non-preferential rules of origin due to the perceived "bottom up" convergence of preferential rules of origin. First, as non-preferential rules of origin "must apply on a MFN basis," they suggests a CMA, which can be more transparent than PTA negotiations given reporting requirements to the WTO Membership.[87] Next, to avoid political holdups, the negotiators should focus on harmonizing rules for goods that already have MFN rates of zero, as well as cooperate on the administration of the rules and on the issuance of certificates of origin.[88] In general, instead of focusing on "easy fixes" to RoO in RTAs, Members should identify the source of these issues and provide a framework for clearer and more efficient non-preferential RoO through a CMA under the WTO – and even "break the

83 Bernard Hoekman and Stefano Inama,'Harmonization of Rules of Origin: An Agenda for Plurilateral Cooperation' (2018) 22 East Asian Economic Rev 3, 5.

84 ibid.

85 ibid 6.

86 ibid 11.

87 ibid 22–23.

88 ibid 22–24.

wall that has separated preferential and non-preferential ROO."[89] At this point, instead of trying to break down walls, let us begin to approach the design of a WTO plurilateral instrument on preferential RoO for 3D printed goods and other tangible goods that have a significant digital input.

4.2 *Designing a RoO Instrument under the WTO*

The first step is to consider whether an agreement on preferential rules can be developed within the WTO framework. As stated in Annex II of the AOR, the Members recognize "that some Members apply preferential rules of origin" and that this leads "to the granting of tariff preferences going beyond the application of paragraph 1 of Article 1 of GATT 1994."[90] Under Annex II, Articles 1.1(4) and 1.2, Members must notify the Secretariat and either the Committee on Regional Trade Agreements or the Committee on Trade and Development of the preferential rules, any judicial decisions and administrative rules, or any modification or additions to existing rules.[91] Yet, some scholars question whether preferential rules are legal measures under GATT Article XXIV either based on a textual analysis of Article XXIV or on the protectionist effect of the rules.[92] It seems to be a bit of puzzle if one considers that under one Annex 1A agreement (GATT 1994) preferential rules are arguably not legal, but another Annex 1A agreement (Agreement on Rules of Origin), recognizes that Members apply such rules.

There are two basic approaches: One, preferential RoO in PTAs are not legal under Article XXIV, and further, there should be no preferential rules. This would end the discussion here. However, preferential RoO are measures that traders across the world deal with on a daily basis. Further, Members continue to design PTAs with preferential RoO. The second argument, and the one that will be followed, is: there is some question as to the legality of preferential RoO under Annex II AOR and Article XXIV GATT 1994; however, given their impact on trade and their potential to cause trade distortions, the WTO, as an organization that promotes liberalized trade, should examine how it could address preferential RoO to reduce their capacity to be used for protectionist purposes and as non-tariff barriers to trade.

---

89 ibid 25–26. See also, Inama, Rules of Origin in International Trade (2022) (n 4) 234–237.

90 Agreement on Rules of Origin (AOR) (15 April 1994) LT/UR/A-1A/7, Annex II arts 1 & 2.

91 ibid arts 1.1(4) & 1.2.

92 Eg, Mavroidis and Vermulst (n 49) 10–11; P Conconi and M García-Santana, L Puccio, R Venturini, 'From Final Goods to Inputs: The Protectionist Effect of Rules of Origin' (2018) 108 American Economic Rev 2335, 2362; Hoekman and Kostecki (n 52) 485–486.

4.2.1 Learning from Ministerial Decisions for RoO for LDCs, the ITA (I & II) and the TFA

Members have shown a willingness to collectively examine rules for preferential rules of origin for LDCs. At the 2013 Bali Ministerial Conference, the Members adopted a Ministerial Decision that established multilaterally agreed upon guidelines for simplifying preferential rules and making them more transparent.[93] The decision provides recommendations on designing rules for the three substantial transformation criteria; for example, (1) when to include or exclude transportation costs using the *ad valorem* method, (2) an across-the-board rule on when non-originating inputs can be deemed to undergo a substantial transformation under the CTH, and (3) taking into account the producing capacity of the LDC when basing a rule on the manufacturing or processing operation method.[94] The Bali Decision includes suggestions on allowing cumulation of materials with LDCs not part of the GSP, simplification of certification of origin procedures, and enhancing transparency by notification of the rules to the WTO.[95] Two years later, at the Nairobi Ministerial Conference, another Ministerial Decision was adopted which includes more detailed provisions on assessing whether sufficient transformation occurs within the LDC and on the expansion of cumulation with other LDCs and GSPs beneficiaries of the preference granting Member.[96] The 2023 Report by the Committee on Rules of Origin (CRO) identifies that almost all preference-granting Members have submitted notifications about meeting the requirements for preferential RoO.[97]

While these Decisions approach a specific issue, preferential RoO for LDCs, they demonstrate 1) the regulation of preferential RoO can be approached within the framework of the WTO, and 2) it is possible to include guidelines for the three substantial transformation criteria within a WTO instrument. The Nairobi Decision permits Members to continue to have sovereignty when designing rules while encouraging them to take into consideration the specific

93 Ministerial Decision, 'Preferential Rules of Origin for Least Developed Countries' (Bali Ministerial RoO Decision) (7 December 2013) WT/MIN(13)/42, WT/L/917 <https://www.docs.wto.org>.

94 ibid para 1.1–1.6.

95 ibid para 1.7–1.10.

96 Ministerial Decision, 'Preferential Rules for Least Developed Countries' (Nairobi Ministerial RoO Decision) (19 December 2015), WT/MIN(15)/47, WT/L/917/Add.1, 1–2.

97 CRO, 'Report of The Committee on Rules of Origin to The General Council on Preferential Rules of Origin for Least Developed Countries (20 November 2023) G/RO/W/223/Rev.2, 2 <https://www.docs.wto.org>.

production capacity and needs of the LDCs.[98] However, this means that the prescriptiveness of the Decision is rather soft. For example, for the *ad valorem* criterion, "Preference-granting Members shall: Adopt a method of calculation based on the value of non-originating materials. However, Preference-granting Members applying another method may continue to use it."[99] With regards to the CTH, "as a general principle," the Preference-granting Member shall, "allow for a simple change of tariff heading or change of tariff sub-heading" and shall eliminate all exclusions or restrictions to CTH rules unless if deemed necessary.[100] Finally, Preference granting Members shall, "to the extent possible, avoid requirements" that impose two criteria for the same product (such as a CTH and *ad valorem* percentage).[101] However, if the Member still maintains a combination, "the Preference-granting Member should remain open to consider relaxing such requirements for that specific product upon request by an LDC."[102] Thus, the Decision continues to give Members a wide latitude of sovereignty in designing rules of origin.

Such language allows Members flexibility in designing rules to be more responsive to the needs of the preference-accepting parties of a GSP, but it does raise questions on how this decision will lead to changes in the design of preferential RoO for GSPs. In 2020, the LDC Group at the WTO submitted a communication to the CRO stating that while some progress has been achieved in terms of transparency, there had not been "parallel progress in implementing the substantive part of the Nairobi Decision, more precisely the paragraphs concerning the substantial transformation and certification requirements."[103] The Group hoped to make "concrete progress" as Members headed towards the 2021 Ministerial Meeting (held in 2022).[104] In advance of the 2024 Ministerial Meeting, the CRO's report identified several instances where preference-granting Members which had not made the suggested changes to simplify the substantive rules (CTH, *ad valorem* requirement, cumulation) to facilitate origin determination.[105] However, the LDC Committee did find that

98 Nairobi Ministerial RoO Decision (n 96) para 1.1 (a)-(b).

99 ibid para 1.1(a).

100 ibid para 1.2 (a)-(b).

101 ibid para 1.4.

102 ibid.

103 LDC Group Communication, 'Submission of LDC to the Committee on Rules of Origin *Ad Valorem* Criterion, (30 October 2020) G/RO/W/202 para 1.1 <https://docs.wto.org> accessed 29 October 2021.

104 ibid.

105 CRO, 'Report' (20 November 2023) (n 97) 4–5.

self-certification programs and changes to the direct transportation rules by some Members, in particular the EU, were examples that could be adopted by the other preference-granting Members.[106]

At this point we can begin to consider whether an WTO Instrument on RoO could be devised for advanced manufactured goods which require a digital file as a necessary input for production. The ITA, TFA, and the Ministerial Decisions share an element in that they focus on relatively narrow areas of trade: a limited range of goods not politically sensitive (ITA), customs procedures (TFA), or LDCs (Bali and Nairobi Ministerial Decisions). Rules for 3D printed goods could apply to a range of goods that are in politically sensitive industries. Members interested in such an Instrument may wish to consider limiting the breadth of goods covered. As the range of goods made with 3D printing and other advanced manufacturing procedures is small relative to the range of goods produced with traditional manufacturing methods, it may be possible for negotiators to focus on a small set of tariff lines. In addition, the negotiators should allow for future expansion of the tariff lines covered by the agreement, as was included in the 1996 Ministerial Declaration on the ITA.[107]

If Members are interested in including the origin of the digital file input as part of the origin analysis, this will require considering what services are origin conferring services. The focus should be on those services that are necessary for the manufacturing of the good, such as the 3D file or a different digital file which instructs a machine to make a good. The value of the design work and other steps performed while creating the file could be cumulated to determine the overall value of the file. However, this should not mean that every email between designers and every mock-up should contribute to the origin conferring value. This could result in a lot of paperwork, damper interest in including the file as part of the origin analysis, and would impose a tracing protocol upon an economy that thrives on fluidity, flexibility, and constant innovation.[108] Since the service input is to be factored into the origin determination, services identified in RoO for goods that do not confer value should also be kept in mind. For example, financial services, logistic services, and advertising services all play a role in the creation, production, or distribution of a good, but they are excluded from contributing value when using the net cost method under the USMCA or CETA.[109] When determining the origin of a good that would be

106 ibid 6.

107 Ministerial Declaration on Trade in Information Technology Products (Singapore) (n 70), annex para 3.

108 Schaffer, 'Trade Law in a Data-Driven Economy' (n 45) 262.

109 USMCA ch 4 art 5(8); CETA Protocols on Rules of Origin and Origin Procedures art 17.

subject to the net cost methods, these services should not confer value on the 3D file to determine the origin of the file. This could help limit the scope of the WTO RoO Instrument.

The rules would also need to confirm whether the legal seat of the service supplier constitutes the origin of a service. Identifying the substantive business operations of a company can be done through accessing government records and databases, and court and administrative interpretations on SBO and on the geographical location of a legal seat can provide guidance.[110] There may be some risk that companies would claim origin based on establishment strategically to qualify for preferential treatment, i.e., claiming origin in the territory of a daughter company or a subsidiary.[111] Thus in the RoO Instrument, the Members could include requirements for proof that the alleged legal owner of the origin conferring input has SBO in the country or territory.

Given the interest in the US, the EU, and the OECD in 3D printing as a means of increasing manufacturing, and the concerns raised by UNCTAD on the impact of 3D printing on production in developing countries, it seems that enough Members would be open to pursuing negotiations. Whether there will be enough Members to reach a Multilateral Decision like the Bali and Nairobi Decisions is questionable given the general challenges that the WTO faces on reaching consensus among the large and varied Membership. It is key, however, that the Members with a significant 3D printing industry or making significant investments in adopting the technology be the foundational members for a plurilateral Instrument.

As multiple sectors use 3D printing and goods with digital file inputs, negotiations for an WTO instrument could face the risk of hold-ups and politically motivated proposals. 3D printed products are inputs in aircraft and vehicles, and entrepreneurs are developing 3D printed food and fabric, products of the politically sensitive agricultural and textile industries.[112] Members with such politically sensitive industries could demand concessions. Members that produce the raw materials, plastics, and metals for ink could have certain bargaining leverage to extract concessions for preferential treatment for unrelated products – there can be no 3D product without the ink. Unlike the ITA which had the advantage of focusing on a rather politically uncontentious industry

110 Mavroidis, *The Regulation of International Trade*, vol 3 (n 1) 301.

111 Barnard with Snell (n 27) 464.

112 Duchêne V and others, *Identifying Current and Future Application Areas, Existing Industrial Value Chains and Missing Competences in the EU, in the Area of Additive Manufacturing (3D printing)* Final Report for the Commission Executive Agency for Small & Medium-Sized Enterprises (Publications Office Eur Union 2016) 18–19 <https://data.europa.eu/doi/10.2826/72202> accessed 8 January 2022.

despite some side negotiations, an instrument on rules of origin for 3D printing could "import" the protectionist motivations that led to the impasse of the HWP on rules for traditionally manufactured goods and animal and agricultural products.

Considering rules for 3D printed goods and advanced manufactured goods provides an opportunity to address one of the key issues with RoO: the global value chain and the need to identify the origin of every part in the chain. The advantage of 3D printing is the reduction of parts to be assembled, such as GE's reduction of the parts of an aviation engine from 855 to 12. If a bicycle is made of fewer parts, the role of non-originating material in each part in the origin determination process may be more easily assessed. This could allow scholars and lawmakers to better examine the purpose and the functionality of cumulation in rules of origin. In addition, cumulation rules designed for goods that have thousands of parts may, when applied to the same type of good with fewer parts, result in preventing the good from qualifying for origin, as perhaps the percentage or value of the non-originating material in the ink is greater than the percentage or value of processing in the territory. Examining rules for advanced manufactured goods may allow us to design cumulation rules that function better in discerning which goods qualify for preferential treatment and also encourage traders to trade under preferential rates.

The role of the WTO would not necessarily be to design the specific rules on cumulation, but to provide guidelines so that cumulation functions to increase trade among the parties of a PTA. For example, the Nairobi Decision encourages Preference-granting Members "to expand cumulation to facilitate compliance with origin requirements by LDC producers" and provides a list of possibilities for expansion.[113] Likewise, a WTO instrument could provide cumulation possibilities for goods produced through advanced manufacturing taking into consideration the unique production methods which differ from traditional manufacturing.

There may not be complete agreement among Members upon detailed guidelines for the *ad valorem* criteria. A country that is a producer of ink or raw materials for ink may find *ad valorem* rules that exclude the 3D file's value favorable. A country that specializes in design of 3D files would not like such *ad valorem* rules. Members specializing in printing would want an *ad valorem* rule that allocates more value in processing and labor rather than in materials. Such issues could arise for other advanced manufacturing techniques which rely on digital technology and innovative or rare raw materials for production

113 Nairobi Ministerial RoO Decision (n 96) para 2.1.

of the goods. Members at least could work together to form guidelines for reducing confusion and inefficiencies when determining the origin of a 3D printed product. Similar to the Nariobi Decision, the WTO RoO Instrument could propose a recommended method for determining origin based on the *ad valorem* criterion, but also allow Members to continue to use other options. If enough Members apply the WTO recommended method, then convergence will occur at a plurilateral level. However, this raises the risk that certain countries with economic and political clout could be instrumental in the designs of guidelines that protect domestic industries or are beneficial to those Members that have already started adopting advanced manufacturing techniques at a widespread level.[114]

4.2.2 Additional Considerations for a WTO Instrument on Preferential RoO for Advanced Manufactured Products

Other topics Members will have to address during negotiations is to what extent the WTO Instrument would reference other WTO instruments (current and future), how the provisions in the Instrument could impact the design of procedural rules in PTAs (such as origin certification requirements), along with maintaining the awareness that as technology advances, the production of goods will change as well. First, the Members should consider the extent the Instrument would be linked to e-commerce instruments. If the moratorium on customs duties on electronic transmissions is made permanent, then there is some need to consider whether the origin of the 3D file should be included in the origin analysis. Members would have to explain that the application of a tariff on the 3D printed good is not a custom duty on the transmission of the 3D file *per se*, but a duty on a finished product based on where most of the value for the product was created.

The Members would also have to consider that RoO for services are based on the GATS. Would the Members include references in the Instrument to the GATS and state that the origin of the 3D file or digital file used in advanced manufacturing should be determined by Article I:2, Article XXVIII, and Article V:6 GATS? Or, would the Members use this negotiation as an opportunity to propose changes, such as the hybridization of the regulation of trade in goods and services? A WTO Instrument on rules of origin for advanced manufacturing products may allow Members to experiment with developing rules that apply to goods and services inputs under one instrument. On the other hand, negotiations would need to consider differences in the GATT and GATS towards

114 Hoekman, 'Urgent and Important' (n 62) 391.

trade liberalization. If the Members apply GATS provisions which provide for origin determination of a service based on the legal origin of the service provider, then they will need to ensure that provisions in the RoO Instrument are consistent with the GATS.

In addition to guidelines on the substantial transformation criteria, the WTO RoO Instrument should also include guidelines on the procedural aspects of determining origin for advanced manufactured products. Legal and economic scholars and companies, great and small, generally recognize that the administrative costs of determining the origin of a good is high. As 3D printing becomes more widespread, exporters and importers when preparing paperwork will have to consider whether printing is sufficient processing to activate a CTH and what HS code a good falls into.[115] Certainly, attempting to understand how a printed part for a vehicle meets the source material and labor value rules under the USMCA will take some guesswork. The WTO RoO Instrument would indicate guidelines for approaching customs determinations, indicating which type of documents are useful for demonstrating where and how the substantial transformation occurred, and establishing protocols for tracing the origin of the 3D file that are not overly burdensome and protect confidentiality and trade secrets. The Members would need to consider granting flexibilities to Developing Countries in implementing the changes to customs procedures proposed in the RoO Instrument.

The Instrument should take into consideration the changes in manufacturing and technology for producing goods for international trade. Destler, in looking at the NAFTA, proposed that for preferential RoO generally, FTAs should include a sunset or review provision.[116] Guidelines could require members to review customs procedures and substantial rules in PTAs given new updates

115 For example, buttons (not covered with textile material) fall into two categories under the HS based on materials. Plastic buttons are HS 9606.21, so buttons made of resin-based ink would fall into this category. Base metal buttons are HS 9606.22, so buttons of metal-based ink would fall into this category. However, scientists are exploring hybrid-plastic-metal inks. Would such printed buttons fall into "other" category for buttons, HS 9606.29? Or, would the classification be determined applying Rules 3 and 4 of the General Rules For the Interpretation of the Harmonized System. WCO, 'General Rules for the Interpretation of the Harmonized System' (n 230); WCO, 'WCO Trade Tools: Harmonized System' (wcotradetools.org) <https://www.wcotradetools.org/en/harmonized-system> accessed 30 October 2021; Shinjiro Umezu and Hirotaka Sato (corresponding authors), 'Metal-plastic hybrid 3D printing using catalyst-loaded filament and electroless plating' (2020) 36 Additive Manufacturing 101556.

116 IM Destler, 'Rules of Origin and U.S. Trade Policy' in Olivier Cadot, Antoni Estevadeordal, Akiko Suwa-Eisenmann, and Theirry Verdier (eds), *The Origin of Goods: Rules of Origin in Regional Trade Agreements* (OUP 2006) 186.

in technologies or manufacturing applied by industrial groups. Indeed, this is one area where continued collaboration with the WCO would be beneficial as updates to the HS code could include new tariff lines for mixtures of materials that constitute 3D printing ink. Standards by industrial organizations with regards to machine set up, operation, and post-processing techniques could indicate how much human labor is generally required and help with indicating how to determine the labor value component for an *ad valorem* calculation. Such review provisions require Members to be willing to commit to making periodic changes to national or regional customs procedures. The USMCA does encourage the Parties to propose additions to the list of parts and components for automotive goods to ensure that the rules on Labor Value Content requirements remain "relevant in light of technological changes and to facilitate the use of originating core parts."[117] As of yet, no significant changes have been made, despite advances in the automotive industry in EV.[118]

In conclusion, a WTO RoO Instrument on preferential RoO for advanced manufacturing products is feasible, but there are several elements required for a successful negotiation of such an agreement. First, the Instrument should be a plurilateral agreement with a core of Members who have a strong interest in reaching an agreement. The Instrument should allow other Members to join, as Members for which advanced manufacturing is still a minor means of production may wish to become a party to the Instrument when their use of advanced manufacturing is more developed. Members should not seek to harmonize the rules, but allow Members to continue to have sovereignty in designing rules for PTAs. It also acknowledges the different industrial capacities of the Members with regards to advanced manufacturing. Such flexibilities may make Members more inclined to become a party of such an instrument. A challenge may arise with regards to concession seeking and side agreements. This could lead to hold ups and eventually a stagnation of discussions, as advanced manufacturing techniques such as 3D printing are used in politically sensitive areas. Further, large economies such as the EU and the US hope to reshore domestic manufacturing by means of 3D printing. Negotiators may feel the pressure of domestic industrial and political policy objectives and attempt to negotiate rules that allow for continued use of preferential RoO as non-tariff barriers.

---

117 USMCA, App, art 3.10.

118 International Union, United Automobile, Aerospace & Agricultural Implement Workers of America (UAW), 'UAW's Public Comment on Operation of the United States-Mexico-Canada Agreement With Respect To Trade in Automotive Goods' Submission No USTR-2023-0013 (17 January 2024) 3 <https://downloads.regulations.gov/USTR-2023-0013-0013/attachment_1.pdf> accessed 23 March 2024.

Members should consider designing provisions for the substantial criteria taking into account the unique allocation of value creation in the raw materials, assembly, human processing, machine processing, and direct costs that advanced manufacturing brings to the production process. This investigation is to ensure that 1) preferential rules still function as a method for sifting-out those goods in which there was no substantial value created in the territory of the parties of a PTA, 2) that the rules do not overly favor one factor of the value chain, for example, the ink producers, the file designers, or the print shop owners, which could favor the domestic industries of one or a few of the parties, and 3) help to prevent rules from being restrictive, because they are designed to limit the geographic pool for materials or limit the ability of assembly shops to source and use 3D printed inputs. Additionally, the negotiators will need to consider the relation of this Instrument to the GATS and any instruments regulating the transmission of digital files if the origin of the 3D file is part of the origin analysis. Finally, the negotiators should encourage simplifying customs procedures as well as adding flexibilities for developing countries to implement the rules and procedures.

5 Tapping into the WTO's Strengths: Assisting the Trade Community with Designing and Complying with RoO for Advanced Manufactured Products

While an instrument on rules of origin for 3D printed goods and goods produced with advanced manufacturing methods would allow the WTO to regulate trade in a digital world, there are other aspects of the WTO that could improve upon the transparency, evenhandedness, and legitimacy of RoO. Indeed, much of what may be sought in terms of assistance in regulating and designing rules is already available to Members; however, it will take a joint effort of the administrative bodies of the Organization as well as Members to make use of these resources.

5.1 *Activity by the Secretariat and the Committee on Rules of Origin*

The WTO has an important role as a font of knowledge creation and technical expertise.[119] As advanced manufacturing is still a nascent, but growing, mode

119 Manfred Elsig, Bernard Hoekman, and Joost Pauwelyn, 'Thinking About the Performance of the World Trade Organization: A Discussion Across Disciplines' in Manfred Elsig, Bernard Hoekman, and Joost Pauwelyn (eds), *Assessing the World Trade Organization: Fit for Purpose?* (CUP 2017) 16–18.

of production, there is time for legal scholars and economists at the WTO to study the technology, experiment to see if rules are more or less restrictive, and provide recommendations for designing these rules.

Information and statistics useful for modernization of preferential RoO could be sourced from the Trade Policy Review Mechanism (TPRM) and the Committee on Rules of Origin (CRO). Elsig, Hoekman, and Pauwelyn note that one important tool of the WTO:

> is the "member-driven" work in the various committees, which allow for clarification, tabling concerns and learning about best practices, and can potentially lead to the elaboration of new regulatory initiatives.[120]

Article 1.2 of Annex II of the AOR requires Members to notify RoO to the Committee on Regional Trade Agreements (which implements the Transparency Mechanism for PTAs falling under GATT Article XXIV and GATS Article V) or the Committee on Trade and Development (which implements the Transparency Mechanism for GSPs).[121] However, the extent of the supervisory effect of these committees is questionable given that of the 500 PTAs notified as of 2021, only 19 notifications resulted in a report from one of the committees.[122] This statistic may result from the fact that the issuing of a report requires consensus and Members may be reluctant to point out inconsistencies in PTAs of other Members when their own PTAs may also not be consistent.[123] In the context of preferential RoO for LDCs, on the other hand, the CRO reported that as of 2023, all preference-granting Members except three had notified their preferential RoO applied to LDCs under non-reciprocal trade agreements.[124]

We could image that an WTO Instrument on rules for advanced manufactured products would include provisions on notifications and transparency and require data on the utilization rate of such rules. Timm Betz and Barbara Koremenos caution that monitoring mechanisms "may infringe on the conception of sovereignty for many states."[125] On the other hand, if states perceive

120 ibid 17.

121 AOR Annex II art 1.2.2; 'Transparency Mechanisms for RTAS' (wto.org) <https://www.wto.org/english/tratop_e/region_e/trans_mecha_e.htm> accessed 3 November 2021.

122 Peter Van den Bossche and Denise Prévost, *Essentials of WTO Law* (2nd edn, CUP 2021) 140–141.

123 ibid 141.

124 CRO, 'Report' (20 November 2023) (n 97) 2.

125 Timm Betz and Barbara Koremenos, 'Monitoring Processes' in Jacob Katz Cogan, Ian Hurd, and Ian Johnstone (eds), *The Oxford Handbook of International Organizations* (OUP 2016) 589.

that there "are no incentives to defect and therefore no incentives to misreport information," then self-reporting can be "an efficient and trustworthy mechanism" while allowing states to "give up a minimum of sovereignty."[126] Examples where states may have an incentive to defect are agreements based on environmental, human rights, and financial obligations, and the requested data may not be reported accurately.[127]

The approach then is designing RoO for advanced manufactured goods so that the parties are encouraged to report data. RoO are available on online platforms[128] as well as on government websites and the rules must be made accessible to traders and customs officers. RoO for advanced manufactured products should balance the need for transparency with the need for states to control commercial policy and regulate the development of technical industries. On the other hand, there may be some hope that self-reporting could prove effective if the data on RoO for advanced manufactured products results in relevant and timely revisions to product specific rules. States could benefit from analyzing utilization rates and use such data to improve trade among PTA parties and third-party countries. In addition to a monitoring mechanism for RoO, the WTO Secretariat could encourage Members to actively self-report by demonstrating examples of the advantages of sharing information on statistics, technical developments, and trade patterns. The CRO, in the context of non-reciprocal preferential RoO for LDCs, encourages Members to cooperate in research on utilization rates with the CRO and to share research conducted separately with the CRO.[129] Such an approach could be applied to all types of rules of origin.

The information on notification of statistical data in the CRO Report (2023) is linked to transparency. The Trade Policy Review Board (TPRB) not only reviews trade policies and practices related to goods, but also to services and IP,[130] information which is relevant to 3D printing and other advanced manufacturing techniques that rely on a digital file. A WTO tool which could stimulate a greater level of transparency on the design and implementation of preferential RoO may lead to an international approach to RoO that factors accountability, predictability, and transparency in negotiations and implementation of RoO. The WTO would also have to convince states that sovereignty

126 ibid 591.

127 ibid.

128 Eg, 'Rules of Origin Facilitator' <findrulesoforigin.org> accessed 31 October 2021.

129 CRO, 'Report' (20 November 2023) (n 97) 9.

130 'The Trade Policy Review Mechanism (TPRM)' (wto.org) <https://www.wto.org/english/tratop_e/tpr_e/tprm_e.htm> accessed 3 November 2021.

costs, which Jonas Tallberg defines as "the reduction in state control associated with transparency and openness,"[131] are low. Such costs can be elevated when "allowing nonstate access to policymaking [is] perceived by states as more threatening in some issues areas than in others, for historical, cultural, and functional reasons," including foreign policy.[132] While RoO are typically associated with a state's commercial policy, they do establish parameters for a state's engagement in foreign trade. The WTO Secretariat must demonstrate that enhancing transparency and openness in the design and administration of RoO through the engagement of nonstate actors like the WTO, researchers and NGOs does not "cost" states much in terms of their sovereignty over commercial and foreign policy.

Tools that apply transparency to shed light upon the sometimes obscure practice of rule design would allow the WTO to provide a framework for the regulation of trade[133] in the digital trading environment. The application of current preferential RoO to advanced manufacturing products, such as 3D printed goods, may not reflect the dynamic and evolving reality of the production and trade of goods in increasingly automated and digitalized global value chains. The issue with relying on the TPRM is that it appears to sometimes go unheeded: notifications may be incomplete, or not submitted on a timely basis, compliance with the TPRB remarks is voluntary, and information on non-tariff barriers is not comprehensive.[134] Betz and Koremenos note that the WTO's TPRM, "which is part of an elaborate and well-equipped international organization, seems to have reached the limits of the WTO's resources and capacities."[135] Thus, increasing the "bite" of the TPRM, at least with regards to preferential RoO may spur Members to design rules that are more efficient and do not distort trade. This may also mean requiring more transparency at the level of the WTO as an institution. As Anne Peters writes:

> Both member states and outsiders, including affected individuals, will only be able to assess the quality of the operations of an international organization and its impact on themselves if they possess sufficient information on those operations. Transparency thereby safeguards member state sovereignty and functions *as a surrogate* [italics original]

131 Jonas Tallberg, 'Transparency' in Jacob Katz Cogan, Ian Hurd, and Ian Johnstone (eds), *The Oxford Handbook of International Organizations* (OUP 2016) 1174.

132 ibid.

133 L Borlini, 'A Crisis Looming in the Dark: Some Remarks on the Reform Proposals on Notifications and Transparency' (2019) 63 QIL, Zoom-out 83, 93.

134 ibid 94–95.

135 Betz and Koremenos (n 125) 590.

> for the lack of democratic and judicial accountability in international organizations.[136]

The WTO should allow access to the information it collects on the design and use of rules of origin and be open about how it assesses such data and develops its recommendations. This may also help Members feel more comfortable in terms of sovereignty in the monitoring or self-reporting processes. Modernization at the WTO is not just confronting digital trade from the angle of e-commerce or hybridization of services, but amplifying and strengthening mechanisms already in place, such as the TPRM.

If it is still too early to begin discussions on a WTO instrument for preferential RoO for advanced manufacturing goods, the CRO could establish research initiatives into on how rules impact the advanced manufacturing environment. The CRO found that changes to direct transportation rules in connection with LDCs by the EU, Australia, and New Zealand, constituted a best-practice that other preference granting Members should adopt.[137] Identifying and sharing best practices in relation to the application of RoO for advanced manufactured goods would benefit all Members. 3D printing has the possibility to shift the dynamics of production at a global level: will reshoring production by 3D printing to northern countries leave southern countries, or countries with a comparative advantage in low labor costs, worse off? If southern countries rely more on tariff revenues than northern countries, how would southern countries interpret RoO in relation to advanced manufactured products to preserve such revenues?

These are questions that can be explored from a trade policy or economic perspective. The benefits of such an exercise can also lead to reflections on changes to trade practice and PTA negotiations, such as the inclusion of deeper provisions in agreements. Additionally, there should be collaboration with the Committee on Customs Valuation and the Technical Committee on Customs Valuation in understanding how the value of the digital service input should be incorporated into the value determination of an advanced manufactured product as RoO chapters refer to the CVA.[138] Finally, the CRO should collaborate with- the WCO and study how it is initiating updates to the HS in response

136 Anne Peters, 'International Organizations and International Law' in Jacob Katz Cogan, Ian Hurd, and Ian Johnstone (eds), *The Oxford Handbook of International Organizations* (OUP 2016) 49.

137 CRO, 'Report' (20 November 2023) (n 97) 6.

138 Eg, in the PEM, "customs value" refers to value as determined under the Customs Valuation Agreement. PEM App 1 art 1(e). ASEAN TIGA also refers to FOB and CIF value of goods under the CVA. ASEAN TIGA ch 3 art 25 (c) and (d).

to changes in trade and manufacturing, such as the addition of a product line and code for additive manufacturing machines.

The WTO could also take an active role in processing and analyzing the preferential RoO in the notified RTAs and understanding how these rules have impacted trade.[139] Donner Abreu looking into the nexus among RoO, the WTO, and PTAs suggests a symbiosis between the multilateral framework and PTA network through more active WTO involvement in providing guidelines for preferential RoO. This derives not only from the repository of information in the WTO, but also from the diversity of the WTO membership.[140] Given these elements and the fact that PTAs will continue to be negotiated by WTO members, Donner Abreu argues that a debate on RoO within the WTO, "would appear to be a positive contribution" both increasing the utilization of market access under PTAs and increasing the participation of third parties in accessing the benefits of liberalization of trade under the PTA.[141] The WTO could assist Members by using its resources and negotiating platform to identify where and how to reduce the costs of RoO.[142] The current approach to the *ad valorem* criterion can discourage producers from adopting more efficient or automated means of production. Advanced manufacturing techniques, such as 3D printing, promise to make manufacturing more efficient by reducing inputs and automating processes. In addition, parties to an PTA may wish to source 3D printed inputs due to their lower costs or better performance, but be constrained by preferential RoO to source local products. The WTO could examine the impact of PTAs on third parties and, as Boonekamp writes, "an agreement in the WTO on important lacunae such as preferential rules of origin … could bring uniformity to how such measures are to be evaluated."[143] The WTO could utilize this platform to explore the impact of advanced manufacturing and preferential RoO on trade and remain a firm anchor in the international trade law system by making progress in multilateral rules for preferential RoO.[144]

5.2 *Collaboration with Participants in Global Trade*

The WTO could assist with making rules of origin less politically murky and more functional by encouraging various participants of global trade to use the

139 Hoekman, 'Urgent and Important' (n 62) 386–387.

140 Maria Donner Abreu, 'Preferential Rules of Origin in Regional Trade Agreements' in Rohini Acharya (ed), *Regional Trade Agreements and The Multilateral Trading System* (CUP 2016) 104.

141 ibid.

142 Boonekamp (n 63) 205.

143 ibid 208.

144 ibid 211.

WTO as a platform for widening the discussion on rules of origin, whether in the form of supporting research on utilization rates or providing an opportunity to non-governmental actors to speak during negotiations or discussions on new rules. However, the invitation to non-governmental actors should be extended with some caution to not allow influence in the design of RoO to lead to trade distortive effects.

There may be some benefits in seeking input from businesses and actors involved in manufacturing and trade. Primo Braga and Hoekman argue that the "purely state-to-state nature of WTO operations is increasingly outdated."[145] This results from the rise of GVCs as a predominant means of manufacturing and a rise in transnational standards initiated by firms, resulting in a greater need for engaging with business organizations.[146] This can be achieved by inviting the business community to participate in Committees for digital trade and preferential RoO as well as more institutional transparency.[147] Hoekman and Nelson argue in their article on 21st trade agreements that for initiatives that "aim to manage economic relations beyond border measures, it is critical that the set of people involved in deliberations go beyond those who have worked on shallow integration agreements," including representatives of international businesses, voters, and consumers.[148] If the labor minimum wage requirement in the USMCA is a precursor to the inclusion of deep provisions in preferential RoO, then the WTO could include industry representatives and consumer representatives in discussions to understand how such deep RoO provisions impact trade. Further, as governments continue to place hopes in advanced manufacturing, especially 3D printing, to reshore manufacturing and bolster the domestic labor pool and economy, the WTO, as a negotiating platform, may be able to temper trade distortive effects of RoO by engaging industrialists, consumer advocates, developing country and LDC advocates, and political bodies in a discussion on the design and implementation of such rules.

Greater involvement of the WTO's technical assistance resources would be beneficial for Members as they examine and design RoO in the context of advanced manufacturing. Elsig, Hoekman, and Pauwelyn identify the WTO's technical assistance resources as one of the services that makes the WTO stand out as an international organization.[149] The term technical assistance generally

145 Primo Braga and Hoekman (n 65) 24.
146 ibid.
147 Hoekman and Mavroidis (n 64) 8.
148 Hoekman and Nelson (n 47) 19.
149 Elsig, Hoekman, and Pauwelyn (n 119) 17.

refers to courses for and technical missions to developing countries.[150] Policymakers, customs officials, and traders in developed and developing economies could also use some help in implementing, interpreting, and complying with RoO.

Currently, on the WTO website, the assistance available to the general public is an online course that provides guidance on "the basic concepts of rules of origin and with WTO disciplines governing their use" and a course titled "Underutilization of trade preferences: blame it on the rules of origin?"[151] The WTO includes webinars inviting experts to discuss developments in the facilitation of obtaining origin certificates or to share the experiences of Members in implementing or using rules of origin. There is also access to academic studies on utilization rates of preferential tariffs and the costs of complying with RoO (though aimed for those already well-versed in RoO). The WTO also supports a search engine called the Rules of Origin Facilitator[152] for over 800 FTAs in force that makes legal documents easily accessible, conveys the number of tariff lines per substantial transformation criteria through graphics and includes materials on the terminology, abbreviations, and basic requirements under the substantial transformation criterion. While admirable in the ease of finding all in one page the rules, certification origin requirements, exceptions, and limitations – for bicycles under CETA, readers are still confronted with this – (CTH + ECT) or (CTH + ALW 50%) – with some definitions, but no example which would be useful to SMEs who have to determine origin on their own. Nonetheless, the WTO has taken steps in making Members and the general public aware of rules, albeit rules that have already been designed and implemented. In April 2024, the CRO met to discuss how to improve the RoO section of the WTO website to "foster more user interaction" and "provide a knowledge hub on rules of origin."[153]

The WTO should also seek the input of customs organizations, researchers at national and regional trade offices, and legal scholars and economists and provide assistance at the design stage. Assistance from the WTO can be useful in providing guidance on the design process. In the context of RoO for advanced manufactured goods, the WTO should seek comments from producers in the

150 Van den Bossche and Prévost (n 122) 17–18.

151 'Rules of Origin' (wto.org) <https://www.wto.org/english/tratop_e/roi_e/roi_e.htm#techass> accessed 7 May 2022, see bottom of page for information on the courses.

152 'Rules of Origin Facilitator' (ITC/WCO/WTO) <https://findrulesoforigin.org/en?culture=en> accessed 17 March 2024.

153 WTO, 'Members review reforms to facilitate participation in rules of origin work' (wto.org 29 April 2024) <https://www.wto.org/english/news_e/news24_e/roi_29apr24_e.htm> accessed 25 October 2024.

advanced manufacturing ecosystem, as they can describe how a finished 3D good is obtained and what processing is carried out. Next, the WTO, perhaps in conjunction with the WCO, should seek input from customs officials, who will have to make determinations on the origin of 3D printed goods and additive manufacturing machines. Then, the drafters will need to decide whether to include the service input as a distinct input or incorporate its value (with clear instructions) into the production process of the 3D printed good.

Having input from technical experts, both from technology industries and customs administration, would assist the WTO in assessing the trade restrictiveness of a technical rule and provide guidance on how to design and interpret rules to minimize trade distortions. For example, information on processing performed by machine and by human at the printing stage could help shape guidance on designing a product specific rule that is not unduly restrictive (i.e. by raising the human labor requirement so high that a printed good can never qualify for origin). Likewise, the CRO could provide guidance to Members interested in adopting advanced manufacturing production for a certain sector on complying with the origin requirements under the RTAs to which they are parties. The CRO can also assist with research on whether a proposed rule or changes to existing rules will result in trade deflection or impair the ability of third countries to trade with members of the RTA due to the restrictiveness of the rules.

5.3 *Bringing Disputes on RoO for Advanced Manufactured Goods to the* DSB

Finally, what role would the DSB have in the regulation of preferential RoO? As there have been no disputes on preferential RoO, it is still unknown what approach a Panel or an AB would take, but we can make some guesses. First, as discussed in Chapter 1, a Panel has already stated Members have much latitude to design non-preferential RoO as long as they meet the requirements of Article 2 of the AOR.[154] It is possible that a Panel would also take the same approach with preferential RoO.[155] As Annex II of the AOR contains no prohibitions on making the rules restrictive, the focus of a dispute may be on whether the rules were clearly defined. In other words, the claimant would have to argue that the Respondent-Member's rules were so unclear as to rise to a violation of Article 3(a) of the Annex, which states that when issuing "administrative

154 Panel Report, *US-Rules of Origin for Textiles and Apparel Products, United States – Rules of Origin for Textiles and Apparel Products* (Panel Report circulated 20 June 2003, adopted 21 July 2003) WT/DS243/R, para 6.23–24.

155 Inama, Rules of Origin in International Trade (2022) (n 4) 820.

determinations of general application, the requirements to be fulfilled are clearly defined."

One could argue that the Complainant-Members of the RTA agreed to the design and language of the rules. Yet, in the USMCA dispute panel, Mexico and Canada argued that the US's interpretation of the RVC roll-up requirements for automotive parts disqualified certain Mexican and Canadian parts from origin status.[156] This suggests that (1) negotiated preferential rules of origin can be the subject of a trade dispute and (2) differing interpretations of the rules impact the ability for Parties to trade within the territory. Finally, a third party to a PTA may argue that the RoO of the PTA impair its ability to trade with Members of the PTA and other Members.[157] As Annex II contains no prohibitions on the restrictiveness of the rules, the third-party Member may claim a violation of GATT Article XXIV; however, Members may be reluctant to do so as the Respondent-Member may counterclaim and point out the inconsistencies in the Claimant's PTAs.

A Member to an RTA may instead claim that the application of the rules by the customs offices of the Respondent-Member is inconsistent or arbitrary, thus impairing its ability to trade under the preferential rules. Article 3(c) of Annex II only references paragraph 1 of Article X of GATT 1994. A Panel would first have to decide to what extent the parties must comply with Article X(1) GATT, which requires that laws, regulations, judicial decisions and administrative rules of general application "are published promptly in such a manner as to enable governments and traders to become acquainted with them." In the Declaration, there is no reference to Paragraph 3 of Article X GATT, requiring Members to "administer in a uniform, impartial and reasonable manner all its laws, regulations, decisions and rulings of the kind described in paragraph 1" of Article X. Puccio argues that the language of Article 3(c) in the Declaration

156 USMCA Panel Report, *United States – Automotive Rules Of Origin* (USA-MEX-CDA-2022-31-01), 14 December 2022, para. 66.

157 This was the argument of the US during the GATT era. The US mission submitted a request for consultations with the European Communities and EFTA resulting from a set of trade agreements concluded between the two parties in 1972. The US argued that that the application of the preferential rules of origin in the set of trade agreements concluded between the EC and the EFTA parties would be "likely to nullify or impair benefits accruing to the United States" under the GATT. United States, 'Rules of Origin: United States-Request for Consultations under Article XXII:1' (31 January 1974) l/3992. This is the only document found via a search of the documents available online at the WTO. Another document indicates that the L/3992 series was scheduled for destruction on 20 February 1976. 'Destructions of Documents' (22 December 1975) L/4281. Documents found at <https://docs.wto.org> accessed 7 January 2022. See also, Hoekman and Inama (n 83) 2, fn 5.

referring only to first paragraph of Article X excludes the application of the third paragraph from rules of origin, i.e., the requirement that they be administered in a uniform manner.[158]

Should a party try to bring a claim under Article X(3)(a) regarding preferential RoO, they would face resistance from *EC-Selected Customs Matters*. In this dispute, the US challenged the European Communities' system of customs administration as a whole under Article X:3(a) and Article X:3(b). In particular, the US argued that differences in penalty provisions and audit procedures by the national custom offices was a violation of Article X:3. The AB found that "the mere existence of differences in laws themselves is not sufficient to show a breach of the uniformity requirement in Article X:3(a) with respect to the administration of European Communities customs law."[159] To establish a claim, the US had to demonstrate that "differences in audit procedures necessarily lead to non-uniform administration of [EC] customs law in particular cases" and the US had not done so before the Panel.[160] The AB emphasized that States can exercise discretion in administering laws without breaching the uniformity requirement of Article X:3: "Different results in the application of a law or provision do not necessarily reflect non-uniform administration of the law itself, but may stem as well from the exercise of discretion in the application of the law or circumstances of the case."[161] Should a Member try to claim Article X:3 GATT 1994 applies to preferential RoO, and that differences in the application of RoO for 3D printed products by customs bodies of the Respondent-Member breach the uniformity requirement of Article X:3, they would have to provide ample evidence of origin determinations in particular cases that lead to a non-uniform administration of customs laws.

Finally, if a new WTO instrument for preferential Roo for advanced manufacturing includes language on reducing trade restrictiveness of the rules, it must be determined if a claim could be brought under that new Instrument. If the Instrument takes the form of a Ministerial Decision, there is some possibility that a claim could be brought under it. For example, in *US-Clove Cigarettes*, the AB upheld a Panel's finding that a Doha Ministerial Decision was a subsequent agreement under the VCLT Article 31.2(a) and thus could fill gaps in the

158 Laura Puccio, '20 Years After Marrakesh: Reconsidering the Effects of Preferential Rules of Origin and Anti-Circumvention Rules on Trade in Inputs and Global Production Networks' 2014 Eur YB Intl Economic L 173, 192.

159 Appellate Body Report, *EC-Selected Customs Matters* (circulated 13 November 2006, adopted 11 December 2006) WT/DS315/AB/R para 216.

160 ibid.

161 ibid; M Matsushita, TJ Schoenbaum, PC Mavroidis, M Hahn, *The World Trade Organization: Law, Practice, and Policy* (3rd edn, OUP 2017) (referred to as Matsushita), 239.

original text, in this instance the Agreement on Technical Barriers to Trade.[162] However, whether any decisions of the CRO could be deemed a subsequent agreement could be problematic as the AB's decision in *US-Tuna II* to find a TBT Committee decision as a subsequent agreement has been controversial to some Members.[163]

If the Instrument takes the form of a plurilateral agreement, it could follow the examples of the ITA and the TFA. The ITA does not include provisions on dispute settlement, but disputes have been brought before the DSB on the basis of Articles II:1(a) and II:1(b) and X:1 and X:2 GATT 1994.[164] Therefore, claims arising from a plurilateral agreement on rules of origin for advanced manufactured products could be brought under the AOR Annex II. The TFA, on the other hand includes provisions in Article 20 on bringing claims to the DSB. In sum, dispute settlement of preferential RoO has yet to be tested at the WTO. Given the proliferation of preferential RoO and their impact on trade, judicial guidance on designing and implementing the rules may be beneficial to the trade community, provided that a Panel or the AB can find a balance between respecting the sovereignty of the Members to design rules to achieve the objectives of the PTA and requiring that such rules contribute to an international law framework that is evenhanded and promotes trade liberalization.

5.4 *RoO for Advanced Manufactured Goods: An Opportunity for the* WTO

While detailed technical rules may be better suited for PTAs given the specific trading environment of the parties, the WTO could use its information resources and negotiating platforms to explore how preferential RoO cause distortive effects and prepare recommendations on rules for global production methods that would also require transparency in the design and implementation of the rules. Adlung and Mamdouh encourage the continued use of the WTO's function as a forum to explore trade issues and as "there are no suitable

162 Appellate Body Report, *US – Measures Affecting the Production and Sale of Clove Cigarettes* (circulated 4 April 2012, adopted 24 April 2012) WT/DS406/AB/R paras 241–268; Matsushita (n 161) 56.

163 Appellate Body Report, *US-Measures Concerning the Importation, Marketing and Sale of Tuna and Tuna Products* (circulated 16 May 2012, adopted 13 June 2012) WT/DS381/AB/R para 372; Matsushita (n 161) 56.

164 Panel Report, *EC-Tariff Treatment of Certain Information Technology Products* (circulated 16 August 2010, adopted 21 September 2010) WT/DS375/R, WT/DS376/R, WT/DS377/R paras 3.1–3.5; In 2023, there were three panel reports issued relating to the India's tariff treatment of information technology goods: case numbers WT/DS582/17y, WT/DS584/14, WT/DS588/14. The Panel ruled in favor of the EU, Japan, and Chinese Taipei. India has appealed the panel reports in connection with the EU and Japan.

other settings … it is therefore essential to resuscitate and promote the WTO's role as a forum for conceptual exploration and exchange."[165] The WTO's role as a forum is necessary, because preferential RoO cause direct and indirect distortive effects on trade, increase costs to trade, and can be utilized to protect domestic markets. Greater WTO involvement in preferential RoO could mitigate the maladies of these rules, while bolstering the WTO's legitimacy as a forum for the regulation of international trade. The WTO must also reassure states that their sovereignty in designing rules is not at risk. However, as Professor Jackson proposed, "in order for the world to cope with the challenges of instant communication" and "fast and cheap transportation," the notion of sovereignty must also be updated to something that "can be called 'sovereignty-modern.'"[166] The world still needs international institutions:

> They increasingly play a larger role in world and local affairs … Clearly a fragmented nation-state sovereignty emphasis will not be able to cope with the world reality that has been imposed on this globe, nor will myopic wishfulness for hegemonic supremacy be workable.[167]

Regarding RoO, a multilateral agreement may not be necessary: by modernizing and improving upon already existing elements of the WTO, the Members can modernize and improve upon preferential RoO as trade becomes more dependent on the production of goods with digital service inputs.

6 Improving the Preferential Rules of Origin System for All States and Traders, Great and Small

While the WTO has an important role in regulating international trade, the development of the design of preferential RoO has occurred through PTA negotiations. Recent activity suggests that states can collaborate in identifying how preferential RoO can be improved. As discussed above, the Bali and Nairobi Ministerial Decisions are examples of such cooperation. Outside of the WTO context, the revisions to the PEM also represent a regional effort to redesign RoO to make them easier to administer and to comply with. Further, the addition of the additive manufacturing machine product line to the HS Nomenclature also suggests that states are also willing to consider updating trade instruments to reflect new products and changes in manufacturing.

165 Adlung and Mamdouh (n 73) 111.
166 Jackson (n 2) 52–53.
167 ibid 53.

While PTAs have costs for traders, there are some benefits to regulating trade in a PTA.[168] These include what Boonekamp refers to as countries "learning by doing" by first entering into trade agreements with geographically close or culturally similar countries.[169] PTAs are innovative in addressing trade-plus issues or in negotiating an approach to trade that conciliates the domestic regulatory policies of the parties.[170] In the area of digital trade, Schaffer notes that PTAs "fill key regulatory gaps for digital trade" and that PTAs allow states to "instill their priorities and values into standards for the digital economy."[171] Given a few signs of international cooperation in terms of preferential RoO and the benefits of PTAs, how could the international trade community as a collection of sovereign states work together to design or apply rules to advanced manufactured products, such as 3D printed goods?

A first step is to investigate trade and technology to minimize any lobbyist pressures on the designers of the rules. US and the EU political bodies aim to boost domestic manufacturing with 3D printing. However, those in the additive manufacturing community in the US point to tariffs on raw materials as limiting their ability to produce goods in the US.[172] Researchers in the EU point to the need to train workers in the technical and digital skills required to design files and operate the printers.[173] Before sitting down to the negotiating table, states should understand first how 3D printing and advanced manufacturing production function and whether support for domestic printers and designers can be achieved through other measures, such as lowering existing tariffs or labor or educational measures separate from any RoO provisions. Flexibilities in the rules should be considered so that they can adapt as manufacturing processes and technology change.

This approach also means increasing the transparency of the negotiation process. As Maria Laura Marceddu notes, the traditional confidential, closed door negotiations are coming under scrutiny by the public.[174] In her research,

---

168 Boonekamp (n 63) 203–206.

169 ibid 204.

170 Hoekman, 'Urgent and Important' (n 62) 386.

171 Shaffer, 'Trade Law in a Data-Driven Economy (n 45) 268.

172 David Shepardson, 'U.S. coronavirus tariff exemptions sought for robots, drones, elevators' (*Reuters* 4 May 2020) <https://jp.reuters.com/article/us-health-coronavirus-usa-china-idUKKBN22G2VK> accessed 1 November 2021; Michael Cao, 'Trade Wars and Tariffs – a 3D Printing Perspective' (*IC 3D Industries* 13 February 2020) <https://www.ic3dprinters.com/trade-wars-and-tariffs-a-3d-printing-perspective/> accessed 1 November 2021.

173 Opinion of the European Economic and Social Committee, 'Living tomorrow. 3D printing – a tool to empower the European economy' (own-initiative opinion) (2015/C 332/05) C 332/36, 8 October 2015, para 3.4.

174 Maria Laura Marceddu, 'Implementing Transparency and Public Participation in FTA Negotiations: Are the Times a-Changin'? (2018) 21 J Intl Economic L 681, 682.

she finds a gradual shift in the US, EU, Canada, Australia, New Zealand, Mexico and Malaysia towards increasing transparency of FTA negotiations. However, she points out that, with the exception of the EU, these nations make texts available after an agreement is reached.[175] While public consultations can increase the legitimacy of the FTA negotiations, key are knowing which stakeholders can better influence negotiations and which non-state actors can effectively and meaningfully engage in technical negotiations.[176] Further, as Inama cautions, the "lack of expertise and the failure of a well-functioning machinery at a domestic level … are the most formidable stumbling blocks to consensus building and sometimes it may lead to fatal mistakes when negotiating rules of origin."[177] With regards to negotiations on the technical rules, it is important for there to be objective and neutral assessments of advanced manufacturing in the territory of the PTA and its potential growth, which can serve as counterpoints to proposals from industry lobbyists. Drafts of the rules should be made available at the very least to custom officials. Ideally, negotiators should provide an explanation on why they designed or selected an *ad valorem* formula or a particular product-specific rule. This may help reduce the risk of the substantial criteria and product-specific rules being unduly restrictive to support a particular industry in one of the states.

It is recommendable to consider aspects of the rules where an internationally shared approach would facilitate trade. One such area are definitions of terms such as simple assembly or simple processing. Given the changes that advanced manufacturing may bring to production, such terms may cause confusion. The US-Japan FTA defines the assembly of 5 or less parts of non-originating material to be simple assembly.[178] Thus, negotiators should consider whether rules that require a minimum number of parts to be assembled are functional rules in the digital production and trade environment. A product may consist of only five 3D printed parts, but that does not necessarily indicate that producing it and assembling those pieces was a simple task. Some of the manual processes which may have been "simple" in traditional manufacturing sectors, such as polishing, require training and skilled handling in advanced manufacturing sectors. Rule designers should find a balance between a one-size-fits all definition for terms such as "simple assembly" and distinct definitions for each type of manufacturing process. If technology advances, but the

175 ibid 699.

176 ibid 700.

177 Inama, *Rules of Origin in International Trade* (2022) (n 4) 825.

178 U.S.-Japan Trade Agreement, Annex II Tariffs and Tariff-Related Provisions of the US, Product-Specific Rules of Origin art 19 (d).

terms and definitions continue to reflect older manufacturing techniques, the rules could leave more and more space to the interpretation of customs offices. For example, the USITC noted that changes to the HS nomenclature resulted in parts for an EV pick-up truck facing different requirements than the same parts for a combustion pick-up and that new and more labor efficient methods of casting aluminum means that the process no longer results in a tariff shift, making it more difficult for these cast aluminum products to qualify for origin under the USMCA.[179]

Thinking about rules for advanced manufactured products also presents an opportunity to reconsider restrictive direct transport rules which can impact utilization rates and form an obstacle to trade.[180] Initially, 3D printing may allow traders to minimize the impact of direct transport requirements by printing inputs in the territory of interest. However, as 3D printing advances, manufacturers of inputs may want to export them, and thus face complicated direct transport documentation.[181] Revisions to the PEM include moving from the direct transport rule to a "more lenient rule of non-alteration" which allows for splitting of consignments in a third country under supervision of a customs official and where there is no doubt of the originating status of the goods.[182] States should consult with each other, the WCO, scholars, and technology companies to understand how goods are made and how to craft language in the rules that facilitates trade and efficient determinations of origin.

Next, states should consider how the value of the 3D file or any significant digital file used to manufacture a good should be included in the origin analysis. This is a discussion that touches upon other legal areas, such as intellectual property rights, corporate law and tax law. These are territorial, despite efforts at establishing international baselines, such as TRIPS, the EU IP Enforcement Directive, the UN Convention on Contracts for the International Sale of Goods,

179 'Report to Congress on The Operation of The United States-Mexico-Canada Agreement with Respect to Trade in Automotive Goods', 1 July 2024, 24 <https://ustr.gov/sites/default/files/2024%20USMCA%20Autos%20Report%20to%20Congress_0.pdf> accessed 23 October 2024.

180 R Soprano, 'Brexit and the EU-UK Free Trade Agreement: Dos and Don'ts When Drafting Rules of Origin' (2019) 18 J Intl Trade L & Policy 96, 104; Pramila Crivelli, Stefano Inama and Jonas Kasteng, 'Using Utilization Rates to Identify Rules of Origin Reforms: The Case of EU Free Trade Area Agreements' (2021) EUI Working Papers RCS 2021/21, 12–13, 15. <https://cadmus.eui.eu/handle/1814/70396> accessed 24 October 2021.

181 Paul Brenton, 'Preferential Rules of Origin' in Jean-Pierre Chauffour and Jean-Christophe Maur (eds), *Preferential Trade Agreement Policies for Development: A Handbook* (World Bank 2011) 172.

182 Commission, 'Guidance: Transitional PEM Rules of Origin' (v1.1–27 August 2024) Brussels, 27 August 2024, TAXUD/A6/AM/MO, 19.

and the OECD's Global Minimum Tax. However, states still retain a significant level of sovereignty in deciding how to regulate trade in IPRs, whether a business has substantive business operations in the territory, and how to tax income. Declaring that a 3D file originates in Country X on the basis that the owner has SBOs in X may subject that file to the intellectual property laws of Country X. By declaring that the owner is a legal person located in Country X, the owner is subjecting itself to corporation laws in X, and may be liable for taxes in X. Thus, if states want to include the digital file as an origin conferring input in an PTA they should consider how assigning origin to a digital file may lead to obligations and rights arising under other areas of national or territorial laws.

Having conducted research, parties negotiating a PTA should consider the content of the rules in connection with their commercial policy objectives and shared objectives for trade. Simplification of the rules means clarity in meeting product specific rules, and can reduce costs in seeking preferential tariff treatment, creating a more level field for participation in trade.[183] Traders would like instructions in "plain English" that clearly explain formulas and expressions such as MaxNOM 50% (EXW).[184] As Jitsuya suggests, a more standardized method of expression would benefit traders.[185] The changes to certification procedures and cumulation requirements in the PEM revisions suggests that states recognize the need to clarify and update the content and the expression of the rules to make them functionable rules. If States do not want to include digital design files, R&D, or engineering activity as independent origin conferring inputs, it would be beneficial for states to design rules to clearly specify how such activity can be included in direct costs for the *ad valorem* criterion. While preferential RoO in different PTAs may continue to be distinct due to the different commercial policy goals of states, a general goal is a more systematic and simplified expression of the rules. This would enable states to retain sovereignty in determining how restrictive the rules should be, while also allowing domestic businesses to benefit from trade under such rules and improve efficiency in manufacturing.

One objective that states can seek to achieve collectively is reducing the restrictiveness of the preferential RoO. Given the differences in the industrial

183 WTO, Summary of Informal Experience-Sharing Session On Preferential Rules Of Origin, held 5 October 2023, available at <https://www.wto.org/library/events/event_resources/devel_0510202315/summary.pdf> accessed 23 March 2024.

184 Interview with Dr. Anna Jerzewska (Milan/Geneva, 22 September 2021). Dr. Jerzewska's website: <https://www.tradeandborders.com> accessed 3 November 2021.

185 Hasegawa Jitsuya,'Standardization of Complex and Diversified Preferential Rules of Origin' (2021) 55 J World Trade 545, 562–564.

capacities, trade flows, and trade policy objectives of each state, rules on reducing restrictiveness would differ in each instrument. A type of restrictiveness that states could agree to reduce, and which would have an impact on GVCs and advanced manufactured parts, is reducing the degree of the restrictiveness that limits input and geographical pools for the parties of a PTA. A rule requiring that a 3D printed good (or a good with 3D printed parts) contain a certain percentage of local content does not impact each producer equally. A producer in a large economy with diversified industries may have less difficulty and costs in meeting that requirement than a producer in a small economy with a narrow industrial sector. Producers in smaller economies may be constrained to pay a high cost for domestic inputs from a firm with a monopoly on the parts or that is inefficient in production methods. Thus, in this example, the PTA should either avoid rules that require a high level of local content or allow for flexibilities in sourcing of third-party content. This is an approach that could be adopted in many PTAs. States should avoid designing a new agreement promising to reduce costs and complexity and to promote technological advancement, only which, due to the restrictiveness of the rules, locks producers into using traditional production methods or source products from domestic industries.

States should also resist increasing the size of RoO chapters without including helpful detailed definitions and lists of what elements can be included in the substantial transformation tests. In 2005, William E James wrote that the New Zealand-Singapore Closer Economic Partnership (2000 CEP), which entered into force in 2001:[186]

> is a model of apparent simplicity in its rules of origin. Instead of hundreds of pages of detailed product specific rules, the agreement adopts the principle of goods wholly obtained in either country as sufficient to confer origin in the case of primary, unprocessed goods and scrap. For goods processed or manufactured in either country it uses a minimum value-added test of forty percent.[187]

186 New Zealand Ministry of Foreign Affairs & Trade, 'CEP Text' (mfat.govt.nz) <https://www.mfat.govt.nz/br/trade/free-trade-agreements/free-trade-agreements-in-force/nz-singapore-closer-economic-partnership/cep-text/> accessed 2 November 2021.

187 WE James, 'Rules of Origin and Rules of Preference and the World Trade Organization: The Challenge to Global Trade Liberalization' in Patrick F J Macrory, Arthur Edmond Appleton and Michael G Plummer (eds) *World Trade Organization: Legal, Economic and Political Analysis* (Springer 2005) 285.

These rules are found in article that consists of 5 subparts and is about 2 pages long.[188] The 2000 CEP agreement includes an 7 page "explanatory" Annex which helpfully provides details on what types of expenditure can be included in labor costs and overhead.[189] Fast forward 16 years later, and the preferential RoO were revised as part of the CEP Upgrade, which entered into force on 1 January 2020.[190] There is now a chapter for preferential RoO. Included are build-up and build-down formulas making the chapter similar in structure to those in USMCA and ASEAN. Gone are the detailed lists of what expenditures can be included in labor and overhead. Added is Annex 3.1 with 324 pages of product specific rules. The New Zealand Ministry of Foreign Affairs and Trade in its "National Interest Analysis" of the upgrade proposes that changes to its "wholly produced or obtained" section aim "to reflect international best practice."[191] A requirement that the last process of manufacture occur in the territory was added to the 40% threshold. These "innovative dimensions of the ROO":

> recognize that in the face of increasing competitive pressures, manufacturers today are seeking to specialize as much as possible, draw on input materials from the most cost effective sources and locate aspects of their business in different places. These features often make it difficult for exports to qualify under traditional ROO.[192]

It will be interesting to monitor the results of this change in the rules and to compare whether utilization rates of the preferential rules increase. One recommendable aspect is to preserve the "explanatory annex" in future agreements, as understanding what falls under labor costs, such as training, and under overhead, such as "research, development, design, and engineering" could be useful for determining the origin of advanced manufactured products under an *ad valorem* method.

188 CEP agreement 2000 art 5.

189 ibid annex 1.

190 Agreement between New Zealand and Singapore on Closer Economic Partnership - Upgrade (entered into force 1 January 2020); New Zealand Ministry of Foreign Affairs & Trade, 'CEP Overview' (mfat.govt.nz) <https://www.mfat.govt.nz/br/trade/free-trade-agreements/free-trade-agreements-in-force/nz-singapore-closer-economic-partnership/cep-overview/#bookmark0> accessed 2 November 2021.

191 New Zealand Ministry of Foreign Affairs & Trade, 'National Interest Analysis' (mfat.govt.nz) <https://www.mfat.govt.nz/assets/Trade-agreements/Singapore-NZ-CEP/National-Interest-Analysis.pdf> accessed 2 November 2021.

192 ibid.

Finally, states should provide assistance to traders as well as collaborate with organizations such as the WCO and ICC. Some customs and trade agencies, like those of the US and EU, provide information. The US published the US Customs and Border Protection Valuation Encyclopedia (1980–2021), a compendium of interpretations and guidance on several key issues in customs valuation.[193] While this information may allow traders to understand how to find the value of a product, there are still other aspects of origin determination that must be considered, such as tracing requirements, certification requirements, and understanding whether a CTH occurred. For example, the CBP offers a publication titled, "What Every Member of the Trade Community Should Know About: U.S. Rules of Origin." It was published in 2004 – and has not been updated.[194] Neither the CBP's website nor the International Trade Administration's website[195] includes information about RoO on the homescreen, instead a search in the search function is necessary. The EU's welcome page to its Access2Markets database does include a RoO self-assessment function.[196] However, the User Handbook on the PEM still references the European Community,[197] and hopefully will be updated once the PEM revisions take effect. If states do not add new definitions to terms or changes to product specific rules for advanced manufactured products in a new RoO instrument or RTA chapter, then they should at least update the materials on trade offices websites to provide an indication of whether 3D printing is sufficient processing or whether training to operate a 3D printing machine can be included in labor costs under the *ad valorem* method.

Some states may not have the financial or organizational resources to create and update guidelines. WTO technical assistance could play a significant role in improving the preferential RoO system for the benefit of all Members. While referencing the Latin American countries, it is possible to apply Estevadeordal and Suominen's words to all countries: "training for exporters and customs

193 CBP, *U.S. Customs and Border Protection Valuation Encyclopedia (1980 – 2021)*, (first Issued 1990, revised December 2021) <https://www.cbp.gov/sites/default/files/assets/documents/2022-Jun/Value%20Encyclopedia%20Dec%202021%20%281%29.pdf> accessed 26 October 2024.

194 CBP, 'Rules of Origin' (1 May 2004) EO13891-OT-122 <https://www.cbp.gov/document/publications/rules-origin> accessed 26 October 2024.

195 USITA, homepage (trade.gov) <https://www.trade.gov> accessed 26 October 2024.

196 Commission, 'Access2Markets' <https://trade.ec.europa.eu/access-to-markets/en/home> accessed 26 October 2024.

197 Commission, Pan-Euro-Mediterranean Convention (PEM) <https://trade.ec.europa.eu/access-to-markets/en/content/rules-origin-pan-euro-mediterranean-convention> accessed 26 October 2024.

about the technical requirements and implementation of rules of origin … would help shorten the learning lags associated with rules of origin [and] reduce the administrative hurdles facing both exporters and customs."[198] Additionally, many states are also members of the WCO. This organization specializes in understanding how products are produced and traded and it shares this knowledge through in-country workshops and capacity building programs.

The WCO Tools website includes a data base on agreements with rules of origin, the HS nomenclature search function, and tools to determine customs values for a product.[199] The WCO dispute settlement system and letters of advice can provide useful interpretations of the HS nomenclature, though non-binding. States can seek consultations on whether a good should be classified under one heading or another or advice on how to address a particular trade topic, such as 3D printed goods, but are not obligated to make changes to their RoO or customs procedures. By collaborating with the WCO, states may be able to give its domestic producers, importers, and exporters clearer instructions on how to participate in international trade. In the end, the most powerful tool that the international trading system can provide to "lift all boats" is clear and easily accessible information on how to comply with rules of origin procedures.

7 Conclusion

The under utilization rates identified by economists and trade scholars, the recognition by the PEM members of the need to simplify and change certificate of origin procedures, and the general challenges faced by traders demonstrates that states should consider collectively how RoO are crafted. The perspective of the WTO's role in regulating preferential RoO and states' sovereignty over these rules needs to become pliant for the international trade system to modernize with changes in manufacturing and trade.

Preferential RoO must discriminate, as that is their purpose, but policymakers in their zeal for promoting commercial policy objectives should take a moment to examine the comprehensibility of the rules implemented to support such objectives. This is a language that must be "spoken" and "understood"

198 Antoni Estevadeordal and Kati Suominen, 'Rules of Origin in Preferential Trading Arrangements: Is All Well with the Spaghetti Bowl in the Americas?' (2005) Economia (Spring) 63, 90.

199 'Welcome to WCO Trade Tools' (wcodtradetools.org) <https://www.wcotradetools.org/en> accessed 2 November 2021.

by all participants in the trading system. The changes to production created by changes in technology provides an opportunity for states to update rules and to provide guidelines on how to apply rules in existing agreements to new types of goods and production methods. Even if 3D printing reshores some manufacturing jobs and produces goods for the domestic market, 3D printed parts may still be part of a GVC chain. Production chains and manufacturing locations are elements of a strategic business plan connected to suppliers, logistics companies, and producers. As Paul Brenton notes, "[r]ules of origin may be an important factor in determining the investment decisions of multilateral firms" and the level of investment can be influenced by whether the rules make it uncertain if preferential tariff treatment will be granted.[200] If a manufacturer with foreign production facilities is uncertain of the tariff treatment of 3D printed products in its main export-territories, it may be reluctant to invest in domestic digital training and advanced manufacturing facilities, despite the encouragement of the state to reshore manufacturing jobs. A state may be protective of its freedom from international oversight to negotiate and design rules for trade agreements, but restrictive rules to promote one set of "deep" objectives may impair its ability to achieve other "deep" objectives, such as training a new digitally-skilled workforce. Thus, a little dose of international cooperation among states and cooperation of states with international organizations may go a long way in making the trading system more beneficial for all producers, importers, and exporters, great and small.

200 Brenton (n 181) 172.

CONCLUSION

A New Horizon for Preferential Rules of Origin

The study of preferential rules of origin is an opportunity to examine both the development of a particular type of trade law and how the international trade law framework could develop in a trade environment increasingly linked to digital technology. First, RoO show an interesting tug-of-war between efforts to make them more complex by the addition of "deep" trade provisions (such as the USMCA) and between efforts to simplify them and make them more trader-friendly (the PEM revisions). Next, RoO can be situated within the debate on whether goods and services trade measures should be merged. In this book, the link between trade law and trade in the digital era is 3D printing, which may bring changes to both how goods are produced and what type of goods are traded internationally. Further, 3D printing can bring into the discussion questions on how a new digital-focused trade framework can sustain (or improve) goals to make global trade more equitable and to make international trade organizations more responsive to changes in trade practices.

Trade law should not be fixed intractably to one point while trade practices advance. This is not necessarily a call for a general evolutionary interpretation of trade law, but rather a proposal to think how trade law could be pliant, allowing for a symbiosis between the advancement of trade and the application of trade measures to these changing practices. This means designing rules that recognize that technology changes often more rapidly than negotiators can design rules. It also requires, however, designers to know how to construct a legal core – a principle or objective – that remains firm so that there is predictability and consistency as trade develops. While preferential RoO would benefit from some flexibility, they should not be too malleable.

3D printing was chosen as a technology, because it is not yet widespread although in use, and so we can still apply the exercise of "what if" without venturing too far off into the hypothetical. What if we apply RoO to 3D printed goods consistently? The main findings are first, if there is not some pliancy worked into preferential RoO in connection with advanced manufactured products, application of preferential RoO may not function in achieving the intended goals of the parties: the design of the rules could inaccurately designate origin, they could be too permissive and let in third party goods or they could be too restrictive and disqualify goods produced in the territory from preferential origin status. Second, the susceptibility of preferential RoO for advanced manufactured goods to protectionist goals demonstrates that there

 | DOI:10.1163/9789004730595_008

is a need for a united effort, whether at the multilateral level or plurilateral level, to find a balance between achieving trade and commercial policy goals and crafting and sustaining a framework that supports producers, traders, and consumers across the globe.

The possibility for states to design or redesign preferential RoO to meet changes in the production and distribution of goods results in part from RoO's rather unique place in international trade law, which the first two Chapters presented. In the first Chapter, the Common Declaration with Regard to Preferential Rules of Origin was introduced, an Annex to the Agreement on Rules of Origin. This Declaration, on the one hand, places preferential RoO at least within the ambit of the WTO. Whether any of the Members can bring legal claims under the Declaration that another Member's preferential RoO impair rights or violate obligations is still an open question. The Declaration does not oblige Members to ensure that their rules are not trade restrictive, only that the requirements are clearly defined and some reporting requirements to the Secretariat are met. The history of the design and application of these rules suggests that Members have received wide latitude in designing these rules with some parameters by the World Customs Organization and the HS Nomenclature. The variety in the design of the rules is seen in Chapter 2. This Chapter presented a brief introduction to the more technical aspects of RoO as well as the administration of these rules in customs offices. However, the main takeaways are (1) that among PTAs there are variations of the wholly produced and substantial transformation criteria for determining the origin of a good, and (2) that these rules evolve from one trade instrument to another. This suggests it could be possible for states, whether in groups of two or three, as a region, or in a plurilateral setting, to at least think about and start upon the design of rules focused on advanced manufactured goods.

In Chapter 3, we identified where the design of RoO drifts away from the objectives of a legal framework that supports predictable and efficient regulation of trade, and then we began to explore how to redirect the design of rules into a framework for digital trade. Issues with transparency and lobbying in the negotiations of the rules can be compounded by the complexity in the wording of the rules. As a result, traders and trade policy specialists struggle to understand the legal obligations established by the rules and how to identify the origin of a product. An important observation was made in this chapter: the restrictiveness that appears in the text in the instrument can be different from the restrictiveness that producers experience when trying to understand and meet the rules. This "effective" restrictiveness becomes apparent when studying the implications of "deeper" trade provisions within RoO chapters. While the inclusion of rules aimed to increase the quality of labor wages or environmental standards shows the ability of states to experiment and develop new rules, such provisions could reduce the options for producers of sources of input or act as a disincentive for the adoption of new and more efficient methods of production.

This tension between qualifying for origin based on *ad valorem* methods that favor labor value and the desire to innovate with less-labor intensive production methods leads us again to 3D printing, as it promises to reduce assembly of parts and the machine does much of the fabrication. From a legal perspective it brings us towards the exploration of whether we should transpose trade rules established within an era of traditional manufacturing into a digital trade framework. In the context of RoO, this could mean reframing how the rules designate inputs that contribute origin conferring value or processing. Regarding 3D printed goods, we must consider whether the 3D file could be a component of the product along with any tangible inputs. This brought us away from RoO for a moment as we had to discuss another area of trade law that is influenced by advances in the technological production of goods: classification of products under GATS and GATT, in other words, is the product a service or a good? While hybridization of goods and services measures is an ongoing debate, this book looked to the GATS and provisions in trade instruments to identify the 3D file as a service.

The goal of the fourth Chapter was to identify where a RoO regime based on traditional manufacturing processes is out of synch with advanced manufacturing and to consider whether service inputs, such as design and development, should be origin conferring inputs of a final tangible good. The wholly produced criterion and the three substantial transformation criteria were explored in the following contexts: (1) the technology of printing a good and (2) the 3D file. The first approach required understanding what makes 3D printing different from traditional manufacturing. We found that there could be the potential for a shift in legal outcome when the substantial transformation criteria are applied to 3D printed goods. The CTH criterion could be too permissive, as all 3D printed goods must undergo a tariff line change, while current language in agreements on assembly and processing may or may not exclude assembly or post-processing of 3D printed goods from substantial processing (origin conferring) status. Under the *ad valorem* criterion, origin could shift from being based on where the most labor value is created to where the ink comes from. Next, the 3D file was considered in the origin analysis. It could be possible to incorporate the 3D file as an input using an *ad valorem* method, but complications arose as to where to designate the origin of the file. The economic origin of a file could be difficult to identify given the global design chain of digital files, while designating origin based on the legal seat of the supplier could fail to identify where most of the work was done of the file. This means making a potential choice, a combined goods-service RoO based entirely on economic origin (but with potentially significant tracing requirements) or a goods/economic + services/legal supplier RoO that combines two approaches to identifying origin. The last choice may be more feasible if it is possible to identify the legal seat of the supplier of the file. Yet, the addition of the file as an input in origin determination could potentially open the door to strategic design of RoO: states with strong service sectors may try to claim origin of the good based on the 3D file if it benefits their domestic industries; likewise, states that want to promote manufacturing may claim that printing in the territory qualifies a good for origin. This presents a new risk to the use of RoO with trade distortive effects within a new digital-based trade framework.

The final Chapter explored how to find a place for preferential RoO for advanced manufactured products in a trade law framework and how states can work together to design rules that both support the goal of giving preferential tariff treatment to goods produced within the territory without impairing trade with third parties. The idea of a WTO Instrument on Preferential RoO was suggested to achieve this goal at a plurilateral level. The first part focused on the importance of identifying the core principles of preferential RoO for advanced manufactured products, like 3D printed goods. This means understanding how these rules could be connected to an e-commerce WTO instrument or e-commerce provisions, but not making the rules dependent on them. Issues of connecting RoO with "deep" regulatory-based trade provisions was also discussed. Next, Members should use the design process to simplify rules on verifying origin. They should craft a set of rules with a central purpose of sorting out how advanced manufactured goods receive preferential tariff treatment, even if digital trade laws are created or modified, while having the flexibility to respond to changes in technological production. Finally, Members should make complying with the rules as streamlined as possible and responsive to the socio-economic position of traders.

Next, the second part of Chapter 5 looked to the design of preferential RoO that are functional yet trader-friendly. First, we experimented with how to achieve the WTO Instrument at a plurilateral level, referencing plurilateral agreements like the ITA and TFA, as well as the Ministerial Decisions on non-reciprocal preferential RoO for LDCs. This led us to find that a WTO Instrument would likely need to focus on a narrow range of goods in order to avoid hold-up issues. Further, we found that the Instrument would likely need to give Members sovereignty in the design of the rules. And so, a question remains on how to include provisions that curtail the use of preferential RoO that have protectionist or trade distortive effects. Next, we looked at how the WTO can provide a forum for the exploration of such rules in the context of PTAs. This in turn, could help the WTO strengthen its position as a resource of trade expertise and as a platform for negotiations. Finally, during negotiations for PTAs states should not only discuss the rules among diplomats, but open the process to trade specialists, industries (with limitations on lobbying), customs officials, and technology researchers. In a single world, the main finding of this second part of the chapter is "collaboration." Allowing those impacted by origin determination to participate in the design of the rules could make the rules more transparent (and comprehensible) and could also strengthen the legal "core." The designers would be able to better understand how to make the rules more predictable and equitable for traders.

These main findings lead into the discussion of "what is the purpose of trade law today." Digital-based production is being adopted by states at various levels of development. The geo-political approach to regulating trade has followed a trajectory from multilateralism towards mega-regional, regional, and bilateral agreements. 3D printing and preferential RoO are two particular examples, one of changes in production, the other in changes to legal provisions on trade. Yet, studying these two examples shows us how, at a more general level, that the trade law community must be aware of how the technological actuality of production when creating an updated framework for trade. We have seen with 3D printing that this means finding a balance: rules must allow for innovation, but still set some parameters to achieve the intended trade policy purpose behind the rules; there must be worked into the rules some method for updating or revising the rules without having to start from scratch as technology changes. Next, we must think of whether trade law could have a greater purpose in the era of digital trade. How can we devise laws and provisions that both achieve policy goals, support innovation, and foster a predictable and equitable trade environment for all? The adoption of 3D printing in developing countries could bring progress in manufacturing and acquisition of digital skills, and the adoption of 3D printing in developed countries could also provide manufacturing jobs. Yet the design of preferential RoO could diminish such benefits if states use the rules to protect or boost domestic goods or services industries. 3D printing and preferential RoO is an example of how trade analysists and trade law experts should consider how rules can impact traders differently based on the level of economic or technical development of a country or region.

Under these considerations, I propose the following regarding a preferential RoO regime for advanced manufactured products. First, I recommend that those interested in incorporating the service input into the origin analysis trace out scenarios on how these rules would be applied by those trading in such goods. This requires a collaboration with trade customs official, industry participants, and economists. If we design an *ad valorem* rule that allows for the 3D file as a distinct input, how does a trader figure out how to comply with the rule and what is the impact on trade in that particular good? Do these results lead to a more transparent, predictable, and equitable trading system? Next, given the complications already arising from GVCs towards origin analysis for goods, designers may want to test out the new rules. Do the intended users of the rules understand them? How can the rules be clear and functional at the same time?

There are several reasons worth consideration for combining RoO for services and goods. This book attempts to present both the positive potential of such an approach with some guidelines (and some cautions) in balancing the legal function of RoO with customs procedures and the manufacturing goals of producers. In his book on RoO, Inama briefly explores whether we have arrived at such a point, not only looking at the iPhone examples of the value of services in producing a good, but also at the role of services in the manufacturing of footwear and the impact on LDCs.[1] With non-electronic goods, services still create more value than the manufacturing stage given R&D and design costs. Here, we start to see an intersection with advanced manufacturing, and the inclusion of digital inputs as key inputs, and the design services behind them. 3D printing is used to produce soles for shoes, by established and start-up companies, with potential impacts on reshoring and sustainability.[2] Digital inputs, and the tangible inputs produced from them, will become key elements of goods, and we have the opportunity to consider now how to recognize this value in the final product while also maintaining support for SMEs and developing countries to participate in trade through preferences or technical assistance.

If such a combined regime is a long-term goal, trade negotiators, trade offices, and customs officials could recognize ways to incorporate the value of design work into the substantial transformation criteria that are already existing. Definitions in the texts could clearly specify that design work value can be incorporated into direct overhead costs. Or, rules could allow a certain percentage of design work in the territory to offset percentages of non-originating materials, so as to allow the value of design work to have more relevance in determining origin. Perhaps it would be possible to consider printing as a step in

1 Stefano Inama, *Rules of Origin in International Trade* (CUP 2022) 238–240.

2 Carolyn Schwaar, '3D Printing Meets the Billion-Dollar Footwear Industry' (Forbes 19 July 2023) <https://www.forbes.com/sites/carolynschwaar/2023/07/19/3d-printing-meets-the-billion-dollar-footwear-industry/?sh=2a67d75652of> accessed 25 March 2024.

the assembly of a product (i.e. it is not minor processing), so that a 3D printed good has more potential to qualify under the CTH and processing operations criteria. Any new rules should be designed with the aim to simplify the process of qualifying a good for preferential origin status.

Additive manufacturing, and advanced manufacturing generally, are linked to several elements that are the focus of regulatory and legislative developments in the areas of sustainability, security, and domestic labor policy. The EU's Carbon Boarder Adjustment Mechanism and the Corporate Sustainability Due Diligence Directive both require an assessment of how a good is made, whether a certain level of carbon emissions is expended or how the production chain meets certain human rights and environmental standards. Yet, RoO do not require this type of tracing to qualify for origin. As discussed in Chapter 3, these policy goals signal a general need in the trade community to understand how to align such goals with a functional and effective RoO regime (both for the substantial transformation criteria and the administrative requirements). Additionally, advanced manufacturing is seen as a way to secure supply chains, not only by reshoring, but by shorting the length of the supply chain or having more control of when and where parts are made. Yet, in addition to the need to train a digitally skilled workforce, the issue of the materials still arises. The EU's Critical Raw Materials Act is aimed at securing access to these materials including the metals used in ink, which as explained in Chapter 4, could have potentially more value than the labor or processing when creating a 3D printed good. How would this policy goal align with the origin determination of such goods, and ultimately the EU's ability to trade under its PTAs? Finally, we come to rise of the focus of security in trade and in trade law. 3D printing can be used to produce weapons and consumer goods; files could be transmitted, thus potentially evading import or export restrictions. The European Economic Security Strategy aims to protect the EU from risks while maintaining its competitiveness. What role would advanced manufacturing have in meeting this policy goal and how would the origin determination of such goods align with it? These are examples only in the EU, but we could imagine similar policy goals of security, sustainability, and boosting domestic manufacturing in other countries. Just look at the Inflation Reduction Act's goal of boosting a green economy, which as reported by the automakers in the US, complicates meeting the Labor Value Content rules of the USMCA.

I conclude with a kind recommendation that legal trade scholars and trade analysts become familiar with rules of origin. In some ways, they are the "bread and butter" of international trade: these rules are applied daily by customs offices throughout the world, and they impact whether traders decide to move goods across borders. In 2021, Alessandro Antimiani and Lucian Cernat proposed a "GVC for LDCs," in which inputs produced in LDCs would remain duty-free across the entire supply chain of a final product.[3] The authors note, "[r]ules of origin would be a critical element in the success of this proposal, and hence sufficient consideration needs to be given to the specific mechanisms and procedures that would govern such a scheme."[4] The authors suggest that rules of origin "do not pose an insurmountable problem" and an analysis of the procedural aspects of rules "could be an additional improvement in the model to better capture the potential impact of this trade policy proposal."[5] In 2023, Cernat highlighted that the EU's digital certification system (TRACES) for meeting organic standards can be tracked along GVCs, which has allowed producers in the agricultural sector in LDCs to increase trade with the EU.[6] Such initiatives in facilitating trade should be complimented by advancements in simplifying the meeting and documenting of origin along supply chains. Likewise, another type of proposal for improving the conditions of trade for LDCs or MSMEs may require an understanding of how to identify the origin of goods produced in such territories or by such firms. Finally, rules of origin continue to be dynamic elements of trade and they make "mainstream" news. The USMCA Panel dispute on the interpretation of Regional Value Content was reported by the Associated Press, Reuters, *The Wall Street Journal*, along with other media outlets. Perhaps the time has come for rules of origin to move, if not to the center, then further from the fringes, of international trade law analysis.

---

3 Alessandro Antimiani and Lucian Cernat, 'Untapping the Full Development Potential of Trade along Global Supply Chains: "*GVCs for LDCss*" Proposal' (2021) 55 J World Trade 697, 700.

4 ibid 712.

5 ibid.

6 Lucian Cernat, 'Promoting a "GVCs for LDCs" approach: the case of digital certification for organic products' (European Centre for International Political Economy October 2023) <https://ecipe.org/blog/gvcs-for-ldcs-digital-certification-for-organic-products/> accessed 25 March 2024.

Bibliography

Books, Chapters in Books, Journal Articles, and Working Papers

Aaronson SA and P Leblond, 'Another Digital Divide: The Rise of Data Realms and its Implications for the WTO' (2018) 21 J Intl Economic L 245.

Aaronson SA and T Struett, 'Data is Divisive: A History of Public Communications on E-commerce, 1998–2020' (2020) CIGI Papers No. 247 <https://www.jstor.org/stable/resrep27511> accessed 3 November 2021.

Abeliansky AL and I Martínez-Zarsoso, K Prettner, '3D Printing, International Trade, and FDI' (2020) 85 Economic Modelling 298.

Acharya R, 'Regional trade agreements: recent developments,' in Rhoni Acharya (ed), *Regional Trade Agreements and the Multilateral Trading System* (CUP 2016).

Adlung R and H Mamdouh, 'Plurilateral Trade Agreements: An Escape Route for the WTO?' (2018) 52 J World Trade 85.

Andrenelli A and J López González, 'Electronic Transmissions and International Trade – Shedding New Light on the Moratorium Debate' (2019) OECD Trade Policy Paper, No. 233 <http://dx.doi.org/10.1787/57b50a4b-en> accessed 23 October 2021.

Andrenelli A and J López González '3D Printing and International Trade: What is the Evidence to Date?' (2021) OECD Trade Policy Paper, No. 256 <https://www.oecd.org/publications/3d-printing-and-international-trade-0de14497-en.htm> accessed 26 November 2021.

Ansong A, 'Single Undertaking, Different Speeds: Pliable Models for Decision-making in the WTO' (2018) 21 J Intl Economic L 395.

Antikainen M and D Jongsma, 'The Art of CAD: Copyrightability of Digital Design Files' in Rosa Maria Ballardini, Marcus Norrgård, Jouni Partanen (eds), *3D Printing, Intellectual Property and Innovation: Insights from Law and Technology* (WoltersKluwer 2017).

Antimiani A and L Cernat, 'Untapping the Full Development Potential of Trade along Global Supply Chains: "*GVCs for LDCs*" Proposal' (2021) 55 J World Trade 697.

Arbabian ME and MR Wagner, 'The impact of 3D Printing on Manufacturer-Retailer Supply Chains,' (2020) 285 Eur J Operational Research 538.

Asakura H, 'The Harmonized System and Rules of Origin' (1993) 27 J World Trade 5.

Baldwin R, '21st Century Regionalism: Filling the Gap between 21st Century Trade and 20th Century Trade Rules' (May 2011) Policy Insight (Centre for Economic Policy Research) <https://cepr.org/publications/policy-insight-56-21st-century-regionalism-filling-gap-between-21st-century-trade-and> accessed 9 March 2025.

Banga R, 'Growing Trade in Electronic Transmissions: Implications for the South' (2019) UNCTAD Research Paper No. 29 <https://unctad.org/system/files/official-document/ser-rp-2019d1_en.pdf> accessed 23 October 2021.

Barnard C with J Snell, 'Free Movement of Legal Persons and the Provision of Services,' in Catharine Barnard and Steve Peers (eds), *European Union Law* (3rd edn OUP 2020).

Betz T and B Koremenos, 'Monitoring Processes' in Jacob Katz Cogan, Ian Hurd, and Ian Johnstone (eds), *The Oxford Handbook of International Organizations* (OUP 2016).

Bhagwati J, *Termites in the Trading System: How Preferential Agreements Undermine Free Trade* (OUP 2008).

Bonneau V and others, 'The disruptive nature of 3D printing' (2017) Digital Transformation Monitor, January <https://ati.ec.europa.eu/sites/default/files/2020-07/The%20disruptive%20nature%20of%203D%20printing%20%20%28v1%29.pdf> accessed 25 October 2021. (archived link).

Boonekamp C, "Regional Trade Agreements and the WTO," in Carlos A Primo Braga and Bernard Hoekman (eds), *The Future of the Global Trade Order* (2nd edn, Eur U Institute 2017).

Borlini L, 'A Crisis Looming in the Dark: Some Remarks on the Reform Proposals on Notifications and Transparency' (2019) 63 QIL, Zoom-out 83.

Brenton P, 'Preferential Rules of Origin' in Jean-Pierre Chauffour and Jean-Christophe Maur (eds), *Preferential Trade Agreement Policies for Development: A Handbook* (World Bank 2011).

Cadot O and C Carrere, J de Melo, B Tumurchudur, 'Product-Specific Rules of Origin in EU and US Preferential Trade Arrangements: An Assessment' (2006) 5 World Trade Rev 199.

Cadot O and J de Melo, 'Why OECD Countries Should Reform Rules of Origin' (2008) 23 The World Bank Research Observer 77.

Calza E and J Soguero Escuer, J Fabiani, G de Prato, 'Advanced Manufacturing Study. Preliminary findings on EU's Advanced Manufacturing industry in the global landscape,' Pub. Office of the EU (2024) <https://publications.jrc.ec.europa.eu/repository/handle/JRC137761> accessed 25 October 2024.

Cernat L and Z Kutlina-Dimitrova, 'Thinking in a Box: A "Mode 5" Approach to Service Trade' (2014) 48 J World Trade 1109.

Ciuriak D and D Bienen, 'Overcoming Low Preference Utilization in Preferential Trade Agreements: Presumption of Origin for Small Shipments' (2014) Trade & Development Discussion Paper No. 02/2014, bkp Development Research and Consulting <https://papers.ssrn.com/sol3/papers.cfm?abstract_id=2460648> accessed 10 March 2025.

Coke Hamilton P and SN Sirmimanne (supervisors), 'What is at Stake for Developing Countries in Trade Negotiations on e-Commerce?: The Case of the Joint Statement Initiative' (2021) UNCTAD: Division on Intl Trade & Commodities & Division on Technology & Logistics <https://unctad.org/system/files/official-document/ditctncd2020d5_en.pdf> accessed 29 October 2021.

Committee on Ways and Means – US House of Representatives, 'Overview and Compilation of U.S. Trade Statues' (2003 edn, US Government Printing Office June 2003).

Conconi P and M García-Santana, L Puccio, R Venturini, 'From Final Goods to Inputs: The Protectionist Effect of Rules of Origin' (2018) 108 American Economic Rev 2335.

Crivelli P and S Inama, J Kasteng, 'Using Utilization Rates to Identify Rules of Origin Reforms: The Case of EU Free Trade Area Agreements' (2021) EUI Working Papers RCS 2021/21, <https://cadmus.eui.eu/handle/1814/70396> accessed 24 October 2021.

Dedrick J and KL Kraemer, G Linden, 'Who Profits from Innovation in Global Value Chains?: A Study of the iPod and Notebook PCs' (2010) 19 Industrial & Corporate Change 81.

Delev C, 'Straining the spaghetti bowl: re-evaluating the regulation of preferential rules of origin' (2022) 25 J Intl Economic L 1.

Deliyanakis N, Lindberg M, Mascalchi E et al. 'Trends in advanced manufacturing R&I – Advanced manufacturing projects and what they tell us about the future of the manufacturing industry' Pub. Office of the EU (2023) <https://data.europa.eu/doi/10.2777/209329> accessed 23 March 2024.

Destler IM, 'Rules of Origin and U.S. Trade Policy' in Olivier Cadot, Antoni Estevadeordal, Akiko Suwa-Eisenmann, and Theirry Verdier (eds), *The Origin of Goods: Rules of Origin in Regional Trade Agreements* (OUP 2006).

Díaz Gavier P and J Gaudalupe Báscones, 'On Article 8.1(b)(iv) of the Customs Valuation Agreement: When is the Value of Certain Services Supplied by the Buyer Relevant for Customs Value (i.e. Engineering, Development, Artwork, Design Work, and Plans and Sketches)?'(2014) 9 Global Trade & Customs J 260.

Dinh D, *Rules of Origin for Services: From the Early Days of GATS to the Era of Servicification* (Edward Elgar 2020).

Donner Abreu M, 'Preferential Rules of Origin in Regional Trade Agreements' in Rohini Acharya (ed), *Regional Trade Agreements and The Multilateral Trading System* (CUP 2016).

Dreier WA, "A Question of Liability: Who's to Blame When Products Developed by Licensees Cause Unforeseen ... ?", reprinted from (2000) New Jersey LJ April 3 <https://norrismclaughlin.com/articles/category/a-question-of-liability-whos-to-blame-when-products-developed-by-licensees-cause-unforeseen> accessed 25 October 2021.

Duchêne V and others, *Identifying Current and Future Application Areas, Existing Industrial Value Chains and Missing Competences in the EU, in the Area of Additive Manufacturing (3D printing)* Final Report for the Commission Executive Agency for Small & Medium-Sized Enterprises (Publications Office Eur Union 2016) <https://data.europa.eu/doi/10.2826/72202> accessed 8 January 2022.

Elsig M and B Hoekman and J Pauwelyn, 'Thinking About the Performance of the World Trade Organization: A Discussion Across Disciplines' in Manfred Elsig, Bernard Hoekman, and Joost Pauwelyn (eds), *Assessing the World Trade Organization: Fit for Purpose?* (CUP 2017).

Erasmus H and F Flatters, R Kirk, 'Rules of Origin as tools of development? Some lessons from SADC,' in Olivier Cadot, Antoni Estevadeordal, Akiko Suwa-Eisenmann, and Theirry Verdier (eds), *The Origin of Goods: Rules of Origin in Regional Trade Agreements* (OUP 2006).

Estevadeordal A and K Souminen, 'Rules of Origin in Preferential Trading Arrangements: Is All Well with the Spaghetti Bowl in the Americas?' (2005) Economia (Spring).

Estevadeordal A and J Harris, K Suominen, 'Multilateralising Preferential Rules of Origin around the World' (2009) IDB Working Paper Series, #IDB-WP-137 <https://publications.iadb.org/publications/english/document/Multilateralising-Preferential-Rules-of-Origin-around-the-World.pdf> accessed 23 October 2021.

Fan Z and J Sotelo, V Sundareswaran, '3D Printing: A Guide for Decision-Makers' (January 2020) World Economic Forum – White Paper <http://www3.weforum.org/docs/WEF_Impacts_3D_Printing_on_Trade_Supply_Chains_Toolkit.pdf> accessed 24 October 2021.

Farrokhina F and C Richards, 'E-Commerce Products Under the World Trade Organization Agreements: Goods, Services, Both or Neither?' (2016) 50 J World Trade 793.

Fink C and D Nikomborirak, 'Rules of Origin in Services: A Case Study of Five ASEAN Countries' in Marion Panizzon, Nicole Pohl, and Pierre Sauvé (eds), *GATS and the Regulation of International Trade in Services* (CUP 2008).

Finger JM, 'The GATT/WTO System and National Trade Policies: Which Comes First?' in Manfred Elsig, Bernard Hoekman, and Joost Pauwelyn (eds), *Assessing the World Trade Organization: Fit for Purpose?* (CUP 2017).

Fleuter S, 'The Role of Digital Products under the WTO: A New Framework for GATT and GATS Classification' (2016) 17 Chicago J Intl L 153.

Flores Ituarte I and SH Khajavi, M Salmi, 'Current and Future Business Models for 3D Printing Applications,' in Rosa Maria Ballardini, Marcus Norrgård, Jouni Partanen (eds), *3D Printing, Intellectual Property, and Innovation: Insights from Law and Technology* (WoltersKluwer 2017).

Foltea M, 'The World Customs Organization' in Marina Foltea (ed), *International Organizations in WTO Dispute Settlement* (CUP 2012).

Forrester IS and T Kaul, 'Tariff Classification,' in Patrick F J Macrory, Arthur Edmond Appleton and Michael G Plummer (eds), *World Trade Organization: Legal, Economic and Political Analysis* (Springer 2005).

Forrester IS and OE Odarda, 'The Agreement on Customs Valuation' in Patrick F J Macrory, Arthur Edmond Appleton and Michael G Plummer, *World Trade Organization: Legal, Economic and Political Analysis* (Springer 2005).

Freund C and A Mulabdic, M Ruta, 'Is 3D Printing a Threat to Global Trade? The Trade Effects You Didn't Hear About,' (2020) World Development Report Policy Research Working Paper, No. 9024 <https://openknowledge.worldbank.org/handle/10986/32453> accessed 26 November 2021.

Gantz DA, 'The United States-Mexico-Canada Agreement: Tariffs, Customs, and Rules of Origin' (2019) Baker Institute Rep. no. 02.21.19.

Gantz DA, 'North America's Shifting Supply Chains: The USMCA, COVID-19, and the U.S.-China Trade War' (2020) Rice U Baker Institute for Public Policy <https://doi.org/10.25613/0gaq-h036> accessed 8 January 2022.

Gebhardt A, and J Kessler, L Thurn, *3D Printing: Understanding Additive Manufacturing* (2nd edn, Hanser 2019).

Geraets D and C Carroll, AR Willems, 'Reconciling Rules of Origin and Global Value Chains: The Case for Reform' (2015) 18 J Intl Economic L 287.

Gereffi G and J Lee, 'Why the World Suddenly Cares About Global Supply Chains,' (2012) 48 J Supply Chain Management 24.

Gladstone J and C Aquilar Flores, 'Free trade agreements: compliance with rules of origin and utilization of preferential tariffs' (2017) 23 Intl Trade L & Regulation 113.

Grant Cohen H, 'What is International Trade Law For?' (2019) 113 The American J Intl L 326, 342.

Guzman AT and JHB Pauwelyn, *International Trade Law* (2nd edn, WoltersKluwer 2012).

Hestermeyer HP and L Nielsen, 'The Legality of Local Content Measures under WTO Law' (2014) 48 J World Trade 553.

Hirsch M, 'Agreement on Rules of Origin' in Rüdiger Wolfrum, Peter-Tobias Stoll and Holger P. Hestermeyer (eds), *WTO – Trade in Goods* (Koninklijke Brill NV 2010).

Holger P. Hestermeyer (eds), 'The Politics of Rules of Origin' in Tomer Broude, Marc L Busch, and Amelia Porges (eds), *The Politics of International Economic* Law (CUP 2011).

Hoekman B, 'Rules of Origin for Goods and Services: Conceptual Issues and Economic Considerations' (1993) 27 J World Trade 82.

Hoekman B, 'Urgent and Important: Improving WTO Performance by Revisiting Working Practices' (2019) 53 J World Trade 373.

Hoekman B and MM Kostecki, *The Political Economy of the World Trading System: The WTO and Beyond* (3rd edn, OUP 2009).

Hoekman B and D Nelson, '21st Century Trade Agreements and the Owl of Minerva' (2018), EUI Working Papers, RSCAS 2018/04 <https://cadmus.eui.eu/bitstream/handle/1814/50964/RSCAS_2018_04.pdf?sequence=1&isAllowed=y> accessed 23 October 2021.

Hoekman B and S Inama, 'Harmonization of Rules of Origin: An Agenda for Plurilateral Cooperation' (2018) 22 East Asian Economic Rev.

Hoekman B and PC Mavroidis, 'WTO Reform: Back to the Past to Build for the Future' (2021) 12 Global Policy (Sup 3).

Hoekman B and C Sabel, 'Plurilateral Cooperation as an Alternative to Trade Agreements: Innovating One Domain at a Time' (2021) 12 Global Policy (Sup 3).

Hoekman B and M Sanflilippo, F Santi, R Ticku, 'Trade, productivity, and services input intensity' *Rev of World Econ* (30 July 2024) https://link.springer.com/article/10.1007/s10290-024-00548-2 accessed 25 October 2024.

Imagawa H and E Vermulst, 'The Agreement on Rules of Origin', in Patrick FJ Macrory, Arthur Edmond Appleton and Michael G Plummer (eds) *World Trade Organization: Legal, Economic and Political Analysis* (Springer 2005).

Inama S, 'Trade Preferences and the World Trade Organization Negotiations on Market Access: Battling for Compensation of Erosion GSP, ACP, and Other Trade Preferences or Assessing and Improving Their Utilization and Value by Addressing Rules of Origin and Graduation?' (2003) 37 J World Trade 959.

Inama S, *Rules of Origin in International Trade* (CUP 2009).

Inama S, *Rules of Origin in International Trade* (CUP 2022).

Inama S and EW Sim, *Rules of Origin in ASEAN* (CUP 2015).

Inama S and P Crivelli, 'Convergence on the Calculation Methodology for Drafting Rules of Origin in FTAS Using the Ad Valorem Criterion' (2019) 14 Global Trade & Customs J 146.

International Chamber of Commerce, 'Business Recommendations on Rules of Origin in Preferential Trade Agreements' (May 2017) Doc. No. 104–89 <https://cdn.iccwbo.org/content/uploads/sites/3/2017/05/ICC-Policy-Statement-on-rules-of-origin-in-preferential-trade-agreements.pdf> accessed 3 January 2022.

Ioannides I, 'The EU-UK Trade and Cooperation Agreement Two Years On: Unpacking Early Evidence' European Parliamentary Research Service (August 2023), 29–34 <https://www.europarl.europa.eu/RegData/etudes/STUD/2023/747433/EPRS_STU(2023)747433_EN.pdf> accessed 23 March 2024.

Jackson JH, 'The Evolution of the World Trading System – The Legal and Institutional Context' in Daniel Bethlehem, Isabelle Van Damme, Donald McRae and Rodney Neufeld, *The Oxford Handbook of International Trade* (OUP 2009).

James WE, 'Rules of Origin and Rules of Preference and the World Trade Organization: The Challenge to Global Trade Liberalization' in Patrick F J Macrory, Arthur Edmond Appleton and Michael G Plummer (eds) *World Trade Organization: Legal, Economic and Political Analysis* (Springer 2005).

Jitsuya H, 'Standardization of Complex and Diversified Preferential Rules of Origin' (2021) 55 J World Trade 545.

Jones VC and L Wong, 'International Trade: Rules of Origin' (2020) Congressional Research Service Report, 3 March <https://crsreports.congress.gov/product/pdf/RL/RL34524/16> accessed 23 October 2021.

Kretz D and E Van de Velde, *Advanced Technologies for Industry – Product Watch: 3D Printing of Hybrid Components*, Report for the Commission Executive Agency for Small & Medium-sized Enterprises (Publications Office Eur Union 2021) <https://data.europa.eu/doi/10.2826/581451> accessed 8 January 2022.

Latrille P, 'Services Rules in Regional Trade Agreements: How Diverse or Creative are They Compared to the Multilateral Rules?' in Rhoni Acharya (ed), *Regional Trade Agreements and the Multilateral Trading System* (CUP 2016).

Low P, 'The Role of Services in Global Value Chains,' in Deborah K Elms and Patrick Low (eds), *Global Value Chains in a Changing World* (WTO Publications 2013).

Mariani P and G Sacerdoti, 'Trade in Goods and Level Playing Field' (2021) Working Paper No. 7/2021, DCU Brexit Institute <https://ssrn.com/abstract=3797021> accessed 23 October 2021.

Marceddu ML, 'Implementing Transparency and Public Participation in FTA Negotiations: Are the Times a-Changin'? (2018) 21 J Intl Economic L 681.

Matsushita, M and TJ Schoenbaum, PC Mavroidis, M Hahn, *The World Trade Organization: Law, Practice, and Policy* (3rd edn, OUP 2017).

Mavroidis PC, *The Regulation of International Trade*, vol. 1 (MIT Press 2016).

Mavroidis PC, 'And You Put the Load Right on Me: Digital Taxes, Tax Discrimination, and Trade in Services' (2020) 12 Trade, L & Development 75.

Mavroidis PC, *The Regulation of International Trade*, vol 3 (MIT Press 2020).

Mavroidis PC and E Vermulst, 'The Case for Dropping Preferential Rules of Origin' (2018) 52 J World Trade 1.

McCollough J, 'The Basics in Valuation of Intellectual Property Assets' Federal Lawyer 64 (August 2017) 7–10.

Meltzer JP, 'Governing Digital Trade,' (2019) 18 World Trade Rev (2Supp) s35.

Micallef JA, 'Digital Trade in EU FTAs: Are EU FTAs Allowing Cross Border Digital Trade to Reach Its Full Potential?' (2019) 53 J World Trade 855.

Miroudot S and C Cadestin, 'Services in Global Value Chains: From Inputs to Value-Creating Activities' (2017) OECD Trade Policy Papers No. 197 <https://www.oecd-ilibrary.org/trade/services-in-global-value-chains_465f0d8b-en> accessed 25 October 2021.

Munro J, 'Pushing the Boundaries of "Products" and "Goods" under GATT 1994: An Analysis of the Coverage of New and Unorthodox Articles of Commerce' (2013) 47 J World Trade 1323.

National Board of Trade – Sweden, 'Trade Regulation in a 3D Printed World: A Primer' (2016) Kommerskollegium 2016: 1.

National Board of Trade – Sweden 'Rules of Origin in the 21st Century' (2020) Kommerskollegium <https://www.kommerskollegium.se/globalassets/publikationer/rapporter/2020/rules-of-origin-in-the-21st-century.pdf> accessed 24 October 2021.

Neeraj RS, 'Trade Rules for the Digital Economy: Charting New Waters at the WTO' (2018) 18 World Trade Rev (2Supp) s126.

Nieß V and S Wende, 'Intellectual Property and Product Liability Challenges in Three-Dimensional Printing' (2017) 6 IEEE Consumer Electronics Magazine October 128.

Neufeld N, 'Great Expectations: How the World Trade Organization's Trade Facilitation Agreement Impacts Trade and Trade Cooperation' (2019) 11 Trade, L & Development 11.

Nordberg A and Schovsbo J, 'EU Design Law and 3D Printing: Finding the Right Balance in a New E-Ecosystem' in Rosa Maria Ballardini, Marcus Norrgård, Jouni Partanen (eds), *3D Printing, Intellectual Property and Innovation: Insights from Law and Technology* (WoltersKluwer 2017).

Osborn LS, *3D Printing and Intellectual Property* (CUP 2019).

Pauwelyn J, 'Comment – Nothing Dramatic (... Regarding Administration of Customs Laws)' (2009) 8 World Trade Rev (Special Issue 1).

Pauwelyn J, 'Taking the Preferences Out of Preferential Trade Agreements: TTIP as a Provider of Public Goods' reprinted in Joost HB Pauwelyn, Andrew T Guzman, Jennifer A Hillman, *International Trade Law* (3rd edn, WoltersKluwer 2016).

Hillman and AT Guzman, JA Hillman, *International Trade Law* (3rd edn, WoltersKluwer 2016).

Peng S, 'A New Trade Regime for the Servitization of Manufacturing: Rethinking the Goods-Services Dichotomy' (2020) 54 J World Trade 718.

Peters A, 'International Organizations and International Law' in Jacob Katz Cogan, Ian Hurd, and Ian Johnstone (eds), *The Oxford Handbook of International Organizations* (OUP 2016).

Primo Braga CA and B Hoekman, 'The Future of the Global Trade Order' in Carlos A. Primo Braga and Bernard Hoekman (eds), *The Future of the Global Trade Order* (2nd edn, Eur U Institute 2017).

Puccio L, '20 Years After Marrakesh: Reconsidering the Effects of Preferential Rules of Origin and Anti-Circumvention Rules on Trade in Inputs and Global Production Networks' 2014 Eur YB Intl Economic L 173.

Reinsch WA and J Caporal, M Waddoups, N Tekarli, 'The Impact of Rules of Origin on Supply Chains: USMCA's Auto Rules as a Case Study' (April 2019) Center for Strategic and International Studies <https://csis-website-prod.s3.amazonaws.com/s3fs-public/publication/190403_Scholl_RulesofOrigin_WEB_v3.pdf> accessed 24 October 2021.

Rimmer M, '*ClearCorrect:* Intellectual Property, 3D Printing, and the Future of Trade' (2019) 23 Gonzaga J Intl L 55.

Sauvé P, 'Life Beyond Local Content: Exploring Alternative Measures of Industry Support in the Context of WTO Accession' (2016) 1 J Int'l Trade 1.

Sauvé P, 'To Fuse, Not to Fuse, or Simply Confuse? Assessing the Case for Normative Convergence Between Goods and Services Trade Law' (2019) 22 J Intl Economic L 356.

Shaffer G, 'Retooling Trade Agreements for Social Inclusion' (2019) U Illinois L Rev 1.

Shaffer G, 'Trade Law in a Data-Driven Economy: The Need for Modesty and Resilience' (2021) 20 World Trade Rev. 259.

Sharma D and A Kumar, 'Methods for Intellectual Property Valuation' in Irene Calboli and Maria Lillà Montagnani ed., *Handbook on Intellectual Property Research* (OUP 2021).

Singh R and S Singh, 'Do Rules of Origin Extend Disproportionate Trade Gains under SAFTA: A Case Study of Bicycle and Textile Industries' (2021) 16 Global Trade & Customs J 59.

Smith F and L Woods, 'A Distinction without a Difference: Exploring the Boundary between Goods and Services in the World Trade Organization and the European Union' (2005) 12 Columbia J Eur L 1.

Soprano R, 'Brexit and the EU-UK Free Trade Agreement: Dos and Don'ts When Drafting Rules of Origin' (2019) 18 J Intl Trade L & Policy 96.

Stabell C and Ø Fjeldstad, 'Configuring Value for Competitive Advantage: On Chains, Shops, and Networks' (1998) 19 Strategic Management J 413.

Suominen K, *Revolutionizing World Trade: How Disruptive Technologies Open Opportunities for All* (Stanford UP 2019).

Tallberg J, 'Transparency' in Jacob Katz Cogan, Ian Hurd, and Ian Johnstone (eds), *The Oxford Handbook of International Organizations* (OUP 2016).

Tuomi J, and S Chekurov, J Partanen, '3D Printing History, Principles and Technologies,' in Rosa Maria Ballardini, Marcus Norrgård, Jouni Partanen (eds), *3D Printing, Intellectual Property, and Innovation: Insights from Law and Technology* (WoltersKluwer 2017).

Umezu S and H Sato (corresponding authors), 'Metal-Plastic Hybrid 3D Printing Using Catalyst-Loaded Filament and Electroless Plating' (2020) 36 Additive Manufacturing 101556.

US Government Accountability Office, 'International Trade: USTR Should Improve Coordination on New Automotive Rules of Origin' Report to Congressional Committees GAO-24-106330 (January 2024) 1 <https://www.gao.gov/assets/d24106330.pdf> accessed 23 March 2024.

US International Trade Commission (USITC), USMCA Automotive Rules of Origin: Economic Impact and Operation, 2023 Report, Pub No 5443, 17 <https://www.usitc.gov/publications/332/pub5443.pdf> accessed 23 March 2024.

Van den Bossche P, *The Law and Policy of the World Trade Organization: Text, Cases and Materials* (2nd edn, CUP 2008).

Van den Bossche P and W Zdouc, *The Law and Policy of the World Trade Organization: Text, Cases and Materials* (4th edn, CUP 2019).

Van den Bossche P and D Prévost, *Essentials of WTO Law* (2nd edn, CUP 2021).

van de Heetkamp A and R Tusveld, *Origin Management: Rules of Origin in Free Trade Agreements* (Springer 2011).

Vermulst EA, 'Rules of Origin as Commercial Policy Instruments – Revisited' (1992) 26 J World Trade 61.

Vermulst EA and P Waer, 'European Community Rules of Origin as Commercial Policy Instruments?' (1990) 24 J World Trade 55, 98.

Weinmann C, 'Trademark Licensors and Product Liability Claims – A European Perspective' (2005) The Trademark Reporter 1394.

Willemyns I, 'GATS Classification of Digital Services – Does "The Cloud" Have a Silver Lining?' (2019) 53 J World Trade 59.

Winslett G, 'Critical Mass Agreements: The Proven Template for Trade Liberalization in the WTO' (2018) 17 World Trade Rev 405.

Winters LA, 'The WTO and RTAs: Is It All Over for Multilateralism?' in Manfred Elsig, Bernard Hoekman, and Joost Pauwelyn (eds), *Assessing the World Trade Organization: Fit for Purpose?* (CUP 2017).

Wong L and KH Kitamura, 'USMCA: Automotive Rules' (2023) Congressional Research Service Reports, 8 December <https://crsreports.congress.gov/product/pdf/IF/IF12082> accessed 23 March 2024.

Wu M, 'Digital Trade-Related Provisions in Regional Trade Agreements: Existing Models and Lessons for the Multilateral Trade System' (2017) RTA Exchange (ICTSD and IDB).

Zampetti AB, 'Democratic Legitimacy in the World Trade Organization: The Justice Dimension'(2003) 37 J World Trade 105.

Zampetti and P Sauvé, 'Rules of Origin for Services: Economic and Legal Considerations,' in Olivier Cadot, Antoni Estevadeordal, Akiko Suwa-Eisenmann, and Theirry Verdier (eds), *The Origin of Goods: Rules of Origin in Regional Trade Agreements* (OUP 2006).

Agreements, Treaties, and International Trade Instruments

African Continental Free Trade Area Secretariat, 'Draft: Protocol to the Agreement Establishing the African Continental Free Trade Area on Digital Trade' (7–10 February 2024) Available at <https://www.bilaterals.org/IMG/pdf/afcfta_digital_trade_protocol_-_9_february_2024_draft.pdf> accessed 20 October 2024.

Agreement between New Zealand and Singapore on a Closer Economic Partnership (CEP agreement 2000) (signed 14 November 2000, entered into force 1 January 2001).

Agreement between New Zealand and Singapore on Closer Economic Partnership – Upgrade (entered into force 1 January 2020).

Agreement between the United States of America, the United Mexican States, and Canada (USMCA) (signed 30 November 2018, entered into force 1 July 2020).

Agreement on Implementation of Article VII of The General Agreement on Tariffs And Trade 1994 (Customs Valuation Agreement) (CVA) (15 April 1994) LT/UR/A-1A/4.

Agreement on Rules of Origin (AOR) (15 April 1994) LT/UR/A-1A/7.

Agreement on Subsidies and Countervailing Measures (SCM Agreement) (15 April 1994) LT/UR/A-1A/9.

Agreement on Trade Facilitation (TFA) (entered into force 22 February 2017) WT/L/940.

Agreement on Trade-Related Investment Measures (TRIMS) (15 April 1994) LT/UR/A-1A/13.

ASEAN Trade in Goods Agreement (ATIGA) (signed 26 February 2009, entered into force 17 May 2010).

ASEAN-Australia-New Zealand Free Trade Agreement (signed 27 February 2009, entered into force 1 January 2010).

ASEAN-India Free Trade Agreement (signed 13 August 2009, entered into force 1 January 2010).

ASEAN-Korea Free Trade Area (AKFTA) (signed 13 December 2005, entered into force 1 June 2007).

Comprehensive and Economic Trade Agreement (CETA) (signed 30 October 2016, some provisions entered into force on 21 September 2017).

Comprehensive and Progressive Agreement for Trans-Pacific Partnership (CPTPP), incorporating Trans-Pacific Partnership Agreement (TPP) (signed 8 March 2018).

Free Trade Agreement between the European Union and the Republic of Korea (signed 10 May 2010, entered into force 13 December 2015).

General Agreement on Tariffs and Trade (GATT 1947) (signed 1 January 1948).

General Agreement on Tariffs and Trade 1994 (GATT 1994) (15 April 1994) LT/UR/A-1A/1/GATT/1.

General Agreement on Trade in Services (GATS)(15 April 1994) LT/UR/A-1B/S/1.

International Convention on the Harmonized Commodity Description and Coding System (HS Convention) (adopted 14 June 1983, entered into force 1 January 1988).

International Convention on the Simplification and Harmonization of Customs Procedures (Kyoto Convention 1973, signed 18 May 1973, entered into Force 24 September 1974).

International Convention on the Simplification and Harmonization of Customs Procedures (as amended) (Revised Kyoto Convention) (entered into force 3 February 2006).

International Convention Relating to the Simplification of Customs Formalities (entered into force 27 November 1924) XXX LNTS 775.

Ministerial Declaration on the Expansion of Trade in Information Technology Products, (ITA Expansion) (Nairobi, 16 December 2015) WT/MIN(15)/25.

Ministerial Declaration on Trade in Information Technology Products (Information Technology Agreement/ITA) (Singapore, 13 December 1996) WT/MIN(96)/16.

North American Free Trade Agreement (NAFTA) (signed 17 December 1992, entered into force 1 January 1994).

Regional Comprehensive Economic Partnership (RCEP) (signed 15 November 2020).

South-Asian Free Trade Area (SAFTA) (signed 6 January 2004, entered into force 1 January 2006).

Tariff Act of 1930, 19 U.S.C. §1592.

The Marrakesh Agreement Establishing the World Trade Organization (15 April 1994) LT/UR/A/2.

Trade Agreement Between The United States of America and Japan (US-Japan Trade Agreement) (signed 17 October 2019, entered into force 1 January 2020).

Trade And Cooperation Agreement Between The European Union And The European Atomic Energy Community, Of The One Part, And The United Kingdom Of Great Britain And Northern Ireland, Of The Other Part, (TCA) (signed 30 December 2020, entered into force 1 January 2021) L 444/14.

Understanding on the Interpretation of Article XXIV of the General Agreement on Tariffs and Trade 1994, <https://www.wto.org/english/docs_e/legal_e/10-24_e.htm> accessed 2 December 2021.

Understanding on Rules and Procedures Governing the Settlement of Disputes (DSU) (15 April 1994) LT/UR/A-2/DS/U/1.

United States – Bahrain Free Trade Agreement (signed 14 September 2004, entered into force 11 January 2006).

United States – Israel Free Trade Agreement (signed 22 April 1985, entered into force 1 September 1985).

United States – Korea Free Trade Agreement (KORUS) (signed 30 June 2007, entered into force 12 March 2012).

Vienna Convention on the Law of Treaties (VCLT) (entered into force 27 January 1980) 1155 UNTS 331.

Drafts, Reports, Communications, and Internal Communications of GATT and WTO – Located at <https://docs.wto.org>

Committee on Rules of Origin, 'Draft Consolidated Text of Non-Preferential Rules of Origin' (11 February 2010) G/RO/W/111/Rev.5.

Committee on Rules of Origin 'Report of The Committee on Rules of Origin to The General Council on Preferential Rules of Origin for Least Developed Countries' (20 November 2023) G/RO/W/223/Rev.2.

Committee of Participants on the Expansion of Trade in Information Technology Products, 'Status of Implementation: Note by Secretariat' (15 March 2024) G/IT/1/Rev.60 <https://docs.wto.org> accessed 23 March 2024.

Committee of Participants on the Expansion of Trade in Information Technology Products 'Minutes of the Meeting of 11 April 2024' (5 July 2024) G/IT/M/80 <https://docs.wto.org> accessed 20 October 2024.

Communication from India and South Africa (10 March 2020) WTO: Work Programme on Electronic Commerce.

'Destructions of Documents' (22 December 1975) L/4281.

General Council Decision, 'Transparency Mechanism for Preferential Trade Arrangements' (14 December 2010) WT/L/806.

Joint Statement Initiative on Electronic Commerce, 'Communication' (26 July 2024) INF/ECOM/87 <wto.documents.org>.

LDC Group Communication, 'Submission of LDC to the Committee on Rules of Origin *Ad Valorem* Criterion' (30 October 2020) G/RO/W/202.

Ministerial Decision, 'Preferential Rules for Least Developed Countries' (19 December 2015), WT/MIN(15)/47, WT/L/917/Add.1.

Ministerial Decision, 'Preferential Rules of Origin for Least Developed Countries' (7 December 2013) WT/MIN(13)/42, WT/L/917.

Ministerial Decision, 'Work Programme On Electronic Commerce' (2 March 2024) WT/MIN(24)/38, WT/L/1193.

Negotiating Group on Non-Tariff Measures, 'Meeting of 30 November 1989' (19 December 1989) MTN.GNG/NG2/14.

Negotiating Group on Non-Tariff Measures, 'Meeting of 14–15 February 1990' (13 March 1990) MTN.GNG.NG2/16.

Negotiating Group on Non-Tariff Measures, 'Points Made in Relation to Rules of Origin: Synopsis by the Secretariat' (13 March 1990) MTN.GNG/NG2/W/54/Rev.1.

Negotiating Group on Rules, 'Compendium of Issues Related to Regional Trade Agreements, Background Note by the Secretariat, Revision' (1 August 2002) WTO doc. TN/RL/W/8/Rev. 1.

Negotiating Group on Rule Making and Trade-Related Investment Measures, 'Rules of Origin, Note by the Secretariat' (6 June 1991) MTN.GNG/RM/W/2.

Preparatory Committee of the United Nations Conference on Trade and Employment, "Report to Commission A by The Sub-Committee on Articles 14, 15, & 24" (15 August 1947) E/PC/T/174.

'Statement by Indonesia: Facilitator's Consultation on Electronic Commerce, MC11 declaration, and other relevant plenary sessions', delivered on 13 December (20 December 2017) WT/MIN(17)/68 .

Technical Committee on Rules of Origin, 'Intersessional Developments Director's Report' (21 December 2018) OC0211E1a.

Trade Negotiations Committee, 'Draft Final Act Embodying the Results of the Uruguay Round of Multilateral Trade Negotiations' (3 December 1990) MTN.TNC/W/35/Rev.1.

Trade Negotiations Committee, 'Draft Final Act Embodying the Results of the Uruguay Round of Multilateral Trade' (20 December 1991) MTN.TNC/W/FA.

United States, 'Rules of Origin: United States-Request for Consultations under Article XXII:1' (31 January 1974) l/3992.

WTO Disputes

Canada-Certain Measures Affecting the Renewable Energy Generation Sector and Canada – Measures Relating to the Feed-In Tariff Program (*Canada-Renewable Energy*) Appellate Body Reports (6 May 2013) 3AB-2013-1, WT/DS412/AB/R; WT/DS426/AB/R.

China – Measures Affecting Trading Rights and Distribution Services for Certain Publications and Audiovisual Entertainment Products, Appellate Body Report (21 December 2009) WT/DS363/AB/R.

European Communities – Customs Classification of Frozen Boneless Chicken Cuts, Appellate Body Report (circulated 12 September 2005, adopted 27 September 2005) WT/DS269/AB/R and WT/DS286/AB/R.

European Communities – Measures Affecting Asbestos and Asbestos-Containing Products, Appellate Body Report (12 March 2001, adopted 5 April 2001) WT/DS135/AB/R.

European Communities – Regime for the Importation, Sale and Distribution of Bananas, Appellate Body Report (9 September 1997, adopted 25 September 1997) WT/DS27/AB/R.

European Communities – Selected Customs Matters, Appellate Body Report (circulated 13 November 2006, adopted 11 December 2006) WT/DS315/AB/R.

European Communities – Tariff Treatment of Certain Information Technology Products, Panel Report (circulated 16 August 2010, adopted 21 September 2010) WT/DS375/R, WT/DS376/R, WT/DS377/R.

Turkey – Restrictions on Imports of Textile and Clothing Products, Appellate Body Report (adopted 19 November 1999) WT/DS34/14.3.

United States – Final Countervailing Duty Determination with Respect to Certain Softwood Lumber from Canada (*US-Softwood Lumber IV*), Appellate Body Report (19 January 2004) AB-2003–6, WT/DS257/AB/R.

United States – Measures Affecting Textiles and Apparel Products, Request for Consultations by the European Communities (3 June 1997) WT/DS85/1.

United States Notification of Mutually-Agreed Solution (11 February 1998) WT/DS85/9.

United States – Measures Affecting Textiles and Apparel Products (II), Request for Consultations by the European Communities (25 November 1998) WT/DS151/1.

Consultations by the European Communities Notification of Mutually Agreed Solution (31 July 2000) WT/DS151/10.

United States – Measures Affecting the Production and Sale of Clove Cigarettes, Appellate Body Report (circulated 4 April 2012, adopted 24 April 2012) WT/DS406/AB/R.

United States – Measures Affecting Trade in Large Civil Aircraft (Second Complaint), Appellate Body Report (12 March 2012, adopted 23 March 2012) WT/DS353/AB/R.

United States – Measures Concerning the Importation, Marketing and Sale of Tuna and Tuna Products, Appellate Body Report (circulated 16 May 2012, adopted 13 June 2012) WT/DS381/AB/R.

United States – Preliminary Determinations with Respect to Certain Softwood Lumber from Canada (US-Softwood Lumber (III)), Panel Report (27 September 2002) WT/DS236/R.

United States – Rules of Origin for Textiles and Apparel Products (Panel Report circulated 20 June 2003, adopted 21 July 2003) WT/DS243/R.

National and Regional Legislation, Judicial Decisions, Administrative Rulings, and Administrative Opinions

Answer given by Ms. Malmström on behalf of the European Commission (14 November 2018) E-004978/2018 <https://www.europarl.europa.eu/doceo/document/E-8-2018-004978-ASW_EN.html> accessed 25 October 2021.

Case C-434/15, *Asociación Profesional Élite Taxi v. Uber Systems Spain SL* [2017] ECLI:EU:C:2017:364.

Case C-509/19, *BMW Bayerische Motorenwerke AG v. Hauptzollamt München* [2020] ECLI:EU:C:2020:694.

*ClearCorrect Operating v. International Trade Comm*ission, 810 F. 3d 1283, Court of Appeals, Federal Circuit 2015.

Commission, 'Notice concerning the application of the Regional Convention on pan-Euro-Mediterranean preferential rules of origin or the protocols on rules of origin providing for diagonal cumulation between Contracting Parties to this Convention," (30 March 2020) OJ 2020/C 322/03.

Commission, 'Guidance: Transitional PEM Rules of Origin' (v1.1–27 August 2024) Brussels, 27 August 2024, TAXUD/A6/AM/MO.

Consolidated versions of the Treaty on European Union and the Treaty on the Functioning of the European Union (TFEU) [2012] OJ C 326, 1.

Council Decision of 14 April 2011 on the signing, on behalf of the European Union, of the Regional Convention on pan-Euro-Mediterranean preferential rules of origin (PEM) (2013) OJ 56 L 54/1.

Council Decision No 2/2005 of the EU-Morocco Association Council of 18 November 2005 amending Protocol 4 to the Euro-Mediterranean Agreement, concerning the definition of the concept of 'originating products' and methods of administrative cooperation [2005] OJ L 336.

Council Directive 2000/31/EC of 8 June 2000 on certain legal aspects of information society services, in particular electronic commerce, in the Internal Market (Directive on Electronic Commerce) [2000] OJ L178/1.

Council Directive 2006/123/EC of the European Parliament and the Council of 12 December 2006 on services in the internal market (Services Directive) [2006] OJ L376/36.

Customs Modernization Act, 19 U.S.C. §1484(a)(1)(B).

Decision No 1/2023 of The Joint Committee of The Regional Convention on Pan-Euro-Mediterranean Preferential Rules Of Origin of 7 December 2023 on the amendment of the Regional Convention on pan-Euro-Mediterranean preferential rules of origin (PEM).

Ministry of Finance Regulation No. 17/PMK.010/2018 on the Second Amendment of Regulation No. 6/PMK.010/2017 on Stipulation of Goods Classification System and Import Duty on Imported Goods ("Regulation 17") [Indonesia].

Opinion of the European Economic and Social Committee, 'Living tomorrow. 3D printing – a tool to empower the European economy' (own-initiative opinion) (2015/C 332/05) C 332/36, 8 October 2015.

Regulation (EU) No 952/2013) of the European Parliament and of the Council of 9 October 2013 laying down the Union Customs Code (recast) (partially entered into force on 1 May 2016) OJ L 269.

US Customs and Border Protection (CBP), Ruling Letter, *Re: Country of origin marking of orthodontic 'aligners'* (1 March 2001) HQ 562012, MAR-05 RR:CR:SM 562012 BLS.

US Customs and Border Protection (CBP),Court Decision, *EOS of North America, Inc. v United States* (10 May 2013) Slip Op. 13–59.

US Customs and Border Protection (CBP),Ruling Letter, *National Commodity Specialist Division, The tariff classification of a Robo 3D Printer from China* (12 September 2017) NY N289281.

US Customs and Border Protection (CBP),Ruling Letter, *re: U.S. Government Procurement; Country of Origin of Storage Infrastructure Solution Systems; Substantial Transformation* (July 16, 2015) HQ H59758, printed in (5 August 2015) 49 Customs Bulletin & Decisions 54.

US Customs and Border Protection (CBP), *Notice of Issuance of Final Determination Concerning Roasted Coffee* (21 November 2017) 82 Federal Register 55387.

US Customs and Border Protection (CBP), *The Tariff Classification of a Smart Speaker from China* (16 October 2019) N306364.

US Congress, S.3431 – Customs Modernization Act of 2023, introduced 7 December 2023.

USMCA Panel Report, *United States – Automotive Rules of Origin* (USA-MEX-CDA-2022-31-01), 14 December 2022.

Online Articles, Newspaper Articles, Website Postings, and Blog Postings

3D Learning Hub, 'How Much Does 3D Printing Cost' (Sculpteo 2024) <https://www.sculpteo.com/en/3d-learning-hub/basics-of-3d-printing/how-much-to-3d-print/> accessed 25 March 2024.

'3D Printers – From Adoption to Scale: A complete 3D Printing Journey' (hp.com 2025) <https://www.hp.com/us-en/printers/3d-printers.html> accessed 11 March 2025.

'3D Printing Technology for Improved Hearing' (sonova.com 2020) <https://www.sonova.com/en/story/innovation/3d-printing-technology-improved-hearing> accessed 24 October 2021.

'About Solvay' (solvay.com) <https://www.solvay.com/en/our-company> accessed 24 October 2021.

'About Us' (home.sandvik) <https://www.home.sandvik/en/about-us/> accessed 24 October 2021.

'Additive Manufacturing: Aviation and Aerospace Industry' (GE Additive) <https://www.ge.com/additive/additive-manufacturing/industries/aviation-aerospace> accessed 24 October 2021.

'Additive Manufacturing Solutions' (solvay.com) <https://www.solvay.com/en/chemical-categories/specialty-polymers/additive-manufacturing> accessed 24 October 2021.

Agenzia delle accise, dogane e monopoli, 'I.V.O. Binding Information on Origin' (adm.gov.it) <https://www.adm.gov.it/portale/en/-informazioni-vincolanti-in-materia-di-origine> accessed 2 December 2021.

Align Technology, 'Align Technology Announces Plans to Assume Operations From Its Manufacturing Services Provider,' (Align Technology Investor Release 22 December 2008) <http://investor.aligntech.com/static-files/de067378-b820-409a-ba5a-fa79087f2fb6> accessed 24 October 2021.

Align Technology 'Align Technology Expands Operations in Costa Rica with New Facilities to Support Continued Long-Term Growth,' (Align Technology Investor Release 25 July 2018) <http://investor.aligntech.com/news-releases/news-release-details/align-technology-expands-operations-costa-rica-new-facilities> accessed 24 October 2021.

'America Makes' (Americamakes.us) <https://www.americamakes.us/about/> accessed 24 October 2021.

Aston R, '3D Printing Done Right' (*Innovation Q*) <https://www.boeing.com/features/innovation-quarterly/nov2017/feature-thought-leadership-3d-printing.page> accessed 24 October 2021.

Brannon I, 'Titanium Production's Perilous U.S. Future' (*Forbes* 29 April 2019) <https://www.forbes.com/sites/ikebrannon/2019/04/29/titanium-productions-perilous-u-s-future/?sh=652a00776a72> accessed 24 October 2021.

Brenner M, 'Navigating Rules of Origin in the New Trade Environment' Proceeding of the 20th Judicial Conference of the United States Court of International Trade (cit.uscourts.gov) <https://www.cit.uscourts.gov/sites/cit/files/MBrenner%20CIT%20Nov182019%20.doc.pdf> accessed 2 December 2021.

Bournias Varotsis A, '3D printing vs. CNC machining' (*3D Hubs*), <https://www.3dhubs.com/knowledge-base/3d-printing-vs-cnc-machining/> accessed 24 October 2021.

Buckberg E, 'Clean vehicle tax credit: The new industrial policy and its impact' Stanford Institute for Economic Policy Research (August 2023) 6 <https://siepr.stanford.edu/publications/policy-brief/clean-vehicle-tax-credit-new-industrial-policy-and-its-impact> accessed 23 March 2024.

'Cassidy, Whitehouse Introduces Bill To Bring U.S. Customs Laws Into The 21st Century, Stop Illicit Trade' (Cassidy.Senate.Gov 8 December 2023) <https://www.cassidy.senate.gov/newsroom/press-releases/cassidy-whitehouse-introduces-bill-to-bring-u-s-customs-laws-into-the-21st-century-stop-illicit-trade> accessed 23 March 2024.

Cao M, 'Trade Wars and Tariffs – a 3D Printing Perspective' (*IC 3D Industries* 13 February 2020) <https://www.ic3dprinters.com/trade-wars-and-tariffs-a-3d-printing-perspective/> accessed 1 November 2021.

CECIMO, 'Press Release: CECIMO Appreciates the Approval of a New Product Nomenclature Standard for Additive Manufacturing Machines' (cecimo.eu 25 April 2019) <https://www.cecimo.eu/news/press-release-cecimo-appreciates-the-approval-of-a-new-product-nomenclature-standard-for-additive-manufacturing-machines/> accessed 24 October 2021.

Cernat L, 'Promoting a "GVCs for LDCs" approach: the case of digital certification for organic products' (European Centre for International Political Economy October 2023) <https://ecipe.org/blog/gvcs-for-ldcs-digital-certification-for-organic-products/> accessed 25 March 2024.

'Certificate of Incorporation' (GE.com 2019) <https://www.ge.com/sites/default/files/GE_Certificate_of_Incorporation_Effective_December_9_2019.pdf> accessed 3 November 2021.

Commission, 'Partnership Council confirms one-off extension of the current rules of origin for electric vehicles and batteries' (ec.europa.eu 21 December 2023) <https://ec.europa.eu/commission/presscorner/detail/en/ip_23_6707> accessed 23 March 2024.

Commission, 'Access 2Markets: Frequently Asked Questions-What is the Harmonized System' (trade.ec.europa.eu) <https://trade.ec.europa.eu/access-to-markets/en/faqs> accessed 2 December 2021.

Commission 'Advanced Manufacturing' (ec.europa.eu) <https://ec.europa.eu/info/research-and-innovation/research-area/industrial-research-and-innovation/key-enabling-technologies/advanced-manufacturing_en> accessed 2 December 2021.

Commission, 'Common Provisions' [for preferential origin arrangements] (ec.europa.eu) <https://ec.europa.eu/taxation_customs/customs-4/international-affairs/origin-goods/general-aspects-preferential-origin/common-provisions_en> accessed 2 December 2021.

Commission, 'EU Customs strategy' (ec.europa.edu) <https://ec.europa.eu/taxation_customs/customs-4/eu-customs-strategy_en?> accessed 2 December 2021.

Commission, 'EU Customs Reform' (ec.europea.eu) <https://taxation-customs.ec.europa.eu/customs-4/eu-customs-reform_en> accessed 23 March 2024.

Commission, 'EU-UK: A New Relationship' (ec.europa.eu) <https://ec.europa.eu/taxation_customs/united-kingdom_en> accessed 5 January 2022.

Commission, 'REX-Registered Exporter System' (ec.europa.eu) <https://ec.europa.eu/taxation_customs/online-services/online-services-and-databases-customs/rex-registered-exporter-system_en> accessed 3 November 2021.

Commission, 'Pan-Euro-Mediterranean Convention (PEM) <https://trade.ec.europa.eu/access-to-markets/en/content/rules-origin-pan-euro-mediterranean-convention> accessed 26 October 2024.

Commission, 'The Pan-Euro-Mediterranean Cumulation and the PEM Convention' (ec.europa.eu) <https://ec.europa.eu/taxation_customs/customs-4/international-affairs/pan-euro-mediterranean-cumulation-and-pem-convention_en> accessed 23 March 2024.

Congressional Budget Office, Cost Estimate for H.R. 5430 (December 2019) <https://www.cbo.gov/system/files/2019-12/hr5430.pdf> accessed 24 October 2021.

Customs and Tariff Bureau, 'Outline for Rules of Origin' (July 2017) Japan Ministry of Finance <https://www.customs.go.jp/roo/english/origin/outline_of_roo.pdf> accessed 2 December 2021.

D'Aveni RA, 'How 3-D Printing Can Jumpstart Developing Economies' (*Forbes* 19 March 2019) <https://www.forbes.com/sites/richarddaveni/2019/03/19/how-3d-printing-can-jumpstart-developing-economies/?sh=12bcfedd4400> accessed 2 November 2021.

Davis J, 'The Strati: a 3D-printed electric car that could be built in 24 hours' *The Guardian* (London, 9 December 2014) <https://www.theguardian.com/technology/2014/dec/09/3d-printed-electric-car> accessed 2 December 2021.

de Sousa A, 'A Realistic Steak is Fake Meat's Holy Grail' (*Bloomberg Business* 22 November 2019) <https://www.bloomberg.com/news/articles/2019-11-22/fake-meat-companies-are-racing-to-3d-print-steaks> accessed 24 October 2021.

Ferrill E and ER Yoches, 'IP Law and 3D Printing: Designers Can Work Around Lack of Cover' (*Wired*) <https://www.wired.com/insights/2013/09/ip-law-and-3d-printing-designers-can-work-around-lack-of-cover/> accessed 25 October 2021.

Fortune Business Insights, '3D Printing Market Size, Share, & Industry Analysis' (Fortunebusinessinsights.com March 2024) <https://www.fortunebusinessinsights.com/industry-reports/3d-printing-market-101902> accessed 23 March 2024.

'GE Nigeria Launches e-learning Portal at Lagos Garage Week 2018' (Africanews.it 7 December 2018), <https://www.africanews.it/english/ge-nigeria-launches-e-learning-portal-at-lagos-garage-week-2018/> accessed 8 March 2025.

Grant M, 'Bill of Materials (BOM)' (Investopedia.com 30 October 2020) <https://www.investopedia.com/terms/b/bill-of-materials.asp> accessed 2 December 2021.

Greenfield D, 'Ford and Nissan Use HP 3D Printing to Address Production Sustainability' (May 2021) Automotion World 20–22. <https://www.automationworld.com/factory/3d-printing-additive-manufacturing/article/21366376/ford-and-nissan-use-hp-3d-printing-to-address-production-sustainability> accessed 10 March 2025.

Hersh AS, 'EPI comments to the Office of the United States Trade Representative on the US-Mexico-Canada Agreement with respect to automotive goods' USTR-2023-0013-0011 Comment Submission (Economic Policy Institute 22 January 2024) https://www.epi.org/publication/us-mexico-canada-agreement/ accessed 23 March 2024.

Heldebrand JM, and SA Martin, R Smith, 'Is Trade the Disrupter or the Disrupted?' (2018) EY Global Trade Symposium Report <https://assets.ey.com/content/dam/ey-sites/ey-com/en_gl/topics/global-trade/global-trade-pdfs/1808-2835224_Global_Trade_Symposium_report_012125-18Gbl.pdf> accessed 23 October 2021.

Hoekman H, and C Lippitsch, M Olarreaga, M Sanfilippo, R Ticku, 'Maximising value-added in Africa exports: Understanding the role of Rules of Origin' *IGC Blog* (International Growth Centre 27 August 2024) <https://www.theigc.org/blogs/maximising-value-added-african-exports-understanding-role-rules-origin>.

'Indonesia Tax Information' (Deloitte 30 April 2018) <https://www2.deloitte.com/content/dam/Deloitte/id/Documents/tax/id-tax-info-apr2018.pdf> accessed 29 October 2021.

International Chamber of Commerce (ICC), 'Builidng Business Engagement ahead of the WTO's 12th Ministerial Conference' (iccwbo.org 24 June 2021) <https://iccwbo.org/media-wall/news-speeches/building-business-engagement-ahead-of-the-wtos-12th-ministerial-conference/> accessed 3 January 2022.

International Chamber of Commerce (ICC), 'Business Recommendations on Rules of Origin in Preferential Trade Agreements' (May 2017) Doc. No. 104–89

<https://iccwbo.org/news-publications/policies-reports/business-recommendations-rules-origin-preferential-trade-agreements/ > accessed 9 March 2025.

International Chamber of Commerce (ICC), 'Certificates of Origin' (iccwbo.org) <https://iccwbo.org/resources-for-business/certificates-of-origin/> accessed 2 December 2021.

International Chamber of Commerce (ICC), 'Chamber Services: Certificates of Origin' (iccwbo.org) <https://iccwbo.org/world-chambers-federation/chamber-services/certificates-of-origin/> accessed 9 March 2025.

International Magnesium Association, 'About Magnesium' (intlmag.org) <https://www.intlmag.org/page/basics_about_mg_ima> accessed 23 March 2024.

International Union, United Automobile, Aerospace & Agricultural Implement Workers of America (UAW), 'UAW's Public Comment on Operation of the United States-Mexico-Canada Agreement With Respect To Trade in Automotive Goods' Submission No USTR-2023-0013 (17 January 2024) 4 <https://downloads.regulations.gov/USTR-2023-0013-0013/attachment_1.pdfz> accessed 23 March 2024.

'Japanese Foreign Trade in Figures' (santadartrade.com July 2021), <https://santandertrade.com/en/portal/analyse-markets/japan/foreign-trade-in-figures?url_de_la_page=%2Fen%2Fportal%2Fanalyse-markets%2Fjapan%2Fforeign-trade-in-figures&&actualiser_id_banque=oui&id_banque=0&memoriser_choix=memoriser> accessed 3 November 2021.

Kenton W, 'Direct Costs' (*Investopedia* 27 June 2020) <https://www.investopedia.com/terms/d/directcost.asp> accessed 24 October 2021.

Kenner JM, 'A Brief Overview of Several Decisions Discussing Substantial Transformation' Proceeding of the 20th Judicial Conference of US Court of Int'l Trade (cit.uscourts.gov), <https://www.cit.uscourts.gov/sites/cit/files/JKenner%20A%20Brief%20Overview%20of%20Several%20Decisions%20Discussing%20Substantial%20Transformation%20final.pdf> accessed 2 December 2021.

King H, 'College student 3D prints his own braces' (CNN.com 16 March 2016) <https://money.cnn.com/2016/03/16/technology/homemade-invisalign/> accessed 24 October 2021.

M Aysha, 'The List of Bicycles Made with 3D Printing Technologies,' (*3D Natives* 22 September 2020) <https://www.3dnatives.com/en/ranking-3d-printed-bikes-220920204/#!> accessed 24 October 2021.

Methenitis WM and K Price Dozier, 'Making Sense of a World in Motion – a Global Trade Perspective' (2016) EY Global Trade Symposium Report, <http://www.goingglobalskills.com/pdfs/making-sense-of-a-world-in-motion.pdf> accessed 23 October 2021.

Ministry of Electronics and Information Technology, 'National Strategy for Additive Manufacturing: Next Generation Digital Manufacturing' (Meity.gov.in 24 February 2022) 1,3 https://www.meity.gov.in/writereaddata/files/Additive%20Manufacturing%20Booklet%2014.02.2022.pdf accessed 23 March 2024.

Mohammadi G, 'The History of CNC Machining, Part I & 2' (*Bantam Tools*) <https://medium.com/cnc-life/history-of-cnc-machining-part-1-2a4b290d994d> <https://medium.com/cnc-life/history-of-cnc-machining-part-2-the-evolution-from-nc-to-cnc-4b9fe1653536> both accessed 24 October 2021.

New Zealand Ministry of Foreign Affairs & Trade, 'CEP Overview' (mfat.govt.nz) <https://www.mfat.govt.nz/br/trade/free-trade-agreements/free-trade-agreements-in-force/nz-singapore-closer-economic-partnership/cep-overview/#bookmark0> accessed 2 November 2021.

New Zealand Ministry of Foreign Affairs & Trade, 'CEP Text' (mfat.govt.nz) <https://www.mfat.govt.nz/br/trade/free-trade-agreements/free-trade-agreements-in-force/nz-singapore-closer-economic-partnership/cep-text/> accessed 2 November 2021.

New Zealand Ministry of Foreign Affairs & Trade, 'National Interest Analysis' (mfat.govt.nz) <https://www.mfat.govt.nz/assets/Trade-agreements/Singapore-NZ-CEP/National-Interest-Analysis.pdf> accessed 2 November 2021.

O'Carroll L, 'UK Carmakers Face Higher Tariffs as EU Rejects Component Plea' *The Guardian* (London, 30 September 2020) <https://www.theguardian.com/politics/2020/sep/30/uk-carmakers-face-higher-tariffs-as-eu-rejects-component-plea-brexit> accessed 2 December 2021.

Office of the US Trade Representative (USTR), 'Key Barriers to Digital Trade' (USTR.gov 31 March 2017) <https://ustr.gov/about-us/policy-offices/press-office/fact-sheets/2017/march/key-barriers-digital-trade> accessed 24 October 2021).

Office of the US Trade Representative (USTR), 'United States – Mexico – Canada Trade Fact Sheet: Rebalancing Trade to Support Manufacturing' (ustr.gov) <https://ustr.gov/trade-agreements/free-trade-agreements/united-states-mexico-canada-agreement/fact-sheets/rebalancing> accessed 2 December 2021.

Office of the US Trade Representative (USTR) 'Report to Congress on The Operation of The United States-Mexico-Canada Agreement with Respect to Trade in Automotive Goods', 1 July 2024, <https://ustr.gov/sites/default/files/2024%20USMCA%20Autos%20Report%20to%20Congress_0.pdf> accessed 23 October 2024.

Page J, 'Determining Origin in a Predetermined World: The Impact of Energizer Battery', Proceeding of the 20th Judicial Conference of US Court of Int'l Trade (cit.uscourts.gov), <https://www.cit.uscourts.gov/sites/cit/files/JPage%20CIT%20Conference%20Article.pdf> accessed 2 December 2021.

Pierce JE, 'IP Strategies for the Rise of 3D Printing' (Venable LLP 14 April 2015) <https://www.venable.com/insights/publications/2015/04/ip-strategies-for-the-rise-of-3d-printing> accessed 25 October 2021.

'Post-elaborazione' (formlabs.com) <https://formlabs.com/it/negozio/post-processing/> accessed 24 October 2021.

Reinsch WA, 'Congressional Testimony: USMCA Automotive Rules of Origin: Economic impacts, Competitiveness Effects, and Relevance' Center for Strategic

& International Studies (CSIS.org 4 November 2022) <https://www.csis.org/analysis/usmca-automotive-rules-origin-economic-impacts-competitiveness-effects-and-relevance> accessed 23 March 2024.

'Results for 'Ultrasonic Bath' (amazon.com) <https://www.amazon.com/Ultrasonic-Bath/s?k=Ultrasonic+Bath> accessed 24 October 2021.

Rubin G, 'How Do You Like Your Beef … Old-Style Cow or 3D-Printed?' *The Guardian* (London, 10 November 2019) <https://www.theguardian.com/technology/2019/nov/10/3d-printed-meat-european-restaurant-menus-environment> accessed 24 October 2021.

Safavian JM, 'Comments Concerning the Operation of the United States-Mexico-Canada Agreement With Respect to Trade in Automotive Goods,' Submission to the USTR (17 January 2024) 1 <https://autosdriveamerica.org/wp-content/uploads/2024/02/2024.01.17-Autos-Drive-America-Comments-to-USTR-on-USMCA-ROO-Operation.pdf> accessed 23 March 2024.

'Solvay in Italia' (solvay.it) <https://www.solvay.it/it/solvay-in/index.html> accessed 24 October 2021.

Schwaar C, '3D Printing Meets the Billion-Dollar Footwear Industry' (Forbes 19 July 2023) <https://www.forbes.com/sites/carolynschwaar/2023/07/19/3d-printing-meets-the-billion-dollar-footwear-industry/?sh=2a67d756520f> accessed 25 March 2024.

SDG Knowledge Hub, 'New Trade Agreement between US, Mexico, and Canada Enters into Force,' (sdg.iisd.org 2 July 2020) <https://sdg.iisd.org/news/new-trade-agreement-between-us-mexico-and-canada-enters-into-force/> accessed 2 December 2021.

Sher D, 'Japanese Additive Manufacturing is Rising' (3D Printing Media Network 7 December 2020) <https://www.3dprintingmedia.network/japanese-additive-manufacturing-is-rising/> accessed 3 November 2021.

Sotelo J and V Sundareswaran, 'Would a Digital Border Tax Slow Down Adoption of 3D Printing?' (*World Economic Forum* 08 January 2020) <https://www.weforum.org/agenda/2020/01/would-a-digital-border-tax-slow-down-adoption-of-3d-printing/> accessed 25 October 2021.

Structo, 'Part I: The Birth of Clear Aligners' (*Structo3D* 18 July 2017) <https://www.structo3d.com/blogs/blog/part-1-the-birth-of-clear-aligners> accessed 24 October 2021.

Tagliabue J, 'Italian Silk Industry Upset by a New U.S. Trade Law' *New York Times* (New York, 10 April 1997) Section D p 4 <https://www.nytimes.com/1997/04/10/business/italian-silk-industry-upset-by-a-new-us-trade-law.html> accessed 6 January 2022.

The White House, 'President Obama Launches Advanced Manufacturing Partnership' (Obama White House 4 June 2011) <https://obamawhitehouse.archives.gov/the-press-office/2011/06/24/president-obama-launches-advanced-manufacturing-partnership> accessed 24 October 2021.

The White House 'Fact Sheet: President Biden Announces New Actions to Strengthen America's Supply Chains, Lower Costs for Families, and Secure Key Sectors' (Biden White House 27 November 2023) <https://www.whitehouse.gov/briefing-room/statements-releases/2023/11/27/fact-sheet-president-biden-announces-new-actions-to-strengthen-americas-supply-chains-lower-costs-for-families-and-secure-key-sectors/> accessed 23 March 2024 (archived link).

Tingvall P and M Rentzhog, 'Is the WTO 3D Printing-Ready?' (2018) Word Trade Rep <https://www.wto.org/english/res_e/publications_e/opinionpiece_by_patrik_tingvall_and_magnus_rentzhog_e.pdf> accessed 2 November 2021.

Understanding CNC Machining' (Thomas Publishing Company) <https://www.thomasnet.com/articles/custom-manufacturing-fabricating/understanding-cnc-machining/> accessed 24 October 2021.

US Court of International Trade, 'About the Court' (cit.uscourts.gov) <https://www.cit.uscourts.gov/about-court> accessed 2 December 2021.

US Customs and Border Protection (CBP), 'Rules of Origin' (1 May 2004) EO13891-OT-122 <https://www.cbp.gov/document/publications/rules-origin> accessed 26 October 2024.

US Customs and Border Protection (CBP), 'What Every Member of the Trade Community Should Know About : Customs Administrative Enforcement Process: Fines, Penalties, Forfeitures and Liquidated Damages' (cbp.gov February 2004) <https://www.cbp.gov/sites/default/files/documents/icp052_3.pdf> accessed 2 December 2021.

US Customs and Border Protection (CBP), 'Accumulation' (cbp.gov 28 May 2014) <https://www.cbp.gov/trade/nafta/guide-customs-procedures/other-instances-confer-origin/accumulation> accessed 2 December 2021.

US Customs and Border Protection (CBP), 'What Every Member of the Trade Community Should Know: Reasonable Care' (cbp.gov September 2017) <https://www.cbp.gov/sites/default/files/assets/documents/2018-Mar/icprescare2017revision.pdf> accessed 2 December 2021.

US Customs and Border Protection (CBP), *'U.S. Customs and Border Protection Valuation Encyclopedia (1980–2021)*, (first Issued 1990, revised December 2021 <https://www.cbp.gov/sites/default/files/assets/documents/2022-Jun/Value%20Encyclopedia%20Dec%202021%20%281%29.pdf> accessed 26 October 2024.

US Customs and Border Protection (CBP), 'Accumulation – Factsheet' CBP Publication No. 1141–0620 <https://www.cbp.gov/sites/default/files/assets/documents/2020-Jun/%2316_Accumulation_USMCA%20Informational%20Fact%20Sheet.pdf> accessed 2 December 2021.

US International Trade Administration (USITA), 'Japan Additive Manufacturing and 3D Printing' (trade.gov 15 June 2020) <https://www.trade.gov/market-intelligence/japan-additive-manufacturing-and-3d-printing > accessed 3 November 2021.

US International Trade Administration (USITA), 'Italy – Country Commercial Guide: Advanced Manufacturing' (trade.gov 23 January 2024) <https://www.trade.gov/country-commercial-guides/italy-advanced-manufacturing> accessed 24 March 2024.

US International Trade Administration (USITA), 'FTA Provisions for Accumulation' (trade.gov) <https://www.trade.gov/fta-provisions-accumulation> accessed 2 December 2021.

US International Trade Administration (USITA), 'FTA Provisions for De Minimis Rule' (trade.gov) <https://www.trade.gov/fta-provisions-de-minimis-rule.> accessed 2 December 2021.

US International Trade Administration (USITA), 'Homepage' (trade.gov) <https://www.trade.gov> accessed 25 March 2024.

US International Trade Administration (USITA), 'Understanding USMCA' (trade.gov) <https://www.trade.gov/usmca-dayone-0> accessed 2 December 2021.

Waters R, 'Google to End Use of 'Double Irish' as Tax Loophole Set to Close' *Financial Times* (London, 1 January 2020) <https://www.ft.com/content/991f11ae-2c51-11ea-bc77-65e4aa615551> accessed 25 October 2021.

'Welcome to WCO Trade Tools' (wcodtradetools.org) <https://www.wcotradetools.org/en> accessed 2 November 2021.

World Customs Organization (WCO), 'Comparative Study on Preferential Rules of Origin' (wccomd.org 2017) <http://www.wcoomd.org/-/media/wco/public/global/pdf/topics/origin/instruments-and-tools/reference-material/170130-b_comparative-study-on-pref_roo_master-file_final-20_06_2017.pdf?db=web> accessed 2 December 2021.

World Customs Organization (WCO), 'Frequently Asked Questions' (wcoomd.org 10 June 2020) <http://www.wcoomd.org/en/topics/nomenclature/overview/harmonized_system_faq.aspx> accessed 2 December 2021.

World Customs Organization (WCO), 'The WCO Has Published the HS 2017/HS 2022 Correlation Tables for the Harmonized System' (wcoomd.org 13 November 2020) <http://www.wcoomd.org/en/media/newsroom/2020/november/the-wco-has-published-the-hs-2017-2022.aspx>. accessed 2 December 2021.

World Customs Organization (WCO), 'Conventions: Summary of Positions' (wccomd.org 1 July 2024) <https://www.wcoomd.org/-/media/wco/public/global/pdf/about-us/legal-instruments/conventions-and-agreements/revised-kyoto/sg0230eb.pdf?la=en> accessed 20 October 2024.

World Customs Organization (WCO), 'Position of Contracting Parties to the Harmonized System Convention and Non-Contracting Party Administrations' (wcoomd.org 7 October 2024) <http://www.wcoomd.org/-/media/wco/public/global/pdf/topics/nomenclature/overview/hs-contracting-parties/positions-of-cp/situation_hs.pdf?db=web> accessed 20 October 2024.

World Customs Organization (WCO), 'Activities and Programmes' (wcoomd.org) <http://www.wcoomd.org/en/topics/enforcement-and-compliance/activities-and-programmes.aspx> accessed 2 December 2021.

World Customs Organization (WCO), 'Amending the HS' (wcoomd.org) <http://www.wcoomd.org/en/topics/nomenclature/activities-and-programmes/amending_hs.aspx> accessed 24 October 2021.

World Customs Organization (WCO), 'General Rules for the Interpretation of the Harmonized System' (wcoomd.org) <http://www.wcoomd.org/-/media/wco/public/global/pdf/topics/nomenclature/instruments-and-tools/hs-nomenclature-2017/2017/0001_2017e_gir.pdf?la=en> accessed 2 December 2021.

World Customs Organization (WCO), 'HS Nomenclature 2022 – Chapter 20' (wccomd.org) <http://www.wcoomd.org/-/media/wco/public/global/pdf/topics/nomenclature/instruments-and-tools/hs-nomenclature-2022/2022/0420_2022e.pdf?la=en> accessed 7 January 2022.

World Customs Organization (WCO), 'HS Nomenclature 2022 – Chapter 84' (wcoomed.org) <http://www.wcoomd.org/-/media/wco/public/global/pdf/topics/nomenclature/instruments-and-tools/hs-nomenclature-2022/2022/1684_2022e.pdf?la=en> accessed 7 January 2022.

World Customs Organization (WCO), 'HS Nomenclature 2022 Edition' (wccomd.org) <http://www.wcoomd.org/en/topics/nomenclature/instrument-and-tools/hs-nomenclature-2022-edition/hs-nomenclature-2022-edition.aspx> accessed 7 January 2022.

World Customs Organization (WCO), 'RILO: A Unique and United Network' (wcomd.org) <http://www.wcoomd.org/-/media/wco/public/global/pdf/topics/enforcement-and-compliance/tools-and-instruments/rilo/rilo-brochure_en.pdf?db=web> accessed 2 December 2021.

World Customs Organization (WCO), 'WCO Trade Tools: Harmonized System' (wcotradetools.org) <https://www.wcotradetools.org/en/harmonized-system> accessed 30 October 2021.

World Customs Organization (WCO), 'What is the Harmonized System (HS)?' (wcoomd.org) <http://www.wcoomd.org/en/topics/nomenclature/overview/what-is-the-harmonized-system.aspx> accessed 2 December 2021.

World Intellectual Property Office, 'Valuing Intellectual Property Assets' (wipo.int), <https://www.wipo.int/sme/en/value_ip_assets/> accessed 25 October 2021.

'World Tariff Profiles 2023' (WTO, ITC & UNCTAD 2023) 2 <https://www.wto.org/english/res_e/publications_e/world_tariff_profiles23_e.htm> accessed 10 March 2025.

World Trade Organization (WTO), 'Briefing note: The Expansion of Trade in Information Technology Products (ITA Expansion)' (wto.org 16 December 2015)

<https://www.wto.org/english/news_e/news15_e/itabriefingnotes161215_e.pdf> accessed 2 December 2021.

World Trade Organization (WTO), 'Event Marks 25th Anniversary of the WTO's Agreement on Rules of Origin' (wto.org 4 March 2020) <https://www.wto.org/english/news_e/news20_e/roi_04mar20_e.htm> accessed 1 December 2021.

World Trade Organization (WTO), 'Members review reforms to facilitate participation in rules of origin work' (wto.org 29 April 2024) <https://www.wto.org/english/news_e/news24_e/roi_29apr24_e.htm> accessed 25 October 2024.

World Trade Organization (WTO), 'Architectural and Engineering Services' (wto.org) <https://www.wto.org/english/tratop_e/serv_e/architecture_e/architecture_e.htm> accessed 24 October 2021.

World Trade Organization (WTO), 'Electronic Commerce' (wto.org) <https://www.wto.org/english/thewto_e/minist_e/mc11_e/briefing_notes_e/bfecom_e.htm> accessed 24 October 2021.

World Trade Organization (WTO), 'Guide to Reading the GATS Schedules of Specific Commitments and the List of Article II (MFN) Exemptions' (wto.org) <https://www.wto.org/english/tratop_e/serv_e/guide1_e.htm> accessed 24 October 24.

World Trade Organization (WTO), 'Information Technology Agreement – an Explanation' (wto.org) <https://www.wto.org/english/tratop_e/inftec_e/itaintro_e.htm> accessed 2 December 2021.

World Trade Organization (WTO), 'Rules of Origin' (wto.org) <https://www.wto.org/english/tratop_e/roi_e/roi_e.htm#techass> accessed 3 November.

World Trade Organization (WTO), 'Schedules of Concessions,' (wto.org) <https://www.wto.org/english/tratop_e/schedules_e/goods_schedules_e.htm> accessed 24 October 2021.

World Trade Organization (WTO), 'Trade Facilitation – Cutting Red Tape at the Border' (wto.org) <https://www.wto.org/english/tratop_e/tradfa_e/tradfa_introduction_e.htm> accessed 2 December 2021.

World Trade Organization (WTO), 'The Trade Policy Review Mechanism (TPRM)' (wto.org) <https://www.wto.org/english/tratop_e/tpr_e/tprm_e.htm> accessed 3 November 2021.

World Trade Organization (WTO), 'Transparency Mechanisms for RTAS' (wto.org) <https://www.wto.org/english/tratop_e/region_e/trans_mecha_e.htm> accessed 3 November 2021.

World Trade Organization (WTO), 'The Uruguay Round' (wto.org) <https://www.wto.org/english/thewto_e/whatis_e/tif_e/fact5_e.htm> accessed 2 December 2021.

World Trade Organization (WTO), 'The WTO and World Customs Organization' (wto.org). <https://www.wto.org/english/thewto_e/coher_e/wto_wco_e.htm> accessed 2 December 2021.

World Trade Organization (WTO), 'What is a WTO Schedule' (*Goods Schedules e-Library*, wto.org) <https://goods-schedules.wto.org/what-is-a-wto-schedule> accessed 24 October 2021.

Zewe A, 'AI-driven tool makes it easy to personalize 3D-printable models' (MIT News 15 September 2023) <https://news.mit.edu/2023/ai-driven-tool-personalize-3d-printable-models-0915> accessed 23 March 2024.

Websites, Presentations, and Miscellaneous Material

Commission, 'Access2Markets' <https://trade.ec.europa.eu/access-to-markets/en/home> accessed 26 October 2024.

Commission, 'My Trade Assistant' <https://trade.ec.europa.eu/access-to-markets/en/home> accessed 1 December 2021 (includes Tariff Calculator).

Harris JT, 'Rules of Origin Preference Utilization' (What Drives the Utilization of Trade Preferences WTO conference 19 May 2021) <https://www.wto.org/english/tratop_e/roi_e/s1_harris19may21.pdf> accessed 1 December 2021.

International Trade Center, 'Rules of Origin Facilitator' www.findrulesoforigin.org accessed 2 December 2021.

Interview with Dr. Anna Jerzewska (Milan/Geneva, 22 September 2021). Dr. Jerzewska's website: <https://www.tradeandborders.com> accessed 3 November 2021.

Martí DF, 'What Drives the Utilization of Trade Preferences? Lessons from the work of the WTO Committee on Rules of Origin; (What Drives the Utilization of Trade Preferences WTO conference 19 May 2021) <https://www.wto.org/english/tratop_e/roi_e/s1_harris19may21.pdf> accessed 1 December 2021.

Trade Facilitation Database (tfadatabase.org 2024) <https://tfadatabase.org/implementation> accessed 20 October 2024.

US Patent No. 4, 575,330 (Apparatus for Production of Three-Dimensional Objects by Stereolithography), Filed 8 August 1984, issued 11 March 1986. <https://patentimages.storage.googleapis.com/5c/a0/27/e49642dab99cf6/US4575330.pdf> accessed 2 December 2021.

USITC, The USMCA Automotive Rules of Origin Motor Vehicle Producer Questionnaire (2024) <https://www.usitc.gov/usmcaautoroo> and https://www.usitc.gov/research_and_analysis/documents/usmca/usmca_auto_roos_questionnaire.pdf> accessed 20 October 2024.

WTO, 'What Drives the Utilization of Trade Preferences' conference held 19 May 2021. Videos and presentations available at <https://www.wto.org/english/tratop_e/roi_e/preference_utilization_190521_e.htm> accessed 3 November 2021.

WTO Summary of Informal Experience-Sharing Session on Preferential Rules of Origin, held 5 October 2023, available at <https://www.wto.org/library/events/event_resources/devel_0510202315/summary.pdf> accessed 23 March 2024.

Index

Printed in the United States
by Baker & Taylor Publisher Services